# THE NIGHTMARE

Books by Henry Kellerman

*Group Psychotherapy and Personality: Intersecting Structures.*

*Group Cohesion: Theoretical and Clinical Perspectives.* (Edited).

*Sleep Disorders: Insomnia and Narcolepsy.*

*Handbook of Psychodiagnostic Testing: Personality Analysis and Report Writing.* (With Anthony Burry).

*Emotion: Theory, Research and Experience.* Vol. 1, *Theories of Emotion.* (Edited: With Robert Plutchik).

*Emotion: Theory, Research and Experience.* Vol. 2, *Emotions in Early Development.* (Edited: With Robert Plutchik).

*Emotion: Theory, Research and Experience.* Vol. 3, *Biological Foundations of Emotion.* (Edited: With Robert Plutchik).

*The Nightmare: Psychological and Biological Foundations.* (Edited).

# The Nightmare

## PSYCHOLOGICAL AND BIOLOGICAL FOUNDATIONS

Edited by Henry Kellerman

Columbia University Press New York 1987

Columbia University Press
New York Guildford, Surrey


Printed in the United States of America

Library of Congress Cataloging-in-Publication Data
The Nightmare: psychological and biological foundations.
Includes bibliographies and index.
1. Nightmares. I. Kellerman, Henry.
BF1099.N53N54 1986 154.6′32 86-13675
ISBN 0-231-05892-6

Book design by J. S. Roberts

# CONTENTS

# ACKNOWLEDGMENTS

IN THIS VOLUME the known parameters of the study of the nightmare are presented. The purpose of creating such a compendium is to provide a comprehensive perspective of the field—from psychoanalysis of the nightmare to its physiology and from an understanding of the nightmare in personality to the effect of nightmares on children. This volume, therefore, is a repository of known research and theoretical understanding of the nightmare with respect to both clinical and laboratory traditions.

In most university graduate programs as well as in medical schools the study of dreams and nightmares has been absent from basic curricula, and this secondary status of the study of dreams has been endemic in the field of mental health the world over. It is only recently—especially with the advent of the sleep laboratory and sleep disorder center—that courses in dreams and nightmares have been included as part of the broad mental health curricula offered at various professional institutions.

In contrast, within the psychoanalytic tradition, exposure to course work on dreams is an established aspect of training, and in many psychoanalytic institutes courses on dream interpretation are considered essential. Such an institution is the Postgraduate Center for Mental Health in New York City.

The Postgraduate Center is a multipurpose mental health center, boasting approximately fifteen training programs, a half-dozen clinics, an active community program, and a fine postgraduate Psychoanalytic Institute, now offering more than 125,000 patient-treatment hours per year—perhaps the largest such institution in the world. The contributors to this volume, all professional psychologists who have researched the field of dreams and nightmares, over two decades were also students of the Postgraduate Center's Psychology Internship Program of which I was formerly the director. We have all benefited from the Center's continuing commitment to the importance of the use of the dream as a clinical tool for understanding the unconscious.

At this time, therefore, during the fortieth anniversary of the Postgraduate Center and the twentieth anniversary of the Center's Psychology Internship Program, thanks are here extended to several individuals who have been especially instrumental in the continuing viability of the Psychology Internship Program and who have helped sustain the nationwide reputation for excellence this program has enjoyed. Appreciation is extended here to Dr. Theodora Abel, Director Emeritus, Department of Psychology, Dr. Anthony Burry, current Director, Psychology Internship Program, Dr. Zanvel Liff, Director, Department of Psychology, and Dr. Harry Sands, Executive Director of the Postgraduate Center.

The founders of the Postgraduate Center who remain at the core of its optimism and inspiration—Dr. Lewis R. Wolberg, Chairman, and Mrs. Arlene Wolberg, Member, Board of Trustees—have always set the tone for the Center's growth and direction. For their untiring efforts and leadership gratitude is extended to Dr. and Mrs. Wolberg from all who have had contact with the Center and benefited from its programs and services.

Finally, I would like to thank Ms. Susan Koscielniak, Ms. Karen Mitchell, and Ms. Elizabeth Sutton of Columbia University Press, who were exceedingly helpful throughout the planning and production phases of this volume.

Henry Kellerman
New York City

# CONTRIBUTORS

HENRY KELLERMAN, Ph.D., is a psychologist and psychoanalyst. He is the author of two dozen papers published in scientific journals and the author and editor of eight books. He has published on the subjects of psychoanalysis, group process and psychotherapy, psychopathology, dreams and nightmares, sleep disorders, emotion and personality, animal behavior, and psychodiagnosis. Several of his works have won awards, and he was the first recipient of the Postgraduate Center for Mental Health Scholar's Award. He has been consulting editor of a number of journals and is currently on the editorial board of the journal *Dynamic Psychotherapy.* He is also editor of the clinical series for Columbia University Press entitled Personality, Psychopathology, and Psychotherapy. In addition, Dr. Kellerman is coeditor of the series of volumes published by Academic Press entitled Emotion: Theory, Research, and Experience.

Dr. Kellerman is a Diplomate in Clinical Psychology of the American Board of Professional Psychology, a fellow of the American Psychological Association, and a fellow of the American Group Psychotherapy Association. He holds postdoctoral certificates in psychoanalysis and psychotherapy and in analytic group psychotherapy from the Postgraduate Center for Mental Health, and in the science of marital and family psychodynamics from New York Medical College, Department of Psychiatry.

Over a span of almost thirty years, Dr. Kellerman has held clinical staff positions and faculty appointments at several hospitals and universities. A former National Institute of Mental

Health fellow, Dr. Kellerman is currently Training Analyst and Senior Supervisor at the Postgraduate Center for Mental Health where he directed psychology internship training for fifteen years.

Dr. Kellerman is in private practice in New York City.

EMILY M. ADAMS, Ph.D., first received her RN degree from Thomas Jefferson University and then her doctoral degree in clinical psychology from the California School of Professional Psychology.

Dr. Adams completed a second psychology internship at the Postgraduate Center for Mental Health in 1983–1984 and trained in the Child and Adolescent Program at the Center. She is now in private practice in Wilmington, Delaware and is a faculty member at the Delaware Technical College.

Dr. Adams is currently preparing a work on widowed persons for publication.

PETER BUIRSKI, Ph.D., is a psychologist and psychoanalyst and holds the Diplomate in Clinical Psychology of the American Board of Professional Psychology. Currently, Dr. Buirski is Professor of Psychology at John Jay College of Criminal Justice of the City University of New York, where he was formerly chairman of the psychology department. He is also currently Director of the Adult Fellowship Postgraduate Training Program in Psychoanalysis and Psychotherapy at the Postgraduate Center for Mental Health.

Dr. Buirski was a psychology intern at the Postgraduate Center for Mental Health from 1968 to 1969. He has published in the fields of psychology, psychoanalysis, personality theory, group theory, and ethology. Dr. Buirski is coauthoring a volume entitled *Bereavement in Children.* He is in private practice in New York City.

MICHAEL JOSEPH DAVIES, Ph.D., was born in Wellington, New Zealand. He attended schools in New Zealand and Australia. He received his doctorate in clinical psychology from the Graduate School of Arts and Sciences of Fordham University. He had previously completed his internship in clinical psychology at the Postgraduate Center for Mental Health in 1975–1976, and then completed a postdoctoral program in psychoanalysis at the Westchester Center for Psychoanalysis and Psychotherapy, White Plains, New York in 1984.

He is in private practice in Mamaroneck, New York and in West Norwalk, Connecticut. Among his publications is *Mental Health as Level of Interpersonal Maturity* (with Alan Grey, 1981).

ARTHUR A. GRAY, Ph.D., was a psychology intern at the Postgraduate Center for Mental Health in 1974–1975 and received a certificate in psychoanalysis and psychotherapy from the Postgraduate Center in 1981. He received his doctoral degree from Teacher's College, Columbia University.

Dr. Gray was formerly Senior Psychologist at Queens Hospital Center's Court Related Program and Staff Psychologist in the Postgraduate Center for Mental Health Child and Adolescent Clinic. He was also formerly Deputy Chairman of the Convention Planning Committee of the Eastern Psychological Association and is a member of the New York Society for Clinical Psychology's Minority Groups Relations Committee.

Dr. Gray is currently working on a book on the subject of intimacy. He is in private practice in New York City.

JUDITH HANLON, Ph.D., received her doctoral degree in clinical psychology from Columbia University. She was a psychology intern at the Postgraduate Center for Mental Health in 1972–1973. She was an Advanced Psychology Fellow at New York Hospital–Cornell Medical Center, Westchester Division and completed psychoanalytic training at the Postdoctoral Program in Psychotherapy and Psychoanalysis at New York University.

Dr. Hanlon is currently in private practice in New York City. She is also a staff psychologist at the Staten Island Mental Health Society, and a supervisor in the Clinical Psychology Program at Teachers College, Columbia University.

LAWRENCE JOSEPHS, Ph.D., received a doctorate in clinical psychology from the University of Tennessee, Knoxville. He was awarded a predoctoral internship in clinical psychology at the Postgraduate Center for Mental Health, 1980–1981.

Dr. Josephs is currently Senior Clinical Psychologist, Essex County Hospital Center. Cedar Grove, New Jersey. He is also currently Assistant Professor of Psychology at the Institute of Advanced Psychological Studies at Adelphi University and a faculty member at the Postgraduate Center for Mental Health. He is a graduate of the Psychoanalytic Institute of the Postgraduate Center. Dr. Josephs has published a number of clinical papers on schizophrenia, Freudian theory, and self-psychology.

DANIEL P. JUDA, Ph.D., completed his undergraduate work at the University of California, Berkeley, and his graduate work at the New School for Social Research in New York City. He received his training in psychoanalysis and psychotherapy from the Postgraduate Center for Mental Health both as an intern in the Clinical Psychology Internship program (1976–1978) and as a Fellow in the Training Program in Psychotherapy and Psychoanalysis.

Presently, Dr. Juda is both in private practice and an Associate Professor of psychology at John Jay College of Criminal Justice of the City University of New York. In addition, Dr. Juda is a consultant to the St. Lukes–Roosevelt Hospital's Crime Victims' Assessment Project. Dr. Juda has published in the areas of psychoanalysis, forensic psychology, and crisis intervention and has been the recipient of the Sidney Blau Memorial Award from the Postgraduate Center for Mental Health and a Meritorious Award from the New York Psychological Association, both for scientific and scholarly papers.

SUSAN KAVALER, Ph.D., is a psychologist and psychoanalyst in private practice in New York City. Dr. Kavaler is a Member of the Faculty at the Postgraduate Center for Mental Health and at the National Institute for the Psychotherapies where she also serves as Supervisor. She is also a Member of the Board of Directors as well as Supervisor and faculty member at the Brooklyn Institute for Psychotherapy. In addition, Dr. Kavaler is a Senior Supervisor and Training Analyst for the International School of Mental Health Practitioners.

Dr. Kavaler was a clinical psychology doctoral intern at the Postgraduate Center for Mental Health in 1973–1974. She is Founder and Chairperson of the National Institute for the Psychotherapies' Professional Association Writing Group and has published papers in scientific and clinical journals as well as chapters in books. Dr. Kavaler is also the recipient of several scholarly awards, including the Honorary Award from the Postgraduate Center for Mental Health, which she won in 1984 and 1985. She is currently at work on a book concerning the female artist from an object relations point of view.

SUSAN KNAPP, Ph.D., is a psychologist and psychoanalyst. She is a faculty member and supervisor at the Postgraduate Center for Mental Health and at the National Institute for the Psychotherapies and the Institute for Contemporary Psychotherapy.

Dr. Knapp was a psychology intern at the Postgraduate Center for Mental Health from 1969 to 1971. She has published several papers in books and scientific journals on the subject of dreams.

Dr. Knapp is in private practice in New York City.

FRANKLIN D. RADDOCK, Ph.D., completed his doctoral training in clinical psychology at the New School for Social Research in New York City. After his phychology internship working with adults and children at the Postgraduate Center for Mental Health (1975–1977), he served as a psychologist and consultant to the New York State Department of Mental Hygiene. There he directed a day treatment program for disturbed youngsters in the Mount Vernon, New York schools, and supervised a clinic for young children and their parents under the auspices of Rockland Children's Psychiatric Center.

Currently, Dr. Raddock directs the Guidance and Consultation Center of Greater New York, a private, comprehensive mental health group, and maintains a private practice in Mount Vernon, New York.

JEANNE M. SAFER, Ph.D., is currently a faculty member, supervisor, and research consultant at the Postgraduate Center for Mental Health, where she was formerly Director of Research. Dr. Safer is also a supervisor at the National Institute for the Psychotherapies, serves as a consultant to several governmental and private agencies, and was on the faculty of the Clinical Psychology Program in the Graduate Faculty of the New School for Social Research in New

York City. She was a psychology intern at the Postgraduate Center for Mental Health from 1972–1974.

Dr. Safer is in private practice as a psychotherapist and psychoanalyst in New York City.

RUTH BERS SHAPIRO, Ph.D., received her B.A. in English from the University of Michigan and her doctorate in clinical psychology from New York University. She was a psychology intern at the Postgraduate Center for Mental Health in 1968–1969, and completed two additional years of clinical training in 1971. Since 1973, Dr. Shapiro has been a member of the Psychology Department at John Jay College of Criminal Justice, City University of New York, where she is an Associate Professor and Deputy Chairperson. She is also an Adjunct Associate Professor of Psychology and Education at Teachers College, Columbia University, and is on the faculty of the Postgraduate Center for Mental Health. She is in private practice in New York and has published articles on child and adolescent development and the psychology of women.

AVA L. SIEGLER, Ph.D., is the Director of the Child, Adolescent, and Family Clinic of the Postgraduate Center for Mental Health and heads its Child and Adolescent Analytic Training Program. She is also on the faculty of the Adult Psychoanalytic Institute.

Dr. Siegler has been an Associate Clinical Professor of Psychology at New York University since 1976, and is a member of the faculty of the New York University Medical School. She was a psychology intern at the Postgraduate Center for Mental Health in 1969–1970.

She currently chairs the National Committee on Child and Adolescent Training and Education of the Division of Psychoanalysis, American Psychological Association.

Dr. Siegler developed and has directed the Prescott Early Intervention Project for Single-Parent Families, a nationally known day care mental health program. She has written and lectured on the impact of the single-parent family on child development, psychological aspects of female development, the analytic treatment of children and adolescents, the psychological development of gifted children, the meaning of fairy tales and myths, the impact of early childhood research upon psychoanalytic theory and practice, and the psychoanalytic theory of human development, and has published in scientific jouirnals. Dr. Siegler has also contributed chapters to edited works. She is currently at work on a volume entitled *The Psychoanalytic Theory of Human Development: A Perspective on the Life Span.*

CARL F. WIEDEMANN, Ph.D., is currently professor of psychology at John Jay College of Criminal Justice of the City University of New York. Professor Wiedemann received his doctorate in clinical psychology from New York University and served a two-year internship in psychology at the Postgraduate Center for Mental Health, 1967–1969.

Dr. Wiedemann has received certificates in the concentrations of clinical psychology and statistics, measurement, research design, and computer applications. His positions at John Jay College have included Director of Research and Director of Faculty Research Computing. Dr. Wiedemann is a consultant in the applications of data analysis and in problems in the psychology of personality to doctoral candidates and to public and private agencies. He has been an active consultant also to a number of agencies in the area of criminal justice.

Most recently, Dr. Wiedemann was appointed to the Doctoral Faculty of the City University of New York, and is the program head for the Ph.D. program in criminal justice at CUNY.

# INTRODUCTION

BEGINNING GRADUALLY ABOUT thirty years ago and accelerating through the past two decades, an upsurge of interest in the study of sleep interruption has appeared. Studies in this area of sleep interruption have generated a greater sense of urgency than ever before among laboratory researchers and clinicians to understand the vicissitudes of sleep and sleep-interruption phenomena. In this new context, not only has the nightmare become a focus of interest among scientists working in sleep laboratories, but this renewed interest has stimulated clinicians to return to the nightmare for a second look.

Although the nightmare is considered a bona fide phenomenon of personality, clinicians have typically assigned it a secondary status on the agenda of important personality manifestations requiring investigation. In this sense, the nightmare has occupied an enigmatic position in the domain of psychology generally and in psychoanalysis especially.

Now, in the mid-1980's—more than thirty years after the landmark finding of the relation of dreaming to rapid eye movement (REM) by Aserinsky in association with Kleitman and Dement—the phenomenon of the nightmare has emerged as a serious arena of clinical interest and research. Before this finding and for almost a century—since the 1900 publication of Freud's classic work *The Interpretation of Dreams*—the nightmare was generally subsumed within the psychoanalytic domain. Yet, the

Freudian or psychoanalytic approach, stressing the importance of disguised wish fulfillment in the dream, is particularly vague with respect to the meaning of nightmares. Consequently, clinical practitioners have had little guidance in understanding the nightmare in terms of actual work in therapy sessions. Although the nightmare usually develops as an outgrowth of the content of conventional dreams, Freud did not provide any fundamental grounding in the theory of nightmare formation or in practical therapeutic applications required to work with patients on nightmares.

Accordingly, in the psychoanalytic field, the literature on nightmares remains scattered. Work by psychiatrists and psychologists is to be found distributed randomly in scores of professional journals. No central repository source has appeared in which a presentation and synthesis of the work on theories of nightmares is provided. The one general attitude regarding the nightmare that exists in popular belief as well as among professional psychotherapists is that the nightmare is synonymous with emotional experiences of terror and dread. This overall attitude persists even though in recent years studies have shown that nightmares are not at all solely dreams of terror or dread. Thus, the need for a foundation volume on the morphology of the nightmare becomes increasingly important because of a growing awareness among clinicians of the relevance of nightmares to the treatment process and the increasing numbers of laboratory studies of non–rapid eye movement (NREM) nightmares and nightmares occurring out of typical REM dreaming phases.

In this book, psychoanalytic and physiological orientations will be presented, along with various traditions in the understanding of the nightmare. In addition, nightmares will be distinguished from anxiety dreams, night terrors, and hypnagogic states. The traditions sampled range from those within an interpersonal framework that reject theories of libido, to analytic theories that accept libido, to others that treat the presentation of all dream material as problem-solving opportunites. A survey of the theories of nightmares should also consider the appearance of episodic dream phenomena during childhood, and this volume, in setting out to survey seminal work of all areas of nightmare study, includes a section on theories of nightmares and night terrors in children.

Still another approach to the study of nightmares represented in this volume may be defined as the study of nightmares in the context of the psychology of personality. In this framework, authors have been concerned with the correlation of personality characteristics, character structure, and symptom patterns of patients with particular nightmares and aspects of nightmares. These studies include those of symbol meaning, recurrent nightmares, and laughing nightmares, to cite just a few.

The volume is organized into five parts. In part 1, "Psychoanalytic and Psychodynamic Theories of Nightmares," theoretical and research contributions in the psychoanalytic and psychodynamic traditions are reviewed. This literature reflects some of the seminal contributions in the field. The historical underpinning of the tradition is also included and constitutes a thorough compendium of the work on nightmares in this psychodynamic tradition.

In chapter 1, Peter Buirski examines the nightmare with respect to many of the central tenents proposed by Freud, including anxiety, drefenses, ego functioning, asggression, and the repetition compulsion. Dr. Buirski also assesses the role of the nightmare in the theory of the dream and wish fulfillment. This overview of the nightmare in psychoanalysis is continued in chapter 2 by the particular analysis of intrapsychic conflict. In this chapter Judith Hanlon traces the evolution of psychoanalysis from its original focus on the influence of the id to a focus more on conflict psychology. Dr. Hanlon shows that the nightmare is currently understood as an expression of conflict, as compared to the early Freudian position on the nightmare as it relates to wish fulfillment and the id. Dr. Hanlon also examines the elements of such conflict in terms of instincts, anxiety, ego, and superego. In chapter 3, Susan Kavaler introduces the context of object relations theory and postulates that in the nightmare, especially, preoedipal fears are most clearly experienced. In the inner world of paranoid and schizoid anxieties, bad objects and pathological object ties threaten the ego. Dr. Kavaler discusses the separation-individuation process as it relates to the nightmare and includes in her analysis the deeper motifs discussed by object relations theorists such as Klein, Fairbairn, and Guntrip as these motifs appear in the nightmare. In chapter 4 Jeanne M. Safer continues to examine the psychoanalytic approach to understanding the nightmare in the light of psychophysiological sleep laboratory research. In this cross-disciplinary context, Dr. Safer distinguishes between anxiety dreams, night terrors, and nightmares and relates some central psychoanalytic concepts such as the function of anxiety, forbidden impulses, oral-aggressive needs, and separation fears to the appearance of the nightmare. Dr. Safer also considers the need for revision of the psychoanalytic focus on thematic aspects of the nightmare on the basis of new laboratory findings. In addition, Dr. Safer introduces the connection between the experience of the nightmare and its function as a possible creative attempt at conflict resolution.

These four chapters by Buirski, Hanlon, Kavaler, and Safer comprehensively cover the psychoanalytic-psychodynamic consideration of the nightmare. Taken together they reveal that the understanding of the nightmare has evolved quite substantially from its modern point of origin in Freud's 1900 publication of *The Interpretation of Dreams.*

In part 2, "Physiological Studies of Nightmare Phenomena," the physiological research tradition and its contribution to the understanding of the nightmare are presented. Included are historical as well as more recent major discoveries in the field. Topics covered include an integration of psychoanalytic and physiological data regarding nightmares, polygraphic studies of nightmares, the difference between dreams and nightmares with respect to physiological measures, and the meaning of level of arousal with regard to nightmares. This review includes the reporting of research findings on NREM nightmares as well as work on the differences between REM and NREM nightmares. Overall research and clinical findings of this physiological tradition are reviewed in order to develop a complete picture of the field. To this end, in addition to the major research, smaller supporting research studies focusing on more delimited variables are also included.

In chapter 5, Carl F. Wiedemann addresses the differences between REM and NREM sleep and relates these states to nightmares and night terrors. Dr. Wiedemann reviews the nature of the sleep cycle and covers a wide spectrum of diverse issues such as the relation of sleep to consciousness, to physiological and psychological integrity, and to the particular sleep disorder of narcolepsy. Night terrors are examined as states of arousal, and REM anxiety dreams are discussed with reference to central nervous system (CNS) growth. Dr. Wiedemann also reviews the literature on REM states in children, discusses other vivid dreamlike experiences such as the hypnagogic hallucination, and provides descriptions of the nightmare and its variants, such as stage 4 night terrors, REM anxiety dreams, stage 2 awakenings, and hypnagogic nightmares. Following Dr. Wiedemann's comprehensive review of sleep and nightmares, Emily M. Adams in chapter 6 further reviews the research, research problems, and results of laboratory studies on the neuropsychology of the nightmare as reported in the literature. In this assessment, Dr. Adams applies standards of experimental design requisites to the research on the sleep cycle, dreaming, and nightmares and reviews the literature on the physiology of nightmares in children. In addition, she includes a discussion of mentation as it applies to dreaming and considers the neural structures of sleep and the role of neurotransmitters and arousal in nightmares. In chapter 7, Lawrence Josephs relates dream reports of nightmares to stages of sleep and distinguishes the nightmare from the night terror. Dr. Josephs' review includes a content analysis of dream reports and nightmares as well as an analysis of the latent content of the nightmare.

The chapters in this second section by Wiedemann, Adams, and Josephs as well as chapter 4 by Safer in the previous section constitute a multifaceted examination of the laboratory and psychophysiological approaches to the study of the nightmare. Taken together, these contributions provide a comprehensive view of this psychophysiological tradition. This section, consequently, reveals the direction research is taking and portrays the enormous strides that have been achieved in this area of research. In addition, a picture is formed of the voluminous amount of new data that has appeared and continues to emerge from the sleep laboratories.

In part 3, "Episodic Dream Phenomena in Children and Adults: Nightmares, Night Terrors, and Anxiety Dreams," the differences between nightmares, night terrors, and anxiety dreams are further considered. Theories of anxiety dreams are reviewed, and the work on clinical differences among disturbed dreams in both children and adults is presented. Proceeding with research on the analysis of night terrors in children, this section then presents work on nightmares in children and adults, findings on the special nature of stage 4 night terrors, and finally, the research on the psychology, neurophysiology, and therapy of night terrors in children.

The aim in this section is to summarize cogently the entire sleep context in children with respect to both environmental and intrapersonal variables. The dimension of episodic dream phenomena and their relation to precipitating and pivotal events is cited, and an overview emerges that differentiates between adults and children with respect to phenomena of nightmares, night terrors, and anxiety dreams.

In chapter 8, Franklin D. Raddock reveals the complex tapestry of nightmares, problem sleep, and difficult bedtime behavior in children. Specific sleep patterns in children, sleep disorders, sleep upset and disturbances, and parent-child interactions as they relate to sleep are presented. Details of sleep disorders and nightmares of the first three years of life, the second three years, and various periods through late adolescence are also presented. Through this exposition, Dr. Raddock provides a context for understanding various problems of nightmares, anxiety dreams, and night terrors in children. In chapter 9, Ruth Bers Shapiro intruduces the psychoanalytic perspective on the subject of anxiety dreams in children and adults. Dr. Shapiro discusses the Freudian view of dreams, anxiety, repressed wishes, and dream censorship and relates these to Freud's structural model and theories of anxiety. Central tenets that are discussed include repetitive traumatic dreams, night terrors, the variety of anxiety dreams, precipitating environmental events, punishment dreams, contemporary theories of anxiety dreams, and psychophysiological investigations of these states. Diagnostic as well as adaptive and ego development considerations are also brought to bear on the subject. In chapter 10, Susan Knapp elaborates the theme of night terrors in children with respect to both emotional and biological factors. Dr. Knapp sorts out the theoretical approaches to the understanding of night terrors including psychodynamic, physiological, and arousal disorder theories. She reviews Freud's writings regarding the dream and the issue of conflict and relates these topics to physiological hypotheses regarding conflict. In addition, Dr. Knapp applies much of the research data from both the psychophysiological and the clinical literature to the subject. Concluding this section, Ava L. Siegler in chapter 11 integrates issues of child development from a psychoanalytic perspective with that of the nightmare experience. Dr. Siegler also considers the nightmare from the perspective of diagnostic considerations, phobic defense, and dream theory, and introduces the idea that the nightmare can also reflect developmental organization and achievement.

In aggregate the chapters in this section form a picture of the clinical, laboratory, dynamic, and physiological organization of differences in various episodic dream phenomena in children. This amalgam of chapters taken together, sets forth the entire nighttime psychology of children, including bedtime behavior as well as sleep disruption phenomena.

In part 4, "Studies of the Nightmare in the Psychology of Personality," a sampling is undertaken of the kinds of papers published on various aspects of the experience of the nightmare as this phenomenon relates to personality functioning. This survey includes work on personality characteristics of nightmare sufferers, the meaning of nightmares in therapy, the nightmare and its relation to hypnagogic hallucinations, and the wide-ranging research on the theory of dreams and nightmares in the psychology of personality. The contribution of this section to the literature is its attempt to present groupings of themes from the field of study relating nightmares to the psychology of personality so that the more salient variables in this realm of research can be distilled.

In chapter 12, Michael Joseph Davies considers the nightmare in terms of its relation to psychopathology and reviews the subject of specific impulses that may characterize the nightmare. In addition, Dr. Davies compares nightmares and dreams and considers the relative extent of their similarities or differences with respect to psychopathology. Dr. Davies also presents significant clinical data to illustrate his conclusions. In chapter 13, Arthur Gray compares the nightmare to phenomena that seem psychopathological, such as hypnagogic hallucinations and sleep paralysis. Dr. Gray also considers the states of anxiety dreams and night terrors and proposes the concept of structuralization as a means of understanding a cluster of related sleep manifestations. In chapter 14, Daniel P. Juda presents data that characterize a segment of the population as nightmare sufferers. Within this special context, he reviews various hypotheses and theories on the meaning of the nightmare. The nightmare sufferer is examined with respect to research data and psychiatric conditions, and psychoanalytic issues such as the repetition compulsion are brought to bear on the subject of the nightmare sufferer. Dr. Juda also discusses specific populations that experience repetitive nightmares.

In reviewing various phenomena of the nightmare and its relation to psychopathology, the work by Davies, Gray, and Juda in this section, taken together, reflects the mainstream thinking on the nightmare in the study of personality.

Part 5, "The Nightmare and the Structure of Personality," consists of four related chapters by Henry Kellerman analyzing a theory of the nightmare in its unique relation to the structure of personality. In this section, the nightmare is viewed as the essential decoder that reveals the various aspects and levels of personality domains as they relate one to the other. The nightmare is seen as a template through which the seeming disorganization, the myriad complexities, overlappings, competing forces, and qualities of the personality suddenly become organized so that the compounded variables are seen to function in the personality in a parsimonious fashion.

In chapter 15, Dr. Kellerman critically assesses psychoanalytic dream theory and crystallizes a series of questions that a theory of the nightmare in the structure of personality needs to address. This introduction is followed in chapter 16 by Dr. Kellerman's proposal of a theory of basic nightmare themes and their relationship to various specific aspects of personality, such as emotions, traits, defenses, and diagnostic propensities. Various clinical vignettes are presented to illustrate these relationships. In chapter 17, Dr. Kellerman further deepens the analysis by relating defense mechanisms to the intrapsychic agency and postulates that nightmare themes reveal the specific intrapsychic purpose of each defense mechanism. The special position of the ego is analyzed with respect to the intrapsychic agency, the personality, and the nightmare itself, and psychosexual development is also considered in order to portray the dynamic interplay of intrapsychic forces. In the final chapter, chapter 18, Dr. Kellerman proposes the cognitive and psychosomatic structures that theoretically complete the nomological network of personality-correlates as this network is revealed through the nightmare.

In chapter 19, a special coda, Dr. Kellerman then concludes this section by recapitulating a series of postulates that were presented throughout the four chapters of this section. These postulates represent a theory that constitutes the only system of nightmares and personality in the literature to link the specific facets of personality with specific nightmare themes in a proposed unified structural theory.

Finally, in an epilogue Dr. Kellerman concludes the book in a manner that reiterates what was said throughout the volume: that nightmares are far more than simply dreams of terror—that they are, in fact, enriched phenomena reflecting what reverberates throughout the personality.

The five sections of this book constitute a comprehensive organization of the field of nightmare study. The field is covered in a manner that permits major theoretical work to be represented as well as providing necessary detail in the form of smaller-scale studies that act as interstitial links in the overall work. Contributors have expanded their reference sections to include other works of interest in their subject areas. The material in this volume can also serve to inspire further knitting together of the disparate areas of applied clinical work and laboratory research in this rapidly expanding field of sleep, dreams, and nightmares.

# PART ONE: Psychoanalytic and Psychodynamic Theories of Nightmares

# 1.

# The Nightmare in Psychoanalysis

PETER BUIRSKI

THE ANALYSIS OF dreams has been a cornerstone of psychoanalytic theory and technique since Freud undertook his own self-analysis. Considering the central position which dreams and their interpretation hold in the history of psychoanalysis, it is remarkable how little attention has been directed to that most dramatic and disturbing of all dream experiences—the nightmare.

While the nightmare differs from other dreams in the intensity of unpleasant or disturbing affect experienced, perhaps the major reason for the neglect of the nightmare in the psychoanalytic literature is that the analysis of the nightmare has traditionally not required any modification or deviation from the orthodox psychoanalytic technique of dream interpretation. Furthermore, the term "nightmare," while common in colloquial parlance, lacks sufficient specificity to be useful in scientific discourse. Frequently included in the variety of dream experiences which are often used interchangeably with the term "nightmare" are anxiety dreams, punishment dreams, post-traumatic dreams, and pavor nocturnus or night terrors.

## The Psychophysiology of the Nightmare

During the past fifteen years, new research techniques for studying the sleeping and dreaming states in the laboratory have revolutionized our understanding of the psychophysiology of the nightmare experience (Fisher et al. 1970; Fisher 1974). The work of Charles Fisher and his colleagues has demonstrated that there are two dramatically different types of "nightmare" experience, one type occurring during REM sleep and the other occurring during stage 4 sleep. These two "nightmare" experiences differ on both the neurophysiological level and on the level of subjective psychological experience. Obviously, prior to this research, psychoanalysts, both theoreticians, and clinicians, were unaware that they were dealing with a variety of different sleep and dream phenomena. With the benefit of the new insights into the psychophysiology of the "nightmare" experience, much that had seemed contradictory or ambiguous in the psychoanalytic literature has been clarified.

In the history of psychoanalysis, the first extensive discussion of the nightmare was found in Ernest Jones's (1951) book *On the Nightmare,* which was written in 1911. According to Jones, there were three cardinal features to a nightmare: intense or agonizing dread; the sense of oppression or of weight on the chest which dangerously threatens the continuation of breathing; and the dreamer's conviction of being helpless or paralyzed. Jones's description of the nightmare was considered definitive for sixty years. Fisher was able to demonstrate that Jones had actually condensed into his definition of the nightmare the subjective experiences emanating from two different psychophysiological stages of sleep. By monitoring the sleep cycles of volunteer nightmare sufferers, Fisher and his colleagues demonstrated that awakening with anxiety occurs during all stages of sleep. However, the most severe type of nightmare experience is confined to the deepest stage of nondreaming sleep, stage 4.

It is characterized by (a) a sudden, cataclysmic breakthrough of uncontrolled anxiety; (b) a sudden loud scream of blood-curdling intensity or cry for help; (c) the passing into an arousal reaction—subject is dissociated, confused, unresponsive, hallucinating; (d) a waking EEG pattern, but subject is not fully alert; (e) the subject frequently being propelled out of bed and moving through the house as though in flight; (f) intense autonomic discharge, heart rate doubling or nearly tripling in 15 to 30 seconds, and respiratory rate and amplitude increasing; (g) difficulty in retrieving content and rapid onset of amnesia for the attack. (Fisher et al. 1970:778)

The overwhelming percentage of reported nightmare experiences however, arise out of REM-stage sleep. Of those subjects who reported anxiety dreams of varying intensity during REM, none of the dreamers experienced the overwhelming panicky feeling that characterizes stage 4. Furthermore, while the REM nightmares were sufficiently disturbing as to cause awakening, they were not accompanied by cries or vocalizations. On the basis of these findings, Fisher (1974) concluded that of the three cardinal features of the nightmare described by Jones, the first, intense dread, is characteristic of a stage 4 night terror, while the remaining two, pressure on the chest and paralysis, are characteristic of REM nightmares.

Distinguishing between stage 4 night terrors and REM nightmares was thought to be important because doubts had been voiced as to whether psychogenic factors trigger the stage 4 night terrors and whether, once triggered, they contain any ongoing mental content (Broughton 1968, 1970). Regarding the presence of a psychogenic triggering factor in stage 4 night terrors, Fisher (1974:187) reported that "the hypothesis may be advanced that episodes can be triggered by either of two different types of stimulation: a) endogenous, in the form of ongoing mental activity during NREM sleep; and b) exogenous, in the form of loud noises or other external stimulation." While there is no question about the presence of mental content in REM dreams, the prevalence of amnesia for stage 4 night terrors has led to speculations that they arise from a psychological void (Gastaut and Broughton 1965). In response, Fisher et al. (1970:762) state: "Against the notion of the nightmare arising from a psychological void is the fact that the psychic content retrieved can be shown to be coherent, psychodynamically organized, related to the subject's pre-existing traumata and conflicts, and to the REM dreams of the same night." This is certainly not an insignificant or petty concern for psychoanalysis, because the essence of the psychoanalytic view of the nightmare or night terror involves discerning the hidden meanings disguised behind the manifest mental content of the dream.

One of the limitations of the sleep and dream psychophysiology research is that the EEG has not been able to differentiate between different types of REM dreams. Thus, we are left to depend on the dreamer's recollections and self-reports in differentiating between anxiety dreams, punishment dreams, and post-traumatic dreams. However, distinguishing between these three different types of disturbing REM dreams has more value theoretically than clinically. From the viewpoint of psychoanalysis, all dream experiences containing mental or sensory content are analyzed in a similar fashion. Whether a psychoanalyst is interpreting a REM nightmare or a stage 4 night terror, the techniques of dream analysis and the assumptions underlying those techniques are constant. Therefore, in the discussion which follows, unless otherwise indicated, the term "nightmare" will be used to include REM anxiety dreams, punishment dreams, post-traumatic dreams, and stage 4 night terrors or pavor nocturnus.

## The Analysis of Dreams and Nightmares

Freud's (1900) seminal work *The Interpretation of Dreams* is the first and very nearly the last word on the psychoanalysis of dreams. In this work, Freud expounds the theory that dreams express the deepest psychological concerns and conflicts of the individual, albeit in disguised or distorted form. During sleep, the normally alert and vigilant ego partially relaxes its defensive functioning. This allows for the emergence into consciousness of certain powerful impulses and wishes which, during wakefulness, are kept under repression in the unconscious by the defensive efforts of the alert ego. These impulses and wishes, because of their threatening, dangerous, or otherwise unacceptable nature, would generate excessive anxiety or promote a loss of self-esteem if they were admitted to conscious awareness in an undisguised form. The major function of the dream, then, is to disguise these emerging unacceptable wishes to the extent that the sleep of the dreamer remains undisturbed. The content of the remembered dream, what Freud referred to as the manifest content of the dream, reflects the ego's attempt to distort or disguise the underlying unconscious content, the latent content, which is always active in the mind of the sleeper.

The ego accomplishes the task of distortion by employing the dreamwork mechanisms of displacement, condensation, secondary elaboration, and symbolic representation. Through the technique of dream analysis, these distorting mechanisms are undone and the manifest dream is revealed to be an elaborate construction designed to disguise the dreamer's unacceptable unconscious wishes. When the dreamwork is successful, the unconscious wishes remain outside the dreamer's conscious awareness and the sleep state remains undisturbed.

The significance of dreams in psychoanalytic treatment is that, through the analysis of the dream, the distortions and disguises of the manifest dream can be unraveled, revealing the latent, unconscious wishes of the dreamer. For this reason, Freud referred to the analysis of dreams as the "Royal Road" to understanding the unconscious mind of the dreamer.

Throughout Freud's life, he maintained his interest in the interpretation of dreams. In his final publication, *An Outline of Psychoanalysis*, Freud stated:

> As the dream-work proceeds, sometimes the unconscious will press forward more successfully and sometimes the ego will defend itself with greater energy. Anxiety dreams are mostly those whose content has undergone the least distortion. If the demand made by the unconscious is too great for the sleeping ego to be in a position to fend it off by the means at its disposal, it abandons the wish to sleep and returns to waking life. We shall be taking every experience into account if we say that a dream is invariably an *attempt* to get rid of a disturbance of sleep by means of a wish-fulfillment, so that the dream is a guardian of sleep. (Freud 1940:170–71; italics added)

While Freud maintained that the function of dreams was to preserve sleep by warding off, through distortion, the emergence into conscious awareness of unacceptable unconscious wishes, he was clearly aware that not every attempt was successful. For Freud, a nightmare results when the dreamwork fails or is incomplete in its action. Such dreams are an expression of immoral, incestuous and perverse impulses or of murderous and sadistic lusts. The dreamer reacts to many of these dreams by waking up in a fright in which case the situation is no longer obscure to us. The censorship has neglected its task, this has been noticed too late, and the generation of anxiety is a substitution for the distortion that has been omitted. In still other instances of such dreams, even that expression of affect is absent. (Freud 1925:132).

## The Determinants of the Nightmare

Nightmares occur to people of all ages. Mack (1970:206) proposed that any theory of the nightmare "must account for the fundamental clinical characteristics of nightmares at any age: the feeling of helplessness and powerlessness; the perception of severe danger; the overwhelming or life and death quality of anxiety; and finally, the threat or actual presence in the dream of violence and destructiveness." Drawing on the theoretical analyses of Mack and others, we can specify six major determinants of the nightmare.

1. *External factors.* Included in a discussion of external factors would be any real environmental events which endanger the dreamer's life or threaten the dreamer with bodily injury. Other disturbing external events would include the loss of a significant person and reverses in the dreamer's life circumstances, such as the loss of employment. While external factors often operate in conjunction with internal factors in contributing to nightmares, they are typically not sufficient determiners on their own.

It is not unusual for the external event which precipitates the nightmare to appear, on a manifest level, to be nonthreatening or even benign. The reason the event served to precipitate the nightmare can only be clarified by analyzing the specific meaning of the event or series of events which led up to the nightmare in the unconscious of the individual dreamer. Typically, the power of an event to precipitate a traumatic response depends on the extent to which the present event finds confirmation in either currently active fears or in the memories of previously disturbing incidents, usually from childhood, which the present event manages to revive.

Occasionally, real traumatic external experiences are relived during sleep in what is referred to as post-traumatic dreams. To the category of post-traumatic dreams should be added those dreams which occur to patients during the course of psychoanalytic treatment whose content contains the revival of forgotten traumatic events from childhood. The phenomenon of post-traumatic dreams appears to pose a thorny problem for the wish-fulfillment theory of dreams. Freud addressed the theoretical problem posed by post-traumatic dreams in *Beyond the Pleasure Principle:*

> The fulfillment of wishes is, as we know, brought about in a hallucinatory manner by dreams, and under the dominance of the pleasure principle this has become their function. But it is not in the service of that principle that the dreams of patients suffering from traumatic neuroses lead them back with such regularity to the situation in which the trauma occurred. We may argue, rather, that dreams are here helping to carry out another task, which must be accomplished before the dominance of the pleasure principle can even begin. These dreams are endeavoring to master the stimulus retrospectively, by developing the anxiety whose omission was the cause of the traumatic neurosis. They thus offered us a view of a function of the mental apparatus which, though it does not contradict the pleasure principle, is nevertheless independent of it and seems to be more primitive than the purpose of gaining pleasure and avoiding unpleasure. (Freud 1920:32)

With the development of Ego Psychology, the explanation was proposed that post-traumatic dreams, through the repeated reliving of the traumatic event during the dreams, represent attempts on the part of the mature ego to master an experience which originally overwhelmed the immature ego (much the way repeated viewings of a horror film will generate decreasing levels of anxiety and shock). Mack (1970) also suggests that, on another level, post-traumatic dreams may serve the function of repeatedly expiating the unconscious guilt of the dreamer.

2. *Instinctual factors.* Instinctual forces lie at the core of all dreams. The manifest dream represents a compromise, forged by the ego, between the unacceptable unconscious wishes of the id and the ego's need to keep these wishes from emerging into consciousness. For the dream to succeed, the forces of defense

must be stronger than the forces propelling the wish into consciousness. A nightmare is an unsuccessful dream; the forces of the unconscious wishes have overwhelmed the strength of the ego's defenses, and the threatening impulses begin to emerge into consciousness. In the face of the threat of the emergence of the unacceptable, the dreamer experiences anxiety or even terror and awakens. These dreams are referred to as anxiety dreams. Awakening from an anxiety dream allows the ego to reassert its defensive strength, which was diminished or relaxed during sleep. While the dreamwork failed to keep the unconscious from emerging into consciousness, awakening now serves that defensive purpose by interrupting the emerging flow of unconscious wishes and allowing the conscious ego to reassert itself.

Whether a dream becomes a nightmare depends, then, on the relative strengths of the unconscious id impulses pushing toward consciousness and the opposition of the ego's defenses. If the ego's defenses are sufficiently strong, the id impulses will be successfully distorted or disguised and the dream will enable the dreamer to continue sleeping. Should the impulses become too strong or the defense become weakened, an anxiety dream could result.

Psychoanalytic understanding of the nature of the instinctual drives involved in the production of nightmares has grown along with general advances in psychoanalytic theory. In *The Interpretation of Dreams*, Freud (1900:585) proposed that nightmares in children "can only be a question of sexual impulses which have not been understood and which have been repudiated." Jones tried to be more specific about the precise nature of the sexual impulses involved in nightmares. While making what today we recognize as a faulty distinction between nightmares and other anxiety dreams, Jones (1951:79) did offer the interesting observation that the nightmare's "essential difference is that its latent content is highly specific and stereotyped. In all cases of anxiety dreams the latent content represents the fulfillment of a repressed sexual wish, usually an incestuous one, but, whereas in nightmares this always relates to the normal sexual act, various perverse sexual wishes come to expression in the other forms of anxiety dreams." By 1925, Freud had already revised his drive theory to include aggression as a primary drive. In a paper published that year, in describing the instinctual impulses involved in precipitating nightmares, he says, "they are an expression of immoral, incestuous and perverse impulses or of murderous and sadistic lusts" (Freud 1925:132). Given the extent of the threatening and dangerous content in nightmares, it is surprising that it took so long for the role of aggression to be appreciated. This seems to have been a case of psychoanalysis forcing the nightmare into the theoretical model of the early drive theory. Only after aggression was recognized by Freud as a primary drive was its operation in forging the nightmare appreciated.

The presence of aggression in the nightmare can be seen in the threat or actual occurrence of violent attacks on the dreamer that are so frequently reported upon awakening. It is uncommon for the nightmare to directly portray the aggressive wishes of the dreamer. Typically, the dreamer experiences himself as the victim of imaginary creatures or forces. Nevertheless, as is true of the presence of libidinal wishes in the dream, the projection or externalization of aggression in the nightmare derives from the dreamer's underlying conflicts over aggressive wishes. The aggressive conflicts of the dreamer often derive from the oedipal or later developmental phases. However, conflicts over aggressive wishes may also derive from experiences or fears of helplessness and vulnerability, abandonment, separation, or loss of love. Regardless of the psychosexual stage or experience from which the aggressive wishes originate, the regressive quality of the nightmare state leads the aggression to be frequently portrayed in savage oral and sadistic imagery.

3. *Developmental factors.* It is Mack's (1970) contention that nightmares are often precipitated by the impulses and struggles appropriate to the current level of psychosexual development. However, Mack recognizes that during sleep, conflicts which are related to earlier developmental phases may be revived. It is not unusual for nightmares to occur during times of important changes in the lives of normal adults. In such cases, Mack suggests that the nightmare may stand out as a landmark of some significant turning point or critical period. For instance, one such critical period might be impending fatherhood. An example of this sort of event was reported by a student who, during his wife's first pregnancy, awoke

in fright from a nightmare in which he saw the doorknob of his front door turning and a huge monster burst into his house.

4. *Ego factors.* Any intense threats to the ego's integrative functions, whether from the external world, the instinctual drives, or the superego, which induce feelings of helplessness may precipitate nightmares. The dreamer's ego may be overburdened by such experiences as the loss or death of an important person, separations even for brief periods from a love object, verbal threats, moves to unfamiliar surroundings, illnesses, bodily injury, hospitalizations, and surgery. When the ego is so overburdened, its defensive functions are diminished and the individual is prone to experience nightmares. One major context in which ego helplessness is found is during the state of sleep. During sleep, the ego's capacity for reality testing is severely curtailed. Furthermore, during sleep, the individual's ego is deprived of external sources of comfort, support, and reality testing which during the waking state might be provided by friends or family. Other ego functions also suffer diminished effectiveness during sleep. The signal function, which during wakefulness can prevent the intensification of anxiety, does not function adequately during sleep. This is a major factor contributing to the experience of overwhelming anxiety in nightmares. While during the waking state, certain ego-defense mechanisms, such as repression and intellectualization, function to bind or ward off anxiety, during sleep their functioning is impaired. Once massive anxiety has built up, the dreamer's only recourse is to wake up, thereby restoring the conditions under which the ego can reestablish reality testing and reinstitute the signal function and the mechanisms of defense.

5. *Superego factors.* Along with anxiety dreams and post-traumatic dreams, a third type of dream, the punishment dream, might also be seen as contradicting the wish-fulfillment function of dreaming. In the case of Little Hans (Freud 1909), the boy is reported to have had an anxiety dream that his mother had gone away and he had no one to coax (cuddle) with. Freud describes this as "a genuine punishment and repression dream" (1909:118). In reconstructing what occurred in little Hans's unconscious, Freud proposed that "the child dreamt of exchanging endearments with his mother and of sleeping with her; but all the pleasure was transformed into anxiety, and all the ideational content into its

opposite. Repression had defeated the purpose of the mechanism of dreaming" (1909:118). At a later date, Freud (1920) suggested that punishment dreams functioned to replace the forbidden wish fulfillment by the appropriate punishment for it. Thus, the punishment dream fulfills the wish of the sense of guilt which arises in reaction to the repudiated impulse. In 1923, Freud explained the process by stating, "Such offensive action as this against the dream can only be ascribed to the critical agency of the ego" (1923:118). Finally, after Freud developed his structural theory in which mental functioning was understood in terms of id, ego, and superego structures, Freud (1932) returned to the defense of his wish-fulfillment theory of dreams with fresh understanding arising from the implications of the structural theory. He stated that "punishment dreams, too, are fulfillments of wishes, though not of wishes of the instinctual impulses but of those of the critical, censoring and punishing agency in the mind" (1932:27). Such dreams, then, satisfy the wishes of the superego, whereas other dreams satisfy the wishes of the id.

6. *Regressive factors.* One of the most prominent features of nightmares is that, in the face of intensified anxiety, there occurs a regression to a state of infantile helplessness. The ego's defensive capabilities become overwhelmed, and the result is the appearance of primitive, primary-process thought patterns featuring projection, externalization, and displacement. Not only are the ego's defensive functions subject to regression, but there also occurs the regressive revival of childhood fears with accompanying feelings of helplessness. Along with the regressive revival of childhood fears, regression with respect to the way significant objects, especially the parents, are represented may occur. Significant objects are represented in nightmares not as the more mature waking ego would view them but in accord with the way a highly ambivalent preoedipal child might have experienced them.

## Summary

Psychophysiological research into the various stages of sleep has revealed that what are colloquially referred to as "nightmares" are the products of two distinct states of sleep: REM and stage 4. The psychoanalytic approach to the analysis of the nightmare, however, does not depend on the sleep stage from which the phenomenon derives. All dreams are understood to be attempts to portray unconscious wishes as being fulfilled. The technical approach for analyzing the nightmare is not appreciably different from that advocated for dreams in general. However, the significance of the nightmare in psychoanalytic theory has to do with the challenge nightmares pose to Freud's wish-fulfillment theory of dreams. Since they appeared to represent an exception to the wish-fulfillment nature of dreams, Freud felt called upon to explain why nightmares did not violate his theory. Through Freud's effort to demonstrate that the nightmare conformed to his theory of dreams, the nightmare contributed to the further elaboration of Freud's ideas on anxiety, the nature of the defenses, the functioning of the ego, the operation of the repetition compulsion, and the important role of aggression in mental life.

## References


Broughton, R. J. 1968. Sleep disorders: Disorders of arousal? *Science* 159: 1070–78.

Broughton, R. J. 1970. The incubus attack. In E. Hartmann, ed., *Sleep and Dreaming*. Boston: Little, Brown.

Fisher, C. 1974. A psychophysiological study of nightmares and night terrors. II. Mental content and recall of stage 4 night terrors. *Journal of Nervous and Mental Disease* 158:174–88.

Fisher, C., J. Byrne, A. Edwards, and E. Kahn. 1970. A psychophysiological study of nightmares. *Journal of the American Psychoanalytic Association* 18:747–82.

Freud, S. *Standard Edition of the Complete Psychological Works of Sigmund Freud*. James Strachey, ed. and tr. 24 vols. London: Hogarth Press, 1953–1974; New York: Macmillan.

1900. *The Interpretation of Dreams*. Vols. 4 and 5

1909. *Analysis of a Phobia in a Five-Year-Old Boy*. Vol. 10.

1920. *Beyond the Pleasure Principle*. Vol. 18.

1923. Remarks on the theory and practice of dream-interpretation. 19:109–21.

1925. Some additional notes on dream-interpretation as a whole. 19:127–38.

1932. *New Introductionary Lectures on Psychoanalysis*. Vol. 22.

1940. *An Outline of Psychoanalysis*. Vol. 23.

Gastaut, H. and R. J. Broughton. 1965. A clinical and polygraphic study of episodic phenomena during sleep. In J. Wortis, ed., *Recent Advances in Biological Psychiatry.* Vol. 7. New York: Plenum Press.

Jones, E. 1951. *On the Nightmare.* New York: Liveright. (Original work published in 1911.)

Mack, J. A. 1970. *Nightmares and Human Conflict.* Boston: Little, Brown.

# 2.

# The Nightmare and Intrapsychic Conflict

JUDITH HANLON

NIGHTMARES HAVE BEEN reported throughout history and across cultures (Mack 1970), and research (Feldman and Hersen 1967) has suggested that they are fairly ubiquitous in the population. It is surprising, then, that psychoanalytic thinkers have devoted relatively little attention to elucidating the dynamics of nightmares. Most writings that do exist tend to address specific aspects of the problem, while few have offered a comprehensive explanation for this phenomenon in the light of modern psychoanalytic theory.

In attempting to outline a nightmare theory, the present chapter takes as its reference point the central psychoanalytic concept of *conflict*. The nightmare would seem to be best understood as arising from a complex interplay of psychic structures and external reality, and as growing out of the range of conflicts and accompanying danger situations which we now know to occur in development. This chapter reviews changing ideas about the nightmare as an expression of conflict, showing how these changes reflect developments in psychoanalysis as a whole since the turn of the century. If the nightmare is a "dream anxiety attack" (Frazier et al. 1975), then explanations of dreaming and of anxiety are also relevant; hence, these are discussed as well. Finally, exceptions to the hypothesis of the nightmare as an expression of conflict are discussed.

Jones (1931), in his early work on the subject, defined the nightmare in terms of three cardinal features: agonizing dread, a sense of oppression or weight on the chest which interferes with respiration, and a conviction of helpless paralysis. Those who followed him, however, seem to have found this definition too limiting. Hartmann (1980:2028) described nightmares as long, frightening dreams that

> usually awaken the sleeper during the second half of the sleep period; and there is a long, vivid recall of a dream ending in a frightening episode; often the dreamer is being chased or being attacked, or a close relative or a loved person is being attacked, or occasionally some catastrophe is threatening the entire world.

Verteuil (1962) identified the nightmare by its chaotic structure and highly disturbing emotions such as dread, horror, loathing, and disgust. An important definitional issue is the distinction between nightmares and night terrors. Kales et al. (1982), among others, argue for a clear distinction between the two, citing both clinical characteristics and sleep laboratory findings. Nightmares, they point out, typically occur in REM sleep, while night terrors occur in slow-wave (stages 3 and 4) sleep. Night terrors are characterized by greater amounts of motility, autonomic discharge, and vocalization than nightmares. Finally, there is vivid and detailed recall of nightmares but not of night terrors. Mack (1970), however, has disputed whether such distinctions really hold up; moreover, he has suggested that the two phenomena lie on a continuum psychodynamically. Of importance here is the fact that the terms are not used to refer to clearly defined phenomena, and are sometimes used interchangeably, in the psychoanalytic literature. For these reasons this chapter will consider the two together and will employ Mack's (1970:2) inclusive definition of the nightmare as "an anxiety dream in which fear is of such intense degree as to be experienced as overwhelming by the dreamer and to force at least partial awakening." The term "nightmare" will be used to refer to what are sometimes called anxiety dreams, punishment dreams, night terrors, and traumatic dreams.

## FREUD'S THEORY OF DREAMING

Freud's theory of dreams was based on the topographic model in which the mental apparatus was seen as divided between the systems "Cs." (conscious), "Pcs." (preconscious), and "Ucs." (unconscious). As spelled out in *The Interpretation of Dreams* (1900), the theory was as follows: in sleep, the mental apparatus is decathected in accordance with the wish of the systems Cs. and Pcs. to sleep. However, the energies of the system Ucs. remain active, threatening to disrupt sleep. The dream is a hallucinated wish fulfillment aimed at discharging these unconscious instinctual impulses in order to preserve sleep. In the mechanism of dream formation the unconscious instinctual impulse attaches itself to preconscious thoughts from the previous day, which also remain somewhat cathected in sleep; together these form a latent dream wish. Because of the conditions of sleep, this wish can be discharged neither in motor action nor in conscious thought. Hence, the latent dream wish must pursue a backward course through the system Ucs. to the sensory rather than to the motor end of the mental apparatus, which accounts for the experience of the dream as visual imagery. In the process of being formed into a manifest dream, the latent dream thoughts are subject to revision and distortion by the laws of primary-process thinking which govern the unconscious. They are also subject to distortion by the intersystemic censor which functions to keep forbidden thoughts from consciousness.

The concept of a psychic censor countering unacceptable thoughts implies some rudimentary notion in this theory of conflict within the mind. However, the greatest stress in Freud's dream theory was on dreams as wish fulfillments which emphasized primarily the id component. This emphasis was consistent with the fact that psychoanalysis had its beginnings as an id psychology. Interestingly, the notion of conflict figured somewhat more prominently in Freud's efforts to explain the distressing dream.

## FREUD'S IDEAS ON THE DISTRESSING DREAM

In *The Interpretation of Dreams* Freud had to respond to the apparent contradiction to his wish-fulfillment theory posed by distressing dreams. He did this in several ways. First, he reminded the reader of the crucial distinction between the manifest and the latent dream. Once subject to interpretation, he claimed, the distressing dream might, like other dreams, turn out to be disguised fulfillments of wishes, the displeasure being a distorted form of a pleasurable wish. In a section added in 1909 he discussed so-called counterwish dreams, dreams in which the subject matter appears to be the frustration of a wish or something unwished for. These, he said, really represented two types of wishes: (1) the wish to prove him wrong, i.e., to disprove his wish-fulfillment theory, as evidenced in the dreams of his patients in a state of resistence; and (2) masochistic wishes, which form part of the sexual constitution of many people. Since masochism was seen at that time as a component of the sexual instinct, its expression in dreams was consistent with a view of the dream as an expression of unconscious sexual wishes.

In his discussion of the anxiety dream from which the dreamer awakens the notion of conflict plays a larger role. In this instance the function of dreaming, to preserve sleep, has failed. The dream process has begun as an attempted wish fulfillment, but

> if this attempted wish fulfillment jars upon the preconscious so violently that it is unable to continue sleeping, then the dream has made a breach in the compromise and has failed to carry out the second half of the task. (Freud 1900:580)

He explained the anxiety in the dream as follows: an unconscious sexual wish has been previously repressed by the Pcs. system with which it has been in conflict. In the state of repression, the pleasurable wish has been transformed into anxiety. When the inhibiting cathexis of the Pcs. is reduced due to the state of sleep, anxiety (previously affect of a pleasurable nature, but transformed through repression) is released,causing the anxiety dream. It is important to note here that Freud's explanation of the anxiety dream draws upon his first explanation of anxiety as arising from accumulated sexual tension due to repression.

As Freud himself noted in 1933, the theory of dreams underwent little revision following *The Interpretation of Dreams* (Freud 1933). However, in his later discussions of dreams, especially distressing dreams, the idea of conflict between different parts of the mind became more explicit. In 1916 he compared the dreamer's relation to his dream to an "amalgamation of two separate people linked by some strong element in common" (Freud 1916:216). The anxiety dream was seen as the undisguised fulfillment of a wish (one "person") which is repudiated by the dreamer (the other "person"). Anxiety awakens the dreamer from sleep, taking the place of the censor, which has failed in this case to protect the dreamer from his wish. Similarly, the punishment dream is understood as representing the punitive wish of the censoring part of the mind aroused in opposition to the instinctual wish fulfillment in the dream. It is important to note the difference between this and the earlier idea of the punishment dream as brought about by masochistic, sexual wishes. Following the introduction of the structural theory in 1923 (Freud 1923a), the punishment dream could be understood in connection with the punitive activities of the superego as a separate structure acting in opposition to id wishes (Freud 1933).

## OTHER EARLY THEORISTS

Jones, in his important volume on the nightmare, explicitly states that the nightmare is "always an expression of intense mental conflict centering about some form of repressed sexual desire" (Jones 1931:44). Noting that all anxiety dreams could be explained in this way, however, he asks what in particular characterized the nightmare in which "dread reaches the maximum intensity known" (ibid.)? His answer is that the nightmare must have its source in the region of maximum repression in the mind; this, he writes, undoubtedly concerns incestuous wishes. He hypothesizes that the nightmare always relates to the normal sexual act, while other anxiety dreams might relate to various other perverse sexual wishes. Like Freud, Jones explains the anxiety in the nightmare in terms of the first theory of anxiety, writing that "the type of emotion designated as Angst is in general closely connected with sexual emotion, and, in particular, with pathological repression of it . . ." (1931:41). Jones's contribution emphasizes the important point that the nightmare is an expression of intense intrapsychic conflict. However, his exclusive emphasis on incestuous wishes and his reliance on the old theory of anxiety seem to minimize the potential usefulness of his propositions.

Early case studies also emphasized conflictual oedipal and incestuous wishes. For example, in 1930 Deutsch presented an account of a 28-year-old man who sought treatment because of impotence, but who had suffered as well from pavor nocturnus and nocturnal enuresis both during childhood and during the course of his analysis (in Deutsch 1965). By "pavor nocturnus" Deutsch seemed to refer to a nighttime anxiety attack with or without recall of dream content, and—especially important in her view—with a particular experience of motor inhibition. In analyzing a dream preceeding an attack of pavor nocturnus in this patient, Deutsch identified intense oedipal wishes associated with the threat of castration. She explained the particular sensation of total motor inhibition as deriving from "inhibition of sexual function . . . carried over . . . to the inhibition of movement altogether" (1965:34).

## Changing Views of Conflict and the Nightmare

Paralleling developments in psychoanalysis as a whole, writings on the nightmare have reflected evolving ideas about the components of psychic conflict—about the content of the underlying instinctual wishes, about the fantasized danger associated with realizing a forbidden wish, about the nature of the experienced anxiety, and about the contributions of ego and superego functioning. This section will review some of these changes, showing the evolution of a more detailed and modern understanding of the nightmare.

### THE INSTINCTUAL COMPONENT

Where once only sexual wishes were seen to underlie the nightmare, recent writings have placed a greater emphasis on the role of aggression. To some degree, aggression had figured in the earlier explanations of the nightmare, specifically as death wishes toward the same-sex parent as a component of oedipal conflict. However, aggression has gradually received more attention in its own right.

Klein's (1932) position on pavor nocturnus provides a kind of transition point. Like Deutsch and other early writers, she saw the night terror as due to an Oedipus conflict (which she, however, dated to a much earlier age). However, in her view, these fantasies had as their nucleus early *sadistic* ideas about parental copulation and represented a fusion of libidinal and destructive impulses. The child's sense of guilt, reflected in the night terror, was derived from sadistic sexual fantasies directed against its parents. Klein stressed that it was not the incestuous wishes themselves which caused conflict but rather the destuctive impulses which were "bound up" with the child's incestuous desires.

Writing later from a Kleinian perspective, Lindsay (1954) likewise emphasized conflict concerning the aggression inherent in sexuality. He presented case material illustrating the relationship between this conflict and night terrors. He showed how the dreamer represented this conflict in terms of his "inner object world" (1954:231). In Lindsay's view, the night terror represented a threat to the ego's existence posed by bad, persecutory objects in the inner world.

Mack (1970) devoted an entire chapter of his book on the nightmare to the subject of aggression. Through detailed clinical case examples, he showed the central role of aggression in nightmares reflecting conflicts from different psychosexual stages. In attempting to understand the nature of the nightmare experience itself, Mack raised an important question: why, if the dream reflects the dreamer's own destructiveness, is the dreamer always the *victim* of aggression in the dream? He suggested that an explanation of this phenomenon lies in a consideration of the extreme danger posed to children—and, by extension, to adult nightmare sufferers, whose nightmares originate in childhood conflicts—by murderous impulses directed toward loved objects on whom they completely depend. The victimization protects the dreamer against the greater threat of destruction of needed objects. Mack also made the interesting suggestion that the central role of aggression in nightmares can explain the observed similarity in their content over a wide age range. This sameness, he wrote, can be seen in part as

> the result of a certain unchanging quality inherent in destructive wishes. Libidinal aims vary according to the level of development, but murder seems always to be murder, and retaliation may be anticipated whether the dreamer is a small child or an adult. (Mack 1970:147–48)

From a psychodynamic if not psychoanalytic point of view, Kales et al. (1982) underscored the role of aggression in the dynamics of two successfully treated night-terror patients. Cason (1935) and Dreistadt (1972) have also stressed aggression as the major conflictual component in the nightmare dream.

Thus, the emphasis in the nightmare literature seems to have shifted from a focus on sexual impulses to a greater consideration of the role of aggression. There has also been a shift from a stress on wishes deriving from the oedipal period to a consideration of impulses associated with earlier phases. Sperling (1974), for example, has emphasized the importance of the pregenital phases and preoedipal relationships in the sleep disturbances and dreams of children. Using rich clinical material, she has suggested a relationship, in particular, between anal-phase conflicts and what she calls Type I pavor nocturnus, characterized by hypermotility, psychotic-like behavior during an attack, and retrograde amnesia (what others have referred to as the "night terror"). She has contrasted this disturbance with "pavor nocturnus Type III"—characterized by the occurrence of nightmares with varying contents from which the child awakens fully, in anxiety, and with a vivid memory of the dream—which she believes to reflect oedipal conflicts. (Sperling's Type II will be referred to in a later section.) Fraiberg (1950) has also underscored the role of anal conflicts in children's nightmares and has presented detailed case material documenting conflicts between the wish to soil, brought out in dreaming, and fear of loss of parental love.

Mack (1970) has noted the prevalence in adults' and children's nightmares of oral themes, reflecting primitive forms of infantile rage and aggression. The nightmare frequently expresses anxiety derived from wishes to incorporate, devour, bite, or eat someone. Mack writes that whatever developmental level the child or adult dreamer may have reached, conflicts tend to be represented in pregenital and especially oral terms; this he sees as an outgrowth of the overall regression characteristic of dreams. In addition to this representation of later conflicts in oral imagery, there is also, according to Mack, a regressive revival in dreaming of early oral conflicts themselves.

## THE FANTASIZED DANGER

Conflicts deriving from the various psychosexual stages include fantasies of danger resulting from instinctual expression. Since the element of danger is so central to the phenomenological experience of the nightmare, it seems important to take note of how this component has been understood by various nightmare theorists. Again, there is an increasing emphasis on the role of earlier developmental phases in the nightmare. Deutsch, in her 1930 paper (in Deutsch 1965), interpreted her patient's nightmare dream of crumbling walls as representing the threat of castration, in keeping with the early emphasis on oedipal conflict. Davison (1945) saw the extreme fear in pavor nocturnus as deriving from a fantasized punishment by death for forbidden wishes. Sperling (1974) and Fraiberg (1950), who addressed anal conflicts in children's nightmares, stressed fear of loss of the mother's love as at the root of the experienced anxiety. Mack (1970) emphasized the reactivation of the earliest anxieties in the nightmare, citing specifically the fear of abandonment or loss of love. According to Mack, in each developmental phase nightmares occur that are associated with the external danger situations characteristic of that period; however, in the nightmare, these are "regressively linked" to anxieties from earlier, and especially the earliest, periods. Hurvich (1985) is in agreement with Mack that the earliest anxieties are activated in the nightmare, but he has proposed that a fear of annihilation or overwhelmed helplessness is an even more basic anxiety than fear of abandonment or loss of love. He views the nightmare and pavor nocturnus as dramatic examples of experiences reflecting annihilation anxiety.

THE NATURE OF THE ANXIETY

Since the nightmare is an intense experience of anxiety during sleep, a satisfactory explanation of its occurrence must include a theory of anxiety. As we have seen, Freud's early theory of the nightmare was based on his first theory of anxiety. According to this theory, anxiety results from a process of direct transformation of dammed-up sexual energy into the affect of anxiety. In this view, anxiety is the result of an organic process following repression of sexual impulses.

Freud proposed a second theory of anxiety in 1926 (Freud 1926), one which is generally accepted by psychoanalysis today.[1] In the second theory anxiety is seen as playing a central role in intrapsychic conflict; hence, an updated theory of the nightmare as an expression of conflict would need to include this view. According to Freud's second theory, anxiety is produced by the ego to signal its perception of danger. This perception is based on the memory of earlier experiences of traumatic anxiety in which the ego is helpless against internal or external dangers. As the ego develops, it can anticipate danger, produce anxiety as a signal, and, finally, institute defensive measures to ward off the impending threat. In the context of intrapsychic conflict, anxiety signals impending danger should forbidden wishes be expressed. Rather than resulting from repression, as the first theory suggests, anxiety, according to the second theory, sets repression in motion.

Few writers have dealt explicitly with the issue of the nature of anxiety in the nightmare. Fraiberg (1950) and Mack (1970), however, have addressed this question, and their ideas seem grounded in Freud's second theory. Fraiberg presented clinical case examples of very young children to elucidate the mechanism of the nightmare. In each case the first onset of sleep disturbance (at about 1 to 1½ years) occurred in relation to a traumatic event. At some point during the second year the mechanism of the nightmare changed; here conflict over the wish to soil played the central role, with anxiety signaling the danger of loss of love. Fraiberg's findings support Freud's second theory of anxiety in that anxiety is first of a traumatic nature and later, as development

1. It is a matter of debate whether he ever totally discarded his first theory, but a discussion of this issue is beyond the scope of this paper.

progresses, functions to signal danger in the context of conflict. Mack has suggested that the explanation for the overwhelming anxiety in the nightmare lies in failure of the signal function to limit the intensity of anxiety, a consequence of the regressed state of the ego during sleep. As indicated earlier, the anxiety in the nightmare, according to Mack, signals a variety of dangers experienced throughout development which are regressively linked to the earliest and most terrifying danger situations of childhood.

## CONTRIBUTIONS OF THE SUPEREGO AND EGO

In *The Ego and the Id* (1923a) Freud put forth the structural theory in which the mental apparatus was seen as consisting of three structures, id, ego, and superego. Arlow and Brenner (1964) have argued for the superiority of the structural over the topographic model in general and, in particular, for the purpose of explaining dreams. They point out that within the topographic theory of dreams the stress was on the dream as an expression of unconscious instinctual wishes. In contrast, a theory of dreams based on the structural model views the dream as an outgrowth of a complex interplay of instinctual wishes, defenses, and punitive wishes, conceptualized as id, ego, and superego functions. Thus, whereas the topographic model points the way to an understanding of the dreamer's instinctual wishes, the structural model is superior in that it provides an understanding of his or her total conflicts. Through use of the structural model, the contributions of ego and superego, not just id, are acknowledged.

One way in which the structural model is useful is that the concept of *regression* can be applied to an understanding of ego and superego functioning as well as to id impulses as expressed in the dream. This is in contrast to the old topographic model which used the concept of regression *from* one system to another to explain the dream's infantile quality. The notion of regression *within* each psychic structure seems to be particularly useful for understanding the phenomenology of the nightmare.

As a demonstration of the superiority of the structural over the topographic model, Arlow and Brenner take the example of the punishment dream. They note that Freud himself (1923b, 1933) applied the concept of superego to an understanding of the punishment dream, replacing the earlier theory of the punishment dream as an expression of masochistic id wishes with the idea of the punishment as emanating from the self-critical agency of the ego. Arlow and Brenner use the notion of superego regression to explain important aspects of punishment dreams. For example, they point out that in these dreams the fantasy of instinctual gratification is far more often accompanied by anxiety than by guilt. What would produce guilt in the mature superego of waking life produces anxiety and a fear of punishment in the regressed superego of sleep. Further, the dreamer is apt to project his conflict onto an external punishing figure which is also characteristic of a childlike or regressed superego. Lastly, superego regression is evident in the fact that the punitive tendencies in the dream are apt to be instinctualized, i.e., to reflect primitive aggressive tendencies. Mack (1970:153), also employing the notion of superego regression, writes similarly of the tendency in the nightmare for the superego to become "infused with early perceptions of the parents as aggressive and retaliative."

Sperling (1974) also looks at superego functioning in an effort to understand distressing dreams. Specifically, she considers superego structure to be the most important element of the Type I pavor nocturnus mentioned earlier. She hypothesizes that this type of nocturnal anxiety attack represents a "split in the superego" (1974:85) whereby pathological pregenital impulses are permitted to be acted out in disguised form via hypermotility. She suggests an interrelation between this symptom and fugue states, amnesia, and certain psychotic states. Kellerman (this book, chapters 15–18) also proposes a theory of the nightmare in which emotions and defenses play a central role in order to regulate fundamental id-superego imperatives of the personality.

Ego functioning would seem to be a crucial dimension in understanding both the proneness to nightmares and the quality of the nightmare experience. Where the ego is weak and undeveloped it would be less able to defend effectively against dangerous impulses, so that the nightmare would be more likely to occur. Thus we might partially explain the frequency of nightmares in children as due to the less developed and more easily overwhelmed ego of childhood. Mack (1965) has suggested that the distinction between night terrors and nightmares lies in the degree to which the reality-testing or integrating functions of the ego are overwhelmed by anxiety in the attack. It follows that the night terror, the most extreme manifestation of anxiety, is particularly common in very young children whose rudimentary egos are especially easily overwhelmed.

Mack (1970) has presented the most thorough discussion of the ego's functioning during the nightmare. Like the superego, the ego regresses as a function of sleep. This helps to explain the experience of not only children but also adult dreamers of being helpless in the nightmare. As noted above, the regressed ego fails to institute adequate defensive mechanisms to limit the intensity of anxiety. Moreover, the regressed ego must rely on primitive defensive operations such as distortion and projection. Regression to primary-process thinking with loss of reality testing contributes to the frequently bizarre and distorted imagery of the nightmare and to difficulty in some cases in reestablishing an orientation to reality even after waking. Finally, the ego's perception of objects is regressed in the nightmare, contributing to the depiction of others in accordance with the threatening and aggressively tinged perceptions of early childhood.

Brenner (1976) has provided a contemporary definition of intrapsychic conflict as comprised of

> (1) wishful striving, (2) anticipated danger, (3) defense and (4) compromise among these. The function of defense is to avoid anxiety in accordance with the pleasure principle. Since current psychoanalytic theory—the structural theory—subsumes drive derivatives under the id, self-punitive trends under the superego and defenses under the ego, one may say that there are two major classes of conflict, those between ego and id and those between ego and superego. In both, anxiety is understood to occupy a key position. It . . . sets an individual at odds with dangerous id or superego derivatives and . . . is responsible for the initiation of the defenses that oppose them. (Brenner 1976:9)

In this section, we have seen how recent writings converge to provide a more complete picture of the way in which the components of conflict are manifested in the nightmare. We have reviewed the contributions of the drives, anticipated dangers, anxiety, and ego and superego to the resultant nightmare experience. We have seen how the nightmare can express not just oedipal incestuous wishes, the old view, but rather a variety of sexual and aggressive impulses from different stages of development. Paralleling this, we have seen how the nightmare can reflect the range of anticipated danger situations arising in development. Anxiety in the nightmare—by definition one of its most important elements—can be understood in terms of its role in internal conflict, as a signal of the impending danger. Finally, we have seen the part in the nightmare played by the ego and superego, functioning at a regressed level during sleep.

## Exceptions to the Theory of the Nightmare as an Expression of Conflict

Having developed the notion of the nightmare as an expression of conflict, we must turn to the question of how comprehensive this explanation is. Do all nightmares reflect internal conflict? In fact, beginning with Freud, dream theorists have acknowledged the existence of certain nightmares which do not grow out of conflict. This section briefly discusses these dreams.

Freud (1920, 1933) wrote that there was one exception to his wish-fulfillment theory of dreams. This was the so-called traumatic dream, a dream in which a traumatic situation of helplessness and fright was relived and repeated during sleep. Examples of this phenomenon had been seen in the traumatic neuroses, which followed accidents involving a risk to life, and in the many cases of war neurosis which Freud saw following World War I. In addition, patients in analysis often reported dreams which seemed to recall the psychical traumas of childhood. The existence of the traumatic dream was a major factor leading to Freud's theory of the repetition compulsion.

According to Freud, a situation was traumatic when excitations from outside were powerful enough to break through a hypothesized "protective shield" (1920:27). An important element in trauma is "lack of preparedness for anxiety including lack of hypercathexis of the systems that would be the first to receive the stimulus" (1920:31). Freud explained the traumatic dream as an attempt to "master the stimulus retrospectively, by developing the anxiety whose omission was the cause of the traumatic neurosis (1920:32).

Thus, Freud acknowledged that wish fulfillment is not the only function of dreaming; the function of some dreams is rather the psychical binding of traumatic impressions. Interestingly, Freud seemed to suggest that these two types of dreams exist in a developmental sequence when he wrote that

> the [wish-fulfilling] function of dreams . . . would not be its original one. . . . If there is a "beyond the pleasure principle," it is only consistent to grant that there was also a time before the purpose of dreams was the fulfillment of wishes. (Freud 1920:33)

Fraiberg (1950) has provided clinical data in support of the idea of a developmental sequence in the function of dreaming. In each of her cases, dreaming appeared originally to be in the service of mastery of trauma through repetition and later to reflect (anal) conflict. It seems important to note that the notion of a developmental sequence of types of nightmare dreams has a parallel in Freud's second theory of anxiety, which views anxiety first as a response to a situation of helplessness and later as a signal in the context of conflict. Just as anxiety as a response to a traumatic situation precedes developmentally anxiety as a signal of danger, so the traumatic anxiety dream might precede the nightmare dream as an expression of conflict.

Sperling's (1974:80) Type II pavor nocturnus is characterized by its sudden onset following a trauma and is "closely related to the traumatic neurosis of the adult." Sperling suggests that part of the function of the traumatic dream lies in the act of awakening from it. By awakening dreamers extricate themselves from the terrifying situation in which they were once passive and helpless.

The rudimentary ego of childhood makes situations of overwhelming helplessness more likely to occur in young children. Nevertheless, there are exceptional experiences in adulthood, such as war or accidents; which can overwhelm the ego and precipitate traumatic dreaming. A comprehensive discussion of the traumatic dream is beyond the scope of this paper, in which the major focus was the nightmare as an expression of conflict. What seems most important here is to acknowledge that not all nightmares can be explained as manifestations of psychic conflict.

## Summary

This chapter has explored evolving psychoanalytic ideas on the nightmare, taking as its point of reference the important concept of intrapsychic conflict. As psychoanalysis itself has moved from an id psychology to more of a conflict psychology, so theories of the nightmare have moved from Freud's early focus on wish fulfillment to a more complex view of the nightmare as an expression of conflict. This paper traced changing ideas on the role of each of the components of conflict—of the instincts, anxiety, fantasies of danger, the ego, and the superego. Finally, it briefly discussed exceptions to a theory of the nightmare as an expression of conflict.

## References


Arlow, J. A. and C. Brenner. 1964. *Psychoanalytic Concepts and Structural Theory.* New York: International Universities Press.

Brenner, C. 1976. *Psychoanalytic Technique and Psychic Conflict.* New York: International Universities Press.

Cason, H. 1935. The nightmare dream. *Psychological Monographs* 45:5.

Davison, C. 1945. Psychological and psychodynamic aspects of disturbances in sleep mechanisms. *Psychoanalytic Quarterly* 14:478–97.

Deutsch, H. 1965. Hysterical conversion symptoms: Pavor nocturnus, bedwetting, impotence. In *Neurosis and Character Types.* New York: International Universities Press.

Dreistadt, R. 1972. A univying theory of dreams, a new theory of nightmares, and the relationship of nightmares to psychopathology, literature, and collective social panic behavior. *Psychology* 9:(4)19–30.

Feldman, J. and M. Herson. 1967. Attitudes toward death in nightmare subjects. *Journal of Abnormal Psychology* 72:421–25.

Fraiberg, S. 1950. Sleep disturbances of childhood. In R. Eissler et al., eds., *The Psychoanalytic Study of the Child* 5:285–309. New York: International Universities Press.

Frazier, S. H., R. J. Campbell, M. H. Marshall, and A. Werner. 1975. *A Psychiatric Glossary.* 5th ed. Washington, D.C.: American Psychiatric Association.

Freud, S. *Standard Edition of the Complete Psychological Works of Sigmund Freud.* James Strachey, ed. and tr. 24 vols. London: Hogarth Press, 1953–1974; New York: Macmillan.

1900. *The Interpretation of Dreams.* Vols. 4 and 5.

1916. Wish-fulfillment, *Introductory Lectures on Psychoanalysis.* 15:213–27.

1920. *Beyond the Pleasure Principle.* Vol. 18.

1923a. *The Ego and the Id.* Vol. 19.

1923b. *Remarks on the Theory and Practice of Dream-Interpretation.* Vol. 19.

1926. *Inhibitions, symptoms, and anxiety.* Vol. 20.

1933. Revision of the theory of dreams, *New Introductionary Lectures on Psychoanalysis.* 22:7–30.

Hartmann, E. 1980. Sleep disorders. In H. I. Kaplan, A. M. Freedman, and B. Sadock, eds., *Comprehensive Textbook of Psychiatry III.* 3rd ed., pp. 2014–29. Baltimore: Williams and Wilkins.

Hurvich, M. 1985. Traumatic moment, basic dangers, and annihilation anxiety. Paper presented at the New York Freudian Society, New York. May.

Jones, E. 1931. *On the Nightmare.* London: Hogarth Press (Original work published in 1911.)

Kales, J. C., R. J. Cadieux, C. R. Soldatos, and A. Kales. 1982. Psychotherapy with night-terror patients. *American Journal of Psychotherapy* 36(3):399–407.

Klein, M. 1932. *The Psychoanalysis of Children.* London: Hogarth Press.

Lindsay, J. S. B.. 1954. Nightmares. *British Journal of Medical Psychology.* 27:224–34.

Mack, J. 1965. Nightmares, conflict, and ego development in childhood. *International Journal of Psychoanalysis* 46:403–28.

Mack, J. 1970. *Nightmares and Human Conflict.* Boston: Little, Brown.

Sperling, M. 1974. *The Major Neuroses and Behavior Disorders in Children.* New York: Jason Aronson.

Verteuil, R. L. 1962. A psychiatric approach to the study of the nightmare. *Canadian Psychiatric Association Journal* 7:151–58.

# 3.

# Nightmares and Object Relations Theory

SUSAN KAVALER

BEYOND REM STATES, and deep into the phenomenological world of horrors, like a Disney World planet or a Twilight Zone paradox, we sink into the preoedipal world of vulnerability in our sleep. Stripped of our daily ego orientation, what creatures do we find there? Where do they come from?

What is the world like for the Kleinian infant—still poised at the stage of paranoid anxiety, milk poisoned by envy and greed; which is felt, however, with a projective twist as retaliation from without. Is this a land we revisit in our sleep?

And what about Ronald Fairbairn's world of black masses and exorcism, where repressed bad objects plot their malign and cancerous plots? Here are our inner Heathcliffs, Iagos, and Richard IIIs—each a synthesis of parental failures, abuse, and frustrations. As we cling to our inner ghosts in Fairbairn's endopsychic world, do we never know it so well as in our sleep? Why Hamlet would rather choose death than the alternative: "perchance to dream."

Following Fairbairn comes Harry Guntrip, who so vividly paints the devouring rage of the schizoid pain. There is no battle of good and evil in his world, just more and more hunger! It's a draining, consuming, vacuum-cleaner sucking of insatiable hunger that can never be fed in the isolated turret where our preoedipal, schizoid part resides—cut off from contact, secluded in the frequent concentration-camp motif of our dreams. The hunger of the split-off true self, the baby closed off in a steel draw, cries unheard except in nightmare dreams and poetic explosions. In *Ariel* the poet Sylvia Plath describes her craving self as "The vivid tulips" that "eat my oxygen":

> The tulips should be behind bars like dangerous animals;
> They are opening like the mouth of some great African cat
> (Plath 1961:11–12)

D. W. Winnicott and Michael Balint continue to define this internal world which dances forth in our dreams, but they look more from the outside. The external view brings us the trauma of the Basic Fault, which leaves a perpetual crack in the Self. It also brings us the baby who can't make it past the transitional stage and the transitional phenomena to authenticity, aliveness, mature dependence—as well as the baby who is stuck in the trap of identification and fusion, remaining undifferentiated and unintegrated. Parental neglect is assumed when "good enough" mother and transitional teddy bears are lacking. Yet, the internal objects are never drawn with the phenomenological pen. Rather, for both Winnicott and Balint, they are implied.

Despite differences among the object relations theorists, however, all the authors mentioned—Klein, Fairbairn, Guntrip, Winnicott, and Balint—were addressing an era that predates the intrapsychic-conflict states of a cohesive and separate self. Unlike Freud, they hypothesized about the preoedipal era without reluctance. In doing so, they were closer to "such stuff as dreams are made on" than the master of dream analysis. This is particularly true when it comes to the nightmare, for in the nightmare experience the most primitive parts of a person erupt.

In their "Preliminary Study of the Personality of the Nightmare Sufferer," Hartmann et al. (1981) suggest that the people who most frequently experience nightmares tend to be more schizoid than not. They lack sturdy, sustained ties with other people, i.e., ties with real external objects. Often insomniac as well, chronic nightmare sufferers tend to be depressive-position failures, who find ambivalence, loss, guilt, and mourning intolerable. They tend to return time and again to the paranoid-schizoid dilemma. In their world, annihilation of the self is a constant threat. The internalized ideal object is assaulted along with the ideal self; and stemming from the extreme schizoid split, the bad objects are very bad indeed. The struggle to preserve the ideal object, which has not yet been modified to the less omnipotent form of the vulnerable good object (and thus has not yet been accompanied by a *modified* bad object) arouses a constant retaliatory strike force from the contrasting malevolence of the bad-object world. The oedipal and latency-age superego has not yet been formed. Horatio's Renaissance Age of Reason has not yet been reached. The Middle Ages continually strike back like Hamlet's ghost, and Hamlet can only cry: "There are more things in heaven and earth, Horatio, / than are dreamt of in your philosophy."

## Nightmares and Psychotherapy

Within the psychotherapy process, the nightmare can play a special role. Even when a patient is not in the class of chronic nightmare sufferers, it is a poignant time in treatment when nightmare experiences as well as memories begin to emerge with some frequency. It is a time of increasing vulnerability for the patient, and it can be a time of increasing contact between patient and psychotherapist. The therapy can be approaching fruition at this time. Yet, there are additional reasons for seeing emerging nightmares as a critical clinical development. For some of these reasons, we need merely look back to Ronald Fairbairn and Melanie Klein.

### FAIRBAIRN'S PSYCHOTHERAPY

Ronald Fairbairn (1952) was explicit in proclaiming the internal world of object relations to be a competitive arena in which tenacious ties to bad internal objects continuously subtract from external object-relational bonds. Following from his thinking, the major goal of psychoanalysis is to release the patient from inner ghosts, so that his innate strivings toward object relations could emerge into the external world of interpersonal relations. In essence, the patient could only come alive, and be present in the world of living, through release from inner-world bondage. Clinging to past and primary parental object ties, the patient would be in constant battle with the therapist to oppose exorcism and release. This was the more true the sicker the patient, for the ties being clung to in the internal world were those particularly derived from bad early life experiences, where frustration and abuse predominated over good, interpersonally contactful experience.

For Fairbairn, real parents are internalized as inner objects only when they are bad, good parents being internalized only as secondary phenomena that work to ameliorate the effects of bad objects within the inner world. Thus, good parents do not have the phenomenological reality that the bad parents have when they are transposed into internal objects; and therefore, they are not sufficient to release the child from bad object cathexis. The child is thus destined to remain half buried within the interior world unless some outside champion appears on the scene. Borrowing from the Catholic Church, Fairbairn declared the psychoanalyst-psychotherapist to be the modern version of an exorcist. He was sometimes to evolve into the patient's champion—although admittedly the odds were against him. In this Fairbairnian scenario, the psychotherapist is both model and wrestler in his role as exorcist. He is the good-object model in the outside world, who can tantalize with goodness, as the internal bad parental objects tantalize with badness. His main asset in this tantalizing role of "model" is in offering "real contact," which Fairbairn believed was the primary goal of the patient's object striving, as opposed to Freud's pleasure-striving, ego-libido. In his alternate role as wrestler, the psychotherapist attempts to wrestle against the patient's resistances. The more the patient clutches his internal bad objects to his breast, the more the therapist strides against the negative transference (the transference projection of the bad objects onto the therapist), with swordlike interpretations, aimed at cutting through the imprisoning internal object bonds. He persists to induce the patient into relinquishing his hold on his internal phantoms. Thus, in his role as wrestler, the Fairbairnian therapist also plays exorcist, although his incantations are cast in psychoanalytic phrases. If the therapist triumphs, malignant inner formations are dispersed, becoming spurious ghosts, devoid of power. The patient is then set free.

In the midst of this wrestling match, the Fairbairnian therapist does battle against intrapsychic defensive processes that guard the static inner world. Repression and splitting are terms that Fairbairn uses interactively, and clearly his meaning for such defenses extends beyond what was termed repression by Freud. Fairbairn is addressing a basic recalcitrance in the psychic system that is preoedipal in origin, extending back to the first year of life, when the pristine ego was first split asunder. In Fairbairn's system, secondary repression is carried out by an already repressed antilibidinal ego, against the libidinal ego and its cathected exciting bad object.

## THE CRUX OF FAIRBAIRN'S THEORY IN TERMS OF BAD OBJECTS

Therefore, in Fairbairn's view, splitting and repression can only be overcome by the release of the bad objects (exciting and rejecting objects). Only when these internal bad objects are released can arrested development advance, because only then can the ego parts (libidinal and antilibidinal egos) that were split off and repressed with them be reintegrated into the central ego, or into what Heinz Kohut (1977) has more recently called the nuclear self. In Fairbairn's view, once this reintegration has taken place, growth through external contact can begin to advance. The central ego can then transverse the transitional stage, from relating through identification (prolonged intrapsychic merger with repressed bad-object residues), to relating as a differentiated self; a self that has graduated from total dependence to mature dependence, which entails mutual interdependence with external object figures.

This is a schematic explanation of Fairbairn's developmental process, and it illustrates how defensive repression and splitting are used in the service of developmental arrest. Critical to further development of self, therefore, are renewed object relations with the external world. The self (Fairbairn's central ego) can only grow through object relations in Fairbairn's system, as is true for the theories of Klein (1975), Guntrip (1969), Winnicott (1965, 1971), Balint (1968), and all other object relationists. In the more current developmental language of Margaret Mahler (Mahler et al. 1975), we would say that the arrests in the separation-individuation phases of development (Balint's Basic Fault) could only be overcome by contact with a good external object. This object could precipitate a mourning process whereby good and bad self parts, and good and bad object parts, could be integrated into a cohesive self structure and a cohesive object structure, which are differentiated from each other. In order for this to occur, the bad experiences from the past need to be consciously experienced, along with the closed-off painful effects that originally caused such experiences to be split off from the conscious nuclear self, or to be repressed out of awareness.

## THE IMPORTANCE OF FAIRBAIRN'S VIEW AS APPLIED TO NIGHTMARES

Going back to Fairbairn, then, it can be seen why the release of bad objects is so central to basic intrapsychic structural change. In addition, the nightmare experience becomes critical as a feature of psychotherapeutic treatment insofar as it serves as an avenue of escape for the repressed bad objects. When these bad objects are brought into awareness, a transition is made from a closed internal system into a conscious self that is an open system, open to developmental process through contact with the external object world.

## NIGHTMARES AND MELANIE KLEIN'S THEORY

In Melanie Klein's (1975) work, a slightly different inner-world struggle emerges and provides us with a different sense of the nightmare's importance. A Kleinian child is not struggling with repressed bad objects that come from bad experiences with real parents. The Kleinian child is struggling with his own badness, in terms of innate death-instinct energy, which manifests itself intrapsychically as "a priori" malevolent images: attacking breasts, intruding penises, sadomasochistic parental intercourse scenes. However, these images are only initially persecutory in nature. Once one transverses the avenue from the paranoid-schizoid position to the depressive position, one begins to sense bad objects as having been spoiled by one's own aggression. Then remorse is felt—sadness, loss, and guilt—and yearnings for reparation come in reaction to the awareness of how one's own envy and greed destroy the good objects within the self.

The task for the evolving Kleinian infant is not, then, the release of bad objects (as it would be for a Fairbairnian child). Rather the task involves the affective reality of feeling good objects (from good real parents) as spoiled, then tolerating the guilt and loss of this psychic reality, and then working through the mourning process. Intrapsychic change comes from "letting go" our blocked depression, and from solidifying connections with one's own internal objects.

What role does the nightmare play in this process? When having a nightmare, we return to the persecutory anxiety of the paranoid-schizoid position in which the very fabric of the self is felt to be threatened. We regress from fears of object loss to a more basic terror in which our self (or Klein's ego) is threatened with annihilation. In nightmares, concern, caring, empathy, and guilt in relation to others are all temporarily lost. We lose the tenuous developmental achievements of the depressive position. In our nightmares, we return to a position in which others are persecutory, unless they are omnipotent and ideal. We care not for them. We are totally preoccupied with self-protection, because we feel as we did prior to various states of self-integration when we could easily dissolve or be wiped out of existence. We are totally helpless without an omnipotent other on which to depend. Along with the threat of annihilation from outside, there are additional threats from the inside, coming from yearnings for merger with the omnipotent ideal object. These yearnings threaten us with death by dissolution. Our basic needs are a threat too, because needing can cause homicidal wrath from our own inner bad objects.

Given this regression to paranoid-schizoid conflicts, the Kleinian developmental task (also the analytic task) cannot be accomplished through mere conscious experience of the nightmare—as it could be in Fairbairn's system, where release of bad objects is a primary goal. However, the return to the paranoid-schizoid position, within the nightmare, can be used therapeutically to get back to the deepest fears of self-annihilation—fears that can continually undermine depressive-position processes of love, integration, reparation, and differentiation. By returning to a stage prior to advanced structural change, we glimpse the basic blocks to personality change. Only when free of intense persecutory anxiety can we tolerate guilt, loss, and the accompanying despair that are essential and perennial components of the mourning process. Only then can the psychoanalytic treatment process proceed.

## Clinical Material

### NIGHTMARES AND OBJECT RELATIONS WORKING THROUGH

The following nightmare was presented by a patient in analysis during an early phase of her treatment:

> My mother appeared before me, with a cold, regal manner of detachment. She almost looked like a statue, because she was so frigid and stoney. She told me that she had something to announce to me. I felt shaky, and very, very small, especially standing in front of her. Even though she was sitting down, she seemed to tower above me. I think I was a very tiny child. I was scared to listen to her, as she pronounced, with accentuated definity that she had decided to die. I heard myself scream wildly, then, raging, almost like an animal. I was screaming, screeching, crying. The more upset I got, the more detached my mother got. It was awful. I felt so needy, and like I was going mad . . . I woke up still screaming, and thrashing around in my bed.

In this nightmare, the basic object relations constellations can be seen and addressed. It appears that the bad-object part of the mother (real or fantasy, according to interpretation) was internalized, and projected out as a persecutory figure. The patient, C., reexperienced a very familiar position of victimization in relation to her mother—a painfully helpless position of total dependence. The patient's early childhood fear that her mother would die was turned into a harsh reality, and the mother became an active persecutory figure through her frigid promise of abandonment.

We can see in this nightmare the basic object relations that characterized the internal psychic structure of the patient and the object relations that characterized the transference projections within the therapeutic relationship, as well as the modus operandi for this patient's current external object relations. These are all additional perspectives to that of the historical parent-child relationship that had become internalized, and each relationship constellation reflects the internalized parent-child object relations unit.

For instance, as treatment progressed, the patient was able to experience, more and more, that she herself was the cold, regal, and detached figure, who bitterly and matter-of-factly dismissed life. She was her own internal bad object, her nightmare mother. It was the coldness, the contempt, and the air of triumph that walled her off from her sorrow, as Melanie Klein so clearly describes in her portrayal of manic controls defending against depressive despair—guilt and loss. Within the nightmare, the anxiety over guilt and loss seemed to be dealt with by denial, and by manic triumph over the needy, hurting part of herself. Inside of her, she had both the mother part and the child part; and one was sadistically controlling the other, as Fairbairn's antilibidinal ego part would control the libidinal ego. In this way, the grief and loss of the child were not experienced so long as her conscious identification was with the hard, cold, withdrawn, and triumphant bad mother in her, or with her antilibidinal ego. However, the nightmare had reawakened the anguish of the child, and her pain and loss could no longer be denied. Experiencing the cold mother part of her, in connection with the hurting child, brought a melting surrender and sorrow. Rage, hurt, and love were expressed as part of a lengthy mourning process. Grief and remorse emerged as the aggressive mother part was felt. The hurting child could not be denied, and the sense of self-injury brought compassion along with remorse. Internal reparation could then be made. In this sense, a Kleinian unfolding took place. Mourning brought a renewed capacity for love, creativity, and object connection through need and love rather than through omnipotent denial and domination.

While this took place internally, parallel processes took place within the analytic relationship, and within the ongoing primary external relationship. Within the transference relationship, in treatment, the tendency had been for the patient to project out, through projective identification, the part of her that was like her internalized bad mother, i.e., cold, withdrawn, and withholding. When she experienced the therapist as being this bad object, she would withdraw and not speak. However, at other times, she would project out the helpless child onto the therapist, disowning her own needs, and her own hunger for the abandoning object. Then, she would portray her contempt and triumph more openly, and aggressive attacks on the analyst would take place.

While this alternating projective-identification process took place in treatment, it simultaneously occurred in her relationship with her boyfriend. She would periodically freeze him out with her contempt, viewing him as the devalued child part of her. She would then see him as a helpless, needy, "dependent schmuck." When she herself became the demanding child, he would be experienced as a rejecting parent, distancing from her, who would not accept her love.

## FAIRBAIRN AND KLEIN IN RELATION TO ILLUSTRATIVE NIGHTMARE

Fairbairn would view the internalized rejecting parent as a highly cathected sadistic object who must be clung to at any cost, despite the masochistic submission required for continued attachment. If this unhealthy, indigestible internal object could be exorcised through the nightmare, the task of "releasing repressed bad objects" could be done. However, it would seem that Fairbairn would view the nightmare merely as a prelude to a whole working-through process of attachment and relinquishment of attachment to the bad internal object, as experienced within the transference relationship.

For Klein, the cold, impassive mother would be a bad internal object, created in the patient's own infantile fantasy. The patient's own aggression is primary in this, the bad object being constructed by her own destructive-drive wishes. Thus, the nightmare could be seen by Klein as a way of formulating, for the patient, her manic defenses against the feelings of guilt and remorse, related to the sense of recognizing one's self as a rejecting mother, or as a demanding and aggressively clinging child. The nightmare expresses the paranoid-schizoid position view of the mother as a persecutory figure. Yet, in Klein's view, the road to health lies in reowning the aggression that has been projected out in the paranoid position (the death instinct deflected outward). Reowning one's aggression means consciously identifying with the projected bad object and reintrojecting it, along with experiencing the painful effects that come with awareness in the depressive position that one's own aggression has hurt and damaged the object. In this nightmare, the child might be seen as damaging the mother by turning her into a withdrawing figure through her own oral wishes to destroy and annihilate with greed and envy. Through envy and greed, the real good mother (external mothers being good in Klein's theory) has been spoiled, and made bad by the child's hungry ravings. Envy of the good object turns it bad, and depletes it through sucking and screaming that devour. Greed is the accomplice of envy. In turning mother bad, the patient can also be seen to become the bad mother as she is internalized through introjection in the depressive position. As the treatment process unfolds, the patient may be confronted with her omnipotent manic control, as portrayed in the nightmare's mother figure. Interpreting this would hopefully, then, lead to the patient's experiencing her own coldness, control, contempt, and devaluing attitude of triumph. Experiencing this means reowning the aggression involved in such control, through the affective awareness of guilt and the pain of loss. The sense of loss and guilt is due to the damaging of the patient's internal object, in terms of turning it bad, and turning it against the self. The depressive working through of the guilt and loss involved constitutes the ongoing mourning process of treatment.

## OBJECT RELATIONS WORK WITH NIGHTMARES, IN RESPONSE TO THE PATIENT'S SUBJECTIVE POINT OF VIEW

The role of the nightmare in working through object relations can be seen again as we look at some clinical cases in which an initial nightmare is reexperienced quite differently at a later stage of treatment. In the case of J., an earlier nightmare of a monster mother became a later experience of the insatiable monster from within. The nightmare was as follows:

I was sitting with my father, outside, in a field. We sat talking. The day was beautiful. But suddenly, the air began to darken and thicken. I heard a noise and looked behind me. A huge-mouthed monster emerged from behind us. I clung urgently to my father, and screamed for him to protect me from the monster. He didn't respond. He sat limp and seemingly powerless . . . The monster began encroaching on us both . . . but before it did, I woke up, crying for help, and sighed with relief that it wasn't really happening.

When this nightmare was first reported by the J., her associations were to the devouring needs of her mother, which had overwhelmed and smothered her at a time when she was left to live with her mother, after her parents' divorce. Her mother was the monster, who had consumed her and prevented her from having any sense of self. She merely reflected her mother's grandiose image, and complied with her needs. She always waited for her father to rescue her from her mother's grasp, but he never did. He seemed impotent in relation to her mother's treatment of her, and for all the years that she remained living with her mother (before college), her father withdrew from her life.

Over the years, as J.'s treatment progressed, she moved from this earlier position as the victim of her internal bad mother, and her interpretation of the nightmare changed as well. She brought up the nightmare again, quite spontaneously, saying, "Do you remember that dream I had about the monster that my father wouldn't protect me from? I used to think the monster was my mother, but now I think it was me. I think it was my hunger. I'm always hungry, no matter how much I get. I always want more." She made this comment at a point in her treatment when she was beginning to "own" her insatiable cravings for food, sex, and power. She had other anxiety dreams and nightmares at this time. Some were of holocaust explosions, as her rage also surfaced. Others were of "savages" attacking her, which reflected her hungry and impulsive cravings and her envy and greed. She also had a nightmare of a "wimpy, dependent, clingy girl," who was being cut, beaten, and bruised by a man. She herself appeared in the nightmare as a friend, who was merely an observer. Yet, in her associations, she was able to own the disowned victim part of her, as well as the disowned sadistic bad object. More and more at this time, and in all the nightmares she mentioned, J. was able to own the bad-object part of her that she had formerly interpreted as her mother. Thus, the working through of the object relations issues in treatment can be seen in terms of the patient's changing associations to nightmares and anxiety dreams. The changes reflected major growth in separation-individuation, and in the working through of abandonment depression effects.

A similar process was reflected in the reinterpretation of an early nightmare by another patient. L. had a nightmare that went as follows:

I was at a restaurant with a whole group of friends. There were all kinds of food on the table. My boyfriend began to tell a story about a dog who ate a cat in front of him. He laughs, and says that he's afraid if he goes to sleep he'll be eaten up. I get terrified, but nobody else seems scared, and this increases my anxiety. Then, I look at the food on the table, and see all kinds of strange fish that look like they're beginning to move. Snails, shrimp, lobsters start to look like they're coming alive again. I suddenly feel alone and shivery. The food seems to be getting bigger. Claws, fangs, and teeth start to come out of the food and move towards me . . . I wake up startled, and find myself shaking.

L's initial associations to this nightmare involve memories of hearing her father tell tales, during her childhood, of food that ate and devoured little children. Her anxieties in reaction to the nightmare all related to fears of being devoured.

Then, several years later in her treatment (following increasing separation, through mourning and loss, similar to the case of J.), L. began to talk of her own greed, and her own craving to devour everything around her. No longer was she the victim of bad objects; she had reowned the bad-object qualities. Recalling the earlier nightmare, she was able to identify with the food, and saw the dream, now, in terms of her own voracious hunger.

## NIGHTMARES OF TRAPS, SUFFOCATION, AND CONCENTRATION CAMPS

At certain points in psychoanalytic treatment, it is not uncommon for patients to dream of being trapped, suffocated, or imprisoned. Fairbairn refers to the channel of transition in maturational development, from the stage of infantile dependence, where identification is the main mode of relation to objects, to that of mature dependence, in which differentiation has been achieved. Fairbairn does not use Margaret Mahler's phrase, "separation-individuation," but basically he talks about the same thing. Speaking of this channel of transition, Fairbairn notes that patients tend to have dreams that depict the developmental journey. They might dream of crossing a channel. They might dream of falling and drowning in the channel. They might dream of flying over the channel. However, if they feel stuck, and are unable to break out of the infantile mode of identification, they might very well dream of being trapped or imprisoned.

Borderline patients, in particular, who are stuck in the trap of identification and merger and who are unable to differentiate and individuate, often have anxiety dreams and nightmares that reflect entrapment or suffocation. Sometimes they dream of concentration-camp images.

Harry Guntrip writes, prolifically, about schizoid patients who relate at an infantile level of identification, and who therefore have a constant life-death, need-fear dilemma, concerning wishes to stay in the womb of security in this regressed state of identification, which turns into a dread of imprisonment and suffocation in the womb. He believes that the "regressed ego" within us all woos us back to a secure objectless womb, deep within our interior world. However, if we succumb to the sirens of security we end up trapped, shut-in, and depersonalized. The fear is as intense as the wish.

A former patient, whose character reflected the undifferentiated schizoid dynamics described by Fairbairn and Guntrip (Guntrip's passive ego identification), had a typical nightmare of entrapment:

> I was in your closet. All your clothes were hanging down on me. It was dark, and I had a hard time breathing . . .

The sense of suffocation woke her up, and she retained the sense of being smothered, of choking. In the dream there are no object relations. There are no persecutory bad objects. However, it is an object relations nightmare, and it is a transference nightmare. Since the closet described is the analyst's closet, the implication is that the patient is trapped inside the analyst's body. Perhaps she is inside the analyst's womb, which would be in keeping with the Guntrip regressed ego's yearning to withdraw to a hallucinated prenatal atmosphere of security. However, the process of entrapment in the womb is also one of developmental arrest, as Fairbairn describes. Since she relates through identification and not as a differentiated self, entrapment is inevitable. It so happens that this patient's nightmare, of being in the therapist's closet, came at a time in treatment when an idealizing transference was turning into a negative or devaluing transference. During the idealization phase, the patient wished to swallow the envied and admired analyst. She introjected aspects of her, and overall she related through identification. As is common with schizoid patients, when actually with me, she had difficulty relating; but when away from me, she would have incessant conversations with me in her head, trying to express her deepest dreams to me in my absence. As treatment continued, more contact occurred, in which, on and off (Guntrip's In and Out solution), she could share her thoughts. Also, instead of being blocked, and withdrawn, she showed more open hostility and contempt. The idealized object was being more openly experienced as the bad object, and the fears in relation to the bad object were of being trapped. Thus, having wished to swallow the analyst, she now saw the analyst as swallowing her, as holding onto her in a regressive symbiosis that bound her to the analyst as her mother continued to bind her. Yet the nightmare does not indicate any active control or persecution on the part of the analyst. Nor does it indicate any active merger or regression into the interior world. The patient is just there, inside the analyst, among the analyst's things. She is there, and doesn't know how she got there. She just knows that she can't breathe well. Has she yearned for withdrawal into this womb-world, as Guntrip suggests, causing her own trauma of being shut away from life? Is she the reluctant victim of a mother who keeps her from moving across the transitional channel to differentiation? Does she withdraw to get away from the mother, or is she withdrawing to stay within the mother? According to Guntrip, the good object will always turn bad, at the schizoid level of the human condition in which passive ego identification leads to suffocation. The more schizoid the person, the more he will turn to further withdrawal to escape the sense of entrapment, rather than struggling through the transitional channel of separation-individuation to differentiation and mature object relatedness. This patient's nightmare suggests the passive withdrawal of a schizoid ego, where the shut-in situation is experienced from the view of a victim. For Fairbairn, however, the patient is always an active participant, clinging aggressively to the bad object to avoid object loss and resulting ego loss or death.

Several other patients show similar nightmare themes of entrapment and suffocation. One woman dreamed of bursting out of her mother's home. She felt an explosive urge to break out of the loneliness. In the nightmare, the mother's house was experienced as suffocating "isolation." Being in mother, then, became being shut away from life. Another female patient dreamed of being back in her mother's house. The house was rocking from side to side, and she tried to stand in the center of it, to balance it. The theme of suffocation emerges more subtly here, as she takes great pains to open the window so that she can breathe better.

Following along with the nightmare theme of entrapment, we come to nightmares that are reported in terms of concentration-camp images. One quite schizoid patient reported a nightmare in which she was under the vigilant observation of a concentration-camp guard. She is thinking of making an escape but is frozen, more from futility than fear. She looks at the male guard, who points his rifle at her, and she thinks how hopeless any escape is. She starts walking, thinking that she should be running toward the gate. She wakes up still with the hovering sense of futility and despair. She knows she must be terrified, but she can't feel it. She just feels hopeless.

Another patient reports a multifaceted dream in which one scene involves being in a concentration camp. It is the same patient who dreamed of an oral monster, and of needing to open the windows so that she could breathe in her mother's house. In this dream, which comes later in treatment, she and her boyfriend enter a room in a dark house, and suddenly they are concentration camp victims. They are emaciated, and look near to death. Yet, just as suddenly as they are trapped in this demise, equally suddenly they get free by walking into the next room of the house. Then they return to normal health and appearance. There seems to be a magical quality of omnipotent denial in this dream that liberates it from the terror of a nightmare. Yet, it also seems a sign of self-growth, in that the helpless entrapment in the earlier nightmares is no longer felt; instead, there is a sense that one can determine one's fate. The patient is less of a passive victim and more in control. As reported earlier, this patient (J.) was able to cross the channel of separation-individuation increasingly in her analysis, and was then able to own the oral-aggressive bad object as part of herself. In doing so, she gains increasing control through the owning of her aggression. In a nightmare that occurred most recently, this same patient speaks of a monster coming up the stairs to kill her. She is with her friends, and she cries for help, asking them to tell her what to do. She is aware that the monster is coming upstairs to murder her, and she is terrified. However, she also is aware, in this nightmare, that she is in control of the monster. Her associations to the nightmare make it clear that she experiences the monster to be her own aggression, particularly her murderous rage that she can turn inward upon herself. Directly following the session in which she reported the nightmare, she became sick. She felt choked up with a sore throat, and felt that she couldn't breathe well. She said that she experienced her sickness as her controlling the monster, turning it inward upon herself. Even though she was identified with the passive victim, who became sick from the monster, she was now also identified with the aggressive victimizer, the persecutory bad object or the antilibidinal ego (Internal Saboteur). The patient's ability to feel in control of the monster indicated the self-growth that had come with differentiation and the increasing owning of her aggression.

The concentration-camp motif, in nightmares, can sometimes reflect a clear conflict over crossing the channel from identification and merger to the side on which differentiation and separation wait. Then the dream is no longer just of entrapment, but also of the entire need-fear dilemma described by Guntrip.

The patient who dreamed that her mother was threatening to die later in treatment had the following nightmare:

I found myself in this strange place. First, I was inside this house, but somehow I knew that if I went into the bathroom I would be put into a hot oven, and would be put to death. I was able to walk outside the house, and when I did I saw this whole free area, with the blue sky above, but all around the free area was this iron gate. Seeing that I was locked in all around, I thought of trying to escape. But then I saw that on the gates, which were surrounding everything, were these huge Chinese bulldogs, which snarled and roared. They had big claws and huge teeth. I knew that if I tried to escape over the gate, I could be torn apart by the Chinese bulldogs. Yet, there was no other way out, and I knew if I stayed I'd have to go back into the house, and eventually into the oven . . . I was terrified, but I knew I would have to try to climb the gates, and to get over them. My only chance was to get past the murderous bulldogs . . . Yet, it looked like either way, I was going to die . . . Then I woke up.

In this nightmare, there seems to be a schizoid "damned if you do, and damned if you don't" dilemma (no way out out of the symbiosis). There is a threat of death by burning, which seems to represent returning to the suffocating womb, and suffering the shut-in schizoid fate of death by regression. Then there is the alternative threat by persecution from the bestial guards of the gate, who can be seen as the antilibidinal ego, turned in against the libidinal ego that needs to escape to the outside world of differentiation and outside object relations. In Fairbairn's terms, the libidinal ego is trapped in a repressed isolation, away from outside relatedness, by the agressive antilibidinal ego, which is fused with the animalistic persecution of the rejecting bad parental objects (Chinese bulldogs). However, the regressive pull toward the inner house, within the gate, can be best understood in Harry Guntrip's terms as the frightened, weak ego that wishes to recede into the security of the objectless womb, away from the persecutory antilibidinal ego and its cathected bad object of the internal object world, and also away from potential outside persecutors (outside the gate, or outside the self). Yet, the lure of the womb also carries the threat of the shut-in schizoid depersonalization, isolation, and entrapment. The prospect of death in an oven can be seen as the loss of ego consciousness, which is the fate of the ego that withdraws from all objects, both external and internal. In this dream, going into the bathroom is experienced as being forced into a hot oven. Guntrip speaks of the suicidal wish to stick one's head in an oven as a reflection of the yearning to regress into the womb for security.

## GUNTRIP'S CONCEPT OF THE "REGRESSED EGO" AS APPLIED TO NIGHTMARES

Deeper than fears of entrapment by either external or internal objects (or by the antilibidinal ego) are fears of the void within, of a deeper inward regression to a featureless place where no objects exist. Patients who give up their internal bad objects can be left with the terror of being isolated, depersonalized, and empty, since they anticipate being left in an objectless state. One patient, who appeared to be operating at a high level of functioning, revealed an inner borderline void within a highly structured personality system. Despite her successful work and social life, she seemed unable to sustain an intimate relationship. It was through a nightmare that the hidden intrapsychic element of a psychic void was most clearly shown, hinting at an answer to the confusing mystery of this woman's character. Although as she grew up this patient had received auxiliary mothering from many of her mother's friends and friends' mothers (which was her way of escaping from an unavailable mother), she still retained an empty hole at her center. Many sophisticated psychic structures were built up through her extrafamilial relationships, but the inner void remained, only to emerge much later in a nightmare. Her younger brother had remained at home with her mother. When in treatment, she dreamed the following dream:

My brother and I were together. The house was deserted for a long time. Then it seemed like the floor opened up and swallowed my brother up, and he was never heard of again.

Guntrip raises the idea of an objectless state, which Fairbairn conceived as impossible. For Fairbairn, no ego (or self) part could exist without an object part attached to it in the inner world. The central ego part had the attached ideal object. The antilibidinal ego had the attached rejecting bad object. The libidinal ego had its exciting bad object. Winnicott (1971) also indicated that there could be no ego without an object by stating that there could be no baby without a nursing mother. Michael Balint (1968) speaks of the primary love that evolves as a harmonious interpenetrating mix-up between self and object. He vehemently disputes and reputes the idea of primary narcissism, since it suggests an objectless state. Guntrip, however, believed differently, and in speaking about a regressed passive ego he theorized that a hidden heart of the self had withdrawn into hiding and was existing in an essentially objectless state. The fantasy of regression into a womb or of part of the baby self being put into cold storage for rebirth at a better time were fantasies volunteered by patients who were particularly schizoid in nature, patients prone to withdraw out of fear. However, withdrawal threatened isolation and ego-depersonalization, so that the objectless regression was also a rendezvous with psychic death. Given this ultimate dread, the most terrifying fate Guntrip could imagine for the human ego is shown in nightmares of empty voids.

Sometimes patients with highly developed characters can reach down to the deepest schizoid dread in nightmares. Yet, the same patient can also touch on Guntrip's higher levels of bad-object relations, both at the level of persecutory anxiety and at the level of depressive anxieties about moral accusers.

One young female patient has had a repeated nightmare in which she and her family are on a boat. It is dark, and they are in the middle of a black sea. The ice below them suddenly begins to break, and their boat begins to sink.

The patient reported this nightmare in association with her fears of closeness. It arose as she spoke of an intense, visceral "No!" which would come up in her just as she was about to yield to a man and to fulfill her wishes for merger. Even though the dream itself is not devoid of objects, the schizoid fear of engulfment in an objectless void is suggested. She speaks of her terror within the nightmare experience in terms of the ice breaking beneath her and of the black sea threatening to wash over the boat (self) which supported her. There is some suggestion of self-dissolution, but the main emphasis is on the devouring and engulfing black void, or black darkness. To yield herself, to let the ice break, would mean some psychic smothering, psychic annihilation. To let the ice break seems to mean to let her icy defenses of manic contempt and control be relinquished. Yet, if she yields to intimacy, she is afraid that her wishes for merger will bring annihilation and psychic death.

Also the fact that it is a black sea that surrounds her, and not just a black void, suggests that letting the ice break will result in death by drowning, which could refer to the endless tears that she is afraid she will cry if she relinquishes her icy false self-contempt and plunges into the depressive-position affects of guilt and loss. In this last respect, the nightmare anxieties suggest a higher level of development than the schizoid level. They suggest depressive-level anxieties. In deferring to Melanie Klein, Guntrip mentions her depressive and paranoid positions as psychic levels that supersede his schizoid level in terms of being higher levels of consciousness and development. He divides Klein's paranoid-schizoid position into two levels, with the fear of persecutory objects being at a higher level than the schizoid fear of emptiness and depersonalization. At the even higher depressive level, he sees the main anxiety being experienced in relation to moral accusers, bad objects who arouse a sense of guilt over aggression.

In the patient just mentioned, all three levels can be seen operating. The nightmare of the black sea suggests mainly schizoid-level fears. In other nightmares, her depressive anxieties are clearer, in terms of fears of moral accusation. In one nightmare, she felt an acute sensation of a whirling light coming toward her and accusing her of something horrible. Then she had a dream in which a Chinese woman threatened to sue her.

In and out of the web of accusatory dreams and nightmares, the same woman has dreams of persecutory bad objects in the form of sadistic sexual abusers. In one particular nightmare, she dreams that a policeman, dressed in an official uniform, is feeding her tunafish, and simultaneously he is torturing her with a sadistic-flavored tone of triumph. As he jams tunafish into her little-girl mouth, he reiterates: "You asked for tunafish, well here's tunafish!"

The patient's associations to this last dream were to forced fellatio and to her grandmother's sadistic and abusive attitudes toward her as a child. Yet, she had converted her persecutor into a man, and she didn't know why. She actively suspects her grandmother of having sexually abused her as a child. She has a fantasy that her grandmother forced her to have oral sex with an adult man when she was a very little girl. Now, her anger at men becomes connected with the persecution in the nightmare.

## PSYCHIC LEVELS: ADULT AND CHILD NIGHTMARES IN THE SAME PATIENT

As can be seen, nightmares can reflect all levels of object relations conflict, and of object relations fears. No patient is exclusively at any one level. In psychoanalytic treatment as adults, some patients have nightmares that reflect and recall earlier childhood nightmares. Patient S. had two nightmares in treatment that brought back earlier nightmares and earlier fears of persecution by bad objects. Initially, she dreamed that her mother was saying some cryptic message, over the telephone, about a penis. Then she was given the telephone, and she dropped it at the point where someone whispered three things that sounded like P. and penises. After reporting this nightmare, S. recalled a childhood nightmare that she had dreamed many times before. It was about a phallic man who crept in through her window, expanded and inflated, and then crept around her childhood apartment. She cried, piercingly, for help, but no one seemed to hear her, even though both her parents were there. Her father sat "benignly" in a living-room chair, with his newspaper in front of his face. As S. ran from her bedroom and into the living room, screaming, her father turned casually toward her and said, "Having fun, honey?" Her mother continued to iron at her ironing board.

These nightmares are particularly interesting in light of the fact that this patient too has suspicions of childhood sexual abuse. She has headaches that can suddenly open up into dissociative states in which she feels like a tiny 3-year-old girl, and has flashing images of her father coming toward her and sticking his penis inside of her. When she allows these flashes, she quickly seals them off and represses them again. She seems to feel flooded with guilt for thinking such thoughts about her father.

S. also had a more recent nightmare that recalled another one from childhood. In the current nightmares, she was out jogging with her kitten, her kitten running beside her:

> I started running faster and faster. I was taking these long dance leaps. It felt wonderful! But then I saw this sharp turn at the end of the path. At each side of the turn I could fall a mile if my foot slipped off the two feet of ground at the turn. I got scared that I was going so fast that I would miss. I told myself I was being melodramatic. I told myself I could put my foot wherever I wanted. Then I missed the two-foot cement spot, and began falling. I couldn't believe it! I told myself that I just had to grab the railing, and then I would be okay. I said to myself, "There's no way you can die out here, when you're running!" Then I tried to grab the railing, and I missed. I kept falling. . . . I woke up feeling this awful sense of horror.

When S. recalled this nightmare, I asked her if the sense of terror in the nightmare reminded her of anything. In response, she told me of a childhood nightmare, which had the same feeling in it:

I and my parents were taken prisoner by a man, in the home we lived in when I was a child. The man wore a handkerchief over his face, and carried a rifle. When a neon sign lit up on one of our hearts, it meant that that person was going to die next. Both my parents were killed, and then the light lit up on my heart. I was going to be killed next. Then I woke up crying, with the same sense of terror as in the recent nightmare.

Harris (1960) wrote about the nature of falling dreams and attacking dreams as reflecting different levels of object relations, as well as reflecting different types of mothers (abandoning versus intrusive mothers). He believed that falling dreams reflect a more primitive level of relating in which one particular mothering person has not yet been cathected. He had a sample of patients who generally would have falling dreams, and another sample that would generally have attacking dreams. My patient, S., had experienced both forms of nightmares, and it is not clear whether abandoning and/or intrusive aspects of the mother are related to the nightmares. However, the sense of terror in the nightmares remains equally intense, whether in falling or being attacked. The sense of impending self-annihilation is prominent in both.

## Summary

Object relations theorists focus on preoedipal fears and conflicts. It is in nightmares that this preoedipal world is most vividly able to emerge. The inner world that reveals itself is one of paranoid and schizoid anxieties, in which persecution and entrapment by bad objects threatens to annihilate a fragile and unformed ego or self. It is a world illustrated by Melanie Klein, Ronald Fairbairn, and Harry Guntrip in their particular views of the internal world of pathological object ties.

Clinical examples of nightmares are analyzed from different theoretical viewpoints, as well as in terms of the working through of object relations dynamics in treatment. The important role of aggression in object relations psychoanalysis is demonstrated, as presented through patients' associations and responses. The importance of the separation-individuation process is emphasized in terms of the reowning of nightmare aggression that is initially experienced as bad-object persecution.

Particular nightmare motifs—traps, suffocation, and concentration camps—are seen to be representative of schizoid-level anxieties in relation to an internal bad-object world. Deeper schizoid anxieties (as described by Guntrip) are alluded to by nightmares of emptiness or black voids. The question is raised whether an inner regression can take place, beyond internal objects, to an objectless state, given nightmares of such character.

Nightmares are also reflective of varying levels of preoedipal anxieties. They remind us that fears of self-loss, or of lost ego-relatedness, can occur in terms of schizoid fears of disintegration, disappearance, or entrapment, as well as in terms of paranoid fears of persecutors or depressive fears of moral accusers. In addition, defenses against depressive-position anxieties of guilt and loss can be shown in nightmares in which manic triumph, control, and contempt appear through sadistic bad-object figures. Also, child terrors can be seen to reappear at adult levels of experience in differing nightmare themes, where the basic effective impact is not altered. Finally, nightmares seem to be indispensable experiences that provide entry to the deepest aspects of object relations development.

## References

Balint, M. 1968. *The Basic Fault.* New York: Brunner/Mazel.

Fairbairn, R. D. 1952. *Psychoanalytic Studies of the Personality.* London: Henley; Boston: Routledge and Kegan Paul.

Foster, J. C. and J. E. Anderson. 1936. Unpleasant dreams in childhood. *Child Development* 7:77–84.

Guntrip, H. 1969. *Schizoid Phenomena, Object Relations, and the Self.* New York: International Universities Press.
Harris, I. 1960. Typical anxiety dreams and object relations. *International Journal of Psychoanalysis* 41:604–11.
Hartmann, E., D. Russ, B. Van der Kolk, R. Falke, and M. Oldfield. 1981. A preliminary study of the personality of the nightmare sufferer: Relationship to schizophrenia and creativity. *American Journal of Psychiatry* 138(6):794–97.
Klein, M. 1975. *Love, Guilt, and Reparation and Other Works, 1921–1945.* London: Hogarth Press.
Klein, M. 1980. *Envy and Gratitude and Other Works, 1946–1963.* London: Hogarth.
Kohut, H. 1971. *The Analysis of the Self.* New York: International Universities Press.
Kohut, H. 1977. *The Restoration of the Self.* New York: International Universities Press.
Lesse, S. 1959. Experimental studies on the relationship between anxiety, dreams, and dream-like states. *American Journal of Psychotherapy* 13(2):442–55.
Mack, J. E. 1965. Nightmares, conflict, and ego development in childhood. *International Journal of Psychoanalysis* 46:403–28.
Mack, J. E. 1970. *Nightmares and Human Conflict.* Boston: Little, Brown.
Mahler, M. S. et al. 1975. *The Psychological Birth of the Human Infant.* New York: Basic Books.
Nagera, H. 1966. Sleep and its disturbances approached developmentally. In R. S. Eissler et al., eds., *The Psychoanalysic Study of the Child* 21:393–447. New York: International Universities Press.
Natterson, J. M. ed. 1980. *The Dream in Clinical Practice.* New York: Jason Aronson.
Plath, S. 1961. *Ariel.* New York: Harper and Row.
Segal, H. 1975. *Introduction to the Work of Melanie Klein.* London: Hogarth Press.
Snyder, F. 1966. Toward an evolutionary theory of dreaming. *American Journal of Psychiatry* 123(2)121–24.
Trossman, H. 1963. Dream Research and the psychoanalytic theory of dreams. *Archives of General Psychiatry* 9:9–18.
Winnicott, D. W. 1965. *The Maturational Process and the Facilitating Environment.* New York: International Univesities Press.
Winnicott, D. W. 1971. *Playing and Reality.* Harmondsworth, Eng.: Penguin.

# 4.

# Psychoanalytic Theory of the Nightmare in the Light of Recent Physiological Research

JEANNE M. SAFER

OVER THE PAST thirty years, a technology has been developed which permits researchers to investigate with precision the physiological processes underlying sleep and dreaming. The sophisticated instrumentation of the sleep laboratory makes it possible to identify precisely when a dream occurs, to obtain immediate and detailed reports of dream content and associations (much of which is forgotten upon awakening in the morning even by the most diligent reporters), and to monitor the organismic state of the dreamer. As a result, what Freud called the "dark and dismal" world of the nightmare has become more illuminated and accessible terrain. It is no longer necessary to rely exclusively on post hoc narrative reports of nightmare sufferers, or theoretical speculations.

Explaining nightmares has always posed a problem for psychoanalytic theory. Freud struggled to reconcile dreams which produce anxiety and terror with his theory of the universally wish-fulfilling function of dreaming, an effort which was only partially successful. Recent physiological research, some of which has been carried out by psychoanalytically trained investigators, has made major and often surprising contributions regarding the nature of such dreams. The findings confirm some psychoanalytic hypotheses, contradict others, and add new dimensions to our understanding of the meaning and function of nightmares. The purpose of this chapter is to report some of the fundamental research and to elaborate its significance and implications for psychoanalytic theory.

## Early Psychoanalytic Approaches to the Nightmare

Before the era of the sleep laboratory and direct observation of dreamers, the clinical and theoretical insights of psychoanalysis were the principal source of scientific data on nightmares. Dreams in which anxiety erupts and awakens the dreamer were apparent contradictions of the wish-fulfilling and sleep-preserving functions which Freud postulated in *The Interpretation of Dreams* (1900). In several categories of nightmares, Freud discovered wishes which had to be disguised because of their unacceptability; hence, dreams in which forbidden sexual or aggressive impulses were blatantly gratified generated anxiety. In such cases, the censor whose purpose is to keep the dreamer asleep has been overpowered by the intensity of the impulse; and the usual distortions of content which permit safe expression, such as symbolization, displacement, and condensation, fail to prevent anxiety.

Freud was also able to discern hidden wish fulfillments in many overtly disturbing dreams. Examples of such dreams are those in which the dreamer is punished for forbidden behavior, in which unacceptable desires are frustrated (counterwish dreams), and those in which worry over another's welfare conceals hostility directed against the victim. The dreams of traumatic neurosis, however, with repetitive content leading to overwhelming and unmodified anxiety, eluded explanation in terms of wish fulfillment and therefore seemed to be a genuine exception to the theory. In *Beyond the Pleasure Principle* (1920), Freud stated that such dreams were attempts to "master the stimulus retrospectively, by developing the anxiety whose omission was the cause of the trauma." By analogy, all nightmares which repeated painful childhood experiences were attributed to the repetition compulsion and the death instinct. Then, at the end of his life, Freud reversed himself and stated in 1933 that all dreams were indeed wish fulfillments, but that some simply failed to transmute pain into pleasure; in these cases, fixation to trauma prevented the dream from fulfilling its function.

Ernest Jones's *On the Nightmare,* first published in 1911, was the first extensive psychoanalytic study of the subject. According to Jones, nightmares are "always" expressions of mental conflict over incestuous desires and depictions of oral-sadistic perceptions of primal scenes of "excessive" power. He explored the autoerotic symbolism of the mounted horse and the werewolf as depictions of incest. Fenichel considered nightmares, like neurotic symptons, to be examples of the return of the repressed. These interpretations have remained essentially unchallenged until the era of the *in vivo* sleep experiment beginning in the 1950s.

## Nightmares and the Stages of Sleep

Laboratory studies have provided documentation of the psychological experience of dreaming and its physiological foundations. Each of the four stages of sleep is known to provide a unique psychophysiological context in which nightmares occur and which they reflect. It has been discovered that "nightmare," the general term for sleep disruptions caused by anxiety, actually constitutes two distinct phenomena. The characteristics of the different types of nightmares, and their psychodynamic significance, reflect the physiological aspects of the stages of sleep in which they occur and about which there is now comprehensive information.

The more common of the two, the classic bad dream or anxiety dream, takes place during REM periods in stage 1 sleep. The vast majority of dreams occur during this neurophysiologically unique type of sleep. REM sleep, also known as paradoxical, activated, or D (desynchronized) sleep, is a period of both intense cortical activity and motor paralysis. As Aserinsky and Kleitman discovered (see Fisher 1965), REM sleep has a specific EEG pattern and bursts of rapid vertical and horizontal eye movements (REMs) which correlate with dreaming. REM periods occur every 90 minutes throughout the night following periods of NREM, or nondreaming, sleep. The length of the cycles increases over the night. Four such cycles, and four dreams per night, are typical; 25 percent of every night, or approximately five years of an average lifetime, is spent dreaming (Fisher 1965).

During REM, which is a combination of light and deep sleep and developmentally the oldest form of sleep, the dreamer can do practically anything but move; the cortex and vegetative systems operate as in the waking state, but the motor system is massively inhibited, and arousal mechanisms as measured by skin resistance are depressed. Blood pressure, heart, and respiration rates tend to increase and, simultaneously, perception of external stimulation (and reality testing) is blocked in the central nervous system. The optic area of the cortex is particularly active, with eye movements following the action of the dream. During dreaming, motor discharge is replaced by hallucinatory perception (Hawkins 1966).

The pervasive motor paralysis during dreaming, which Freud hypothesized, is one of the most striking features of REM sleep. Immobility resulting from loss of muscle tone and of reflex activation of the limbs prevents dreamers from physically acting out their dreams (Fisher 1965). Gross body movements signal the end of dreams (Trosman 1963). An intriguing fact from the psychoanalytic standpoint is the presence in males, from infancy to senescence, of periods of penile erection and detumescence synchronous with REM periods—a phenomenon absent only during anxiety dreams. Recent research (Fisher et al. 1983) has demonstrated analogous patterns of sexual arousal in females, but not so specifically tied to REM periods. The meaning of sexual arousal during sleep is unclear.

Most nightmares occur approximately 20 minutes into a long stage 1 sleep period in the second half of the night, but are possible during any REM period. They can last for 20 minutes; it has been discovered that dream time approximates clock time

(Hawkins 1966). The most severe anxiety dreams happen within 3 minutes of REM onset, but there is evidence that the longer a dream lasts, the more likely it is to turn into a nightmare.

A considerably rarer and more pathological form of nightmare known as night terror, pavor nocturnus, or incubus attack takes place during NREM sleep. This type of sleep accounts for 75 percent of the night, and has three stages, known as stages 2, 3, and 4, with stage 4 the most physiologically quiescent and the deepest. Slow-wave EEG patterns characterize these sleep phases. It is during stage 4 that the most horrific nightmares occur, as well as the other major disturbances of sleep including somnambulism, enuresis, and bruxism (Fisher et al. 1970).

The deepest nondreaming sleep of stages 3 and 4 occurs in the first few hours of the night when fatigue is greatest, about 25 percent of the night's sleep. This is a time of physiological restitution, when all body functions slow down. In stage 2 sleep, which accounts for 50 percent of the night's total and takes place in the last half of the night, the mind is neurologically at rest. A form of nightmare more severe than the REM anxiety dream but less overwhelming than a full-fledged night terror occurs during this phase.

Mental activity continues throughout much of nondreaming sleep. These images, thoughts, and ruminations are experienced as qualitatively different from dreams, and more like secondary-process thinking and preconscious day residues.

Seventy percent of night-terror episodes happen during the first NREM period of the night, with the most severe preceded by the most stage 4 sleep. The barriers to the expression of the most deeply repressed conflicts would theoretically be lowest, and the ego least defended, at this time.

## The Physiology and Psychology of Nightmares

The common REM nightmare and the rare night terror, while often similar in content, differ strikingly in their physiological correlates and in their psychodynamic significance. An important characteristic of the REM nightmare, which is considered by psychoanalytic theorists (Mack 1970) to be an anxiety attack during sleep, is the absence of the usual physiological concomitants of anxiety. These dreams, in contrast to night terrors, occur during sleep in the midst of ongoing REM, and terminate on arousal. Only occasionally do manifestations of autonomic activation such as sweating, racing pulse, and hyperventilation accompany these dreams. Nightmares with sexual content are most likely to produce autonomic changes; themes of anger and loneliness do not, unless they evoke anxiety for particular individuals. Cardiac and respiratory rates, when they do accelerate, do so gradually. In the sleep laboratory, heart rates increased from 76 to 92 beats per minute, and respiration from 18 to 30 breaths per minute before spontaneous arousal in the most severe instance recorded (Kahn et al. 1978).

In addition to the limited autonomic involvement in REM nightmares, there is little screaming, and the occasional verbalizations tend to be subdued. Dream content is usually vivid and elaborate, and the dreamer is easily calmed and quickly lucid if awakened. Two of Jones's three classic symptoms, paralysis and the feeling of oppression on the chest, can occur in REM nightmares. These symptoms are related to the physical state of the organism during REM sleep.

The limited degree of physiological involvement and autonomic arousal in REM nightmares is thought to be a buffer against overwhelming anxiety; this "de-somatization," as Max Shur called it (Fisher et al. 1975) modulates anxiety by moderating its physiological manifestations. Diminishing the intensity of the anxiety responses decreases potential disruptive effects, keeps the person asleep, and prevents anxiety from becoming physically expressed panic. So effective is desomatization in reducing and aiding in the mastery of anxiety that REM dreams during the same night and with the same content as night terrors may not even arouse fear. The salutary effects of desomatization, however, break down if anxiety is intense enough.

Since REM anxiety dreams often progress over 20 minutes, there is time for abundant dreamwork to take place, and content is often complex and disguised. Several studies (Kales et al. 1980; Hartmann et al. 1981) have explored the content of recurrent REM nightmares. In order of precedence, the most common themes were found to be fear of falling and fear of attack, fear of death, and, less frequently, fear of choking or suffocation. While children most often dream of being chased, attacked, or wounded by animals which symbolically represent both themselves and their parents, the adult variant is attack by an unknown, usually male, intruder.

Mack (1970) states that all nightmares regardless of severity or place in the sleep cycle have as their manifest theme danger and helplessness, and as their latent content conflict and fear regarding destructive aggression, sexuality linked with annihilation, loss of identity, and loss of objects. The intensity of the nightmare depends on the severity of trauma and the resilience of the ego.

If REM nightmares are dream anxiety attacks, then the night terrors which occur in NREM sleep are encapsulated psychotic episodes (Fisher et al. 1974). Suddenness and dissociation are their distinguishing features. There is no preparation, no evidence of any physiological change prior to onset, and then massive, precipitous, and overwhelming reactions, all of which seem to vanish within several minutes.

Night terrors are among the most terrifying experiences human beings can endure. The preverbal fears of childhood are vividly replayed in uncontrollable anxiety of panic proportions. The attacks are said to "arise out of" stage 4 sleep (Fisher et al. 1974) because the symptomatology begins on arousal and is accompanied by an EEG pattern like that of awakening (alpha). Rapid and dramatic physiological changes take place, including extreme tachycardia, rapid breathing, apnea, and such signs of intense autonomic activation as sweating, hypermotility, and somnambulism. The precipitous increases in cardiovascular rate suggest that the body is behaving as in a fight-flight syndrome.

Episodes typically begin with cursing and blood-curdling screams of "animal-like intensity" (Fisher et al. 1974). Tapes of the screams of victims played at a scientific meeting were described as "one of the most chilling ever recorded, a series of solos in terror" (ibid.). The sufferer calls for help, attempts to flee, is propelled from bed, and in the sleep laboratory often tries to tear off electrodes. Heart rates can escalate twice or three times normal in 15 seconds. Night-terror episodes are the occasion for the greatest sudden accelerations of heart rate possible in humans, with instances of increases from 64 to 152 beats in 30 seconds. The episodes are brief in duration, usually 2 minutes, but 3 to 5 can occur in one night.

Elaborated dream content was retrievable only 10 percent of the time in the laboratory, and is typically violently aggressive and terrifying. There is often one scene, image, or idea which causes the panic. Upon awakening, the dreamer tends to be confused, disoriented, unresponsive to external stimuli, and hard to calm. The experience is typically rapidly dissociated and rerepressed, with a "striking and surprising" return to sleep within 4 minutes (Fisher et al. 1975).

It is hypothesized that in susceptible individuals the most deeply repressed conflicts, often with oral-sadistic content, emerge in the physiological quiescence of deepest sleep. Paradoxically, sufferers of night terrors tend to have peaceful REM sleep. It is an achievement indicating increased ego strength when in psychotherapy they begin to have REM nightmares (Fisher, personal communication, 1984).

Because of the nature of brain activity in slow-wave sleep, the content of night terrors is more conceptual and less visual than that of REM nightmares, though many of the themes are similar: being crushed, emtrapped, abandoned, choked, or killed. Fear of aggression by others against the self was the most commonly reported topic in the comprehensive investigation of Fisher and his colleagues (1965, 1970, 1974, 1975), which included data from 750 NREM nightmares from 12 subjects over 5 years. Recall was significantly better than previously reported. In the sleep laboratory, the most severe episodes involved content of being crushed or strangled by sudden forces, things closing in, or choking or swallowing objects. Aspects of the laboratory situation were often incorporated into the terrors, resulting in such themes as having the body infused with frightening substances by laboratory personnel. Content was often related to REM dreams of the same and surrounding nights, indicating that the images are psychodynamically meaningful to the dreamer.

The themes and images reported by Fisher's subjects resemble Winnicott's (1965) list of the infant's "unthinkable anxieties." These included an abandoned baby carriage about to roll down an incline, being stepped on, being abandoned in a rowboat by a person who disappears, and the room closing in. Subjects claimed that the theme of dangerous animals, such as being pursued by man-sized cats, was common at home, but this did not occur in the laboratory. In an example of a stage 2 nightmare cited by Kahn et al. (1978), which is a less severe form of NREM terror, the subject moaned and reported upon spontaneous awakening having dreamed of receiving a severed human leg as a Christmas gift.

Subjects who could recall content reported that their thoughts had caused them to scream and panic. This confirms that frightening thoughts precede physiological arousal, rather than occurring as a result of excitation. The centrality in night terrors of themes of persecution, which involves use of the defenses of projection and externalization of aggression, suggests an underlying paranoid personality organization in these subjects.

Psychodynamically, night terrors contain preoedipal as well as oedipal derivatives, often related to the child's violent distortions of sexuality and projection of intense murderous, oral-sadistic impulses.

The etiology of night terror is obscure. It has been attributed to severity of trauma in childhood or adulthood, and to psychopathology and organic factors. The conditions for onset of the episodes are the progressive deepening of stage 4 sleep in the early hours of the night. It is proposed that the ego regression and loss of reality testing which accompany the deepest sleep lead in susceptible individuals to the uninhibited, unmodulated release of terrifying repressed primitive impulses. The precipitous onset of the symptom does not permit preparation, which increases the anxiety response as in a traumatic neurosis. In addition, the rapid dissociation, re-repression, and amnesia which often occur may prevent the subject from integrating or resolving any of the conflicts which the night terrors express.

Organic causes for night terror have not been demonstrated, but there are possible predisposing genetic factors, since the symptom is more common in identical twins, and is associated with other sleep disturbances. Males suffer from night terrors twice as frequently as females, with the greatest frequency of occurrence corresponding to the oedipal and early latency years from 5 to 7, leading to the psychoanalytic hypothesis that castration fear is connected to the symptom. The lower arousal threshold in deep sleep shown by night-terror sufferers is similar to the autonomic responses found in concentration-camp victims and soldiers suffering from combat neurosis.

As Fisher et al. (1970) note, Broughton has argued that the major sleep disturbances are actually disorders of arousal, which occur out of a "physiological void" in stage 4 sleep, and that the psychological content of the terrors is actually a post hoc elaboration of the physiological reactions. Harkening back to the James-Lange theory of emotions, he attributes feelings of panic to responses to increased heart rates. Fisher and his colleagues were able to demonstrate the existence of psychodynamically meaningful mental content preceding the physiological symptomatology. They contend that night terrors are not dreams at all, but brief, encapsulated, reversible episodes of paranoid psychosis caused by an ego deficit in the ability to control anxiety. However, Hartmann (1984) reports findings which contradict this conclusion. His examination of the MMPI profiles of 18 night-terror sufferers revealed no elevation of scales indicative of psychosis. Most had quite normal profiles. In fact, he notes that the two patients with the most severe night-terror conditions in his experience, one of whom caused several deaths during an episode, were well-defended, rigid obsessional characters.

## Physiological Evidence and Current Psychoanalytic Perspectives

What is the relationship between the burgeoning physiological data on the phenomena of nightmares and contemporary psychoanalytic theory? Thirty years of research in the physiology and psychology of dreaming in the sleep laboratory have lead to revisions in some of the classic psychoanalytic interpretations of nightmares. It is now known that in both REM and NREM nightmares, preoedipal themes predominate over oedipal themes; Jones's insistence on incest conflicts as the ubiquitous cause of nightmares has not been borne out by research, although his emphasis on oral-sadistic aggression seems to be supported. It is also likely that feelings of powerlessness are more important causative factors than sexuality. The significance of separation anxiety is suggested by the decrease in severity of nightmares if the person sleeps with a light on. Anxiety was usually also less intense in the laboratory, where another person was always present.

Analytic authors have stressed the sexual origins of nightmares, but, according to Mack (1970), even so it is still necessary to explain why sexuality should be experienced as so overwhelming and destructive. He argues that one cannot attribute all violence in dreams to sexuality any more than in waking. When oedipal conflicts do occur in nightmares, it is because sexuality has become unconsciously fused with annihilating aggression, and early infantile fears of merged impulses are revived. According to Mack, "nightmares uniquely convey conflict over murderous impulses and primitive sexuality and capture the experience of helplessness in relation to forces within and without which threaten to overwhelm and destroy the dreamer and his world."

Freud's notion of anxiety dreams as representing failures of censorship and breakthrough of instinctual wishes where the dream content has undergone little distortion also requires revision in the light of physiological findings. There are actually great variations in distortion, often within the same dream. When content is undisguised, it has often been found to represent actual external threats to the dreamer (Mack 1970). There is also little physiological evidence of a clear discharge function in nightmares. Cycles of sexual arousal tend to be inhibited during anxiety dreams.

It is unclear whether the most terrifying nightmares, both recurrent REM anxiety dreams and night terrors, are efforts at mastery, or whether instead they are fixations or regressions which prevent mastery of anxiety. Fisher et al. (1970) assert that the mastery function in night terrors is questionable, since these symptoms occur when the ego is most deeply regressed and without resources to defend itself. They consider this phenomenon a massive failure of the ego to control anxiety by the usual means, which is via REM anxiety dreams.

Post-traumatic nightmares and night terrors do not permit integration of trauma because it is continuously relived in a regressed state. However, Mack states that such dreams are nonetheless efforts to limit and confine anxiety to sleep, to circumscribe the disorganizing effects of massive anxiety on the personality. Without such dreams, a person would be more burdened during the day, and waking functioning more impaired. Hence, severe nightmares are a continuous effort to compartmentalize or neutralize anxiety. They are, in Mack's words, acts of "desperate creativity" which occur when conflicts are too intolerable to permit successful resolutions. One of the most striking pieces of evidence of the self-preservative function of nightmares is the fact that aggression in these dreams, even the most destructive, rarely has the self as the agent; by rendering the self as the victim rather than as the perpetrator of violence, the dreamer preserves the object of the aggression and protects the self from retaliation.

Studies in the sleep laboratory have led to important revisions and extensions of the psychoanalytic understanding of nightmares. The conflicts and anxieties which these dreams express are now seen as predominantly preoedipal, with separation, abandonment, and oral rage the principal themes. Current thinking holds that it is the fusion of internal and external aggression with sexuality, rather than sexual desire itself, which is experienced as overwhelming and terrifying.

Another important development consonant with recent work in ego and self psychology is the emphasis on the creative rather than the pathological aspects of the nightmare, and its role in maintaining personality integration and daily functioning by releasing anxiety and by expressing in its intense imagery attempts to resolve the unresolvable. The fact that the dreamer is rarely the perpetrator of violence is now seen as an indication of the need to preserve relationships with significant figures at all costs.

Hence, continuing research into both the nature and the meaning of frightening dreams has led to an increased appreciation of the adaptive resources of human beings, as well as more understanding of the sources of their deepest fears.

## Summary

This chapter summarizes psychophysiological sleep-laboratory research and examines the implictions for psychoanalytic approaches to understanding nightmares. Data from studies of sleep and dreaming indicate that there are two types of nightmares which occur in different phases of sleep and which reflect the physiological properties of these phases: the common anxiety dream, which occurs in REM sleep, and the rare night terror, which arises out of the deepest, nondreaming phase of sleep.

During REM sleep, motor paralysis prevents the dreamer from acting out the dream, but the cortex is highly activated. REM nightmares are elaborately symbolic, often lengthy experiences which are usually remembered vividly, and which terminate upon awakening. They serve a distinct function in releasing anxiety associated with forbidden impulses, usually of an oral-aggressive nature. Other common themes include separation and feelings of helplessness in the presence of inner or outer dangers.

In contrast to the common nightmare, the night terror resembles an encapsulated paranoid psychosis more than a dream. These episodes, which are among the most frightening human beings can experience, occur when the person is in a stage of physiological quiescence during which, theoretically, the most deeply repressed mental content emerges. They start with screams of terror, and the victim is frequently propelled out of bed in an attempt to evade attackers. Night-terror attacks, which can recur several times a night for years, cannot be integrated or resolved because they are presumably rapidly dissociated and re-repressed.

Several aspects of psychoanalytic theory of nightmares need to be revised in the light of evidence from these psychophysiological studies, which included immediate reports of dream content. Early preoedipal anxieties were found to be more prevalent in nightmare imagery than was previously thought; Jones and others had emphasized the centrality of incestuous themes from the oedipal phase. Data from the sleep laboratory indicate that the most common themes are separation anxiety, helplessness, and fear of being overwhelmed by oral aggression fused with sexual impulses and fantasies. Current theoretical formulations focus on the creative aspects of nightmares as attempts to "resolve the unresolvable" and to preserve daily functioning and maintain personality integration by releasing anxiety.

## References


Fisher, C. 1965. Psychonalytic implications of recent research on sleep and dreaming. *Journal of the American Psychoanalytic Association* 13(2):197–303.

Fisher, C., J. Byrne, A. Edwards, and E. Kahn. 1970. A psychophysiological study of nightmare. *Journal of the American Psychoanalytic Association* 18(4):747–833.

Fisher, C., E. Kahn, A. Edwards, D. Davis, and J. Fine. 1974. A psychophysiological study of nightmares and night terrors. *Journal of Nervous and Mental Disease* 158(3):174–87.

Fisher, C., E. Kahn, A. Edwards, D. Davis. 1975. A psychophysiological study of nightmares and night terrors. I. Physiological aspects of the stage 4 night terror. In L. Goldberger and V. Rosen, eds., *Psychoanalysis and Contemporary Science.* Vol. 3. New York: International Universities Press.

Fisher, C., H. D. Cohen, C. Schiavi, D. Davis, B. Furman, K. Ward, A. Edwards, and J. Cunningham. 1983. Patterns of female sexual arousal during sleep and waking: Vaginal thermo-conductance studies. *Archives of Sexual Behavior* 12(2):97–122.

Friedmann, C. 1980. *Nightmares.* In J. Natterson, ed., *The Dream in Clinical Practice.* New York: Jason Aronson.

Freud, S. *Standard Edition of the Complete Psychological Works of Sigmund Freud.* James Strachey, ed. and tr. 24 vols. London: Hogarth Press, 1953–1974; New York: Macmillan.

1900. *The Interpretation of Dreams.* Vols. 4 and 5.

1920. *Beyond the Pleasure Principle.* Vol. 18.

1933. *New Introductionary Lectures on Psychoanalysis.* Vol. 22.

Hartmann, E. 1984. *The Nightmare.* New York: Basic Books.

Hartmann, E., D. Russ, B. Van der Kolk, R. Falke and M. Oldfield. 1981. A preliminary study of the personality of the nightmare sufferer: Relationship to schizophrenia? *American Journal of Psychiatry* 138(6):794–97.

Hawkins, D. 1966. A review of psychoanalytic dream theory in the light of recent psycho-physiological studies of sleep and dreaming. *British Journal of Medical Psychology* 39:85–104.

Jones, E. 1931. *On the Nightmare.* London: Hogarth Press. (Original work published in 1911.)

Kahn, E., et al. 1978. Night terrors and anxiety dreams. In A. Arkin, et al., eds., *The Mind in Sleep: Psychology and Psychophysiology.* Hillsdale, N.J.: Lawrence Erlbaum Associates.

Kales, A., C. R. Soldatos, A. B. Caldwell, D. S. Charney, J. D. Kales, D. Markel, and R. Cadieux. 1980. Nightmares: Clinical characteristics and personality patterns. *American Journal of Psychiatry* 137(10):1197–1201.

Mack, J. 1965. Nightmares, conflict, and ego development in childhood. *International Journal of Psychoanalysis* 46(4):411–27.

Mack, J. 1970. *Nightmares and Human Conflict.* Boston: Little, Brown.

Schonberger, S. 1946. A clinical contribution to the analysis of the nightmare-syndrome. *Psychoanalytic Review* 33(1):44–69.

Trosman, H. 1963. Dream research and the psychoanalytic theory of dreams. *Archives of General Psychiatry* 9(1):9–18.

Winnicott, D. W. 1965. *The Maturational Processes and the Facilitating Environment.* New York: International Universities Press.

# PART TWO: Physiological Studies of Nightmare Phenomena

# 5.

# REM and Non-REM Sleep and Its Relation to Nightmares and Night Terrors

CARL F. WIEDEMANN

OUR UNDERSTANDING OF nightmares has been profoundly affected by the extensive research that has been done over the past thirty years on sleep and its disorders. With the advent of the sleep lab where subjects can be studied under controlled conditions, knowledge of the sleep cycle has been both increased and refined. Researchers such as Broughton (1968), Fisher et al. (1968, 1970, 1973, 1974), Dement (1972), Kahn et al. (1973), and Kales et al. (1975) have been able to differentiate among nightmares by the stages of their occurrence in the sleep cycle and to develop theories about their diverse etiologies and functions based on this means of classification.

The discovery of rapid eye movement sleep by Aserinsky and Kleitman in 1953 provided the basis for a whole new way of studying sleep, and dreams. At first it was thought that all dreams, including nightmares, occurred only in REM sleep. Mendelson et al. (1977) report that Aserinsky and Kleitman found dream recall in only 9 percent of subjects awakened from NREM sleep, whereas about 75 percent of those who were roused during REM periods could describe vivid dreams. Dement and Kleitman (1957) hypothesized that this small amount of NREM recall represented "delayed recall of earlier unreported REMP *[sic]* dreams" (see also Foulkes 1962).

However, Foulkes, in one of the first systematic studies of mentation occurring in the different stages of sleep (1962) found significant evidence both that NREM dream recall was much higher than heretofore believed (54 percent) and that there was a qualitative difference between REM and NREM mentation in general which made the hypothesis of delayed REM recall untenable. Fisher et al. (1974), in a replication of Foulkes's study, also found a high rate of NREM recall in his subjects (58 percent). He also pointed out that the nature of the dream content in REM and NREM periods appears to differ. In crude terms, REM mentation is bizarre and dreamlike while NREM is more thought-like.

Foulkes suggested that this difference reflects a developmental progression in which the thinking and memory processes which form much of the content of NREM mentation gradually evolved into REM content characterized by affective involvement, vivid visualizations, physical movement, and a much less direct connection between the dream material and the waking life of the dreamer.

Foulkes (1978) has also pointed out, however, that these are fairly gross distinctions and that they will be affected by several factors, such as the amount of elapsed sleep, the presence or absence of rapid eye movements during REM periods sampled, and the dreamer's personality. For example, because late night dream reports tend in general to be more vivid and lengthy than early ones, reports from the earliest REM periods during a night may closely resemble those from NREM periods later the same night, and vice versa. Further, Molinari and Foulkes (1969) found qualitative differences in mentation within REM sleep itself, depending on whether subjects were awakened during the episodes of intermittent bursts of rapid eye movement, REM-M, or those in which eye movement was quiescent, REM-Q. They found REM-M mentation to contain more "primary visual experience," while REM-Q was closer in kind to NREM mentation, i.e., characterized by "secondary cognitive elaboration."[1] Finally, it has been shown that in subjects whose waking mentation reflects bizarre ideation, as measured by the MMPI, both REM and NREM dream reports are relatively bizarre and unpleasant.

The study of nightmares as specifically REM and NREM events really began with the work of Broughton (1968), who discovered that the severest form of nightmare, distinguished by its terrifying appearance to the observer, belonged to NREM rather than REM sleep. From this, standard classifications of nightmares have been established through use of EEG measurements. Taub et al. (1978) list these as: (1) stage 4 night terrors; (2) REM anxiety dreams; (3) stage 2 awakenings; (4) hypnagogic nightmares (anxiety arousals in sleep-onset stage 1 or in stage 1 later in the night). As Keith (1975) notes, while nightmares can usually be classified clinically, they are always identifiable encephalographically.

Stage 4 night terrors and REM anxiety dreams account for the vast majority of nightmares in the general population. Their etiology, physiology, and psychogenesis have been studied in some detail in normal (Taub et al. 1978), nightmare-prone (Broughton 1968; Fisher et al. 1970, 1973; Kahn et al. 1973; Johns 1975; Kales and Kales 1975; Keith 1975), and special populations such as victims of war neuroses (Greenberg et al. 1972; Schlosberg and Benjamin 1978) and children (Caldwell et al. 1970; Mack 1970; Schroeder et al. 1972; Gulleminault and Anders 1976; Benoit et al. 1978).

We now know quite a bit about their specific characteristics and their occurrence in the sleep cycle. This information has raised other questions about their purpose or function. What follows is an attempt to delineate what is currently known about nightmares within the framework of REM and NREM research and to present some of the hypotheses that have been developed to connect physiological data with psychological concepts.

1. A later study by Bosinelli, Cicogna, and Molinari (1974) confirmed and extended these findings. They also found greater feelings of self-participation during REM-M dreams than REM-Q or NREM, indicating that cognition plays a role in dream production. Exploration of the role of cognition in dreaming has been a major thrust of Foulkes' work as well.

## The Sleep Cycle: REM and NREM Sleep

Mendelson et al. (1977) have provided one of the clearest overviews of the sleep process, based on a summary of the research. During a normal night REM and NREM sleep alternate in a complex pattern of increasing and decreasing phases. In an ideal cycle, wakefulness is followed by a NREM period lasting for 70 to 90 minutes. The sleeper moves progressively deeper into sleep, beginning with stage 1, which is said to arrive when alpha waves, signals of the waking state, become less than 50 percent, replaced by slower beta and theta waves. Stage 2 is reached when spindles (brief bursts of rhythmic cycles) and K complexes (a high-amplitude negative wave followed by a positive wave) appear along with theta and some slow, high-amplitude delta waves. Stage 3 is characterized by between 20 and 50 percent of delta waves and stage 4 by 50 percent of delta or slow waves. Stages 3 and 4 are often jointly labeled slow-wave sleep.

The longest period of slow-wave sleep occurs early in the night, during the first cycle. The sleeper gradually returns to stage 2 sleep, then enters the first and briefest REM period of the night. In REM sleep the EEG wave pattern resembles the mixed pattern found in stage 1; however, a marked decrease in muscle tone and the appearance of conjugate rapid eye movements distinguish REM from stage 1. As the night continues, stages 3 and 4 sleep progressively decrease while REM sleep gradually lengthens from an initial 10 minutes or so to perhaps 30, occupying about 25 percent of total sleep time or about 1½ hours per night. Stages 3 and 4 sleep each take up 10 percent of the night's total, stage 1 5 percent, and stage 2 almost 50 percent of total sleep time.

The majority of recalled dreams take place during REM sleep, especially during the longer REM period late in the night. However, dreams—and nightmares—can occur at all times of night, in all stages of sleep (Fisher et al. 1970). It is likely, as Kales and Kales (1975) have pointed out, that recall is higher late at night precisely because REM periods are longer and sleep is made up of "lighter" sleep levels.

Mendelson et al. (1977) focus on a central issue in sleep research, the concept that sleep is to be viewed as an active process made up of three physiologically different states of consciousness: waking, REM, and NREM sleep. It is believed that some form of mentation exists in all three states (Mack 1970). The very act of going to sleep is increasingly described in active terms. Johns (1975), for example, recently hypothesized that sleep occurs when psychic input to the arousal-promoting system is reduced by interaction with the sleep-promoting system found in NREM sleep. He suggested that a third neuronal system associated with REM sleep also comes into play, further regulating the sleep cycle.

The function of REM and NREM sleep has, of course, been the object of much speculation. Fisher et al. (1970) concluded that slow-wave sleep provides the body with the means of recuperating from fatigue. Their subjects' heart and respiratory rates were somewhat lower, more stable, and less variable in stages 3 and 4 sleep than in REM periods. Slow-wave sleep during the first two hours of the night is also the time when the greatest amounts of growth hormones are secreted (Kales and Kales 1975). REM sleep, largely because of the high rate of recall (usually put at 70 percent), is closely associated with the study of dreams. Studies summarized by Mendelson et al. (1977) appear to show that sleep deprivation creates REM "pressure"—that is, a need for increased REM sleep.

In a study of naturally short and long sleepers, Oswald (1969) found that consistently short sleepers had a very high proportion of both REM and stage 4 sleep with brief REM latencies (i.e., NREM periods preceding REM sleep). A possible implication was that they compensated in this way for their decreased total sleep time. Long sleepers got about the same proportion of stage 4 sleep as the short sleepers but much more total REM sleep. Efforts to relate REM sleep to personality type or physical need or the quality of sleep have been inconclusive, according to Mendelson et al. (1977), who cite conflicting studies such as those of Webb and Agnew (1969) and of Hartmann (1970). However, one possible conclusion is that the varied amount of REM sleep reflects the need to dream in different individuals.

This is partially supported by Greenberg's study of war neurotics (Greenberg et al. 1972). Greenberg found that high scores on an instrument which evaluated "defensive strain" were associated with increased pressure to dream, as reflected in shortened REM latencies. The study found a less clear correlation between the amount of time spent in REM sleep and amelioration of tension. Greenberg concluded that there is some sort of connection between psychodynamic and physiological events and suggested that REM sleep might be an avenue to understanding the nature of unconscious processes.

## Dreams and Nightmares

REM sleep is known to be age related, attaining its peak in infancy, remaining high in childhood, then gradually dropping and leveling off before declining in old age (Mendelson et al. 1977). Mack (1970) notes that the higher percentage of REM sleep in childhood is generally believed to be related to a greater amount of dream activity than is found in adults. Mack cites Roffwarg's work linking REM sleep to neuronal differentiation and maturation of immature portions of the brain through active stimulation of them by the earlier-maturing lower centers. Connecting this to Fisher's concept that dreams may be necessary to discharge tensions and anxiety, Mack hypothesizes two interrelated functions of dreaming in general: it may be that when external stimuli cannot, for some reason, be adequately assimilated, they are carried into the child's sleeping central nervous system activity and are experienced as dreams; conversely, some of the affective and perceptual content of dreams which seem to represent attempts to master impulses may carry over into the growth of ego functions during waking. In both cases REM sleep could be said to play a role in building the central nervous system.

The nightmare dream has received particular attention in the sleep lab as part of research interest in disorders of sleep. Experiments with drug use and withdrawal have produced nightmares which seem to be associated with a rebound in REM sleep after its artificial suppression (Kales and Kales 1975; Firth 1974; Johns 1975). Most simply defined, a nightmare is a frightening dream from which the dreamer wakes spontaneously because of mental content associated with anxiety that can range from the fairly mild to the severe (Taub et al. 1978). They often contain material that reflects aggression, disruptive elements, and signs of castration anxiety, according to Taub. Mack (1970) describes them as an "encapsulated" state lying between normal dreams and acute psychoses. However, unless they occur frequently, nightmares are generally considered to be natural sleep events that arise in response to as yet unidentified stimuli (Kales and Kales 1975; Johns 1975; Taub et al. 1978).

## Night Terrors

The night terror (also called pavor nocturnus and incubus attack) has been of major interest to sleep researchers, perhaps because of its dramatic appearance. Although its occurrence in the general population is relatively rare, it is the most common childhood sleep disorder seen by pediatricians, according to Guilleminault and Anders (1976). The term is also used for the minority of post-traumatic sleep reactions which occur in NREM sleep (Fisher et al. 1973).

The night terror is terrifying to the observer. Broughton's (1968) depiction of the event is standard in the literature: the person, usually a child, sits up abruptly in bed and screams loudly, often in a bloodcurdling tone. No matter what is done to comfort victims, they remain inconsolable and unreachable for perhaps 10 minutes in children and 1 to 2 minutes in most adults before they seem to regain consciousness. It is common for victims to have no memory of the attack then or in the morning and to return to sleep immediately afterwards. Guilleminault and Anders (1976) point out that this is clearly different from REM anxiety dreams, which are usually associated with such vivid memories of dream content that children may be afraid of going back to sleep or even to bed for several nights afterwards.

All descriptions of night terrors emphasize the overwhelming nature of the panic, the attempts to fight or flee seen in bodily movement, and the utterances that may include cries for help and calls for mother (Fisher et al. 1970; Arkin 1981). These profoundly disturbing symptoms have led to theories that night terrors are indications of psychological disturbances, particularly when they begin or continue into adulthood (Johns 1975). Fisher et al. (1970), for example, compared night terrors to brief, reversible psychotic episodes, theorizing that they represent "a sudden cataclysmic breakthrough of uncontrolled anxiety."

The understanding of night terrors took a giant step forward with Broughton's (1968) discovery that they belong specifically to stage 4 sleep rather than, as had previously been thought, to the REM part of the cycle. Even more specifically, they arise during arousal from slow-wave sleep in the first or second NREM periods (Kahn et al. 1973). The physiological attributes of the terror attack underlie the abruptness and intensity of the autonomic discharge involved: the heart rate doubles or even triples very abruptly (Arkin 1981); breathing becomes more rapid and irregular with the same swiftness; skin resistance decreases, which signals heightened autonomic activity (Fisher et al. 1973); perspiration, glassy staring, obvious distress, and vocal sound accompany these signs (Guilleminault and Anders 1976). Concurrently the EEG shows an abrupt shift from delta to alpha waves, suggesting an apparent return to wakefulness (Fisher et al. 1973). However, the subject displays mental confusion and disorientation rather than a return to lucidity, as well as a lack of response to external stimuli. The episode is followed by amnesia and little recall of dream content (Broughton 1968).

From his examination of the physiological processes found in night terrors, Broughton (1968) theorized that they are not dreams at all but rather what he termed *disorders of arousal,* sharing certain features and a common symptomology with somnambulism and enuresis, with which they often occur. All are characterized by their paroxysmal nature, lack of responsiveness to externals, automatic quality, and amnesia after the event, according to Guilleminault and Anders (1976), who also found a positive family history and greater incidence among males than females for these and related sleep disorders.

Fisher et al. (1970, 1973), who extended the investigations of Broughton and his colleague Gastaut, pinpoints the night-terror scream as ushering in the arousal reaction. One of the most striking features of the attack, discovered in the sleep lab, is that it seems to arise out of what Fisher et al. (1973) called a "physiological vacuum." That is, the sleep preceding it is physiologically quiescent. Kahn et al. (1973), for example, found no measurable physical changes before the sudden onset of the attack. They suggested that some sort of frightening dream content might appear abruptly to "ignite" the arousal reaction.

Fisher et al. (1970) found a correlation between greater lengths of stage 4 sleep, larger amounts of delta waves, and slower respiration preceding an arousal and the severity of the night terror. This seemed to suggest that the deeper the preceding sleep, the more intense the attack. Fisher attempted to link this to the idea that ego regression may well be affected by the depth of stage 4 sleep, allowing the eruption of massive anxiety, attached to earlier traumas of either childhood or recent origin, because of the body's fatigue and accompanying decrease in vigilance. From this Fisher hypothesized, somewhat like Broughton, that the stage 4 night terror is not so much a dream as a pathological formation produced by a rift in the ego's capacity to control anxiety.

In a study that attempted to identify differences between children with night terrors and those without, Benoit et al. (1978) concluded, in contrast to Fisher, that the night-terror group had significantly shorter stage 3 and 4 sleep than the normal subjects, particularly during the first three hours of the night. This study found "modification" in the early REM periods also—for example, the first full REM sleep was delayed, preceded by a number of atypical partial REM periods. The duration of the first REM period (which depends on REM latency and place in the cycle) was no longer than in normal subjects; however, the duration of subsequent REM periods were very similar to those recorded for normals. The study concluded that children with night terrors show a deficit in slow-wave sleep, especially during the first three hours of the night. This appears to be accompanied by difficulty entering REM sleep at the beginning of the night. The significance of this is unclear, since the REM rhythm of normal children varies much more with age than that of adults. However, as Benoit points out, the subsequent normalization of the sleep cycle during the later night is paralleled by the relative absence of night terrors then.

All victims of night terrors, as Fisher et al. (1973) have said, are sleep talkers. Keith (1975), in a review of sleep disorders, cites the hypothesis that episodes of sleep talking connected with night terrors suggest the presence of mental content in stage 4 dreams, although it may be difficult to retrieve. This material, which could be neutral in itself, may produce sudden terror by touching on an extremely conflictual area and releasing extreme anxiety (Fisher et al. 1974; Kahn et al. 1973). Arkin (1981) has done extensive work on somniloquy, building on the studies of Broughton, Fisher, and others. He cites the views of Broughton and Fisher that the outbreaks of panic called night terrors are due to some sort of physiological overstimulation combined with unknown psychological variables. He also cites Dement's (1972) hypothesis that night terrors are precipitated by a sudden eruption of phasic activity in NREM sleep, as well as Benoit and Adrian's study which found a relationship between the difficulty children with night terrors have in establishing REM sleep and the presence of night terrors early in the night. From this Arkin has theorized that night terrors arise as "manifestations of out-of-normal-context REM sleep components into slow-wave sleep"—that is, they represent the intrusion of REM sleep into NREM parts of the cycle. He cites as evidence the theory that psychoactive drugs such as diazepam, commonly used to treat night terrors in adults, also tend to reduce REM sleep parameters. Arkin suggests that Broughton's (1968) characterization of night terrors as excessive startle reactions may explain the initiating mechanism. Fisher et al. (1973) demonstrated, for example, that the sound of a buzzer could provoke terror arousals in some subjects awakened by it during stage 4 sleep. Arkin (1981) offers the idea that something startling the speaker produces emotion which gives rise to night terrors by neural processes occurring in stage 4 sleep.

This is as purely physiological an etiology as has been developed for night terrors. The relationship of the physiological and psychological understanding of night terrors has been very difficult to establish. Broughton (1968) first raised the issue by concluding that it was virtually impossible to decide whether the occasionally retrievable images associated with night terrors preceded the attack or arose in response to cardiorespiratory changes which produced panic. He used the phrase "psychological void" to suggest that the symptoms were due primarily to abnormal physiological reactions during slow-wave sleep.

In general, physiologists have been very reluctant to link observations of physical processes to psychological explanations. Studies cited by Fisher et al. (1970), such as those done by Kurth and Kales and Jacobson, suggest that organic factors such as central nervous system immaturity and forms of brain damage may play a role in the etiology of at least childhood night terrors. Hersen (1972), reviewing studies on the physiological correlates of nightmares, presents evidence that homeostatic imbalances may be the source of the night terror. An article on "Night Terrors" (1974) in the *British Medical Journal* hypothesizes that night terrors occur when anxiety arousals and wakefulness arousals are erroneously activated at the same time. The authors do not believe these have a psychological origin.

On the other hand, the possibility of connecting physical and psychological phenomena has continued to fascinate researchers. According to Fisher et al. (1973), for example, Broughton himself later came to a more psychologically oriented explanation of night terrors, theorizing that chronic psychic conflicts can produce physiological changes in some "predisposed" people, altering the normal arousal reaction. Fisher's own conclusion (Fisher et al. 1970, 1973) was that night terrors are a pathological process arising in NREM sleep and represent signs of the ego's inability to control intense anxiety. He believed that some external stimulus probably triggered the arousal reaction in those subjects whose stage 4 arousal threshold was lower than in REM sleep (the opposite of the normal pattern). In other predisposed individuals night terrors might be set off by internal ongoing NREM mentation (Fisher et al. 1974). In both cases, Fisher theorizes, night terrors may be related to generalized past traumas which erupt during arousal.

The view that night terrors are psychological responses to trauma has found some corroboration in Kellerman's (1979) study of leukemic children with night terrors. Their symptoms were successfully eliminated through behavioral therapy which sought to lessen anxiety around separation from families and medical procedures and to reinforce regular sleep patterns.

The mental content of night terrors has been difficult to ascertain because of the characteristic amnesia that follows the attack. However, many subjects who were awakened during stage 4 night terrors were able to recall content of two basic kinds, according to Fisher et al. (1970): (1) ongoing, occurring just before or simultaneously with the scream; (2) elaborated, occurring subsequent to the scream during the confused period following arousal. The content itself revolved primarily around threats of violence directed at the dreamer, or fears of being entrapped, falling, or left alone (Fisher et al. 1974). Fisher attempted to establish some concordance between the verbal content of sleep utterances during night terrors and recalled mental content, but the results were inconclusive. More recently, Taub et al. (1978), in reviewing the evidence, returned to the theory that most of the mental content reported can be attributed to physiological responses during awakening—that is, the experience of anxiety or terror is produced by the tachycardia and electrodermal activation that occur.

Keith (1975), who has summarized much of the more recent research on night terrors, concluded that it is still unknown why certain people are prone biologically to abnormal arousal patterns associated with stage 4 sleep. We have not moved much beyond Broughton's (1968) original formulation that some preexisting constellation of physiological changes somehow predisposes subjects to arousal disorders of various kinds, whether it be somnambulism, enuresis, night terrors, or some combination of these. As Broughton points out, this formulation may help to explain the common symptoms seen in such sleep disturbances, but it does not uncover the initiating mechanisms.

Numerous attempts have been made to relate and compare stage 4 night terrors to REM nightmares. Keith (1975) cites research which appears to show that themes which are reported during stage 4 awakenings are often present in REM anxiety dreams of the same night. The chief difference he noted between the two forms of nightmares was that REM dreams had a better means of tempering and modulating anxiety than night terrors. Taub (1978) concluded from his study of the subject that REM nightmare content is characterized by more anxiety, physical activity, actual violence, and visual imagery than NREM mentation. This parallels the finding of Fisher et al. (1970) that night-terror content is filled with threats and fears, rather than acts of aggression. Fisher et al. (1973) cite some evidence that there is no necessary distinction between nightmares and night terrors; however, in general, the term "night terror" continues to be reserved for nightmares in stage 4.

Mack (1970) distinguishes REM anxiety dreams from night terrors both physiologically, according to the sleep stage they occur in, and psychologically, by the intensity of the terror and smaller amount of recalled content in the latter. NREM sleep seems to make the dreamer more vulnerable to sudden and fairly massive eruptions of anxiety and repressed hostility, according to Mack.

## REM ANXIETY DREAMS

The vast majority of nightmares belong to the category of REM anxiety dreams, including what are commonly referred to as "bad dreams" (which may or may not result in spontaneous awakenings; Kales and Kales 1975), and the larger percentage of post-traumatic arousals (Fisher et al. 1973). Frequent and recurrent nightmares are relatively rare in the general population. Children are believed to have nightmares more often than adults (Mack 1970), and these are thought to be related to developmental stages and to be transient phenomena. Furthermore, there is some evidence that anxiety dreams occur more in females, which according to Hersen (1972) may reflect their greater fearfulness. Swanson and Foulkes (1968) found a correlation between REM anxiety dreams in females and the menstrual cycle, with the greatest amount of self-reported "dream unpleasantness" occurring repeatedly during menses. Nightmare victims do not necessarily suffer from other sleep disorders, although REM anxiety dreams can occur in combination with them (Johns 1975). Greenberg et al. (1972), in a review of the research, concluded that sporadic nightmares are apparently normal events, not reflective of psychological disturbance.

Anxiety dreams belong specifically to the REM phases of the sleep cycle. The most easily retrievable of these dreams occur during the later part of the night when REM periods become longer. REM sleep is a time of increased autonomic reactiveness and intense cellular activity in the cortex and other parts of the central nervous system, accompanied by 30 to 50 percent more blood flow than NREM phases (Mack 1970). According to Melnechuk (1983), many researchers now accept Hobson and McCarley's theory that activity in REM sleep may be prompted by periodic self-excitatory behavior by the neocortex. This seems to have developed from the finding cited by Broughton (1968) that some sort of cerebral activation affects the neocortex in REM sleep.

Electrographically, REM sleep is characterized by a considerable increase and fluctuation in heart and respiratory rates with a concomitant increase in the number of eye movements (Fisher et al. 1970). REM is also referred to as "paradoxical sleep" because of the apparent contradiction between the return to alpha waves, as in the waking state, and a decrease rather than increase in muscle tone, which produces motor paralysis. Immediately before the nightmare occurs, there seems to be a gradual rise in cardiorespiratory rate (Kahn et al. 1973). With the onset of REM sleep, according to Hawkins, as discussed by Mack (1970), inhibitatory impulses in the brainstem reduce the activity of the motor neurons so that motor discharge is hindered at the same time as sensory portions of the central nervous system become more alert. It is as if preparations are being made to wake up, but the sleeper goes into another sleep phase instead.

During the nightmare itself, which may continue for several minutes, only mild to moderate autonomic discharge may occur (Fisher et al. 1973). On awakening, the heart and respiratory rate quickly return to normal (Fisher et al. 1970) and the sleeper comes to full wakefulness by all means of measurement (Arkin 1981). Broughton (1968) noted that lucidity and cerebral reactivity to visual stimuli return almost immediately on arousal, in sharp contrast to the mental confusion and nonresponsiveness seen in stage 4 nightmares.

Within the REM nightmare itself a fundamental quality appears to be the feeling of being helpless and powerless, in danger of being destroyed. The body is typically unable to move or make sounds because of the motor paralysis (Arkin 1981). Dream content is episodic, illogical, hallucinatory (Melnechuk 1983). Fisher et al. (1970) discussed another basic feature of this form of nightmare, what they called the dissociation between subjectively experienced anxiety and the objectively measured physiological responses. In general, the amount of anxiety felt in the dream bears no correlation to cardiorespiratory rates or eye movement response. Similarly, post-REM physical changes seem to have more to do with bodily movement on awaking than with any emotional reactions. Fisher theorized that this desomatization serves to control anxiety by disconnecting the physiological response from the psychological content.

As discussed earlier, the need for REM sleep has been studied extensively in the context of REM deprivation. A certain amount of REM sleep does seem to be required (Melnechuk 1983). It appears that the brain chemistry on which sleep is based is directly affected by the selective deprivation of REM sleep and by certain psychoactive drugs (Oswald 1969). After a period of general sleep deprivation, the recovery period often shows an increased percentage of both REM and stage 4 sleep, which is known as rebound sleep. Individuals who are sleep deprived sometimes show changes in mood and performance as well as transient neurological symptoms, according to the Mendelson et al. (1977) review of the literature. Kales and Kales (1975) concluded that the body seems to have great pressure to recover stage 3, stage 4, and REM sleep, in that order. Only in REM sleep deprivation, however—whether created through waking subjects up or administering drugs that suppress REM sleep—does the rebound sleep appear disturbed, with multiple wakings and numerous bad dreams (Oswald 1969; Kales et al. 1970; Firth 1974; Kramer 1979). One theory cited by Mendelson et al. (1977) is that REM deprivation leads to increased cortical excitability, which may be associated with nightmare production. Mack (1970) refers to evidence that an unusually high percentage of REM sleep occurring in a subject seems to be associated with the presence of nightmares. At this point, however, the relationship of REM excess or deprivation to anxiety dreams still remains obscure (Johns 1975).

The biochemical basis of nightmares—in particular the roles that neurotransmitters may play in producing anxiety dreams—has been discussed in some detail by Hartmann (1984). Focusing on studies which link administration of medications such as reserpine, the beta-adrenergic blockers, and cholinergics to the appearance of frequent nightmares, he points out that all these drugs either abnormally reduce or intensify the activity of certain neurotransmitters which seem to undergo similar but less drastic changes during REM dream periods. Nightmares, according to this formulation, result when these transmitters—specifically serotonin and norepinephrine, which normally decrease, and acetylcholine, which increases—are for some reason altered to a greater degree than usual during REM sleep.

Hartmann further speculates that a fourth neurotransmitter, dopamine, plays a key role in producing nightmares rather than dreams. Although dopamine, unlike the other brain chemicals cited, does not appear to change during normal REM periods, Hartmann found that administering L-Dopa to increase the level of dopamine in subjects also significantly increased the likelihood of vivid anxiety dreams. Dopamine has been implicated in sleep arousal and in some psychoses, both of which appear to be linked to more frequent nightmares. Hartmann has hypothesized that subjects who suffer frequent nightmares may be intrinsically more reactive to increased dopamine and that this may reflect a greater vulnerability to psychosis as well. However, what might cause any of the four neurotransmitters to alter their normal behavior during sleep, or what the specific interrelationship among them might be, is not yet known.

What is the significance of REM dreaming, including nightmares? A variety of theories have been offered. Liddon (1967), in an overview of the subject, begins with Freud's conception that the sleeper experiences inhibited motor movement in anxiety dreams which reflects a conflict of will rather than wish fulfillment. Jones linked this conflict specifically to sex. Liddon goes on to connect Fisher's discovery of a cycle of penile erections in REM periods to the possible emergence of psychic conflict around the sexual drive. Most research (Mendelson et al. 1977), however, has come to consider this a purely physiological event. Liddon's own theory was that dreams become nightmares when the potential for anxiety that arises in REM periods is dealt with unsuccessfully because of the failure, for some reason, of psychological mechanisms.

Hersen (1972) raised the question of a possible correlation between the frequency of nightmare occurrences and elevated levels of manifest anxiety. He found a significant relationship between subjects' conscious concerns about death and the presence of nightmares. However, this finding has not been corroborated by others, he acknowledged. Schroeder et al. (1972) cite Feinberg's work suggesting that REM may be a physiological index of central nervous system impairment, since he found a correlation between percentage of REM sleep and IQ. Greenberg et al. (1972) discussed studies of REM deprivation which seemed to demonstrate a marked alteration in subjects' ego defenses with the loss of REM sleep. This led to the hypothesis that dreaming serves to reconstitute such defenses and that nightmares may be examples of dreams that do not do this successfully. Crick and Mitchison (1983), have proposed the theory that REM sleep represents the mind's way of erasing false or useless memories that interfere with rational thought. Some of these memories, which represent aberrant or "parasitic modes" of brain activity, reach consciousness as dreams and are disposed of in this way. They thus act as correctives to distorted thought processes through weakening the synapses in which these are stored (Melnechuk 1983). Crick and Mitchison even propose that the function of REM sleep is to remove undesirable modes of interaction in networks of cells in the cerebral cortex.

## REM States in Children

One of the most fruitful ways of studying nightmare phenomena has been through children. As Mack (1970) points out, even infants appear to dream. REM states seem to be closely related to central nervous system development and differentiation, as well as to the development of psychological functioning, reflected, for example, by the capacity to distinguish internal from external perceptions and experience. Schroeder et al. (1972) cite Berger's work on the biological function of REM sleep, which seemed to link it to the maintenance of binocular eye movements. Schroeder hypothesized from this that sleep disturbances may be connected in some way to visual-motor dysfunction.

Mack (1970) theorized that young children tend to have more nightmares because of their stage of development. He noted that in infancy REM periods tend to be active, with body movements accompanying the conjugate eye movement. By age 2, however, this activity has already been decreased and peripheral motor blocking is evident. By age 5 or so movement in REM sleep tends to be limited to occasional twitches. These observations led Mack to conclude that a conflict develops between the motor blocking mechanism and vivid internal images that arise and call the body to action. The result is a disturbing dream.

According to Mack (1970), the nightmare may also be a survival mechanism of the species. He summarizes Snyder's "sentinal hypothesis," which postulates that REM sleep, because it is accompanied by a state of heightened arousal, serves an alerting or warning function in the central nervous system. Perhaps nightmares represent the mind's constant awareness of possible danger in the environment. Mack cites experiments which suggest that the content of nightmares may be related to innate fears in response to external stimuli and that they may be of phylogenetic rather than individual origin. The fact that children so often dream of being attacked by animals may reflect ancient realities. Thus, nightmares which rouse the sleeper to a state of alertness may originally have had a protective function. Mack goes on to hypothesize that humans have adapted this mechanism to cope with psychic conflict that arises when the ego feels helpless in sleep. The resultant anxiety acts as a signal to warn the ego of possible danger and wake the dreamer up. In sum, the function of REM anxiety dreams may often be, as Mack says, to guard the sleeper rather than the sleep.

## Nightmares Occurring in Other NREM Periods

Fisher et al. (1970) provide a number of useful points of comparison between the REM anxiety dream and stage 4 night terror which imply that they represent the extremes of a continuum. To resummarize briefly, REM nightmares are characterized by controlled anxiety, almost complete motor paralysis, and arousal out of a complex, vivid dream. Night terrors are associated with uncontrolled anxiety, hypermotility and vocalization, and difficulty in recalling both mental content and the attack itself.

Two other forms of nightmare have been identified according to the sleep stage in which they occur: the stage 2 awakening, which lies between REM and stage 4 nightmares in severity of reaction, and the hypnagogic hallucination, which occurs at sleep onset at the beginning of the night or following a later arousal (Fisher et al. 1970). Very little appears to have been written about the stage 2 nightmare. It is sometimes accompanied by low vocalizations and some bodily movement. Before awakening the sleeper shows no change in heart or respiration rate, as in stage 4 arousals, and only a moderate increase on awakening, as in REM anxiety dreams (Fisher et al. 1970). Stage 2 nightmares can occur in individuals who have bad dreams in REM and stage 4 as well, although stage 2 dreams are rarer than either of these (Fisher et al. 1973).

Schlosberg and Benjamin (1978) found that victims of combat fatigue showed a prevalence of recurrent nightmares occurring in stage 2, which seemed to be part of a larger pattern of sleep anomalies, including chronic insomnia. The REM sleep of these subjects was rare and short, stage 3 was shortened, and stage 4 absent; most sleep remained in stages 1 and 2. Muscle tone stayed high throughout the night, as did the total number of awakenings. Subjects often felt they had not slept at all. Schlosberg and Benjamin agree with Fisher (1973) that this form of nightmare is essentially a stage 4 night terror that occurs in stage 2 because of the absence of stage 4 sleep. Interestingly, they note that one subject who showed the most violent night-terror-like responses also had no REM periods.

Hypnagogic hallucinations resemble night terrors in their intensity, yet they are associated more closely with REM sleep in that they tend to appear in subjects who show REM periods at sleep onset without going through the normal latency period (Liddon 1967). Citing Bulow and Ingavar's work, Liddon points out that changes in respiratory rate at sleep onset take place more rapidly than usual, producing apnea. It may be that this physical event leads to the sensation of being suffocated or crushed by a frightening object or person sitting on the chest, which is the classic description of these dreams. Sleepers can normally be awakened from them by being touched or called (Mendelson et al. 1977). At times individuals pass directly from hypnagogic hallucinations into REM sleep, where the hallucinations may be experienced as recurring nightmares (Guilleminault and Anders 1976).

These hallucinatory dreams are seen to occur in febrile children especially and are a common symptom of narcolepsy, along with cataplexy and sleep paralysis. Researchers have commented on the similarity between the low muscle tone of the REM period and of sleep paralysis ("Terrors of Sleep" 1971). Mack (1970) suggests that sleep paralysis may represent a state in which the motor inhibitions associated with REM sleep somehow become dissociated from it. Liddon (1967) questions whether hypnagogic hallucinations might be REM anxiety dreams that somehow intrude into the sleep onset period.

## Summary

The more we learn about sleep, dreams, and nightmares, the more subtle and complex are the interactions we seem to uncover. Sleep is now perceived as an active state, a continuation of consciousness in an altered form. The cycle of REM/NREM sleep is widely believed to play an important role in maintaining the physiological and psychological integrity of the whole organism (Mack 1970). Night terrors are generally regarded as disorders of arousal rather than dreams per se. Why they occur in certain individuals remains unknown. Studies have raised the possibility of a relationship between night terrors and some forms of epilepsy (Schlosberg and Benjamin 1978; Montplaisir et al. 1981). Montplaisir reported, for example, that an epileptic patient given a right temporal lobe lobectomy was relieved of both clinical seizures and night terrors (but not REM nightmares). Broughton (1982) has studied the effect that a neurological disease such as narcolepsy may have on the dream process, especially on the characteristic intensification of nightmares that occurs.

REM anxiety dreams represent another area of study. The relationship of REM sleep to central nervous system growth and of nightmares to the preservation of daytime functioning during times of crisis or developmental changes (Mack 1970) has been the subject of speculation. In general, after some early attempts to link the psychology of dreams and the biological functions of sleep (Liddon 1967; Broughton 1968j; Fisher et al. 1970, 1973, 1974), the physiological and psychological approaches have tended to diverge. Mack (1970), Hersen (1972), and Johns (1975), among others, have warned that we must be extremely careful about drawing conclusions regarding any connections between physical and psychic events. Recent research appears to be focused on drug and disease-related REM/NREM nightmares, in a continued attempt to clarify their etiology and function. But much about the mechanism of these phenomena remains to be discovered.

One of the few new tools that has been developed to study dreams—and by extension nightmares—is the Scoring System for Latent Structure (SSLS) devised by Foulkes (1978), based on principles of cognitive analysis similar to those used by psycholinguists. The purpose of the SSLS is to allow researchers to "undertake comparative studies of dream-work in different psychophysiological states," moving beyond what Foulkes considers to be often a reductionist biological perspective to an attempt to integrate study of the dream process per se with exploration of the dreamer's private meanings and individual patterns. The SSLS would seem to offer one possible means of bringing together physiological and psychological research, refining both our understanding of the ways mentation varies across the sleep cycle and of what that signifies.

## References


Arkin, A. 1981. *Sleep Talking: Psychology and Psychophysiology.* Hillsdale, N.J.: Lawrence Erlbaum Associates.

Benoit, O., F. Goldenberg-Leygonie, and M. Marc. 1978. Sleep in children with episodic sleep phenomena: A comparison with the normal child. *Electroencephalography and Clinical Neurophysiology* 44(4):502–12.

Bosinelli, M., P. Cicogna, and S. Molinari. 1974. The tonic-phasic model and the feeling of self-participation in different stages of sleep. *Giornale Italiano di Psicologia* 1(1):35–65.

Broughton, R. 1968. Sleep disorders: Disorders of arousal? *Science* 159(3819):1070–78.

Broughton, R. 1982. Neurology and dreaming. *Psychiatric Journal of the University of Ottawa* 7(2):101–10.

Caldwell, D., A. Brane, and P. Beckett. 1970. Sleep patterns in normal and psychotic children. *Archives of General Psychiatry* 22(6):500–3.

Crick, F. and G. Mitchison. 1983. The function of dream sleep. *Nature* 304:14, 111–14.

Dement, W. 1972. Sleep and dreams. In A. Freedman and H. Kaplan, eds., *Human Behavior: Biological, Psychological, and Sociological.* New York: Atheneum.

Dement, W. and N. Kleitman. 1957. The relation of eye movements during sleep to dream activity: An objective method for the study of dreaming. *Journal of Experimental Psychology* 53:339–46.

Firth, H. 1974. Sleeping pills and dream content. *British Journal of Psychiatry* 124:547–53.

Fisher, C., J. Byrne, and A. Edwards. 1968. NREM and REM nightmares. *Psychophysiology* 5(2):221–22.

Fisher, C., J. Byrne, A. Edwards, and E. Kahn. 1970. A psychophysiological study of nightmares. *Journal of the American Psychoanalytical Association* 18(4):747–82.

Fisher, C., E. Kahn, A. Edwards, and D. Davis. 1973. A psychophysiological study of nightmares and night terrors. I. Physiological aspects of the stage 4 night terror. *Journal of Nervous and Mental Diseases* 157(2):75–98.

Fisher, C., E. Kahn, A. Edwards, D. Davis, and J. Fine. 1974. A psychophysiological study of nightmares and night terrors. 3. Mental content and recall of stage 4 night terrors. *Journal of Nervous and mental Diseases* 158(3):174–88.

Foulkes, D. 1962. Dream reports from different stages of sleep. *Journal of Abnormal and Social Psychology* 53:339–46.

Foulkes, D. 1968. *A Grammar of Dreams.* New York: Basic Books.

Greenberg, R., C. Pearlman, and D. Gampel. 1972. War neuroses and the adaptive function of REM sleep. *British Journal of Medical Psychology* 45(1):27–33.

Guilleminault, C. and T. F. Anders. 1976. The pathophysiology of sleep disorders in pediatrics. II. Sleep disorders in children. *Advances in Pediatrics* 22:151–74.

Hartmann, E. 1970. What is good sleep? In E. Hartmann, ed., *Sleep and Dreaming.* Boston: Little, Brown.

Hartmann, E. 1984. *The Nightmare.* New York: Basic Books.

Hersen, M. 1972. Nightmare behavior: A review. *Psychological Bulletin* 78(1):37–48.

Hilakivi, I., J. Makela, A. Leppavoori, and P. Putkonen. 1978. Effects of two adrenergic beta-receptor blockers on the sleep cycle of the cat. *Medicine and Biology* 56(3):138–43.

Johns, M. 1975. Sleep and hypnotic drugs. *Drugs* 9:448–78.

Kahn, E., C. Fisher, A. Edwards, and D. Davis. 1973. Mental content of stage 4 night terrors. *Proceedings of the Eighty-first Annual Convention of the American Psychological Association.* Montreal, Canada. 8:499–502.

Kales, J. and A. Kales. 1975. Nocturnal psychophysiological correlates of somatic conditions and sleep disorders. *International Journal of Psychiatry in Medicine* 6(1–2):43–62.

Kales, A., T. Preston, T. Tan, and C. Allen. 1970. Hypnotics and alterd sleep-dream patterns. I. All-night EEG studies of Glutethimide, Methyprylon, and Pentobarbital. *Archives of General Psychiatry* 23(3):211–18.

Keith, P. 1975. Night terrors: A review of the psychology, neurophysiology, and therapy. *Journal of the American Academy of Child Psychiatry* 14(3):477–89.

Kellerman, J. 1979. Behavioral treatment of night terrors in a child with acute leukemia. *Journal of Nervous and mental Diseases* 167(3):182–85.

Kramer, M. 1979. Dream disturbances. *Psychiatric Annals* 9(7):50–68.

Liddon, S. 1967. Sleep paralysis and hypnagogic hallucinations: Their relationship to the nightmare. *Archives of General Psychiatry* 17(1):88–96.

Mack, J. 1970. *Nightmares and Human Conflict.* Boston: Little, Brown.

Melnechuk, T. 1983. The dream machine. *Psychology Today* 17(11):22–34.

Mendelson, W., J. C. Gillin, and R. Wyatt. 1977. *Human Sleep and Its Disorders.* New York: Plenum Press.

Molinari, S. and D. Foulkes. 1969. Tonic and phasic events during sleep: Psychological correlates and implications. *Perceptual and Motor Skills* 29(2):343–68.

Montplaisir, J., M. Laverdiere, J. Saint-Hilaire, J. Walsh, and G. Bouvier. 1981. Sleep and temporal lobe epilepsy: A case study with depth electrodes. *Neurology* 31:1352–56.

Night terrors. 1974. *British Medical Journal* 4(5936):63. October 12.

Oswald, I. 1969. Sleep. *Experimental Medicine and Surgery* 27(1–2):65–79.

Schlosberg, A. and M. Benjamin. 1978. Sleep patterns in three acute combat fatigue cases. *Journal of Clinical Psychiatry* 39(6):546–49.

Schroeder, S., C. Schroeder, and B. Ball. 1972. Sleep disturbance in children with visual-motor deficits. *Perceptual and Motor Skills* 34:695–700.

Swanson, E. and D. Foulkes. 1968. Dream content and the menstrual cycle. *Psychophysiology* 4(3):373–74.

Taub, J., M. Kramer, D. Arand, and G. Jacobs. 1978. Nightmare dreams and nightmare confabulations. *Comprehensive Psychiatry* 19(3):285–91.

Terrors of sleep. 1971. *British Medical Journal* 4(786):507–8. November 27.

Webb, W. B. and H. W. Agnew. 1969. Measurement and characteristics of nocturnal sleep. In L. A. abt and B. F. Riess, eds., *Progress in Clilnical Psychology.* Vol. 8. New York: Grune and Stratton.

# 6.

# The Neuropsychology of Nightmares

EMILY M. ADAMS

IT IS HARD to imagine the complex interactions, psychological and physiological, which are thought to occur in the brain during sleep when someone is sleeping quietly. On the other hand, observing someone in the midst of a night terror, hearing screams pierce the still air and watching legs and arms flail involuntarily as the person's heart and lung rate accelerate rapidly, one knows that a great deal is happening—not only physically but also psychologically. The aim of this chapter is to present the theories underlying the neuropsychology of nightmares. Implicit in this aim is the belief that the brain's biology is in some way related to the complex cognitive and affective experiences noted by observers and sufferers alike of nightmares and night terrors.

## The Neuropsychology of Sleep

Unlike other bodily systems, for example, the lungs, heart, and gastrointestinal systems, the brain does not become quiet, functioning at a generally reduced rate, during sleep. This discovery of the awake brain was made as the result of controlled laboratory studies conducted by Dement and Kleitman, who are pióneers in the field of sleep research. Dement and Kleitman (1957) discovered, after collecting electroencephalogram readings (brain-wave activity) and recording the amount and frequency of each sleeping subject's eye movements, that sleep really is two separate processes: non–rapid eye movement sleep (NREM) and rapid eye movement sleep (REM).

According to Dement and Kleitman, NREM sleep is a cycle with four distinct stages which lasts approximately 90 minutes. This cycle repeats itself until the individual awakens. However, they also observed that throughout this cycle, periods of rapid eye movement (REM sleep) occur which reflect the state of dreaming. Dement and Kleitman, using the EEG readings as well as eye movement as criteria, established a means of describing and classifying the four stages of the NREM sleep cycle.

## The Sleep Cycle

The early sleep before the first stage of NREM sleep is characterized by an EEG reading of shifting, near-alert electrical brain-wave activity. Quickly, as the individual slips into stage 1 NREM sleep, the EEG pattern changes. It changes to one of low voltage and rapid rate (the electrical activity in the brain at this moment is not intense) and the actual rate of the brain waves is very rapid. Stage 2 NREM sleep follows very quickly. In appearance and by comparison, this stage is very similar to the brainwave activity which occurs in stage 1 NREM sleep. Sleepers, at this point, can be easily aroused. They appear to be sleeping peacefully: their breathing is regular and quiet.

Stages 3 and 4 and the deepest stages of NREM sleep. During these latter stages of sleep, the EEG pattern changes from one of low voltage to one of high voltage and from the previous pattern of high frequency to a pattern of low frequency, i.e., the brain wave activity is now very intense and the waves, much slower, more pronounced in their appearance. During these two stages, sleepers' respirations and pulse rates can fluctuate considerably, especially in stage 4 sleep. Occasionally, sounds are uttered by the sleeper. As previously mentioned, these stages of the sleep cycle last approximately 90 minutes and continue to recur until the individual awakens.

The EEG pattern for REM sleep is similar to the EEG pattern which characterizes early, pre-stage 1 NREM sleep. The electrical activity in the brain during REM sleep is one of low voltage and a rapid rate. REM sleep has also been described as alert and active sleep and as "D" state sleep (Hartmann 1966). Dement and Kleitman (1957) also indicate that REM sleep contains mentation as well as dreaming. They observed that 74 percent of subjects when awakened during REM sleep were able to recall their dreams. However, when the same subjects were awakened during NREM sleep, the amount who could recall dreams dropped to 7 percent. These findings appeared to confirm that mentation and dreaming occurred primarily during REM sleep. In recent years, largely due to the advances in technology and measurement techniques, the construct of mentation has been more clearly understood and shall be discussed in the following section.

## Mental Activity and the Sleep Cycle

Mentation, a term frequently seen in the literature, can be somewhat confusing as it is used to include affective experiences such as anxiety and panic and to include cognitive operations such as memory and thinking. The concept of mentation is also used to describe both conscious and unconscious states. Consequently, when these processes are discussed under the term mentation it is not always apparent which aspect of mental activity, in dreams and in the sleep cycle, is being discussed. For example, researchers agree that mental activity occurs in both REM and NREM sleep. Breger (1967) characterizes the mentation of REM sleep as containing bizarre, fantasy-related content which is highly accessible to the individual's recall. In contrast, NREM mentation, according to Breger, is fragmented and concrete, literal, in its content. Breger suggests that these two processes may be distinct and separate from one another. Foulkes (1966) points out that the issue is not do we or do we not have different kinds of mentation. Rather, the issue may be how mentation is measured. Using only subject recall as an outcome criterion for the presence of mentation is insufficient because subjects will differ in their ability to recall. Further, using subject recall as the central criterion for the presence of mental activity confuses the issue. This criterion of recall does not indicate whether or not mentation has in fact occurred (Foulkes 1966). Considering both points of view regarding the relative importance of recall as a central criterion for the presence of mentation, several important questions have been raised. First, recall as a mental activity requires a constant level of arousal, similar to the level of arousal which is evident, according to EEG readings, during REM sleep. If this needed state of arousal has not been achieved, can it be said that no mentation or mental activity has occurred simply because the subject cannot recall material? The answer to this question is that EEG indication of arousal in stages 3 and 4 sleep implies that arousal is episodic. Therefore, memory processes such as recall will not be present in the same reliable way as recall occurs when the pattern of arousal is more consistent, as it is in REM sleep.

The EEG evidence of arousal during NREM stage 3 and 4 sleep indicates that the arousal activity is episodic. Thus, arousal appears to be necessary in order for information to be stored in memory, which in turn is necessary for recall to occur. Quite possible, this episodic arousal activity observed in these latter two stages of NREM sleep does indicate the presence of cognitive and affective activity. However, because this arousal is not consistent and perhaps not of sufficient intensity to activate memory, cognitions and affective experiences do not become stored in memory. If they are stored in memory, they may be recorded only as bits and pieces or as the fragments that Breger (1967) describes as NREM mentation. Thus, it seems that recall as a central criterion in the measurement of mentation turns out to be unreliable. The issue of arousal therefore, is of vital importance to the consistent appearance of recall as a component of mentation. The issue of arousal is also important throughout the organization and functioning of neural structures during sleep and waking and shall be examined in the following section.

## Neural Structures of Sleep

Sleep, arousal, and waking are mediated by a network of projections located throughout the brain and brainstem. In the lower brain, Jouvet (1967) discovered that the pons and medulla are involved in REM sleep. The reticular activating system, also located in lower brain structures with projections into the cortex, also mediates REM sleep and plays a significant role in maintaining arousal states in the brain. Messages, however, are not simply sent to the cortex via these systems. The thalamus, a primary sensory relay system, conveys information to and from both the higher cortical centers and also relays messages to the lower brain centers. Although this complex circuitry is necessary to maintain the balance between sleeping and waking and for the maintenance of arousal, neurotransmitters are equally important.

There exist, quite possibly, hundreds of neurotransmitter systems. The effects these neurotransmitters may have on the brain are still largely unknown. More specifically, neurotransmitter effects of emotions, cognitions, sleep, waking, and arousal are also unknown. The effects of neurotransmitters on arousal will be more thoroughly considered in the discussion of nightmares, night terrors, and arousal.

In the following section nightmares and night terrors will be considered with respect to their neuropsychological underpinnings.

## The Neuropsychology of Nightmares and Night Terrors

Many biological explanations of nightmares, such as oxygen deprivation and gastrointestinal disturbances, have been refuted. Recently, researchers have investigated the possibility that nightmares may be due to disorders of arousal which may be affected by aberrations in neurotransmitters or in the brain amine systems.

Broughton (1968) on the basis of his early research on somnambulism and enuresis, which he defined as disorders of arousal, hypothesized that nightmares were also disorders of arousal. Broughton states that the night terror which occurs in stage 4 sleep is most assuredly a disorder of arousal. He found that subjects who experienced night terrors experienced significant autonomic arousal, including involuntary movement and accelerated heart and respiratory rates, and that occasionally these individuals made verbal utterances. Broughton believed that night terrors were physiological and tend to occur in physiologically predisposed individuals. According to Broughton, the individual experiencing night terrors does not experience any sort of dreamlike consciousness or mentation. He believed that any report of mental activity subsequent to a night terror was the subject's attempt to rationalize the experience.

Fisher et al. (1968, 1969) replicated Broughton's studies, confirming many of Broughton's assertions about night terrors. However, these authors also reported significant differences. For instance, subjects who experienced night terrors did not show significant signs of autonomic arousal. In fact, their sample of subjects showed a trend toward autonomic slowing before and initially during the night terror. According to Fisher, as the night terror proceeds, the subjects do show an increase in autonomic arousal. They also found that subjects experiencing night terrors reported mentation of a terrifying nature. Fisher did not see this as an attempt on the subject's part to rationalize the experience. These authors found evidence of nightmare activity in all stages of sleep, including REM sleep; the latter they called REM anxiety dreams.

Fisher et al. (1968, 1969) suggest then that the differences between night terrors and REM anxiety dreams (nightmares) are quantitative rather than qualitative and that both involve physiological aberrations, particularly in the arousal mechanism, which produce psychological as well as physiological symptoms.

The anxiety-dream sufferers were, according to Fisher et al., in a state of heightened arousal. Their EEGs indicated patterns consistent with arousal. These individuals, when in this state of arousal, may or may not experience slight increases in heart and respiratory rates.

Fisher et al. (1968, 1969) believe that this state of arousal represents a state of physiological readiness which the authors refer to as desomatization. They believe that this physiological process acts like a signal to psychological mechanisms, which then become engaged to help the individual ward off anxiety.

Consequently, because of this desomatization, the individual, during an anxiety dream, experiences psychological and physical discomfort, but such experiences do not reach the magnitude of terrifying panic and physical discomfort reported by subjects who had experienced night terrors.

Desomatization, according to Fisher et al., does not occur in stage 4 night terrors because the arousal during this stage of sleep is more episodic. Consequently, the amount of arousal present in this stage does not appear to be sufficient to engage the desomatization process described as occurring during REM sleep. As a result, the night-terror sufferer experiences anxiety without any protective barriers, an anxiety experienced as panic.

Fisher et al. agreed with Broughton's assertion that night terrors are a disorder of arousal. However, unlike Broughton, the authors also include in their classification system nightmares as anxiety dreams. Fisher et al. maintain that anxiety dreams are due to aberrations in arousal during REM sleep. They do not agree with one of Broughton's primary assertions, that is, night terrors occur only in physiologically predisposed individuals. They believe that nightmares and night terrors are due to disorders in the arousal mechanisms of stage 4 and REM sleep which lead to psychological as well as physiological changes (Fisher et al. 1968, 1969).

Hartmann (1966) replicated many of the Fisher et al. studies. He too found evidence of nightmares occurring in NREM as well as in REM sleep, which he refers to as S-sleep and D-sleep, respectively. However, Hartmann's more recent contributions, as a result of his investigation of the effects of certain drugs, reserpine, the effect of drug withdrawal, benzodiazene tranquilizers, and the effects of alcohol withdrawal, are quite important to understanding the role arousal seems to play in nightmares and night terrors.

## The Role of Neurotransmitters in Nightmares

Hartmann found that generally the subjects he studied experienced prolonged periods of D-state sleep (REM sleep) and frequent periods of waking in the above drug-induced conditions. Hartmann hypothesized that normally norepinephrine is repaired during D-state sleep. However, owing to biochemical interference, the normal balance between brain amines or the neurotransmitters is affected. This, suggests Hartmann, leads not only to an interference with storage but also to a state of hyperactivity on the cellular level. As a result, the mechanism of arousal is altered, producing a variety of disturbances, as increase in bizarre dream content, and an increase in frequency of nightmares. He suggests that the brain amine system which appears to be most implicated in this process is the catacholamine norepinephrine. Hartmann arrived at the conclusion that the level of norepinephrine increases in subjects who had been given reserpine, an antihypertensive, and in subjects who were taking inderal, a beta blocker. In addition he observed this same phenomenon in subjects who were withdrawing from benzodiazepine tranquilizers and alcohol.

This research on the effects of various drugs and drug withdrawal indicates that a neurotransmitter, norepinephrine, has a direct affect on the arousal state. Hartmann's (1984) research indicates how neurotransmitters can also affect dreams and nightmares by influencing dream content.

Hartmann (1984) discovered that the level of dopamine (a neurotransmitter) is elevated in nightmare sufferers. This finding regarding dopamine and nightmares is intriguing because elevated levels of dopamine have also been associated with psychotic episodes and these episodes have content that is similar to the content of nightmares. Hartmann believes that the primary affect of dopamine is not on the arousal mechanisms found in D-state sleep but rather that dopamine is responsible for increasing the vividness of dreams. This means, then, that for individuals experiencing nightmares, there appears to be a significant increase in the level of dopamine, suggesting that the neurotransmitters play a significant role in the appearance of nightmares. In the previous section it was shown that norepinephrine affects nightmares by directly interfering with the arousal mechanism. Dopamine, on the other hand, affects the content and intensity of the nightmare.

A final neurotransmitter related to behaviors described by Broughton (1968) and Fisher et al. (1968) is acetylcholine. Excessive amounts of acetylcholine have frequently been associated with psychological changes: confusion, agitation, slowing of motor functions, and nightmares.

Increased levels of acetylcholine are also associated with profound physical changes directly affecting the parasympathetic branch of the autonomic nervous system, i.e., decreased heart rate, decreased pulse rate, and eventually, paralysis of respiratory muscles. Hartmann's (1984) investigations confirmed that nightmare activity increases when levels of acetylcholine in the brain increases. Thus, again, the neurotransmitter is a major variable in the appearance of the nightmare.

## Drugs and Sleep Disturbance

Drugs have also been used to treat sleep disturbances. For example, antidepressants have been used with enuretic children, and minor tranquilizers have been used to relieve traumatic stress symptoms thought to be related to nightmares. Antidepressants and minor tranquilizers are thought to reduce delta activity, which is associated with stage 4 sleep (Fisher et al. 1973; Flemenbaum 1976; Beitman and Carlin 1979). The reduction of delta activity in stage 4 sleep appears to be related to the reduction of the report of nightmares. Alcohol ingestion is also associated with reports of reduced nightmare activity, as is barbiturate ingestion. The increased incidence of nightmare activity during alcohol withdrawal is considered to be a rebound phenomenon (Hartmann 1984).

Many of the studies on the effects of drugs on nightmare activity are inconclusive, largely because small samples were used and the preferred method for controlling confounding variables, the double-blind technique, was not always used. In some instances, these research findings are confounded because the subjects selected not only suffered from nightmares but also had psychiatric diagnoses.

## Conclusion

On the basis of the research and literature examined here, it appears that nightmares occur throughout the sleep cycle and also during REM sleep. There is disagreement, certainly, on the point, but this view has become accepted. Moreover, most researchers no longer accept fully Broughton's (1968) position that night-terror victims are physiologically predisposed and that there is no mental activity during night terrors. Researchers following Broughton's original premise, that night terrors were disorders of arousal, have both supported and refuted certain aspects of his earlier studies and certainly expanded upon the role that arousal plays in nightmares and night terrors. Hartmann's research has provided intriguing hypotheses about the role neurotransmitters may play in the arousal mechanism and thus directly on the content of dreams. It seems that in the further exploration of nightmares and night terrors from a neuropsychological perspective, it will be necessary to replicate present research. It also appears that the reliance on small samples, the unavailability of appropriate control groups, and the inconsistency between measurement devices and the criteria used for measurement have limited the internal and external validity of these studies. However, as pioneer research, these studies have more than amply opened the door to hypothesis testing and to more controlled observations. These studies have been of immeasurable value in furthering our understanding of nightmares and night terrors.

## Summary

In this chapter, the neuropsychology of sleep, mentation during sleep, and neural structures related to sleep and dreaming were reviewed. With this information as a basis, the neuropsychology of nightmares and night terrors was addressed. Evidence was presented largely indicating that nightmares and night terrors are primarily due to disorders of arousal which may occur throughout the NREM sleep cycle and also during REM sleep. Several factors, including the interference of normal neurotransmitter functioning, seem to have an effect on these arousal mechanisms. Further, there is evidence to refute original assertions that nightmares and night terrors are primarily physiological reactions occurring solely in physiologically predisposed individuals. Although this point remains open to investigation, it is fairly well accepted that nightmares and night terrors involve psychological changes as well as physiological ones. Many of the findings reported are based on studies which, in spite of their intriguing findings, seem nonetheless affected by experimental methodological issues which certainly may decrease the validity of data. At this point the amalgam of studies seems to be generating a body of underlying data of the nightmare that include psychological as well as physiological structures.

## References

Arkin, A. 1970. Rebuttal to Fisher et al. In E. Hartmann, ed., *Sleep and Dreaming.* Boston: Little Brown.

Beitman, B. D. and A. S. Carlin. 1979. Night terrors treated with imipramine. *American Journal of Psychiatry* 136(8):1087–88.

Breger, L. 1967. Function of dreams. *Journal of Abnormal Psychology,* vol. 72, no. 5.

Broughton, R. J. 1968. Sleep disorders: Disorders of arousal? *Science* 159:1070–78.

Broughton, R. J. 1970. The incubus attack. In E. Hartmann, et., *Sleep and Dreaming.* Boston: Little, Brown.

Colman, C. and J. McGaugh. 1980. *Behavioral Neuroscience.* New York: Academic Press.

Dement, W. C. 1966. Psychophysiology of sleep and dreams. In S. Arieti, ed., *American Handbook of Psychiatry.* Vol. 3. New York: Basic Books.

Dement, W. C. and N. Kleitman. 1957. The relation of eye-movements during sleep to dream activity: An objective method for the study of dreaming. *Journal of Experimental Psychology* 53:339–46.

Fenichel, O. 1945. *The Psychoanalytic Theory of Neurosis.* New York: Norton.

Fisher, C., J. V. Byrne, and A. Edwards. 1968. NREM and REM nightmares. *Psychophysiology* 5:221–22.

Fisher, C., J. Byrne, A. Edwards, and E. Kahn. 1969. REM and NREM nightmares. *Psychophysiology* 6:252.

Fisher, C., E. Kahn, A. Edwards, and D. Davis. 1973. A psychophysiological study of nightmares and night terrors. The suppression of stage 4 night terrors with diazepam. *Archives of General Psychiatry* 28(2):252–59.

Flemenbaum, A. 1976. Pavor nocturnus: A complication of singly daily tricyclic or neuroleptic dosage. *American Journal of Psychiatry* 133(5):570–72.

Foulkes, D. 1966. *The Psychology of Sleep.* New York: Scribner's.

Gastaut, H. and R. Broughton. 1965. A clinical and polygraphic study of episodic phenomena during sleep. In J. Vostis, ed., *Recent Advances in Biological Psychiatry.* Vol. 8. New York: Plenum Press.

Hartmann, E. 1966. Dreaming sleep (the D-state) and the menstrual cycle. *Journal of Nervous and Mental Disease* 143:406–16.

Hartmann, E., ed. 1970. *Sleep and Dreaming.* Boston: Little, Brown.

Hartmann, E. 1984. *The Nightmare.* New York: Basic Books.

Hersen, M. 1972. Nightmare behavior. *Psychological Bulletin* 78:37–48.

Jones, E. 1949. *On the Nightmare.* London: Hogarth Press. (Original work published in 1911.)

Jouvet, M. 1967. Neurophysiology of the states of sleep. In G. Melenchuk and O. Schmidt, eds., *The Neurosciences.* New York: Rockefeller University Press.

Klackenberg, Gunnae. 1982. Somnambulism in childhood: Prevalue, course, and behavioral correlates. *Acta Paediatrica Scandinavia* 71:495.

Mack, J. 1970. *Nightmares and Human Conflict.* Boston: Little, Brown.

# 7.

# Dream Reports of Nightmares and Stages of Sleep

LAWRENCE JOSEPHS

THIS CHAPTER REFLECTS the convergence of two major areas of dream research: the psychological content of dreams and the physiology of dreaming. Each approach to dream research has a long tradition and has developed an extensive body of knowledge. The convergence of these two areas of investigation has led to significant and fascinating findings in regard to the study of the nightmare (incubus) and the night terror (pavor nocturnus).

## Dream Reports and Content Analysis of Nightmares

In reviewing the literature, Mack (1965) cited some of the definitional difficulties in the study of the nightmare. He noted that authors have employed a variety of terms in this area of investigation, such as "bad dream, unpleasant dream, anxiety dream, nightmare, and night terror." In regard to children, pediatricians have distinguished the night terror from the nightmare by the greater intensity of the child's panic, the persistence of disorientation and terrifying hallucinations after rousing, and by the greater difficulty encountered in trying to comfort the child (Bakwin and Bakwin 1960; Mack 1965; Nelson 1959). Mack (1965) defines the "nightmare" as an anxiety dream in which there is at least partial awakening. He reserves the term "night terror" for a variant of particular intensity in which there remains some inability to identify the dream images as arising from within even after awakening.

Ernest Jones (1931), in his 1911 book *On the Nightmare*, attempted the first systematic content analysis of the nightmare. Jones noted three regular psychic contents of every nightmare: (l) "In every instance, there is a sense of oppression and helplessness, and the extent to which these are carried, varies according to the violence of the paroxysm" (1931:20); (2) "The sense of stifling oppression of the chest of an overpowering weight that impedes the respiration often to the extreme limit of endurance" (1931:21); (3) "The utter powerlessness amounting to a feeling of complete paralysis, which is the only response of the organism to the agonizing effort that it makes to relieve itself of the choking apprehension" (1931:22). In terms of the variability of the content of nightmares, Jones stated that "the modifications which nightmare assumes are infinite but one passion is almost never absent—that of utter and incomprehensible dread" (1931:17). One limitation in the collection of the mental content of nightmares relates to the difficulty of finding the right words to describe the rich visual and emotional content of the dream: "It is not often realized that most descriptions of Nightmare given by its victims are an inarticulate and feeble echo of the dread reality" (1931:13–14).

Although Jones cited the innumerable types of content in nightmares, there does seem to be some developmental progression of danger situations that are portrayed in anxiety dreams. Despert (1949) reported that children ages 2 to 5 produce dreams with well-individualized themes, although there are commonly occurring contents. Two 5-year-olds mostly reported dreams of being bitten, devoured, and chased. Despert noted that the content represents an intense fear of being destroyed in a specific way that never includes the types of hostile interchanges that the child may have actually experienced in real life, such as being hit, kicked, pinched, pushed, scratched, etc. These dreams often contain accounts of escaping danger, never of fighting it. Two-year-olds typically express the fear of being bitten, devoured, and chased without naming the agent, while 3, 4, and 5-year-olds would identify powerful, destructive animals. Foster and Anderson (1936) noted that unpleasant dreams in children ages 5 to 9 were most often about strange or bad people and about such impersonal dangers as war, fire, and electricity. Between 9 and 12, the disturbing content relates to difficulties surrounding themselves and their friends. Their findings corroborate Despert's in that children 5 and under tend to have unpleasant dreams concerning animals. In contrast to these findings about anxiety dreams, studies of dreams of preschool children, latency-age boys, and normal as well as emotionally disturbed adolescent boys revealed that the content of typical (e.g., nonanxiety) dreams was realistically related to the activities of waking life, and relatively free of bizarre symbolism and unpleasant affect (Foulkes et al. 1969). The authors suggested that dreams only become relatively more bizarre and unpleasant for children with some dysfunction in the waking personality.

Cason (1935) reported that the most frequent subjects for nightmares of normal adults were "death and murder, home and family, miscellaneous people, and accidents." For normal children, the most frequent subjects were animals, being chased, miscellaneous people, and falling. "Feeble-minded" institutionalized patients frequently reported animals, death and murder, being chased, falling, and home and family. Thus, the content of their nightmares tended to combine contents that are common in children and in adults. Feldman and Hyman (1968), studying nightmare reports in adults, reported that nightmares usually contain themes of catastrophe in which the victim is typically the self. The danger is frequently in the form of death, physical injury, or social affront. Attempts at coping are typically unsuccessful, but the final danger is often avoided by an abrupt awakening.

Of Jones's three common features of nightmares, only the feeling of agonizing dread has been commonly reported by other investigators. Contrary to Jones, who stressed the feeling of paralysis, many researchers have found night terrors to be associated with somnambulism (Fisher et al. 1970; Mack 1965; Schur 1969; Sperling 1958; Stern 1951). In summary, many authors believe that the content of a nightmare can include any situation of danger.

Young children tend to report danger situations involving being attacked by animals. With progressing age, the danger becomes more related to people and to personal situations. The variety of danger situations is innumerable, but for individuals certain types of danger situations may be repetitive.

Another variable in psychological content which has considerable import is the intensity of the anxiety in the nightmare. On one end of the continuum is the anxiety dream, which does not result in awakening. According to Mack (1965), the typical nightmare can be considered to be an anxiety dream that results in awakening. At the other end of the continuum is the night terror of children and adults which in addition to awakening may be associated with somnambulism, screaming, confusion, and hallucinations. Night terrors have been noted to have qualities reminiscent of psychosis (Sperling 1958). Research into the physiology of dreaming has revealed that in addition to the difference in psychological intensity between the nightmare and the night terror, there are also clear-cut physiological differences which can be measured.

## Stages of Sleep and Their Relation to the Nightmare and Night Terror

In investigating the physiology of sleep, Dement and Kleitman (1957a) described four stages of EEG activity that occur during sleep. They noted that EEG activity in sleep demonstrates a cyclical nature. Stage 1 sleep was the "lightest" stage, while stages 3 and 4 were associated with "deep" sleep. Sleep began with a rapid shift from stage 1 to 4 shortly after sleep onset. After varying amounts of time stage 4 would yield to stages 3, 2, and 1. This sequence recurs cyclically throughout sleep. Stage 1 sleep recurs about every 90 minutes and constitutes about 25 percent of total sleep. Stages 3 and 4 occur mostly during the first few hours of the night and constitute 25 percent of total sleep. Stage 2 makes up the sleep of much of the last half of the night, about 50 percent of total sleep time.

Dement and Kleitman (1957a) discovered that consistently and exclusively associated with stage 1 EEG activity were bursts of rapid eye movements (REM). Subjects who were awakened during stage 1 EEG activity concurrent with rapid eye movements regularly reported dream content (Dement and Kleitman 1957b). Other investigators have consistently confirmed this finding that dreaming is associated with stage 1 REM sleep. Foulkes (1962) discovered that although recall of dreams was most likely following REM awakenings made well after REM onset, dream reports can be elicited with some degree of success during any stage of sleep. Foulkes suggested that reportable mental activity is always present in the sleeping human. He described how mental activity shifts cyclically during sleep "from the conceptual to the perceptual mode of experience, a shift from fragmentary and disjointed content to elaborated and integrated content, and increasing distortion and decreasing reality contact of content" (Foulkes 1962:15). Stages 2, 3, and 4 appear to contain much more secondary-process thinking and are more related to recent memory and to current daily preoccupations.

Gastaut and Broughton (1965) and Broughton (1968) noted that most pathological manifestations of sleep, such as night terror, sleepwalking, most sleep talking, enuresis, and bruxism, are not associated with REM sleep but rather are associated with arousal from slow-wave sleep (stages 3 and 4). The night terror is associated with increases in heart and respiratory rates, mental confusion and disorientation, automatic behavior, relative nonreactivity to external stimuli, poor response to efforts to provoke behavioral wakefulness, amnesia for the somnambulistic episode, and only fragmentary recall of apparent dreams, or none at all.

These pathological symptoms of slow-wave sleep are, according to Broughton (1968), "disorders of arousal." He suggested the possiblility that the night terror arises out of a "psychological void." He suggested that night terrors are caused by marked physiological abnormalities and that any mental content elicited during an attack may be created to make sense out of the intense physiological arousal. Thus Broughton (1970) did not view the night terror as being related to ongoing non-REM mentation or content of a conflictual nature that may serve as a trigger for such a severe physiological response.

Subsequent to Broughton's seminal work, other investigators have studied in the laboratory both the physiological and the psychological characteristics of night terrors and nightmares. Fisher et al. (1968) noted that night terrors typically occur during stage 4 sleep and often occur during the first non-REM period. Fisher et al. (1970) noted that 70 percent of stage 4 night terrors occur in the first hour and a half of sleep. The night terror is ushered in by a loud scream of blood-curdling intensity or a call for help. There is a sudden breakthrough of intense, uncontrolled anxiety. After the scream, the subject passes into an arousal reaction in which he appears to be dissociated, confused, unresponsive to the environment, and hallucinating. Many subjects were somnambulistic during severe stage 4 night terrors. The investigators discovered that the deeper the sleep, the more intense the night terror and that subjects with stage 4 night terrors would have quiet and peaceful REM sleep.

Fisher et al. (1970) confirmed the findings of Broughton and Gastaut that it is difficult to elicit psychic content from the night terror. Subjects tended to have amnesia for both the experience of the night terror and the content. Frequently subjects did not remember screaming and would return to sleep almost immediately. Fisher et al. (1970) did find content which occurred prior to the scream, during the scream, and afterward during the confused hallucinatory state. Ongoing content was not elaborate but typically related to a single vivid scene, such as falling, being crushed, choking, etc. The authors noted that the content appeared to be psychodynamically organized, related to subjects' preexisting conflicts and to REM dreams of the same night. Thus Fisher et al. (1970) disputed Broughton's notion that night terrors arise out of a psychological void. These authors found the incidence of the stage 4 night terrors to be low; only 4 percent of 200 subjects complained of recurrent nightmares.

Again, Fisher et al. (1970) noted that most frightening arousals subjectively experienced as nightmares are actually REM anxiety dreams. The authors noted that in REM anxiety dreams subjects' reports of anxiety of fairly great intensity were not associated with autonomic discharge. The authors believed that there was a "desomatization" of anxiety in the REM nightmare. This finding stands in marked contrast to the stage 4 night terror in which there is tremendous physiological arousal. In REM anxiety dreams, if the anxiety passes a certain threshhold, the desomatization reaction breaks down, autonomic responses are activated, and the subject may wake up. The content of REM nightmares was found to be well elaborated and more complex than that of the night terror.

In further study of the content of the stage 4 night terror, Kahn et al. (1973) found 58 percent recall of content following night-terror arousals, which is similar to recall percentages obtained for awakenings during NREM sleep (Foulkes 1962). The authors believed that a considerable amount of the content was unique and unusual, not directly related to the laboratory, and unlikely to be elaborated in the postarousal period. The REM nightmare shows a gradual acceleration of heart and respiratory rates during sleep immediately prior to spontaneous arousal (Fisher et al. 1970), whereas the night terror does not manifest any comparable change during sleep, just before the sudden onset of the episode. Kahn et al. (1973) suggested that in the stage 4 night terror frightening content does not build up gradually as in the REM anxiety dream, but rather occurs suddenly, immediately triggering the arousal reaction. Kahn et al. (1973) suggested that ongoing neutral NREM mentation touches upon an intense conflict which triggers the subsequent night terror.

Fisher et al. (1973) noted that spontaneous arousal with reports of mental content associated with anxiety can occur at any time of night from all stages of sleep. The authors found that they could artificially induce night terrors in subjects who were prone to night terrors by sounding a buzzer. A buzzer sounded during REM sleep produced only mild arousals and no nightmares. They noted that night terrors actually do not occur during sleep but in a dissociated state with an EEG characterized by waking alpha rhythym. The REM anxiety dream and REM nightmare develop during sleep, and generally endure for 5 to 20 minutes before spontaneous awakening occurs. The authors believed that the "desomatization" of anxiety preserves sleep during REM anxiety dreams, and that during REM sleep only a small autonomic change may occur before awakening. They felt that the question of a possible organic factor in night terrors is still undecided. The authors concluded: "The night terror is not a dream at all in the ordinary sense but a symptom, a pathological formation emerging from NREM sleep brought about by a rift in the ego's capacity to control anxiety. Although the REM nightmare shows attempts at mastery of the traumatic experience, the night terror seems to be a manifestation of the failure of mastery, which may explain why it may endure unchanged and unabated for periods of a quarter of a century" (Fisher et al. 1973:96). Hartmann (1984:248) in summary of the literature suggested that the biology of the REM anxiety dream and nightmare is essentially an intense form of the biology of dreaming in general: "All of this then suggests that the nightmare is an especially long, intense, and vivid dream arising out of a physiologically long and intense dream period."

In a follow-up study, Fisher et al. (1974) examined further the mental content of stage 4 night terrors. The most common themes were fear of aggression by a person or persons, things closing in or being entrapped in a small area, fear of falling, fear of being left alone, and fear of choking. Animals played little role in the reported night terrors.

In comparing the contents of nightmares and night terrors, Fisher et al. (1970) noted that naked manifestations of aggression are more marked in the night terror: traumatic events of either recent or childhood origin rarely appear in undisguised form either in nightmares or in night terrors. They noted that symbolization, displacement, and condensation appear in both the nightmare and the night terror.

## Latent Content of Nightmares

In anxiety dreams, nightmares, and night terrors, the content of the danger situation is typically of a persecutory or annihilatory threat directed toward the self. Thus far, we have been discussing what Freud (1900) called the "manifest content" of the dream, the verbalized report of the dream. In *The Interpretation of Dreams*, Freud (1900) described how the "latent content," that is, the presumed underlying unconscious meaning of the dream, could be discovered. He divided the dream into elements (parts of the manifest dream) and gathered the patient's associations to each element. The associations eventually led to the latent thoughts which brought to light the unconscious meaning of the dream.

Jones (1931), relying upon mythology, folklore, and historical sources, gathered that the latent content of nightmares was always an expression of an intense conflict centering about some form of a repressed incestuous desire. Jones emphasized phallic and oedipal themes. The anxiety felt in the dream was thought to be derived from castration anxiety.

Mack (1965), in his review of the literature, noted how other authors have described other types of unconscious conflicts underlying nightmares. Freud (1918), in discussing the case of the Wolf Man, related the fear of death to the childhood fear of being eaten. Schonberger (1946), employing anthropological sources, described how in primitive myths nightmares may be explained as punishment for oral-sadistic impulses. Despert (1949) suggested that the self-preservation instinct alone was involved and threatened in the earliest anxiety dreams recorded. Fisher et al. (1974:186) formed the impression that the latent content of the night terror related to "pregenital and Oedipal content relating to primal scene experiences or fantasies with the projection of intense murderous oral sadistic impulses."

It is puzzling that even in the night terror, in which there is a massive failure to control anxiety, traumatic events rarely appear undisguised, and that aggressive or sexual wishes are rarely acted upon but almost always projected so that a persecutory situation becomes the reported content. Despert (1949) notes that in preschool children parents always appear in benevolent roles, the child rarely displays an openly hostile or sexual attitude toward the parents, and the child always flees from danger rather than fights it. Thus, in the anxiety dream and night terror of childhood there is rarely an enactment of aggressive or sexual wishes; rather, a persecutory situation is the predominant content.

From a conflict-defense model of intrapsychic functioning in which the expression of drives and wishes needs to be defended against, nightmares and night terrors would largely be viewed as projections or punishments for aggressive and sexual wishes emanating from various levels of development. It remains puzzling that the manifest content would not reflect these wishes directly, especially in the case of the night terror, in which there is apparently no ability to control the development of anxiety. Hartmann (1984), in his investigation of the personality characteristics of frequent nightmare sufferers, discovered upon psychological testing that these individuals did not suffer from an excess of aggressive drive but rather were persons with thin boundaries, such that normal fears and angers get through more and become more vivid and frightening for them than for most of us (1984:105). The work of Atwood and Stolorow (1984) sheds some light on the finding that the content of nightmares and night terrors characteristically represents a situation in which the dreamer is in imminent danger. The authors proposed as a supraordinate principle of human motivation the need to maintain the organization of experience, especially of the experience of the self. They proposed that experiences of the self find symbolization in the concrete perceptual images of dreams, lending a feeling of conviction to that self-experience. Thus Atwood and Stolorow would view nightmares and night terrors as dreams which vividly reify the experience of self-endangerment and thereby bring the state of the self into focal awareness with a feeling of conviction and reality that can only accompany sensory perception. The night terror, as often noted, is so real that the person may somnambulistically act out his defense against the imagined threat. Atwood and Stolorow would suggest that such an experience reflects both the encapsulation of the danger to the self and a concretizing effort at self-restoration. The capacity for concrete symbolization underlies the construction of hallucinations and delusions as well as of artistic creations. Hartmann (1984:135) noted that both schizophrenic patients and artists suffer a higher frequency of nightmares than most persons.

Returning to a consideration of anxiety dreams and nightmares in children, hostile animals or monsters can be seen as the concretizing symbolizations par excellence of children's fears of self-dissolution. Children must develop beyond animism and learn to differentiate animate from inanimate and human from animal, as well as self from other. Parents represent the ultimate in affirming who the child is and in preserving the continuity of the experience of self. Thus, despite the conflicts with or disappointment with parents in real life, in dreams the parents continue to represent benevolent security. As development proceeds and animistic thinking recedes, mistreatment by other people would be viewed as the main danger to the self. Since, as Freud suggested, the "ego" is foremost a "body ego," danger to the sense of self is most readily concretized as a danger to the physical body, which is the most common danger reported in the content of nightmares.

The night terror represents a concretization to the point of a hallucinatory experience which may be acted upon. In the night terror there is a greater loss of reality testing than in the nightmare, so that the fantasy seems real. Mack (1965) has reported how in night terrors in young children the hallucinatory images may continue into the next day and that the child tends to consider the night terror a real experience rather than a dream. Differences in the physiology of the various stages of sleep seem to account for the extent to which the self-experience may be concretely symbolized. The "desomatization" of stage 1 REM sleep appears to ensure that the concretization will not extend beyond the sensory-perceptual level of experience. In stage 4 there appears to be no desomatization or inhibition of motility, so that the concretization may extend into the motoric, as evidenced in the screaming, sleep talking, and somnambulism associated with night terrors.

## Summary

In summary, nightmares can be defined as anxiety dreams in which there is at least partial awakening. Both anxiety dreams and nightmares typically occur during stage 1 REM sleep. In contrast, the night terror occurs exclusively during stage 4 sleep. Whereas in nightmares the anxiety dreams are well elaborated and complex, with only minimal autonomic arousal before awakening, in the night terror the content of the dream is a single terrifying and vivid scene accompanied by intense autonomic arousal. In addition, night terrors are often accompanied by somnambulism, screaming, confusion, and hallucinations. Both nightmares and night terrors most frequently depict a situation of imminent physical danger. The content of these situations of danger varies with the age of the dreamer, beginning with the threat of attack by animals in the dreams of young children and progressing to situations involving people and personal experience with advancing age. Traditionally the theoretical explanation for these persecutory scenarios was that they represented either the projection of or the punishment for forbidden sexual or aggressive wishes. Recent developments in the psychology of the self suggest that persecutory scenarios in nightmares and night terrors may also reflect through concrete symbolization the reification of the experience of self-endangerment.

The nightmare and the night terror were seen as embodying the actualization of man's deepest fears. The REM nightmare is a common occurrence in children and adults that appears to serve an adaptive purpose in the working through of various anxieties and fears. The stage 4 night terror, in contrast, occurs in a rather small percentage of children and adults whom it may plague for years. Paradoxically, the night terror represents the most complete inability to master anxiety while concurrently reflecting perhaps the most vivid actualization of the experience of human terror.

## References


Atwood, G. E. and R. D. Stolorow 1984. *Structures of Subjectivity: Explorations in Psychoanalytic Phenomenology.* Hillsdale, N. J.: Lawrence Erlbaum Associates.

Bakwin, H. and R. Bakwin, 1960. *Clinical Management of Behavior Disorders in Childhood.* Philadelphia: Saunders.

Broughton, R. J. 1968. Sleep disorders: Disorders of arousal? *Science 159:* 1070–78.

Broughton, R. J. 1970. The incubus attack. In E. Hartmann, ed., *Sleep and Dreaming.* pp. 188–92. Boston: Little, Brown.

Cason, H. 1935. The nightmare dream. *Psychological Monographs* 46:5.

Dement, W. and N. Kleitman. 1957a. Cyclic variations in EEG during sleep and their relation to eye movements, bodily motility, and dreaming. *Electroencephalography and Clinical Neurophysiology* 9:673–90.

Dement, W. and N. Kleitman. 1957b. The relation of eye movements during sleep to dream activity: An objective method for the study of dreaming. *Journal of Experimental Psychology* 53:339–46.

Despert, J. L. 1949. Dreams in children of preschool age. In R. Eissler et al., eds., *The Psychoanalytic Study of the Child* 4:141–81. New York: International Universities Press.

Feldman, M. J. and E. Hyman, 1968. Content analysis of nightmare reports. *Psychophysiology* 5:221.

Fisher, C., J. V. Byrne, and A. Edwards. 1968. NREM and REM nightmares. *Psychophysiology* 5:221–22.

Fisher, C., J. V. Byrne, A. Edwards, and E. Kahn. 1970. A psychophysiological study of nightmares. *Journal of the American Psychoanalytic Association* 13:747–82.

Fisher, C., E. Kahn, A. Edwards, and D. Davis, 1973. A psychophysiological study of nightmares and night terrors. I. Physiological aspects of stage 4 night terror. *Journal of Nervous and Mental Disorders* 157:75–98.

Fisher, C., E. Kahn, A. Edwards, D. Davis, and J. Fine, 1974. A psychophysiological study of nightmares and night terrors. III. Mental content and recall of stage 4 night terrors. *Journal of Nervous and Mental Disorders* 158:174–88.

Foster, J. C. and J. E. Anderson, 1936. Unpleasant dreams in childhood. *Child Development* 7:77–84.

Foulkes, D. 1962. Dream reports from different stages of sleep. *Journal of Abnormal and Social Psychology* 65:14–25.

Foulkes, D., J. D. Larson, E. M. Swanson, and M. Rardin. 1969. Two studies of childhood dreaming. *American Journal of Orthopsychiatry* 39:627–43.

Freud, S. *Standard Edition of the Complete Psychological Works of Sigmund Freud.* James Strachey, ed. and tr. 24 vols. London: Hogarth Press, 1953–1974; New York: Macmillan.

1900. *The Interpretation of Dreams.* Vols. 4 and 5.

1918. *From the History of an Infantile Neurosis.* Vol. 17.

Gastaut, H. and R. Broughton. 1965. A clinical and polygraphic study of episodic phenomena during sleep. In J. Wortis, ed., *Recent Advances in Biological Psychiatry,* pp. 197–221. New York: Plenum Press.

Hartmann, E. 1984. *The Nightmare.* New York: Basic Books.

Jones, E. 1931. *On the Nightmare.* London: Hogarth Press. (Original work published in 1911.)

Kahn, E., C. Fisher, A. Edwards, and D. Davis, 1973. Mental content of stage 4 night terror. *Proceedings of Eighty-First Annual Convention of the American Psychological Association* 8:499–500. Montreal, Canada.

Mack, J. 1965. Nightmares, conflict, and ego development in childhood. *International Journal of Psychoanalysis* 46:403-28.

Nelson, W. E. 1959. *Textbook of Pediatrics.* Philadelphia: Saunders.

Schonberger, S. 1946. A clinical contribution to the analysis of the nightmare syndrome. *Psychoanalytic Review* 33:44–70.

Schur, H. 1969. Hallucinations in children. In M. Kanzer, ed., *The Unconscious Today: Essays in Honor of Max Schur.* New York: International Universities Press.

Sperling, M. 1958. Pavor nocturnus. *Journal of the American Psychoanalytic Association* 6:79–94.

Stern, M. 1951. Pavor nocturnus. *International Journal of Psychoanalysis* 32:302–9.

# PART THREE: Episodic Dream Phenomena in Children and Adults: Nightmares, Night Terrors, and Anxiety Dreams

# 8.

# Nightmares, Problem Sleep, and Peculiar Bedtime Behavior in Children

FRANKLIN D. RADDOCK

WHILE IT MAY often be true, to quote Moore and Ucko (1957:333), that "A sleepless baby [or child] is a reproach to his guardians," a complete appraisal of children's sleep difficulties must include consideration of psychological development and the physiology of sleep, as well as a discussion of parental practices. With these three considerations in mind, the plan of this chapter is to review the general sleep patterns of children and the better-defined sleep disorders, and finally, to consider the etiological role of individual development and family problems in children's sleep difficulties.

## Children's Sleeping Patterns

We commonly talk of ourselves as "going to sleep" or of a child being "put to sleep," as if we must pass through a mysterious door into some dark, special place. But perhaps the door swings the other way. For human beings, especially at birth, "becoming alert" and the phenomenon of the conscious state may be the special figure constructed upon the ground of the more general state of sleep. For we are born sleeping more than half of each day, which gradually decreases to less than 8½ hours each day by age 16 (Ames 1964; Kleitman 1939; Nagera 1966).

Studies of premature infants have indicated that increasingly well-defined states of sleep develop, with fewer "transitional sleep states" and less irregular activity, as gestation advances (Parmelee et al. 1967). A cycle of more active periods of sleep (associated with rapid eye movements, REM sleep), alternating with more quiet periods develops (Aserinsky and Kleitman 1955; Anders and Guilleminault 1976). By age 2 years, EEG sleep-phase organization resembles that of an adult (Anders and Guilleminault, 1976).

While asleep, the newborn spends about 50 percent of the time in active, REM sleep, which declines by adulthood to about 20 percent (Anders and Guilleminault 1976). It is likely that dreams and nightmares, which begin, conservatively, about the second year of life, occur mostly during REM periods (Fisher and Dement 1963). Newborns, usually, have 5 to 6 randomly distributed periods of wakefulness with lengthening and less numerous periods of sleep and wakefulness (Ames 1964; Parmelee et al. 1964). The number of sleep periods or naps decreases rapidly in the first year; by 1 year, there is usually one long nap between 11 A.M. and 2 P.M., which is gradually given up around school age (Ames 1964).

Sleep periods and nap periods rapidly form day-awake, night-asleep periodicity which may be seen as early as the third week of life (Nagera 1966). Underpinned by neurological maturation by approximately 13 weeks a stable diurnal cycle is established, and "settling" occurs where the infant sleeps for a five-hour period after midnight (Moore and Ucko 1957).

In infancy, REM cycles are shorter (50 to 60 minutes) than in adults (90 to 100 minutes) (Anders and Guilleminault 1976). Also, the onset of the first REM cycle usually appears sooner in infants than in older children. Roffwarg et al. (1964) reported that REM onset is within one hour after sleep onset in 2–3-year-olds but about 3 hours after sleep onset in 4–5-year-olds, which they attribute to the presumed greater physical activity of the older children and therefore the greater need for recuperative, quiet sleep. If 4–7-year-olds do spend more time in stage 4, non-REM sleep at sleep onset, this might be a factor in accounting for the relatively common occurrence in this age range of sleep disturbances associated with non-REM sleep, i.e., night terrors, sleepwalking and -talking, and enuresis (Ames 1964; Fisher et al. 1974; Kales et al. 1981).

Ames (1964), in a study of middle-class children, has documented changes in bedtime trends and time of awakening throughout childhood. The infant of 40 weeks will usually fall asleep after nursing and sleeps from 6 P.M. to 6 A.M., with occasional night awakenings. The 18-month-old goes to sleep from 6 to 8 P.M. and is much less resistant to going to sleep than the 2½-year-old. No doubt to their parents' pleasure, however, the 2½-year-old may sleep later (after 6–8 A.M.) than the 18-month-old. Once the child is awake, in this age range, one parent must be also, in general. It is not until about 5 years that the typical child may entertain and toilet himself, except for short periods in the morning.

Disturbances of sleep or related behaviors are estimated to be very common (25 percent) in the infancy and preschool period (Kales et al. 1970). The 2-year-old may wake up easily and from 2–3 years, there may be elaborate bedtime rituals, night awakenings, and attachments to treasured objects.

Treasured objects (e.g., a blanket, pillow, stuffed animal, or doll), at least in one study of middle-class families, were used by half of all children after age 1—even until age 13 years—with a peak usage at ages 3–4 years. Disruptions or delays in going to sleep may occur if the object is not available, until there is a usual gradual detachment from the object (Ames 1964; Beltramini and Hertzig 1982; Sherman et al. 1981).

Ames (1964) reported that the 6-year-old is more easily put to bed and is a sounder sleeper (generally sleeping from 7 P.M. to 7 A.M.) than the preschooler. There are fewer nightmares and associated night awakenings after age 6. From about 8 to 12 years of age, the child may dawdle before going to sleep. By ages 10–11, there may be a period of presleep activity or worrying or radio before the 8:30 to 9:30 P.M. bedtime. By age 12, good dreams outnumber the bad, and by age 14, there is less presleep activity, more concern for caring for the body and obtaining enough sleep, and increased getting to sleep on time (10 P.M.). The child is now definite about establishing his own sleep and wakening hours. Repeated calls by parents and conflict may occur, especially in relation to getting up.

In summary, the shifts in sleeping patterns and the disturbances in sleep in childhood are substantial—enough to test the patience and flexibility of parents who, we presume, wish to obtain their 8 hours of uninterrupted sleep, taken according to their customary schedule.

## Sleep Disorders in Children

The Autumn 1979 issue of the journal *Sleep* was devoted to an extensive diagnostic classification of sleep and arousal disorders. While this classification is currently expected to be revised by 1987, for the purposes of this discussion disordered sleep may be classified as too long (hypersomnolence), too short (insomnia), or disturbed by episodic events that occur within non-REM (the NREM dyssomnias) or within REM sleep (Anders and Guilleminault 1976). Hypersomnolence and insomnia are quite rare in childhood—less than a few percent of childrens' sleep disorders (Anders and Guilleminault 1976; Shirley and Kahn 1958).

### INSOMNIA AND HYPERSOMNIA

Insomnia may be associated with illicit drug use, dependence on hypnotic, sedative drugs, or sometimes with family problems or the absence of the primary caretaker or an adequate substitute (Anders and Guilleminault 1976; Spitz 1965). Disturbed sleep, especially night awakenings, may also be associated with physical illness, febrile illness, and psychologically related illness, such as childhood asthma (Kales et al. 1968, 1970). Excessive sleep or hypersomnia may be related to depression, to prescribed or illicit sedative use, or to school-related difficulties (Herskowitz and Rosman 1982; Shirley and Kahn 1958).

There are two rare disorders of excessive daytime somnolence (EDS) which may afflict children; narcolepsy and sleep apnea syndrome. The hallmark of narcolepsy is the sleep attack in which the almost irresistible urge to fall asleep is followed by a period of sleep, typically lasting about 15 minutes (Herskowitz and Rosman 1982). Most narcoleptics first develop the syndrome after age 16, by young adulthood; but it has been estimated that between 5 and 20 percent develop the disorder before ages 10–11, and many sufferers previously had been long-sleepers earlier in childhood. The disorder is not usually a problem until the child reaches school age, where the episodes of sleep interfere with work. Sufferers of narcolepsy and sleep apnea syndrome may have numerous microsleep episodes of perhaps 5–15 seconds, which precede the sleep attacks and which interfere with attention and memory in school learning.

There are several associated features of the narcolepsy syndrome. In cataplexy, which is pathognomonic of narcolepsy, there is full or partial loss of muscle tone, particularly in the jaw or neck muscles, usually lasting a few seconds to a minute but sometimes longer. The narcopleptic may also suffer from hypnagogic hallucinations, which are vivid, usually frightening images occurring at sleep onset. In rare cases, there may be sleep paralysis in which the person cannot move for several minutes to a half-hour or more, until the "spell is broken" when the person is touched or hears a sound. Other environmental stimulation can also end the episode, if it does not conclude spontaneously (Anders and Guilleminault 1976; Ferber 1985; Herskowitz and Rosman 1982; Kellerman 1981). Ferber (1985) has suggested that the sudden turning on of the paralysis may be a kind of sudden switching in a portion of REM-sleep mechanisms, i.e., the muscle paralysis which is characteristic of REM sleep.

In the sleep apnea syndrome, repetitive apneic episodes (even 50 per hour) occur where breathing stops, perhaps for 20 seconds or more, but only when the child is sleeping. In most cases, the breathing stops because of an upper airway narrowing or collapsing, which restricts the airflow and which is usually related to enlarged tonsils or adenoids, to fatty deposits associated with obesity, or to a physical malformation (Ferber 1985). Anders and Guilleminault (1976) have also suggested that a neurologically based breath discordination may be involved in some cases, which they believe may also be at the root of sudden infant death syndrome. In sleep apnea, loud snoring occurs at night associated with the breath blockage, excessive daytime somnolence, and morning headaches which are related to the lower blood-oxygen levels concomitant with the apnea, and sometimes with enuresis. The disorder, which usually affects males, can lead to the behavioral symptoms of irritability, inattentiveness, and hyperactivity alternating with unscheduled naps in the daytime (Anders and Guilleminault 1976; Herskowitz and Rosman 1982).

## EPISODIC SLEEP DISTURBANCES

Sleep disturbances which occur in the form of nocturnal episodes may be generally categorized as either associated with quiet, NREM sleep (the NREM dyssomnias, such as night terrors, sleepwalking and -talking, and bedwetting) or active, REM sleep (i.e., bad dreams, nightmares).

The NREM dyssomnias are nonpsychotic, paroxysmal events associated with sudden physiological arousal in which there is nonresponsiveness or diminished awareness of the environment. There may be automatic actions and retrograde amnesia for the experience. Generally, the NREM dyssomnias occur during the first hour of sleep in the NREM sleep period just prior to the emergence of the first REM period (Anders and Guilleminault 1976; Caldwell et al. 1970). The NREM dyssomnias appear to be both disorders of physiological arousal which occurs during slow-wave, stage 4 NREM sleep and disorders where deep-seated mental conflict or anxiety can lead to the arousal during sleep (Broughton 1960; Fisher et al. 1974).

Night terrors (pavor nocturnus) occur, it has been estimated, in 1 to 3 percent of children ages 1–14, mostly males, with the greatest occurrence between ages 5 and 7 years (Fisher et al. 1974). There also appears to be a genetic contribution, and family history is often positive for night terrors. Many preschoolers have one or a few night terrors which never recur (Fisher et al. 1974; Herskowitz and Rosman 1982).

In the night terror, the child may sit suddenly upright (automatic action), and begin screaming in a terrified manner. A very rapid, sudden physiological arousal with rapid breathing (tachypnea), rapid heart rate (tachycardea), and intensive autonomic activation (perspiration, vocalization, distress, glassy staring, inconsolable) may also occur. (Anders and Guilleminault 1976; Herskowitz and Rosman 1982). Parents may actually exacerbate the episode if they attempt to console the child (Kales et al. 1980). The child is difficult to arouse and does not remember the incident after wakening (retrograde amnesia) (Fisher et al. 1974). Violent movement is sometimes associated with night terrors as the individual attempts to defend against the attacking agent (Kales et al. 1981). Sleepwalking may also be associated with the episode, and in both disorders, particularly sleepwalking, the child's safety may be in jeopardy (Herskowitz and Rosman 1982).

The high incidence of night terrors in the preschool years has been widely reported (Ames 1964; Fisher et al. 1974; Mack 1965). The disturbance is associated with the child's poor capabilities in controlling aggressive feelings related to toilet training, compliance with parental strictures, or oedipal conflicts—all of which occur at a time when the child has few resources for dealing with inner tensions and relies on the parent for comfort (Adam 1964; Fisher et al. 1974; Mack 1965). Perhaps the high incidence of the disorder in the 2–7 age range is related to the maturation of psychoneurological structures wherein brain centers controlling arousal and emotions (aggression, fear, sexuality-pleasure) become increasingly linked to higher cortical areas which are beginning to exert executive, inhibitory, and modulatory influences. But these influences are not sufficient to produce the less chaotic functioning of the latency years. The night terror, then, may be a normal disturbance of development underpinned by psychoneurological events, at lease in the cases of many young children. Such a view, however, must account for research findings which relate night terrors particularly to NREM sleep. Ferber (1985) has suggested that stage 4 sleep is very deep in young children and there may be an abrupt transition from stage 4 sleep to the next sleep phase. During transitions, the child may partially arouse as if half-asleep and half-awake at the same time. The child may sleepwalk, talk, or thrash. With advancing age, neurological maturation gradually smooths the sleep phase transition.

Sleepwalking (somnambulism) and sleep talking (somniloquy) occur mostly in schoolage children and are often not serious conditions. Kales et al. (1968) estimate that 15 percent of children between 5 and 12 years of age have had one sleepwalking episode and that it occurs in about 1–6 percent of the general population. It occurs more frequently in males and is often associated with nocturnal enuresis (Anders and Guilleminault 1976). In such an episode, the eyes are glassy and efforts to communicate usually result in mumbled speech (Anders and Guilleminault 1976). Sleepwalking episides are not acting out of a dream, the Kales and their colleagues (1968) have asserted, since, for one thing, dreaming occurs chiefly in REM sleep.

Secondary nocturnal enuresis, or bedwetting, is highly prevalent in children (10–15 percent of all 3-year-olds to 3–4 percent of those age 12) and is, generally, defined as occurring in children beyond age 3 where the child has been dry for some time (Anders and Guilleminault 1976; Kales et al. 1981). Bedwetting occurs more frequently in males, in families where the parents have been bedwetters, in lower SES families (such families often start toilet training later, perhaps reflecting disorganization), in families reporting financial hardship, in children in public care, in fatherless families, and in overcrowded families (Blomfield and Douglas 1956; Essen and Peckham 1976; Ferber 1985). As with other NREM dyssomnias, the children are difficult to arouse during or after the episode. If dreams are reported of floods, rivers invading the room, and so forth, it is believed that these dreams occur during the REM period following the episode, and that is when the children may wake up (Anders and Guilleminault 1976; Despert 1949; Kales et al. 1981). If a boy gets out of bed, he may urinate into a closet, boot, toy chest, or other partially enclosed area. Many younger children will then return to sleep without really waking (Ferber 1985).

## THE NIGHTMARE AND DISTURBANCES IN REM SLEEP

Bad dreams are very frequent in the range 1–8 years (about 40 percent of children) and diminish, substantially, by about 9–12 years of age (22 percent) (Foster and Anderson 1936). Foster and Anderson (1936) suggested that the content of unpleasant dreams was similar to the content of children's fears, such as the fear of animals in preschoolers. Nightmares are bad or frightening dreams that awaken the child, may lead to the child's seeking parental comfort—especially in younger children—and are much more prevalent than night terrors, as well as lasting longer into adolescence (Shirley and Kahn 1958). One study of middle-class children reported that almost 40 percent of the 4–5-year-olds studied evidenced nightmares at least once every two weeks (Beltramini and Hertzig 1983).

The occurrence of nightmares has been associated with many "triggers" such as sexual molestation, assassination of family members (author's cases), burns, cruelty or brutalization by parents or others, verbal threats or warnings, febrile illness (the nightmares occur after the fever subsides), other illness, hospitalization, surgery, injury, fatigue, sibling rivalry and birth of a sibling, an anticipated move, actual occurrence or concerns about separation from or death of loved ones, radio, TV, or movie programs, conflicts with playmates, fears exhibited during the day, misconceptions which confuse sleep with death, concerns of particular developmental periods, such as toilet training and oedipal concerns, and drug use (Despert 1949; Ferber 1985; Foster and Anderson 1936; Hartmann 1984; Herskowitz and Rosman 1982; Kales et al. 1981; Mack 1965, 1970; Roberts and Gordon 1979). Compared to adults, children are less likely to develop repetitive nightmares which "replay" for years after a traumatic experience, as Hartmann (1984) described in cases of combat veterans.

Children's nightmares frequently reflect concerns which are characteristic of the developmental period (including advances), the level of object relations, and the configuration of sexual and aggressive tendencies. The child under 2 years old, for example, may have nightmares reflecting separation-individuation and oral themes, such as those involving frightening machines like the vacuum cleaner's sucking and noise (Fraiberg 1950; Mack 1970).

Several factors may combine to make young children's experience of the nightmare particularly disturbing to them: (1) the intensity of sexual and aggressive wishes and developmental tasks that face them; (2) their unsophisticated comprehension of the origins of dreams and nightmares (following Piaget, the child first believes that the dream is real, though possibly its pictures are of air or light, then the child theorizes that origination is from inside the body before the dream appears outside, and finally the child believes in origination from the eye or head); and the immature capacities of the ego (3) for reality testing (there really is a tiger in my bed!), (4) for defensive tactics within the dream experience itself, such as identification with the aggressor (the child of 9 or 10 years may dream of fighting back, instead of simply being the victim of attack), or (5) for an increased cognitive capacity for disguised, symbol formation (Despert 1949; Mack, 1965, 1970). With advancing development, by age 11–12 years, there is much less disturbance of sleep by nightmares (Ames 1964; Mack 1970).

### OTHER SLEEP DISTURBANCES OF CHILDREN

There appear to be a number of nocturnal experiences which do not fit neatly into the categories discussed above. For example, Herskowitz and Rosman (1982) described a 3-year-old who, in a panic, was seen rubbing imagined bugs from her arms while sitting up and asleep (tactile hallucinosis). I have observed a 7-year-old in a trance-like state able to act out commands to row a boat during sleep in bed. Another 6-year-old boy acted out complete fight sequences including speaking and without the motor inhibition characteristic of REM sleep. These clinical observations suggest that much research remains to be done is describing and categorizing childhood sleep disturbances.

## Psychological Development, Parent-Child Interaction, and Nightmares

Children's sleep disturbances are often associated with parental difficulties which may be triggered by particular, normal developmental hurdles that their offspring come to face. In this section, we shall examine the role of parent-child interaction in sleep difficulties, in the context of the child's developmental tasks.

Some parent-child interaction patterns which relate to sleep disturbances may be more obvious than others. For example, parents may frighten a child with their own fears. One 3-year-old boy, concerned with oedipal issues and castration anxiety, whose mother was afraid of birds, had a bad dream about a bird pecking off his nose (Mack 1970).

Some parents may be insensitive to the need for a gradual, low-key transition into sleep—the need to be sure the child avoids frightening TV shows and exciting activities before bedtime (Adam 1964; Pasulka 1979). Or, they may be unsympathetic to their child's fears and refuse to leave a small light on or the bedroom door open for the crying preschooler (Herskowitz and Rosman 1982). Some parents may become angered at their own children's cries or believe that they are being punished by the child with the sleep disturbance. Still others may, in handling the child's nightmares, employ "the hallucinated attackers described by their children to manipulate and control them, threatening that the monsters or ghosts would return in the night if they did not behave" (Mack 1970:230; Hirschberg 1957). Thus, the parent may blur the distinction between dream and reality and not foster the development of reality testing in the child (Mack 1970). Mack (1970) maintains, also, that physically abusive environments may lead to difficulties in the development of the capacity to reality-test the dream, since the bad dream and the environment seem so much alike, so threatening.

With the child's developing capacity to test the dream-reality distinction, his dream attackers retreat into the nether corners of his room. Ames (1964) reported that the 2½-year-old fears the dark and small bugs or animals in his bed. By 5–6, the animals are out of the bed but in the room, and by 7–8 years, the spies and robbers have retreated to the shadows. The fact that there are such fears is much less important than the attitudes that are conveyed and the methods of coping that are taught. But, there are many more subtle difficulties in the parent-child interaction related to sleep problems.

Parents may too rigidly or too quickly require their children to go to sleep, just as they may rigidly counteract the perceived transgressions in toilet training or other areas, and this rigidity may provoke balking in going to sleep in the younger child and problems in awakening in the older child (Hirschberg 1957; Nagera 1966). Fraiberg's (1959:155) remarks on learning self-control could easily apply to learning good sleep habits: "The slow education for control demands much more parental time and patience at the beginning, but the child who learns control in this way will be child who acquires healthy self-discipline later."

Parental rigidity or lack of patience may be contrasted with parental undercontrol and excessive flexibility—allowing too much decision-making on the child's part. A child who sets his own bedtime may tend to go to sleep and awaken later and later. Then, the child may be overly tired if, for example, he gets up for school without enough sleep. Ferber (1985) has recently stressed the importance of sleep-awake cycles and circadian rhythms in the understanding of certain children's sleep problems. For children whose sleep-awake patterns and biological clocks are running too far behind or too far in advance, a gradual resetting of the clock may be accomplished by having the child go to sleep earlier or later each day. Otherwise a child's inner clock may be at an "awake-energize setting" when it is time to fall asleep. Regular, parentally directed routines help maintain a regular 24-hour rhythm and schedule. Ferber also noted that there is actually a 25-hour circadian rhythm which reinforces a tendency to go to sleep later and later each day.

Parental overpermissiveness may serve to encourage and perpetuate children's sleep difficulties in other ways. Parents who have ambivalent feelings toward their child set up inconsistent guidelines. They may, then, encourage dependent behavior that leads to increased crying, demands, delays in going to bed, and night awakenings (Healy 1972). Many researchers have pointed to the wisdom of having a child sleep in his own bed (e.g., Foster and Anderson 1936; Shirley and Kahn 1958). A child's overinvolvement with either parent may be related to a wish to disturb the parental union, which may be subtly encouraged by the parents (Vogl 1964).

The application of too much tender loving care by parents, consequent to the undesirable sleep behavior, can increase the probability of that behavior. Roberts and Gordon (1979) documented a case of a 5-year-old burn victim whose nightmares were reinforced by parents and hospital staff. Other examples of parenting problems and their etiological role in sleep difficulties will be reviewed below.

SLEEP DIFFICULTIES IN THE FIRST YEAR OF LIFE

Before discussing the role of the parent-child interaction in the sleeping difficulties of the first year, it is important to acknowledge that not all infants are born alike. There are individual differences in the sleeping patterns of neonates, some of whom may develop irritable sleep within a few days (Bernal 1973). The premature infant displays a more restless, active, irregular, and less-defined sleeping pattern than the full-term infant (Parmelee et al. 1967). In addition, research suggests that infants of heroin-addicted mothers, infants at risk for CNS abnormalities, infants of mothers who have had long labors, infants who have suffered anoxia or birth trauma, or infants of mothers who were under great emotional tension during pregnancy may be more restless in sleep, show less well-defined sleep patterning, be delayed in settling, or cry excessively (Anders and Guilleminault 1976; Bernal 1973; Moore and Ucko 1957; Nagera 1966; Shirley and Kahn 1958).

Given the individual differences in sleeping patterns of infants in general, the proper maternal response to a difficult sleeper is sometimes not easy to determine. There is some evidence to indicate that great maternal responsiveness and patience to a wakeful, tense baby may actually prolong the sleep difficulty, as may too great unresponsiveness or rigidity (Bernal 1973).

In the infant's first year, there are major changes in sleeping schedules which can test the patience and flexibility of parents who are losing sleep and who must accommodate to their children's schedules. However, this accommodation is not one-sided. We know that the infant is gradually time-conditioned by the caretakers to fit into the sleep-awake patterns and routines of the family (Shirley and Kahn 1958). The parent may modify the infant's pattern of night awakenings or even the adaptation to day-night periodicity, for example, by altering feedings or feeding water, or by developing a consistent feeding-bathing-playing routine.

Usually, the parents are asleep at night, which plays a role in the infant's prolongation of the night-asleep period. Nevertheless, the timing of the development of the diurnal cycle and settling are, for the most part, biologically determined (Nagera 1966; Parmelee et al. 1964; Shirley and Kahn 1958). It may be that the age of settling is more biologically determined but the night awakenings are more environmentally determined and related to parental handling (Anders 1979). Parental handling also plays an important role in the delicate balance and flow between sleep states and states of consciousness or alertness.

Early in infancy, wakefulness is brought on, primarily, by physiological discomfort, such as hunger or thirst. The infant wakens when it is hungry and may fall asleep after a feeding or a fatiguing bath. By about 3 months of age, EEG alpha rhythms are established, and as the baby wakens from delta wave, somnolent sleep to the alert alpha state because of a discomfort such as hunger, the mother, like a pied piper, may "capture" the infant in an increasingly comfortable and intriguing alert state, during feeding or play. Thus, she exerts some control over the sleep-awake cycle and the development of consciousness (Nagera 1966). But she will fail to have appropriate, positive control if she cannot maintain a certain level of comfort for her child.

Babies require reassuring routines and comfortable conditions. If basic processes such as sleeping, feeding, and alertness occur under conditions of discomfort, the infant's development can be negatively affected. As Finch and Kemph (1964) pointed out, the feeding-sleeping-waking cycle of comfort-discomfort is a building block of ego formation, and if the infant is allowed to remain in too uncomfortable a state, later instinctual control, interpersonal relationships, and sleep may be affected negatively. The parent who is suffering from great anxiety, depression, or addiction, who is unprepared for the responsibility of parenthood (e.g., the teenage mother) or is suffering from other disturbances may subject the infant to great inconsistencies in handling, and thereby delay the normal sleep pattern development and trigger increased night awakenings (Anders and Guilleminault 1976; Fraiberg 1959; Nagera 1966).

The parent who is overresponsive, overanxious, or overindulgent may actually provoke increased dependent behaviors such as crying, demands, and night awakenings in the child (Healy 1972). There is some evidence that too much play and contact (over 20 minutes) and too little play and contact (below 10 minutes) beyond the required nursing time may be related to sleep difficulties in infancy (Anders and Guilleminault 1976; Bernal 1973; Nagera 1966). Unfeeling play may also be related to sleep difficulties (Nagera 1966).

Children come to favor and associate certain conditions with falling asleep. If these favored conditions—"sleep associations"—include the parent's presence (e.g., holding or lying in bed) or parental actions (e.g., rocking or feeding), the child does not learn to fall asleep alone, preferably in a quiet, darkened room. Indeed, the child may virtually come to require the parent's presence or ministrations in order to fall asleep easily (Ferber 1985).

When a parent excessively rocks the baby, walks the floor, feeds or otherwise ministers to the child, wakefulness can be encouraged (Shirley and Kahn 1958). At a very early age, infants begin to develop the ability to comfort themselves, though in limited ways, a development which the overanxious parent may overlook. After the third month, Nagera (1966) suggests, the infant begins to be capable of self-gratifying maneuvers such as hand-to-mouth movements and can comfort himself and sleep through the night more readily. By 6–9 months, the infant can tolerate more minor discomforts, including some separation from the mother (Fraiberg 1959).

The specific anxiety that prompts a parent to be overresponsive is an individual matter; but some mothers feel unworthy (a narcissistic involvement) in allowing the young infant to be "part of her" (fear of fusion) (Hirschberg 1957). The mother may ultimately have concerns about her own body integrity but believes that the baby's body integrity is threatened. One mother of a 6-month-old with frequent night wakenings constantly checked and fussed over the baby, thereby waking it up (Sperling 1955). The constant checking may have been a compulsive mechanism to undo any possible harm that reflected the mother's ambivalent wish for harm.

Too little stimulation from an angry or rejecting mother can provoke hypersomnolence in a child (Hirschberg 1957). The response to a completely rejecting mother, in infancy, can be to fall into a sort of vegetative state (Finch 1964). Spitz (1965) proposed that if a mother is both hostile and pampering, the inconsistent treatment can produce prolonged rocking behavior in infants. Both rocking and head banging often occur while the child is falling asleep or during night awakenings. The rhythmical behavior can be a method of securing the parent's return to the child (Ferber 1985). Ferber (1985) suggested that an anxious child may rock or head-bang to cope with scary fantasies. The rocking is also autoerotic or pleasurable. Rocking may also be a self-calming device, as illustrated by the case of Maria, who at age 1 rocked in her crib and by age 2 would crawl out of her crib and rock in a chair until she grew calm and fell back to sleep.

Besides the association between the pampering-hostile parental handling and rocking, Spitz (1965) discussed children in their first year who had very unresponsive mothers or who were absent from their mothers for extended periods and who, therefore, suffered from two "emotional deficiency diseases." In an anaclitic depression, the child has been apart from its mother for 3–5 months without a suitable substitute; while in marasmus, the situation continues and the infant may die. In both conditions, severe insomnia is a symptom.

These disorders occur during the period of attachment to the primary caretaker, the primary socialization period. While this is a period when the child first learns to love, to paraphrase Fraiberg (1959), it is also period of increased experiences of anxiety based upon the fear of separation from the mother. Several researchers have noted that there is often an increase in night awakenings in the period of approximately 8–18 months which corresponds to the period of primary attachment (Ames 1964; Moore and Ucko 1957; Nagera 1966).

Fears of separation and stranger anxiety may be associated with sleep disturbances in the first year, according to Kales et al. (1970). To illustrate, Fraiberg reported the case of an 8-month-old girl who developed severe, prolonged, and terror-stricken night awakenings, which began after the girl awoke one night to find the face of a completely unknown baby-sitter. Mack (1970) also noted that the earliest nightmares, in the second year of life, occur in relation to situations involving strangers and separation from the parents.

In sum, infantile sleep difficulties are often founded in the more overt aspects of the parent-child interaction. Sleep disturbances of the first year of life are not quite the complex psychological affair that they are in the second and third years.

SLEEP DISTURBANCES IN THE SECOND YEAR OF LIFE

Most sleep disturbances in the 1–3 year age range are transient phenomena associated with normal development (Nagera 1966). To paraphrase Anna Freud, in the second year of life, falling asleep has become very much a psychological affair, rather than a purely physical affair. Several psychoanalytic observers have suggested that the act of falling asleep involves the withdrawal of interests into the self—reproducing the primary narcissism of the suckling infant (Nagera 1966; Windholz 1942). Also, the development of an attachment to the primary caretaker brings with it the anxiety of separation from that beloved person and separation from the newfound exciting world that the caretaker has introduced the child to (Fraiberg 1959; Freud 1965). The toddler's demands for the mother to sit with him, cuddle, read another story, or hold the hand are ways of avoiding separation (Nagera 1966). A consistent routine associated with bedtime—the same surroundings, noise level, manner of being put to sleep—all may serve to reassure the child during the psychological separation of sleep (Finch and Kemph 1964). The "bedtime soliloquy," or constant chatter before sleep, of the child over 1 year is the normal attempt of the child to recreate in words the objects and significant others that he must anxiously give up to sleep (Fraiberg 1959).

Increasingly, as language development proceeds, language—self-talk—may be used by the child as a means of calming himself so that he can enter a more relaxed state before falling asleep. There is a process that children learn of controlling their anxiety and falling asleep—a process of gradually learned self-control. James, at the age of 14 months, could be calmed before going to sleep by saying, "It's all right," or "That's all right," sometimes while being held and comforted. Soon afterwards while crying about the separation during sleep, he began to repeat, "That's all right!"—calming himself if he began to cry. Children can be taught how to fall asleep. James was told to "lie down, put your head on the pillow, close your eyes, and go to sleep," which he did. At a very early age, he began to use language to direct his falling asleep.

Nagera (1966) recalled that with increasing language development, the ego can bind anxiety by meaningful, reassuring thought processes. The child can more easily fall asleep if his mother is absent by repeating, sometimes with her inflection, what his mother said, such as (Nagera's examples) "Mummy went to the cinema," "Mummy holidays" or "Mummy will be back soon." Probably, the availability of self-calming mechanisms in the child's repertoire also promotes the capacity to reality-test the dream under conditions of lessened anxiety.

When the child is closer to age 2, being told directly to go to sleep may increase the child's resistance, since the child can now anticipate the separation that will ensue. I have utilized a play scene of stuffed animals falling asleep in the crib or bed or stories about falling asleep, to suggest less directly the act of falling asleep (somewhat akin to embedded hypnotic suggestion).

Sleep disturbances in the second year may also herald a developmental advance, such as walking or bowel control. Mack (1965) reports nightmares relating to these advances. Toilet training that occurs too early also may lead to sleep disturbances. For example, Fraiberg (1950) reports the case of a girl who began toilet training at 8 months of age. At 14 months, the girl would lie awake, rigid and tense in her bed, fearful that she would soil herself and lose her mother's love or approval.

Fraiberg (1950) has also reported cases of children around 1 year of age who had been beaten by siblings or engaged in rough or sexually provocative play (kissed and rubbed all over), victimized by other children, who developed fearful night awakenings. The threat to the child's safety or security is an aspect of sleep disturbances.

## SLEEP DISTURBANCES IN THE THIRD YEAR OF LIFE (2–3 YEARS)

By 2–2½ the problem is being put to sleep, while by 3–4, problems shift more to later night awakenings (Ames 1964). The preschool years are years of a very active fantasy life; yet the ability to test the reality-fantasy or reality-dream distinction is not yet fully developed (Kales et al. 1981; Mack 1965). As a result, the 2-year-old may believe that there actually is an alligator in the bed when it is dark. The young preschooler has limited capacity to deal with the inner tensions of the age, and the lack of capacity to cope with anxiety may be expressed in night terrors (Mack

1965). Some nightmares and night terrors may relate to the previous day's fears (Despert 1949).

The anxiety of separation from the parent is still an important one for the 2–3-year-old, and with advancing cognitive development, the child may think up numerous, almost obsessional and compulsive ways to keep the parent with him and to put out of action the dangers associated with the idea of sleep: the blatant request to sleep in the parent's bed, the request for toileting or drinks, the calls to the parent to come back ("curtain call behaviors"), the prolonged or repeated just-one-more-bedtime story, the special blanket placed in a special way, the special goodnight kiss (a hug-and-a-kiss-and-a-growl-and-a-squeak!), the particular way to brush the child's teeth, the "sit-with-me's" or the "you-forgot-to-cuddle's!" (Ames 1964; Finch et al. 1964; Friend 1956; Mack 1965; personal observation). If the child reacts with violence when the sleep ritual is violated then, Vogl (1964) suggests, there is a neurotic sleep ceremonial.

The 2–2½-year-old has a sense of identity closely linked to body concept, and in sleep, it has been proposed, there is a dissolution of that identity and concept (Fraiberg 1959; Friend 1956). Treasured objects, such as soft clothes, pillows, blankets, a piece of wool or a soft toy animal, may relieve the anxiety over the instability of formation of the body image and accompanying body disintegration anxiety, as the child may hold the object against its skin—some suggest representing the mother's skin (Friend 1956). There may be considerable night wakening during early preschool years related to these anxieties.

Separation anxiety may be at issue in either disturbed or too perfect falling asleep. In a study of the sleep behavior of 2-year-olds, Ragins and Schachter (1971) suggested that mothers who were anxious about their children's sleep and who were unable to comfort their children tended to react harshly to the child and/or covertly encourage the sleep disruptions. Their children tended to fall asleep extremely rapidly, i.e., in less than 10 minutes like an infant, or extremely slowly—taking over an hour. The authors suggest that a 2-year-old who has no trouble with sleep at all may be retreating from the separation issue, which portends later problems. The average 2-year-old is tended to for about a half-hour before falling asleep (Ames 1964).

Regarding the causes of sleeping problems, the whole issue of behavioral compliance and the active teaching of parentally acceptable behavior has been underestimated in the 2–3-year period in some overemphasis on toilet training, which also requires compliance. To paraphrase Despert (1949), the child's bad dreams about huge engines overrunning him may be related to the general demands for compliance by the parents. Certainly, the whole process of toilet training—which has the special distinction of requiring control over one's bodily functions—is intimately related to the more general process of the teaching of parentally approved behavior. This close relationship may be seen in the example of James, age 2 years and 10 months, who upon being requested to go upstairs to take a bath, refused and while urinating stated emphatically, "I'm peeing in my pants!" But, falling asleep, too, involves both control over bodily events (e.g., relaxing, brain-wave states) and compliance with parental wishes and routines.

In the 2–3-year age range, the child's growing sensitivity to issues of sexuality may figure increasingly prominently in sleep disturbances. Children may pretend to be asleep while actually spying on the parent's sexual acts if they are in the same room or nearby (Finch and Kemph 1964). Fraiberg (1950) reported the case of a 2-year-old with night awakenings and clinging to her mother after witnessing sexual intercourse.

Toward the end of the 2–3-year period, with the development of the oedipal phase, children's desire to sleep in the parental bed or have a parent, often of the opposite sex, come to their room may be associated with oedipal wishes to disturb the parental union and have the opposite-sex parent for themselves (though an inverse oedipal relationship has also been suggested) (Nagera 1966; Vogl 1964). Herzog (1980) studied twelve little boys, ages 18–28 months, who suffered from nightmares or night-terror-like experiences and who would call for their daddies at night. Their mothers could not comfort them. Rather, only the father's presence could comfort them. Herzog suggested that the syndrome occurred in boys whose fathers had left the home (through separation, etc.), and it was suggested that the children believed that it was their own uncontrolled aggression that eliminated their rival. The boy's attainment of the mother—for example, through the mother's taking the child into her bed—only confused the child further and exacerbated the situation.

Sibling rivalry can occur as soon as the child perceives that he must share his parent's affections or caretaking; and the aggressive wishes that ensue can find expression in nightmares (Mack 1970).

## SLEEP DISTURBANCES AT 3–6 YEARS

Sleep disturbances in the 3–6-year period are often elaborations upon the central themes which developed earlier, such as the beginnings of oedipal concerns, learning self-control, and sibling rivalry. Nagera (1966) maintained that consistent sleep disturbances after age 3 were indicative of neurotic conflicts. Several researchers have reported that the years 5–7 are years in which children are very much troubled by nightmares and are the years highest in the incidence of night terrors (Ames 1964; Fisher et al. 1974). It may also be that the separation from parents, the academic demands, and the social requirements of school, which begin at age 5, relate to the increased sleep disturbances.

From 3 to 5 seems to be a neurologically timed period when sexual and aggressive neurological structures become increasingly linked to higher-cognitive cortical structures. Infantile sexuality appears to figure prominently in the sleep disturbances of the age. Windholz (1942) suggested that the temptation to masturbate, which is usually suppressed during the day, can cause sleep disturbances. Nagera (1966) reported the case of a 5-year-old girl who refused to go to bed because "sleep was dirty" and related her refusal to anxiety about masturbation.

In the 3–6 age range, direct viewing of sexual activity or being subject to sexual activity is particularly associated with the development of sleep disturbances (Deri 1942; Mack 1970; Nagera 1966). Nagera (1966) described a 3-year-old child who could not sleep alone, even with sedation, after witnessing sexual intercourse and believing that his mother had been hurt.

In the 3–6 period, with the development of oedipal dynamics, the opposite-sex parent needs to accept the child's infantile sexual advances, yet not be too rejecting or too seductive. The same-sex parent needs to tolerate a reasonable amount of aggression but remain affectionate to the child without being too rigidly punitive (Finch and Kemph 1964; Sperling 1955). Parental seductiveness can lead to sleep disturbances. For example, the father of one 4-year-old girl often slept with his daughter, kissed her rather than his wife before he went to work, and walked around the house naked. The girl developed night terrors in which snakes threatened her (Mack 1965). In this case, the mother also lacked the skills to enforce discipline effectively, which seems to have the result of increased aggressive attacks in the child's dreams and night terrors. The overstimulated aggressiveness is turned back on the child at night (Mack 1965).

In the oedipal phase, the same-sex parent may perceive the child's hostile or aggressive rivalry behavior as a disrespectful transgression, and it is probably also likely that the parent's strictness in such cases extends to other areas, such as toilet training, as well as to the management of the sleep disturbance itself (Hirschberg 1957). Some parents may discipline the child during sleep time, thereby encouraging the child to stay up.

Apart from the oedipal relationship, the parent who is too punitive and who attempts to dominate or control the child in a manner which does not respect the child's personal integrity (and there are sexual or sadistic overtones in this) may engender much hostility in the child which may be expressed in the form of a sleep disturbance. The following clinical vignette is one such illustration.

Tanika's adoptive mother constantly teased her 4-year-old daughter and attempted to control her behavior rigidly. The mother would force the girl to go to bed, and Tanika would transgress by coming out of the bedroom. The mother would check and recheck the girl and Tanika would lie awake for her chance to leave the room again, whereupon she would be forced back to bed. This sequence could continue for hours.

The importance of aggressive proclivities in parents is apparent in some parents who are overly concerned that harm may befall their children. Hirschberg (1957) has suggested that such parents may become overinvolved in their children's sleep rituals in order to counteract their own unacceptable harmful wishes. They may prearrange bedclothes, continually cover the child, or be excessively concerned about light or noise. Some parents may encourage a child's staying awake by their overconcern with the child's soiling or wetting while asleep (Hirschberg 1957; Nagera 1966). Bedwetting, in general, is common in this age range.

After age 3, about 10–15 percent of all children are enuretic (Kales et al. 1981). Ferber (1985) suggested that most cases of enuresis are not caused by emotional factors but rather are related to either a form of arousal disorder which occurs during or just after NREM sleep or to the child's not having learned to recognize the sensations produced by a full bladder or a partially full, contracting bladder. However, Kales et al. (1981) associated secondary enuresis with a need to regress or for more attention, as when a sibling is born. But it is important to ask further, why is there a need to regress or to seek attention? The answer may be found in the child's hostility or anxiety, particularly over separation from a significant other. Also, parental control needs to be considered. As a hostile act, bedwetting or wetting oneself, in general, causes the parent a great deal of work (laundry, loss of sleep, changing clothes or bedclothes) and thwarts the parent's wishes. As an act of anxiety, bedwetting brings a parent back to the child's room. One girl who was taught to act lovingly whenever she felt hostile toward her little sister and others discharged her suppressed hostility through bedwetting (Fraiberg 1959).

A number of factors underlying problem sleep in the 3–6 period are similar to those of earlier periods. For example, sibling rivalry is still an important issue. Similarly, traumatic events may also play a role in sleep disturbances of this age range, as the following case illustrates:

Five-year-old Marsha was sexually molested by a 16-year-old boy who stated that he would murder her mother if she "told." Subsequently, Marsha was afraid to fall asleep lest her mother be hurt. Marsha also had nightmares which recapitulated the incident.

Finally, parental insistence that a child play quietly in bed may also lead to increased awakenings or difficulty falling asleep as the association between bed and quiet sleep is broken (Shirley and Kahn 1958). This is similar to the circumstances of the adult insomniac who finds interesting activities and exciting things to do while staying awake in bed.

SLEEP DISTURBANCES AT 7–12 YEARS

With the increasing cognitive development of the child and the decrease in the emotional turmoil of the oedipal years, there are fewer nightmares and night terrors during the 7–12 age range. In general, sleep is sounder, though there may be an increased resistance to being put to bed which reflects the child's attitude toward any parent-imposed task (Ames 1964). In psychoanalytic thinking, with the repression of the oedipal, libidinal, and aggressive strivings, by about age 7, the compulsive rituals of the preschooler are less necessary. There are sleep rituals in this period, but they involve such things as sleep position and the desire to wear particular pajamas or to have a particular clock (Finch and Kemph 1964). However, for the child who has not successfully resolved the situation of emotional conflict in the oedipal years, we may see behavior rituals, but ones which are suitable to the expanding world and cognitive development of the older child. One 12-year-old, upon retiring, had her window curtains arranged carefully, table cloth placed exactly, and the clocks at a certain distance (Nagera 1966). Except for the high incidence of sleepwalking and talking in the 7–12 range, in general, sleep disturbances of this period are more adult-like (Anders and Guilleminault 1976; Nagera 1966).

Beginning at about age 10–11, there may be a half-hour of radio, daydreaming, and worrying before going to sleep (middle-class Ss) which declines in later years (Ames 1964). Some children read extensively before going to bed, which Nagera (1966) believes is a defensive maneuver that avoids the impulse to masturbate or to fantasize about masturbating.

The older child's more sophisticated cognitive-emotional mechanisms which serve to preserve sound sleep have also been reported by other clinical observers. For instance, Mack (1970) suggests that by age 4, the child is firm in the understanding that a dream is not real. During ages 6–8, the child can reassure himself within the dream that he is only dreaming and can even awaken himself. Mack also reports that older children are capable of "identifying with the aggressor" within the dream and can assume aggressive characteristics in the dream to fight back against the dream attackers. Selman's (1971) research in cognitive social reasoning has indicated that there is an advance in perspective-taking skills in the preteen years, and it may be that the child can view himself more objectively in the role of the victim and also assume the role of the victimizer. Thus, cognitive development, in the case of the dream terror, is ultimately responsible for the reduced fear and anxiety.

In the dreams of children ages 7–12, we also sometimes see the dynamics and conflicts seen in children of younger ages, such as oedipal conflicts, castration anxiety, and parental overseductiveness and overindulgence. But, in the older child, dreams manifest more disguised and symbolic content (Mack 1970). Oedipal dynamics may also be at the root of sleep disturbances other than nightmares or bad dreams. For example, Sperling (1955) reported the case of a 10-year-old girl who, from the age of 2, had constant night awakenings and severe insomnia. At age 2, the child had usurped her mother's place in the parental bed and the father played with her frequently whenever she awoke. Also, believing that the child had a very small stomach, the mother had fed her constantly through the night from the time the child was an infant.

## SLEEP DISTURBANCES IN ADOLESCENCE (12–18 YEARS)

Ames's (1964) study of middle-class children reported that adolescents have fewer instances of disturbed sleep than any other age group. There is an increasing insistence on going to sleep later (10:30–11 P.M.) reflecting, in part, the growing independent stand that the adolescent should determine his own routines. Teenagers may go to sleep later and later until their entire sleep phase and biological clocks shift (Ferber 1985). Excessive parental rigidity may provoke increased rebelliousness on the part of the adolescent in the form of going to sleep still later.

The adolescent may be in conflict with his parents for waking up too late, and the 14-year-old may require repeated calls, and so forth, to be awakened (Ames 1964). The later bedtime hour, which leads to increased tiredness, may be at the root of the later awakening. But a number of other factors have also been suggested, notably: the adolescent's own striving for increased independence and adult privileges (Finch and Kemph 1964); sleep deprivation associated with poor time management as the adolescent begins to learn to cope with increased academic, social, and athletic activities which may also lead to sleepiness during the day (Herskowitz and Rosman 1982); and the possibility that with puberty, increased sexual wishes are passively coped with in sleep (Friend, 1956).

During puberty, there is a resurgence of sexual and aggressive strivings and a rekindling of masturbatory and old oedipal conflicts (Finch and Kemph, 1964). Neurotic anxiety over these issues may be related to sleep difficulties. Monroe and Marks (1977) reported that adolescent poor sleepers who complained of sleep difficulties and had difficulty falling asleep, according to their therapist's ratings, were high in neuroticism and measures reflecting anxiety (phobias, fears, obsessions, anxiousness) and depression. The "poor sleepers" were more introverted than "good sleepers" and tended, it was suggested, to direct their own aggressive wishes toward themselves. Ferber (1985) too has suggested that children who are in rigid control of their angry and sad feelings during the day tend to have more NREM dyssomnias (arousal difficulties) as if the feelings work their way out under the conditions of lessened wakeful control that exist in NREM sleep. One "controlled" 17-year-old boy would jump out of bed and occasionally mumble a phrase such as "I've got to kill him" (Ferber 1985:157) after his parents had divorced and his father remarried.

But there are cases where the threat to the individual's security comes more clearly from without. For example, in one clinical study of young adolescents, sleep disturbances were associated with a feeling of threat to the children's security or existence (Adam 1964). In one case, the mother threatened suicide. In another case, siblings had been killed.

## Summary

This chapter has reviewed the major varieties of and etiology of children's sleep disturbances. First, common sleeping patterns and the development of REM and NREM states are discussed. There are substantial shifts and disturbances of sleep throughout normal childhood development—such as the shifting napping or sleeping patterns of infants or the occurrence of night terrors or nightmares in the preschool child. Second, the major sleep disorders of childhood are described, such as disorders of excessive sleep (e.g., narcolepsy and sleep apnea syndrome), disorders of too little sleep (insomnia), and episodic sleep disorders (e.g., night terrors, sleepwalking, bedwetting, nightmares). As children grow older, they are typically less subject to disturbed sleep; the cognitive- and ego-developmental, emotional, and psychosexual factors accounting for this are discussed.

A substantial portion of the paper is devoted to the chronological adumbration of the role of parent-child interaction in the etiology of sleep disorders at different ages from birth to adolescence. The role parents play in teaching their children to calm their anxieties (self-calming) and to learn how to master the process of falling asleep are also reviewed. It was concluded that most nonorganic sleeping difficulties or peculiarities in bedtime behavior of particular children can be understood in the context of psychological development, parental practices, the physiology of sleep, and maturational changes in sleep patterns.

## References

Adam, R. 1964. Two aspects of the pathology of sleep in children: Personality features in children with sleep disturbances. In E. Harms, ed., *Problems of Sleep and Dreams in Children.* New York: Pergamon Press.

Ames, L. 1964. Sleep and dreams in childhood. In E. Harms, ed., *Problems of Sleep and Dreams in Children.* New York: Pergamon Press.

Anders, T. 1979. Night-waking in infants during the first year of life. *Pediatrics* 63(6):860–64.

Anders, T., and C. Guilleminault. 1976. Sleep disorders in children. *Advances in Pediatrics* 22:151–74.

Aserinsky, E. and N. Kleitman. 1955. A motility cycle in sleeping infants as manifested by ocular and gross bodily activity. *Journal of Applied Physiology* 8:11–18.

Beltramini, A. and M. Hertzig. 1983. Sleep and bedtime behavior in preschool aged children. *Pediatrics* 71(2):153–58.

Bernal, J. 1973. Night waking in infants during the first 14 months. *Developmental Medicine and Child Neurology* 15:760–69.

Blomfield, J. and J. Douglas. 1956. Bedwetting: Prevalence among children aged 4–7 years. *Lancet* 1:850–52.

Broughton, R. 1960. Sleep disorders: Disorders of arousal? *Science* 159:1070–78.

Caldwell, D., A. Brane, and P. Beckett. 1970. Sleep patterns in normal and psychotic children. *Archives of General Psychiatry* 22:500–3.

Deri, F. 1942. Symposium on neurotic disturbances in sleep. II. *International Journal of Psychoanalysis* 23:56–59.

Despert, J. 1949. Dreams in children of preschool age. In R. Eissler et al., eds., *The Psychoanalytic Study of the Child* 4:141–81. New York: International Universities Press.

Erickson, M. 1941. On the possible occurrence of a dream in an 8-month-old infant. *Psychoanalytic Quarterly* 10:382–84.

Essen, J. and C. Peckham. 1976. Nocturnal enuresis in childhood. *Developmental Medicine and Child Neurology* 18:577–89.

Ferber, R. 1985. *Solve Your Child's Sleep Problems.* New York: Simon and Schuster.

Finch, W. and J. Kemph. 1964. The etiology of sleep. In E. Harms, ed., *Problems of Sleep and Dreams in Children.* New York: Pergamon Press.

Fisher, C. 1965. Psychoanalytic implications of recent research on sleep and dreaming. *Journal of the American Psychoanalytic Association* 13:197–303.

Fisher, C. and W. Dement. 1963. Studies on the psychopathology of sleep and dreams. *American Journal of Psychiatry* 119:1160–68.

Fisher, C., E. Kahn, H. Edwards, and D. Davis. 1974. A psychophysiological study of nightmares and night terrors. I. Physiological aspects of the stage 4 night terror. *Psychoanalysis and Contemporary Science* 3:317–97.

Foster, J. and J. Anderson. 1936. Unpleasant dreams in childhood. *Child Development* 7:77–84.

Fraiberg, S. 1950. On the sleep disturbances of early childhood. In R. Eissler et al., eds., *The Psychoanalytic Study of the Child* 5:285–309. New York: International Universities Press.

Fraiberg, S. 1959. *The Magic Years.* New York: Scribner's.

Friend, M. 1956. Panel on sleep disturbances in children. *Journal of the American Psychoanalytic Association* 4:514–25.

Freud, A. 1965. *Normality and Pathology in Childhood.* New York: International Universities Press.

Hartmann, E. 1984. *The Nightmare.* New York: Basic Books.

Healy, A. 1972. The sleep patterns of preschool children. *Clinical Pediatrics* 11(3):174–77.

Herskowitz, J. and N. Rosman. 1982. *Pediatrics, Neurology, and Psychiatry.* New York: Macmillan.

Herzog, J. 1980. Sleep disturbance and father hunger in 18- to 28-month-old boys. In A. Solnit et al., eds., *The Psychoanalytic Study of the Child* 35:219–33. New Haven: Yale University Press.

Hirschberg, J. 1957. Parental anxieties accompanying sleep disturbance in young children. *Bulletin of the Menninger Clinic* 21(4):129–39.

Kales, J., A. Jacobson, and A. Kales. 1968. Sleep disorders in children. In L. Abt and B. Riess, eds., *Progress in Clinical Psychology.* New York: Grune and Stratton.

Kales, A., C. Soldatos, and J. Kales. 1970. Childhood sleep disorders. In S. Gellis and B. Kagan, eds., *Current Pediatric Therapy.* Philadelphia: Saunders.

Kales, A., C. Soldatos, and J. Kales. 1981. Sleep disorders: Evaluation and management in the office setting. In S. Arieti, ed., *American Handbook of Child Psychiatry* 2d ed., vol. 7. New York: Basic Books.

Kellerman, H. 1981. *Sleep Disorders: Insomnia and Narcolepsy.* New York: Brunner/Mazel.

Kleitman, N. 1939. *Sleep and Wakefulness.* Chicago: University of Chicago Press.

Mack. J. 1965. Nightmares conflict and ego development in childhood. *International Journal of Psychoanalysis* 6(4):403–28.

Mack, J. 1970. *Nightmares and Human Conflict.* Boston: Little, Brown.

Maenchen, A. 1942. Symposium on neurotic disturbances of sleep. IV. *International Journal of Psychoanalysis* 23:59–62.

Monroe, L. and P. Marks. 1977. Psychotherapists' descriptions of emotionally disturbed adolescent poor and good sleepers. *Journal of Clinical Psychology* 33(1):263–69.

Moore, T. and L. Ucko. 1957. Night waking in early infancy. *Archives of the Diseases of Childhood* 32:333–42.

Nagera, H. 1966. Sleep and its disturbances approached developmentally. In R. Eissler et al., eds., *The Psychoanalytic Study of the Child* 21:393–447. New York: International Universities Press.

Parmelee, A., W. Wenner, Y. Akiyama, M. Schultz, and E. Stern, 1967. Sleep states in premature infants. *Developmental Medicine and Child Neurology* 9:70–77.

Parmelee, A., W. Wenner, and H. Schulz. 1964. Infant sleep patterns from birth to 16 weeks of age. *Journal of Pediatrics* 65:576–82.

Pasulka, P. 1979. The responsibilities of the night child care worker. *Child Care Quarterly* 8(4):303–6.

Ragins, N. and J. Schachter. 1971. A study of sleep behavior in two-year-old children. *Journal of the American Academy of Child Psychiatry* 10(3):464–80.

Roberts, R. and S. Gordon. 1979. Reducing childhood nightmares subsequent to a burn trauma. *Child Behavior Therapy* 1(4):373–81.

Roffwarg, H., W. Dement, and C. Fisher. 1964. Preliminary observations of sleep-dream patterns in neonates, infants, children, and adults. In E. Harms, ed., *Problems of Sleep and Dreams in Children.* New York: Pergamon Press.

Selman, R. 1971. Taking another's perspective: Role-taking development in early childhood. *Child Development* 42:1721–34.

Sherman, M., M. Hertzig, R. Austrian, and T. Shapiro. 1981. Treasured objects in school aged children. *Pediatrics* 68(3):379–86.

Shirley, H. and J. Kahn. 1958. Sleep disturbances in children. *Pediatric Clinics of North America* 5:629–43.

Sperling, M. 1955. Etiology and treatment of sleep disturbances in children. *Psychoanalytic Quarterly* 24:358–68.

Spitz, R. 1965. *The First Year of Life.* New York: International Universities Press.
Vogl, M. 1964. Two aspects of the pathology of sleep in children: Sleep disturbances in neurotic children. In E. Harms, ed., *Problems of Sleep and Dreams in Children.* New York: Pergamon Press.
Windholz, E. 1942. Symposium on neurotic disturbances in sleep. I. *International Journal of Psychoanalysis* 23:49–52.

# 9.

# Psychoanalytic Perspectives on Anxiety Dreams in Adults and Children

RUTH BERS SHAPIRO

FREUD CONSIDERED *The Interpretation of Dreams* his most significant work. Toward the end of his life, he wrote of the reassurance which the theory of dreams offered him during periods of intellectual uncertainty.

> I myself found it [dream theory] a sheet-anchor during those difficult times when the unrecognized facts of the neuroses used to confuse my inexperienced judgment. Whenever I began to have doubts about the correctness of my wavering conclusions, the successful transformation of a senseless and muddled dream into a logical and intelligible mental process in the dreamer would renew my confidence of being on the right track. (Freud 1933)

Throughout his writing Freud (1916–17, 1933) expressed frustration that professionals as well as laymen were remarkably resistant to grasping the fundamental principles of dream theory. In his view, they consistently misread and rejected the basic proposition that dreams always contain the fulfillment of an unconscious wish. The overriding importance of the wish-fulfillment hypothesis remained an important issue for Freud, who returned to it whenever he expanded, modified, or restated his theory of dreams (Freud 1900, 1901, 1916–17, 1920, 1933).

## Anxiety Dreams and the Wish-Fulfillment Hypothesis

The question of dreams which are unsettling, saddening, disturbing, or frightening occupied Freud throughout his life. He referred to them as anxiety dreams, not nightmares. Often, his explication of anxiety dreams appears in the context of a hypothetical dialogue in which he anticipates that disturbing dreams will be used as evidence against the wish-fulfillment theory. His apprehensions proved accurate: Brenner (1974) reports that anxiety dreams have been used for half a century to discredit Freud's position. Freud characteristically responded to this anticipated criticism by demonstrating the variety of ways in which dreams which are manifestly disturbing are simultaneously wish fulfilling. It is not surprising that Freud—eager to establish the power and primacy of the unconscious in mental life—often wove his formulations regarding anxiety dreams into the fabric of a larger argument. Nonetheless, the view of anxiety dreams which emerges from Freud's work as a whole offers a comprehensive approach to the psychodynamics of such dreams, provides the theoretical underpinning for later investigations of anxiety dreams in adults and children, and, in some instances, anticipates current psychophysiological findings.

Freud's (1900) chief formulations about anxiety dreams can be found in *The Interpretation of Dreams,* one of two texts which Freud updated as his theory expanded. In *The Interpretation of Dreams* he examines the interplay between repressed wishes and dream censorship which produces anxiety dreams, investigates typical dreams associated with anxiety, defines punishment dreams, and discusses pavor nocturnus, or the night terrors of children. Furthermore, in detailing the work of the dream censorship and in describing the role of anxiety in dreaming, Freud anticipates formulations about psychic structures and processes elaborated in the structural model (1923) and in the revised theory of anxiety (1926).

A concise reiteration of the dynamics of anxiety dreams appears in the *Introductory Lectures* (1916–17) and in the *New Introductory Lectures* (1933). In *Beyond the Pleasure Principle* (1920) Freud raises an exception to the wish-fulfillment hypothesis. He concludes that disturbing dreams which recall scenes of traumatic events are not compatible with the wish-fulfillment theory. This modification accompanies Freud's introduction of the concepts of the repetition compulsion and death instinct. A summary of Freud's exploration of anxiety dreams affords a view of evolving theory. For example, dream censorship, originally posited as one aspect of a permanent censoring mechanism operating to keep unconscious wishes out of awareness, is eventually seen as an aspect of superego and ego functioning (Laplanche and Pontalis 1973). This chapter will follow the development of Freud's ideas and relate his hypotheses and formulations to contemporary psychoanalytic inquiries into anxiety dreams.

## Dreamwork and Dream Censorship

From the start, Freud described anxiety dreams as a product of internal conflict and compromise, a view which in its broad outlines is consistent with current psychoanalytic thinking (Altman 1969; Brenner 1976). Dreaming permits the expression of a repressed wish at the same time as it preserves sleep. Sometimes, however, this dual purpose cannot be accomplished, and sleep is disturbed or interrupted by anxiety. The conditions which cause anxious arousals, elicit feelings of distress or sorrow, or give the dreamer an uneasy feeling for some time following the dream occupy an important place in Freud's theory of dreams.

In chapter 7 of *The Interpretation of Dreams,* Freud indicates that an anxiety dream arises when a repressed wish and the preconscious repudiation of that wish are not properly balanced and the unacceptable impulse comes too close to consciousness. Ordinarily the dream censorship "brings about the distortion of dreams; it does so in order to prevent the generation of anxiety or other forms of disturbing affect." (Freud 1900:267) The mechanisms of the dreamwork—condensation, displacement, representability, and secondary revision—produce the distortions which conceal the forbidden wish.

> The dream process is allowed to begin as a fulfilment of an unconscious wish; but if this attempted wish-fulfilment jars upon the preconscious so violently that it is unable to continue sleeping, then the dream has made a breach in the compromise and has failed to carry out the second half of its task. (1900:580)

When the dream censorship is functioning in an optimal fashion, the content of an unacceptable impulse and the affect associated with the impulse are sufficiently disguised to be kept out of awareness. When the dreamwork is not successful or is only partially successful in concealing either or both of these components, anxiety is produced. Two brief examples follow.

A dream in which the content of the repressed wish is not adequately hidden is reported by a young woman. She dreams that her male therapist issues a warning to her: *"You have to be careful not to turn out like S. You know she had sex with her father and then with her brothers."*

The patient awoke with a sense of panic; she felt as if there had been a loud explosion in her head. She was disturbed by the dream for several days. In the dream, the presumed repressed incestuous wishes are only partially concealed. The disguise is particularly transparent since the dreamer had two older brothers, was highly identified with her childhood friend, and was being directly warned by her therapist. Despite these close parallels, the dreamer did not consciously realize that the forbidden acts in the dream corresponded to her own impulses. She was, instead, struck by how strange it was to be dreaming about someone she had not seen in more than twenty years, as she was struck by the "horrifying" news she had been given about her friend. After a series of dreams involving the same theme, she could acknowledge that the panic reflected her own conflicts.

The experience of anxiety is a reflection of the patient's distress at the forbidden impulses which are veering close to consciousness. At the same time the anxiety serves to disguise the affect originally associated with the repressed wish. By concealing the pleasurable aspect of the wish, the anxiety protects the dreamer from a troubling piece of self-knowledge. The dreamer's response to the dream involved shock and dismay at hearing such a terrible thing. Her anxiety reassured her that she finds such acts reprehensible, not desirable.

A second example of an anxiety dream involves a senior partner in an accounting firm describing a dream in which the content of the wish is distorted but the affect is not repressed. *"An important client of mine came to the office. I was on the telephone and couldn't speak to him right away. He asked M for a copy of a new ruling. M gave it to him. I was furious."* The dreamer continues, *"I woke up sweating. I couldn't go back to sleep. I kept thinking about ways to get M fired if he acted in such an unprofessional way."*

The manifest content of the dream reveals little reason for the eruption of anxiety: the episode in the office is innocuous. However, the dreamer's childhood rage at having been usurped by a younger brother has not been repressed. The dreamwork has disguised the circumstances which gave rise to the anger, but the quality of the original affect remains intact. Freud (1916–17) suggests that it is easier to distort the content of a wish than the affect connected to it and stresses that in mental life, affect and content can exist independently from each other. Anxiety accompanies the dreamer's wish to destroy his younger brother. At the same time, the intensity of the anxiety serves a defensive function. By waking the dreamer, anxiety prevents him from expressing his destructive impulses more fully in the dream. "Anxiety dreams are as a rule also arousal dreams: we usually interrupt our sleep before the repressed wish has put its fulfilment through completely in spite of censorship" (Freud 1916–17:217).

## The Role of Anxiety in Dreams

Freud originally conceived of anxiety as dammed-up sexual energy associated with an unconscious wish: the libido vested in the unconscious impulse provides the energy for the dreamwork. However, even in the earliest version of the *The Interpretation of*

*Dreams,* Freud indicated that anxiety connected to dreams could serve a variety of purposes—including that of alerting the dreamer to a psychologically dangerous situation. Anxiety could disguise or enhance the disguise of a forbidden impulse, or, by waking the dreamer, could protect him by ending the dream before the impulse was clearly elaborated or revealed. The view of anxiety as a signal of impending distress articulated in this early text remains a cornerstone of the psychoanalytic theory of psychopathology.

## Typical Dreams Associated with Anxiety

Freud's discussions of typical dreams illustrates his view that anxiety plays a variety of roles in dreaming. Typical dreams are part of our common experience: dreams of missing a train, facing a difficult examination, having a tooth pulled, appearing undressed in public, losing a loved one, etc. Initially Freud indicated that such dreams are particularly resistant to interpretation through associations. Nonetheless, he pointed out the common wishes and inhibitions expressed in such dreams. In "embarrassing dreams of being naked," for instance, the universal desire of childhood to show oneself undressed is enacted while the dreamer experiences shame. Shame or anxiety is a reaction to the wish *and* protects the dreamer from knowing that he retains an early impulse to exhibit himself. In 1914, after consolidating his position on the presence of universal symbols in dreams, Freud indicated that such symbols often permit access to the meaning of typical dreams and are especially useful when associations fail to lead to the latent dream thoughts as may well be the case when dreams are laden with symbols.

That Freud visualized the defensive purpose of anxiety is affirmed in his discussion of dreams concerning the death of a loved one. Dreams in which a loved person dies fall into two categories: those in which there is sorrow attached to the death and those in which there is no grief. The second group, he argues, are not relevant because in these dreams the manifest content of a death is used to conceal some other wish which varies from individual to individual. To illustrate Freud offers the example (one he used frequently) of a woman who dreamed that she saw her nephew lying in a coffin. The latent dream thoughts involve the wish to encounter a man she had met at the funeral of another nephew, not a death wish. However, when dreams involving the death of a loved one are accompanied by distress, anxiety is produced because the unconscious wish for a death is blatantly satisfied in the dream. The destructive wishes expressed in such dreams are believed to be rooted in the sibling and oedipal rivalries of childhood. These dreams belong to the group of dreams discussed earlier in which the content of the wish is not sufficiently hidden. Again, anxiety is a reponse to unacceptable wishes *and* serves to disguise them.

Anxiety plays a different role in typical examination dreams. Dreams in which someone is either required to take an exam he has already taken or fails an exam he has already passed usually have the same meaning for all dreamers. Such dreams revive memories of having been punished for misbehavior or failures in childhood and arise when one has acted badly or expects to be unsuccessful. This explanation stresses the importance of day-to-day experiences on anxiety dreams, a position emphasized by later theorists (see the section on anxiety dreams in children). An additional explanation, added in 1909, suggests that examination dreams illustrate a particularly subtle form of wish fulfillment.

Using an observation made by Stekel that people always dream about exams which they have passed, not those which they have failed, Freud offers the following analysis. Such dreams occur when the dreamer is confronting a new task and is unsure of the outcome. The anxiety experienced in the dream reflects a day residue. After awakening the dreamer is consoled by the thought that he has in fact already passed the exam in question and does not need to worry.

The dreamer recapitulates an old anxiety—one which is no longer appropriate—in order to convince himself that the contemporary anxiety is also inappropriate. By displacing the contemporary anxiety onto the past, he attempts to satisfy the wish that there is nothing to worry about in the present, that things will work out well as they once did. Interestingly, these interpretations focus on preoccupations which are to a large extent conscious and downplay the contribution of early impulses. In this sense they anticipate the role of ego and superego functions in dreaming which have been elaborated in recent psychoanalytic thinking.

## Punishment Dreams

Another class of anxiety dreams, those in which the dreamer finds himself in a clearly disturbing, terrifying, or humiliating situation, is delineated in *The Interpretation of Dreams* and discussed in later works on dreams. Freud agrees to call these dreams punishment dreams, but emphasizes that they too represent wish fulfillments. They satisfy the part of the personality which recoils from certain impulses and deems them worthy of punishment. It seems possible that some examination dreams may fall within this category. Such dreams gratify a masochistic wish and may, in addition, satisfy other impulses. In a 1919 addition to *The Interpretation of Dreams,* Freud amended the description of punishment dreams to include developments in the theory of psychic structures.

> Thus punishment-dreams indicate the possibility that the ego may have a greater share than was supposed in the construction of dreams. The mechanism of dream-formation would in general be greatly clarified if instead of the opposition between 'conscious' and 'unconscious' we were to speak of that between the 'ego' and the 'repressed'. (Freud 1900:558)

And, in 1930, he added a footnote stressing the relevance of the superego, "one of the later findings of psychoanalysis" (p. 558) to such dreams.

The idea that an aspect of the psyche reacts to protect the individual from awareness of an objectionable wish while another demands payment for such impulses anticipates the current psychoanalytic view that dreams are the product of a compromise between id, ego, and superego forces.

## Contemporary Views of Anxiety Dreams

The interplay of intrapsychic forces can be seen in the following dream which may be designated as a punishment dream but also reveals characteristics of the dreamer's defensive operations and affords a picture of the balance between impulse, defense, and superego prohibitions:

*I was sitting in the front seat of a car with my father driving. It was an old Pontiac. My mother and sister were in the back seat. The scenery was beautiful. My father went up a curvy road to the top of a mountain. There was going to be a beautiful view. My mother screamed "Watch out!" My father crashed into a tree. I was flung out and pinned against the tree by the car. I was paralyzed and woke up screaming.*

A 27-year-old man awoke in terror from this dream following a gratifying sexual experience with a young woman whom he admired. A small piece of the interpretive work done with this dream is used for illustration. Associations to the scenery included a series of childhood memories in which his mother and sister changed into bathing suits and everyone went swimming together. Contact with the family members in the water was exciting and pleasurable.

It is proposed that efforts by the ego to disguise and deal with erotic feelings toward mother and sister and competitive strivings toward father are seen in many aspects of the dream. Thus the beautiful curves of the women are represented by the mountains and road; the attempt to distance himself from the women and identify with the father are seen in the seating arrangements. By yielding the driver's seat, the dreamer retreats from certain aspects of the oedipal struggle. Clearly negative and positive presumed oedipal wishes appear in the dream, and to some extent the arrangements are wish-fulfilling as well as defensive. Despite these attempts by the ego to strike a compromise between oedipal strivings and acceptable pleasures, it is further proposed that internalized prohibitions against such strivings are aroused. The conclusion of the dream seems to indicate that brutal punishment inflicted by father—one which will interfere with sexual activities—is mandated by the superego.

The exciting sexual encounter of the previous evening had stirred deeply rooted sexual and aggressive wishes. At this point the patient was not able to fully distinguish contemporary feelings of sexual pleasure and conquest from those associated with the figures of his childhood. The identification with his father which bolstered his sense of competence and offered him satisfaction in his professional life could not protect him from superego censure in situations which produced intense sexual arousal. Similarly, his love of hiking and travel remained unconflicted as long as it could be kept isolated from erotic fantasies and the hostility and fear of retribution accompanying them. Following an experience of intense stimulation, the ego could not negotiate a successful compromise and anxiety erupted.

Compromise is rooted in efforts of the ego to maintain an equilibrium which protects the individual from anxiety. Altman (1969) maintains that the psychoanalytic process with its goal of dismantling maladaptive defenses creates temporary ruptures in this equilibrium which may provoke an increase in anxiety dreams. While the experience of an anxiety dream is stressful, working on the dream in an analytic setting permits the ego to confront and potentially integrate conflictual material. The anxiety dream "by concretizing anxiety and placing it in perspective, prepares the patient to bear distress in the face of the upsurging unconscious" (Altman 1969:98). Anxiety dreams may also indicate that the analyst, by making premature interpretations, has pushed the patient to examine material which the ego is not able to integrate. Such anxiety dreams are an artifact of the psychoanalytic process which may serve valuable diagnostic and therapeutic functions. However, Altman stresses that each step in the analysis which reveals unconscious material elicits anxiety in some form which will persist until there has been a reordering of the balance of intrapsychic forces.

The impact of the therapists' interpretation of dreams on dreaming is discussed in different but complementary terms by Palombo (1978), who hypothesizes that dreaming serves an adaptive function in relation to memory. Using an information-processing model, he suggests that dreams facilitate the integration of new experiences into the permanent memory structure by linking them with relevant experiences of the past. The analysis of a dream provides the dreamer with new information which is incorporated in subsequent dreams and leads to modifications of the sense of self and others obtained in childhood.

The dream discussed earlier in which a woman is warned by her analyst not to turn out like her friend was the first in a series of dreams which followed the type of progression suggested by Palombo. In subsequent dreams, the patient was involved with symbolically incestuous figures in a number of ways. Although she awoke from these later dreams with considerable anxiety, she was neither horrified nor profoundly troubled by the dreams on the days following them, as she had been after the first dream. She herself identified the figures in the dreams as representations of her father, and was able to recall feelings of possessiveness and jealousy in reaction to him. A range of emotions, once banished to the unconscious, could be worked through and integrated. Analyses of these dreams gave her access to a clearer, more fully elaborated view of herself and her relationships with her father and brothers.

## Night Terrors and Traumatic Dreams

Freud's attention to night terrors, or pavor nocturnus, and to post-traumatic dreams, two additional types of anxiety dreams, is particularly noteworthy in the light of current psychophysiological research and investigations of the role of anxiety dreams in children and adults. In these instances we are reminded once more of Freud's assiduous efforts to make a distinction between similar but not identical phenomena. In 1895, Freud described night terrors as an attack of hysteria or anxiety which takes place during sleep. In the earliest version of *The Interpretation of Dreams* he offered an explanation of the circumstances which might lead to "night terrors accompanied by hallucinations . . . which are so frequent in children" (1900:585). Freud reasoned that such an outburst of anxiety may occur when a child has witnessed intercourse between adults and has not been able to integrate his reactions to such a scene.

He speculated that research into such experiences would demonstrate a correlation between night terrors and an intensification of sexual drive which could be brought about *either* by sexually stimulating situations or by shifts in the child's psychological development. In 1900, he wrote that he did not have sufficient evidence to affirm this hypothesis, but by 1919, he added that a great deal of data corroborating his view had appeared in writings of psychoanalysts.

In *Beyond the Pleasure Principle,* Freud addresses the phenomenon of frightening dreams which repeat traumatic episodes. The individual suffering from a traumatic neurosis recapitulates scenes of an accident; the soldier relives grim events of the war; the psychoanalytic patient is brought back to painful situations of childhood. This tendency to recall traumatic situations perplexed and troubled Freud. Such repetitions were not consistent with the function of dreaming. This class of dreams could not be adequately explained as wish fulfillments and did not serve the pleasure principle: "These dreams are endeavouring to master the stimulus retrospectively, by developing the anxiety whose omission was the cause of the traumatic neurosis" (1920:32).

The explanation of trauma in *Beyond the Pleasure Principle* anticipates the distinction between automatic and signal anxiety elaborated in 1926, although Freud was not yet consistent in maintaining this distinction. Freud postulated that trauma occurs when the individual has no forewarning of a distressing situation or the circumstances are of such devastating dimensions that preparation would not help. He is overwhelmed by the situation. The compulsion to repeat such devastating events in dreams reflects a mental function "independent" of and "more primitive" than the pleasure principle. The terror aroused by traumatic situations needs to be modified, brought to manageable proportions before the pleasure principle can be dominant. The motive to recall distressing events involves more than an interplay between repressed wishes and reaction against those wishes. The return to devastating experiences represents an attempt to integrate the trauma.

## Psychophysiological Investigations of Traumatic Dreams, Nightmares, and Night Terrors

Current research supports Freud's clinical impressions that certain disturbing dreams are qualitatively different from others. However, the question of the role of dreams in mastering anxiety is a complex one and remains the subject of considerable investigation. Data from the sleep laboratory and from clinical observations indicate that some disturbing dreams involve adaptive psychophysiological mechanisms while others represent a dramatic failure to contain anxiety.

Recent psychophysiological investigations of sleep and dreams indicate that night terrors and *some* post-traumatic dreams do belong to a particular class of psychophysiological events (Fisher et al 1970, 1973). Dream research reveals two distinct types of frightening sleep disturbances: those which arise in REM sleep (stage 1) and are by far the most prevalent, and those which occur during NREM sleep (Fisher et al. 1970, 1973; Kales et al. 1980). Although either experience might be called a nightmare by the dreamer, contempory theoreticians have begun to reserve the term "nightmare" for profoundly disturbing anxiety dreams occurring in REM sleep (Fisher et al. 1970, 1973; Mack 1970; Kales et al. 1980). *The difference between anxiety dreams and nightmares is a quantitative one and depends on the subjective evaluation of the dreamer.*

Night terrors, on the other hand, refer to the massive eruption of anxiety associated with arousal from slow-wave NREM sleep. Stage 4 arousal reactions are the most severe sleep disturbances. Night terrors of children and of adults (many of which originated in childhood) and some post-traumatic dreams belong to this group. The post-traumatic dream also occurs in REM sleep (Fisher et al. 1973; Greenberg et al. 1972; Blitz and Greenberg 1984). Whether a trauma will result in a night terror or a REM nightmare cannot be predicted, since neither the extent of the trauma nor the psychological health of the individual adequately accounts for the outcome. However, Fisher et al. (1973:96) suggest that a REM nightmare is the more likely development because night terrors are "relatively rare while conflict and trauma are ubiquitous." Night terrors occur infrequently. It has been estimated that between 1 and 5 percent of children experience them and that the incidence in adults is much lower (Kales et al. 1968). Nightmares are a common experience in childhood and not unusual in adults (Kales et al. 1980).

Although nightmares and night terrors are now defined in terms of the stage of sleep in which they arise, they can for the most part be easily distinguished outside of the sleep laboratory (Fisher et al. 1970, 1973; Kales et al. 1980). Nightmares develop during REM sleep, involve a lack of motility, and consist of an elaborate dream sequence which may last from 5 to 20 minutes.

The distinction between the physiological correlates and the adaptive aspects of REM nightmares and night terrors is striking. In REM nightmares, the dreamer's subjective experience of anxiety may be correlated with slight increases in respiratory, cardiac, or eye-movement rate. However, about one-half of the time, REM anxiety dreams are not accompanied by increases in autonomic functioning. Interestingly, individuals who have highly alarming stage 4 arousals often have undisturbed, peaceful REM sleep on the same night, even when the night terrors and REM dreams involve the same material. Fisher and his coworkers hypothesize a desomatization mechanism during REM dreams which diminishes the physiological concomitants of anxiety and may protect the individual from experiencing overwhelming anxiety in a number of ways. The desomatization mechanism may preserve sleep by diminishing the level of anxiety during an anxiety dream. It may minimize the extent of the disturbance if sleep is interrupted or may interfere with the development of secondary anxiety as a reaction to increased heart rate or respiration. The anxiety in REM dreams is generally contained and controlled.

The anxiety in night terrors is massive and out of control. The characteristics of this "sudden, instantaneous, cataclysmic event" are enumerated by Fisher and his coauthors (1970:780, 1973): (1) an anguished, bloodcurdling scream or cry for help; (2) a rapid acceleration of autonomic discharge—heart rate may double or triple in 15 to 30 seconds; (3) a state of arousal marked by disorientation and hallucinations; (4) motility or somnambulism, which may involve a flight response; (5) an EEG pattern indicating wakefulness although the individual is not fully alert; (6) difficulty in remembering what was dreamed, and onset of amnesia for the entire experience. When the content in such an awakening is remembered it usually consists of a single frightening image.

Fisher and his coauthors conclude that *while REM nightmares appear to involve adaptive integrative mechanisms which help the dreamer deal with internal conflicts and past traumas, night terrors represent the inability of the ego to cope with anxiety.* Research which examines the content of dreams in relation to the dreamer's life situation (Breger et al. 1971; Greenberg and Pearlman 1975) indicates that REM dreams provide a channel for internally negotiating problematic emotions and circumstances. Furthermore, there is evidence that REM sleep facilitates the capacity to perform complex tasks in waking life (Pearlman 1982).

Someone in the throes of a night terror is utterly helpless and panic striken. The crucial ego functions have failed him. Since night terrors arise when the ego is in a severely regressed state, when the defenses and reality testing are weakened, such traumatic dreams cannot be described as attempts to master anxiety. Rather, they may be thought of as "a symptom, a pathological formation . . . brought about by a rift in the ego's capacity to control anxiety" (Fisher et al. 1973:96). Night terrors which begin in childhood may continue for decades into adult life, suggesting that this type of anxiety remains unmodulated, inaccessible to the expanding resources of the ego.

## Traumatic Nightmares and Narcissistic Disorders

Blitz and Greenberg (1984:105) report that most traumatic nightmares associated with traumatic war neuroses take place during REM sleep and consist of scenes closely related to terrifying experiences:

> The incidents appear *unintegrated* with or unelaborated by the veterans' current or previous experiences. This lack of integration in the nightmare appears to have parallels in the traumatized person's sense of himself. The veteran frequently reports feeling that he has lost something of himself. . . . Current relationships and accomplishments do not

appear to be able to mitigate the sense that something has shattered inside.

In reviewing the psychodynamic literature concerned with war neuroses, they conclude that such traumatic disorders as well as traumatic nightmares are more likely to occur in people who have never established a well-articulated, separate identity and who have defined themselves through merger with others. Individuals suffering from narcissistic structural deficits in Kohut's sense have great difficulty integrating traumatic experiences either in their waking lives or during REM sleep. The adaptive potential of dreaming is often unavailable to them.

Blitz and Greenberg emphasize the relevance of Kohut's position that some dreams reflect the condition of the self and are not particularly accessible to interpretation in terms of conflict. Nightmares in which the dreamer's life is threatened "can be interpreted as mental representations of an imperiled self, that is a self that is potentially fragmenting" (1984:118). In working with such dreams, they argue, it is crucial to attend to the dreamer's experience of himself as vulnerable, deteriorating, and subject to annihilation rather than to the symbolic meaning of the dream. The manifest dream communicates its deepest meaning. The authors report that such interpretive work is effective and that subsequent dreams will show the integration of traumatic events. Their formulations offer a seemingly useful way of viewing traumatic neuroses and traumatic dreams. However, the work of Fisher and Mack, among others, indicates that traumatic dreams also reflect internal conflict. It would seem that a comprehensive therapeutic approach should attend to both problems of the self and struggles between impulse and defense.

Mack (1970) warns against making simplistic determinations about which dreams serve an adaptive function. He suggests, for instance, that if someone suffers from a lifetime of repetitive nightmares we cannot assume that the nightmare does not offer protection from anxiety. Perhaps it permits the dreamer to relegate to the sleeping state a conflictual area which would otherwise disturb his daily functioning. The complex relationship between the eruption of massive anxiety in dreams (dreams designated as nightmares) and other psychological variables has been examined by Hartmann (1984). He posits that a tendency toward nightmares is associated with sensitivity to both physical and interpersonal stimuli, creativity, and vulnerability to psychopathology. He concludes that individuals who suffer from nightmares seem to be characterized by "thin or permeable boundaries" which may interfere with the differentiation between sleep and wakefulness, fantasy and reality, and self and other.

## Children's Anxiety Dreams

Freud (1900) originally proposed that the dreams of young children represent simple wish fulfillments which are easily understood if we are familiar with the child's daily life. In early formulations he vacillates between presenting a rather idyllic view of children's dreams in which longings for sweets and family expeditions are satisfied and suggesting that children are particularly vulnerable to anxiety dreams. Although he consistently maintained that children may have undisguised, undistorted dreams reflecting their daily experiences, he soon amended the notion that there is a clear distinction between the dreams of children and those of adults, indicating that children's dreams are often the product of conflict and compromise and contain distortions (1909, 1916–17). Undisguised wish-fulfillment dreams, on the other hand, occur in adults also: the dreams of starving prisoners and explorers attest to this. In the description of night terrors discussed above, Freud clearly suggests that events in the child's life as well as conflicts arising out of developmental changes may lead to dreams of intense anxiety.

## Ego Development and Anxiety Dreams

Contemporary psychoanalytic investigations of anxiety dreams in children and adolescents focus on the comparative effect of intrapsychic conflicts, developmental shifts, and environmental circumstances. Fraiberg (1950), Nagera (1966) and Mack (1965, 1970) stress the importance of investigating the sleep disturbances of early life in relation to normal maturation and ego development. Nagera argues that disruptions in sleep, especially during the second year of life when they are commonplace, reflect anxieties consistent with the immature ego of that period. At this time instinctual conflicts should be thought of as playing a negligible or secondary role.

Any eruption of anxiety, including those connected with sleep, needs to be evaluated in terms of the ego's ability to comprehend, internalize, temper anxiety, and interpret reality. A child of 12 to 18 months (the last three months coincide with the early rapprochement stage described by Mahler et al. [1975]) is particularly vulnerable to trauma, since these ego functions are rudimentary, emotional object constancy is not yet established, and the distinction between dream life and reality is unclear. Anxiety dreams and nightmares of this period develop because the ego is unable to adequately integrate the child's daily experiences. Routine separations as well as painful or troubling events may lead to anxiety. Stabilization of object ties and the increased use of language at the end of the second year facilitate the child's capacity to tolerate anxiety.

In Nagera's view conflict becomes a more prominent source of anxiety dreams and sleep disturbances as the ego develops. The instinctual demands associated with particular stages of development as well as the child-rearing tactics of the parents and the unconscious conflicts of the parents may all contribute to sleep disturbances and anxiety dreams. Whether or not such disturbances will develop into neurotic symptoms depends on a range of internal and external conditions.

Fraiberg (1950), Mack (1965, 1970), and Ablon and Mack (1980) take the position that even at one year anxiety dreams stem from a subtle interplay between the child's drives, level of ego functioning, and daily experiences. Examining the dreams and life circumstances of children under 2 who suffered from sleep disturbances, Fraiberg found that anxiety dreams are the product of an interaction between the young ego's vulnerability to trauma and conflicts of the anal period. Initially, night waking from an anxiety dream follows a traumatic episode—one in which the child feels terror and helplessness. The ego cannot moderate the level of anxiety. Painful separations from a parent, attacks by an older child, or primal scene experiences might lead to such feelings. "The dream mechanism in the early stages of such sleep disturbances is likened to that of the traumatic neuroses in which the dreamer is brought back to the scene of the trauma and the dream work supplies the conditions of apprehension and anticipation which had failed in their protective functions at the time of the original event" (Fraiberg 1950:308).

Toilet training precipitates conflicts between the wish to soil and fear of loss of parental love. If, during this period, the child is subject to disturbing experiences which leave him feeling helpless and unprotected, his anxiety over parental disapproval is exacerbated. In such cases dreams expressing anal impulses may well lead to anxious arousals, since the consequence of satisfying such wishes fills the child with dread. If such an internal struggle is not alleviated—if parental imperatives for control or the traumatic external conditions are not altered—the anxious awakenings can become more severe and can disrupt the child's day as well as his sleep patterns. In addition, failure to strike a balance between impulse and defense at one psychosexual stage increases the likelihood that the conflicts of subsequent stages will be incorporated into the sleep disturbance.

In studying the nightmares of children from infancy to advanced latency who did not have serious pathology, Mack (1965) focused on the content of the dreams and on the circumstances in which they occurred. In addition, he asked how the child mastered the anxiety of the dream, both within the dream and in response to the dream, and he examined the structural changes in dreams in relation to ego development. He returned to these issues in a comprehensive work on nightmares (1970). Mack concluded that *nightmares reflect conflicts and anxieties of a particular developmental stage and may indicate that a child is about to take an important developmental step. The manifest and latent content of the nightmare also express earlier conflicts which are revived in sleep.*

Often, for instance, conflicts associated with later developmental stages are depicted in oral terms in a nightmare (Mack 1970). In such instances, the struggles around devouring and being devoured, characteristic of the early years of life, are replayed in the nightmare. Such a revival of early conflicts, in Mack's view, accounts for the similar quality of nightmares throughout the life cycle. During the day, a sense of reality and the presence of supportive figures help protect the child from experiencing massive anxiety: during sleep he is open to such anxiety. Mack also confirms the finding that objectively threatening circumstances become intertwined with inner conflicts and unrealistic fears.

Nightmares of the first two years seem to leave the child overwhelmed by fear and incapable of modifying his distress without help from his parents. A 2–3-year-old can prepare himself for possible anxious disruptions of sleep by bedtime rituals. As the child's reality testing improves, he is able to reason with himself in order to control his panic. Between 6 and 8, the child is able to reassure himself while he is dreaming that "It's only a dream" or to wake himself out of a frightening dream. Mack (1970) indicates that it would be incorrect to describe such defensive measures as being directed against the unacceptable impulses expressed in the dream rather than against the nightmare or anxiety associated with it. He argues that the nightmare itself can have a profound influence on the dreamer and that he needs to cope with its effects.

The development of the ego offers the child additional skills to deal with the anxiety generated by a dream and allows for greater complexity in the structure of the dream. Even the dreams of 2–3-year-old children contain considerable symbolic displacements, condensations, and distortions which disguise the conflictual material in the dream and diminish the anxiety associated with it. Mack considers these mechanisms "amongst the earliest defensive operations of the immature ego, a kind of 'desperate creativity' aimed at reducing and mastering instinctual tension" (1965:425). As the child matures, the disguises of the dreamwork become more intricate, and the core issues may be far from obvious. Other aspects of the child's growth are also reflected in the content and structure of the dream. Evolving object relations and sexual differentiation are reflected in a shift from inanimate objects to animals to part objects to complete human figures. As the superego develops, defensive procedures are accelerated and "the oedipal 'principals' retreat once more behind a variety of totems, masks, costumes, and other disguises" (ibid.). Mack hypothesizes that the ego's ability to conceal forbidden impulses coupled with the child's enhanced reality testing contributes to the decline of nightmares during latency.

While Mack (1965, 1970) and Ablon and Mack (1980) caution against assuming that anxiety dreams involve a purposeful motive to master anxiety, they propose that anxiety dreams and nightmares offer a way to evaluate the child's capacity to deal with the internal and external forces with which he has to cope. Distressing dreams may indicate mastery and developmental progress or they may point to areas of trauma and conflict which leave the child open to massive anxiety and deficient ego functioning.

## Summary

Psychoanalytic formulations regarding anxiety dreams run parallel to the development of psychoanalysis as a whole. Freud was preoccupied with the question of disturbing dreams throughout his life. Eager to demonstrate that distressing dreams did not contradict the wish-fulfillment hypothesis, he articulated numerous ways in which the interplay between repressed wishes and dream censorship could result in an anxiety dream. His investigations of the role of censorship and the role of anxiety in dreams anticipate formulations about psychic agencies and processes contained in the structural model and the revised theory of anxiety. The view of the anxiety dream was amended to include the role of the ego and eventually of the superego.

Contemporary psychoanalytic theorists conceive of the dream as a compromise effected between id, ego, and superego forces. The dream offers a view of the dreamer's intrapsychic struggles and his reactions to the circumstances of his life. Anxiety indicates a disequilibrium, which needs to be evaluated in the context of the internal and external environment. If we examine a series of anxiety dreams reported in psychoanalytic sessions, for instance, a progressive integration of repressed material may be discerned.

Freud conceived of repetitive traumatic dreams as exceptions to the wish-fulfillment theory, as operating outside the pleasure principle. He noted that night terrors might also be the consequence of overwhelming stimulation. Current psychophysiological research distinguishes between anxiety dreams occuring in REM sleep and the uncontrolled night terrors of NREM sleep. The term "nightmare" is reserved for profoundly disturbing REM dreams. REM nightmares appear to involve adaptive mechanisms, while night terrors represent the inability of the ego to cope with anxiety. Post-traumatic dreams are usually REM nightmares. It has been suggested that susceptibility to such repetitive dreams bespeaks problems in individuation and sense of self.

The study of anxiety dreams in children confirms Freud's impressions that daily events, conflicts, and trauma have a profound influence on the dream life of children. Contemporary researchers hypothesize that anxiety dreams, in particular, reflect both current and earlier developmental conflicts and struggles and provide a measure of the child's level of ego functioning.

## References

Ablon, S. L. and J. E. Mack. 1980. Children's dreams reconsidered. In A. Solnit et al., eds., *The Psychoanalytic Study of the Child* 35:179–217. New Haven: Yale University Press.

Altman, L. L. 1969. *The Dream in Psychoanalysis.* New York: International Universities Press.

Blitz, R. and R. Greenberg. 1984. Nightmares of the traumatic war neurosis: Implications for theory and treatment. In H. J. Schwartz, ed., *Psychotherapy of the Combat Veteran,* pp. 103–23. New York: Spectrum.

Breger, L., I. Hunter, and R. Lane. 1971. *The Effect of Stress on Dreams.* Psychological Issues Monograph, no. 27. New York: International Universities Press.

Brenner, C. 1974. *An Elementary Textbook of Psychoanalysis.* New York: Anchor Press.

Brenner, C. 1976. *Psychoanalytic Technique and Psychic Conflict.* New York: International Universities Press.

Fisher, C., E. Kahn, A. Edwards, and D. Davis. 1973. A psychophysiological study of nightmares and night terrors. *Journal of Nervous and Mental Disease* 157:75–98.

Freud, S. *Standard Edition of the Complete Psychological Works of Sigmund Freud.* James Strachey, ed. and tr. 24 vols. London: Hogarth Press, 1953–1974; New York: Macmillan.

1895. On the grounds for detaching a particular syndrome from neuresthenia under the description "anxiety neurosis." 3:87–117.

1900. *The Interpretation of Dreams.* Vols. 4 and 5.

1901. On dreams, *The Interpretation of Dreams.* 5:629–86.

1909. *Analysis of a Phobia in a Five-Year-Old Boy.* Vol. 10.

1916–17. *Introductory Lectures on Psychoanalysis.* Vol. 5.

1920. *Beyond the Pleasure Principle.* Vol. 18.

1923. *The Ego and the Id.* Vol. 19

1926. Inhibitions, symptoms, and anxiety. 20:75–172.

1933. *New Introductionary Lectures on Psychoanalysis.* Vol. 22.

Greenberg, R. and C. Pearlman. 1975. REM sleep and the analytic process: A psychophysiologic bridge. *The Psychoanalytic Quarterly* 44:392–403.

Greenberg, R., C. A. Pearlman, and D. Gampel. 1972. War neurosis and the adaptive function of REM sleep. *British Journal of Medical Psychology* 45:27–31.

Hartmann, E. 1984. *The Nightmare.* New York: Basic Books.

Kales, J. D., A. Jacobson, and A. Kales. 1968. Sleep disorders in children. In L. E. Abt and B. F. Riess, eds., *Progress in Clinical Psychology,* pp. 63–75. New York: Grune and Stratton.

Kales, A., R. Soldatos, A. B. Caldwell, D. S. Charney, J. D. Kales, D. Market, and R. Cadieux. 1980. Nightmares: Clinical characteristics and personality patterns. *American Journal of Psychiatry* 137(10):1197–1201.

Laplanche J. and J.-B. Pontalis. 1973. *The Language of Psychoanalysis.* New York: Norton.

Mack, J. E. 1965. Nightmares, conflict, and ego development. *International Journal of Psycho-Analysis* 46:403–28.

Mack, J. E. 1970. *Nightmares and Human Conflict.* Boston: Little, Brown.

Mahler, M. S., F. Pine, and A. Bergman. 1975. *The Psychological Birth of the Human Infant.* New York: Basic Books.

Nagera, H. 1966. Sleep and its disturbances approached developmentally. In R. Eissler et al., eds., *The Psychoanalytic Study of the Child* 21:393–447. New York: International Universities Press.

Pearlman, C. 1982. Sleep structure variation and performance. In W. Webb, ed., *Biologic Rhythms, Sleep, and Performance.* New York: Wiley.

Palombo, S. R. 1978. *Dreaming and Memory.* New York: Basic Books.

# 10.

# Night Terrors in Children and Adults: Emotional and Biological Factors

SUSAN KNAPP

NIGHT TERRORS—PAVOR NOCTURNUS in children and incubus in adults—are dramatic episodes during which the sleeper suddenly erupts into what looks like a psychotic state. He or she may scream, cry, and thrash about, and often appears to be hallucinating some kind of mortal danger. Physiological changes include marked increase in heart rate, rapid and irregular deep breathing, dilated pupils, profuse sweating, and erratic and often violently heightened motility as the sleeper appears to attempt to fight or flee. Stern (1951:302) referred to these episodes as "one of the most striking manifestations of anxiety in human life." Gardner (1932:187) offers a vivid description of one of these episodes given by the mother of a 3-year-old boy:

> Last night his eyes were glazed and staring and his teeth were tight together with his lips drawn back and they were blue looking. He screamed *for half an hour* before we could make out what he was saying. The first word we got was "airplane." Then he started his old formula: "My hands, oh they hurt, help me, my hands, my hands." He finally quieted a little, but sobbed and sobbed. Then he started in again. This time it was "Go away, I don't love you [Mother.] I want my own Daddy. I want

Daddy." His daddy was holding him the entire time. Suddenly he jumped and relaxed. Daddy said he had looked at him as if he had never seen him before, and then smiled and cuddled down in his arms.

Night terrors are often confused with nightmares. The latter tend to occur with much more frequency and are common at all stages of life. Night terrors, on the other hand, can occur during adulthood but are for the most part a problem of children. The major distinction between the two, however, has been based on the elaborate content that the dreamer can provide upon waking or being awakened from the midst of a frightening dream or nightmare. In contrast, it is extremely difficult to rouse or comfort a sleeper during an episode of night terrors. These episodes usually last for only a few moments, but they can continue for up to 20 minutes. Then, almost as suddenly as the episode began, the sleeper falls back into a quiet sleep. There may be repeated episodes during the night, and yet the sleeper usually experiences total amnesia upon awakening the next morning. Fisher et al. (1974), however, found that if the sleeper spontaneously awakens at the end of an episode, it is possible in 65 percent of these instances to gather some mental content of the episode. This mental content, in most instances, is only a single frightening feeling or sensation such as falling, choking, being crushed, etc.

Other differences include the stages of sleep during which the two phenomena occur. Night terrors generally appear shortly after the onset of sleep and are confined to NREM or stage 4 sleep. More specifically, they take place during arousal from stage 4 sleep. Nightmares, on the other hand, take place during the REM stage of sleep and can occur throughout the night. Moreover, the tendency for night-terror episodes to disappear in most instances as the child grows older has led many writers, such as Broughton (1968), to call them an arousal disorder due to delayed maturation of the central nervous system. Thus there has been a trend in the literature for some writers to characterize the nightmare as more of a psychological disorder, while night terrors are seen as a more straightforward physiological disorder whose psychological content is somewhat epiphenominal. Table 10.1, taken from Keith (1975), summarizes these findings.

TABLE 10.1. A Comparison of Night Terrors and Anxiety Dreams

| | *Night Terrors* (Pavor nocturnus: classic "nightmare" of E. Jones; incubus attack: dreams of the traumatic neurosis) | *Anxiety Dreams* ("Bad" dream: common nightmare; REM nightmares) |
|---|---|---|
| EEG characteristics | Occurs in stage 4 sleep with arousal to an awake (alpha) pattern; 70% are in the first non-REM period of the night. | Occurs during REM sleep; no particular time of night. |
| Physiological characteristics | Very rapid changes, with increase in pulse usually over 108; rapid breathing; periods of apnea; intense autonomic activation (Sweating, mydriasis, etc.). | Gradual increase in pulse, usually into the 90s; little autonomic activation. |
| Motility | Always great activity (thrashing, sitting up), and often somnambulism. Children more active than adults. | Lesser movement; no somnambulism; decreased muscle tone. |
| Verbalizations | Almost always present at onset and usually during the episode. May include screaming. | May be present, but subdued. |
| Mental content | Single overwhelming feeling or memory; elaborate dream only 10%; violently aggressive, terrifying content. | Elaborate, vivid, longer duration; lesser anxiety; more disguised dynamics. |
| Mental state if awakened | Confused, disoriented, unresponsive to the environment; hard to calm; usually amnesic. | Lucid very quickly; can be calmed, clear memory of the dream. |

SOURCE: Paul Keith, "Night terrors: A review of the psychology, neurophysiology, and therapy," *Journal of the American Academy of Child Psychiatry* 14:479, © 1975 by American Academy of Child Psychiatry; reprinted by permission of the author and publisher.

## Incidence

Reports of children suffering from night terrors begin occurring regularly in the medical and psychiatric literature in the late 1800s. These early references establish that night terrors are a long-standing, identifiable syndrome in children. The overall incidence of night terrors is not, however, particularly high. J. Kales et al. (1968) report at least one incidence of night terrors in all children between the ages of 5 and 12 years of age. Clardy and Hill (1949) in a study of 100 children from an inpatient psychiatric unit found a 7 percent incidence of night terrors. These findings seem to be consistent with those of other researchers. When one looks at a sample of children who have been specifically identified as suffering from sleep disorders, the numbers understandably get much higher. Anthony (1959) looked at this type of population and found that in children from 4 to 7 years of age, 63 percent suffered from night terrors. The percentage dropped to 24 children between the ages of 8 and 10 and to 13 in children between 11 and 14. Anthony (1959) and J. Kales et al. (1968) report the incidence of night terrors in all children at from 1 to 4 percent. They further state that their occurrence in adults is much rarer—a finding that other writers seem to support.

It is not surprising that attitudes of parents versus professionals toward the incidence of night terrors in children differ considerably. Many professionals see this disorder as a temporary childhood idiosyncracy which they feel the child will outgrow. Parents, on the other hand, are often quite upset by the child's apparent distress. Some professionals do, however, see these episodes as potentially serious. Keith (1975) for example, states that in those instances in which night terrors occur as often as 3 to 4 times a week over a period of months, the episodes should be seen as evidence of serious pathology. Moreover, almost all writers consider that night terrors in adults are quite serious.

## Etiology

Theories as to the etiology of night terrors can be roughly divided into those in which a psychodynamic explanation is and is not attempted. Before Freud there were a variety of explanations ranging from demonic possession to various physical syndromes. Freud's writing on dreams began a new way of looking at this phenomenon. Freud (1895) saw night terrors in adults to be a kind of anxiety attack, while those in children had an element of hysteria in addition to being part of a general anxiety neurosis. In his *Interpretation of Dreams* (1900:585) he tied these attacks to sexual impulses which the child did not understand and was attempting to repudiate:

> Investigations would probably show a periodicity in the occurrence of the attacks, since an increase in sexual libido can be brought about not only by accidental exciting impressions but also by successive waves of spontaneous developmental processes.

Jones (1931) in the early 1900s was the first of Freud's followers actually to treat a case of pavor nocturnus in an adult. He saw the patient's problem as being due to psychosexual conflict. He was, however, reluctant to discuss pavor nocturnus in children because he felt that not enough was known about infantile sexuality.

Other psychoanalysts accepted Freud's position and found support for it in their work. A number of 1930s studies show this Freudian orientation. Waelder (1946) reported a successful analysis of a 7-year-old boy suffering from pavor nocturnus. She found that the attacks expressed the typical conflicts aroused by a rather dramatic oedipal triangle. Following Freud's theory of the relationship between sleep and symptom formation, Waelder proposed that night terrors were a symbolic expression of the child's conflictual feelings which were allowed to emerge by the lessening of repression under the conditions of sleep. Deutsch (1951) stated that night terrors are one of the most common neurotic symptoms of childhood. "Pavor nocturnus is *par excellence* the most intense expression of that infantile anxiety which lets us see the difficulties which even a normal child has to contend with in his psychological development" (1951:32). Deutsch reported on a case of a young man suffering from pavor nocturnus who had also had attacks during his childhood. She believed that oedipal conflicts were the source of these attacks, but she also stressed the importance of conflicts related to masturbation. She felt that a sense of immobilization is, for example, an attempt to avoid masturbation and the punishment that it would prompt. Gardner (1932) reported on 15 cases of childhood and adolescent night terrors. Using psychoanalytic play-therapy techniques, he gathered data which led him to believe that the threat of mutilation was at the root these episodes. Klein (1963), reporting on her treatment of several young girls, stated that their night terrors were a repetition of their daytime anxiety attacks. Klein interpreted these attacks as representing oedipal aggression and the fear that it creates. Later, Mack (1965) pointed out that, in addition to reflecting current conflicts in the child's life, pavor nocturnus attacks, like dreams, include earlier conflicts which have become reactivated.

Stern (1951) offers an interesting explanation for the physical sensations such as choking, inability to move, etc. Like Deutsch, Waelder, etc., he believes that night terrors are the result of intense sexual impulses experienced during sleep which arouse a level of anxiety too great for the child's ego to master. Stern hypothesizes that because the child is unable to discharge this massive anxiety, he experiences a catatonic reaction in response to the psychogenic shock that the anxiety creates. This "catatonic reaction" explains the physical symptoms which, Stern says, the sleeper then links to the content of the dream, making it seem even more real.

Sperling (1958) divided night terrors into three distinct types. Type 1, or the psychotic type, begins in the second or third year of life and may go on through puberty. Children who fall into this category are subject to sexual overstimulation from the parents, siblings, or other members of their environment. In response to this overstimulation, the child begins to act out sexually. This acting out is met with harsh repression, and a vicious circle is created in which the child internalizes two conflicting sets of values. The night terrors then become the arena in which the forbidden sexual and aggressive impulses are allowed to emerge in contrast to their rigid repression during the day. Sperling compares these night terrors to certain psychotic and fugue states. When these episodes continue through adolescence, the child invariably goes on to develop serious character disorders, perversions, or psychoses.

The second type or type 2 night terrors are called the traumatic type because they begin in response to acute physical or emotional trauma. They can occur in a child of any age and are quite similar to dreams of adults who are suffering from traumatic war neurosis. In the night terror the child recreates the original trauma, but then, by awakening, is able to gain a measure of mastery, in that escape is now possible. Sperling feels that the prognosis for this kind of night terror is also similar to that of traumatic war neurosis in that, if there is subsequent pathological development, the child may develop neurotic, psychosomatic, or psychotic disturbance. Sperling calls type 3 night terrors the neurotic type. She sees these as almost identical to the adult night terrors described by Jones. Keith (1975) points out, however, that what Sperling is calling neurotic night terrors are in fact not night terrors at all. Rather they are typical REM sleep anxiety dreams in which oedipal conflict leads to the formation of a dream.

## Research Findings

Researchers using sleep laboratories have been able to provide a major source of information about sleep disorders. This information augments and in some instances poses questions regarding the data gathered by psychoanalytic investigation. In these laboratories subjects can be continuously monitored as to their various physiological changes, sleep stages can be carefully followed, and all behaviors can be observed and recorded. Attempts to explain night terrors as stemming from physiological as opposed to psychodynamic factors have always been part of the literature. These have included explanations linking night terrors with gastrointestinal infections (Still 1900), migraine headaches (Shackle 1928), and diseased adenoids (Agrell and Axelsson 1972).

A. Kales et al. (1980) studied the families of 52 patients who suffered from either or both sleepwalking and night terrors. They determined that hereditary factors predispose the individual to develop one or both of these syndromes. They further state that the expression of the trait may indeed be influenced by environmental factors. In an earlier paper J. Kales et al. (1979) had suggested that febrile illness was a potential causal factor in provoking a tendency toward night terrors and sleepwalking. Other epidemiological studies, including that by Hallstrom (1972), lend further support to the genetic predisposition theory.

J. Kales et al. (1980), in a study of 40 adults who suffered from night terrors, evaluated personality patterns of these adults and found that they exhibited "an inhibition of outward expression of aggression and a predominance of anxiety, depression, obsessive compulsive tendencies and phobicness." Moreover, these researchers decided that, while night terrors in children seem to have clear relationship to genetic and developmental factors, they believe that "their persistence and especially their onset in adulthood are . . . related more to psychological factors" (1980:1413). These findings as well as those from sleep-laboratory experiments suggest the interplay of physiological and psychological factors in night terrors.

Gastaut and Broughton (1965) were the first researchers to report actual data gathered during a night-terror episode. One of their most startling discoveries was that night terrors arise out of stage 4 sleep. Since dreams do not occur in stage 4 sleep but only in REM sleep, and since nightmares are clearly a kind of dream, Gastaut and Broughton's findings made it clear that there are fundamental differences between night terrors and nightmares. Gastaut and Broughton further found that, during episodes of night terrors, in addition to a marked tachycardia, there was hypernea, and occasionally brief but complete apnea. They proposed that the apnea accounted for the individual's phenomenological sensation of suffocating. Hartmann (1984:254), however, states that recent data from studies of sleep apnea have demonstrated that a reduction of the oxygen supply to the brain does not lead to the formation of nightmares. Finally, Gastaut and Broughton (1965), in a study which included 5 adults, 1 adolescent, and 7 children, observed that children who suffered from night terrors rarely displayed daytime anxiety, while the opposite was true for adults.

EEG findings from Gastaut and Broughton's research also provided valuable information. Because these findings showed a sudden shift from slow-wave or delta activity to an awake or alpha rhythm pattern, Broughton (1968, 1970) described night terrors as a "disorder of arousal." By disordered arousal Broughton meant that while the sleeper's EEG reading corresponds to a waking state, his mental state is confused and there is evidence of impaired or diminished cerebral reactivity. In contrast to the normal clear-headedness that most individuals experience upon awakening, this sleeper shows the physiological signs of being awake without really being so. Instead he shows "a continuation of responsiveness typical of nonREM sleep" (Broughton 1968:1074). Moreover, there appears to be some inhibition of visual pathways. Broughton feels that it is this postarousal confusional state that leads to the seemingly bizarre symptoms of night terrors. He suggests that those individuals who suffer from what he calls classical sleep disorders "appear to manifest physiological changes which predispose them to attacks," and that these physiological changes "may be enhanced during some nights, culminating in an attack" (1968:1076).

Thus Broughton is proposing that the origin of night terrors is a biological anomaly which, for reasons unknown, predisposes certain individuals to suddenly go from deep sleep to a state of incomplete arousal. The question that arises is whether this state of arousal is triggered by a shift in psychological defense which allows for the emergence of threatening psychological content and its attendent anxiety. Broughton agrees that this biological-psychological interaction is indeed quite possible, and this is obviously the position that a psychoanalyst would be inclined to take. Broughton points out, however, that it is quite difficult to evaluate this position because of the difficulty in determining whether the frightening mental content that is gathered upon arousal is actually an attempt to make sense of the disturbing physiological changes. These physiological changes, such as tachycardia and hypernea, are part of the "disordered arousal" that he feels in inherent in the night-terror episode. He adds,

> The possibility must even be entertained that such disorders arise from a "psychological void," and that even the symptoms specific to the attack types are due to abnormally marked physiological responses during the recurrent slow-wave arousal episode (bladder contraction, producing enuresis; sensorium impairment, leading to somnambulism; cardiorespiratory changes, giving rise to terror). (Broughton 1968:1077)

It is the old argument about whether the man is running because he is scared or scared because he is running. Moreover, Broughton suggests that in the instance of night terrors it is an argument which may be unanswerable. He believes that any mental activity which may or may not have existed in the slow-wave sleep before the attack would probably be erased upon arousal, just as the attack itself is erased. Therefore, he states that "We may be faced with a biological example of the indeterminacy principle" (ibid.).

Fischer et al. (1973b, 1974) support most of Broughton's basic physiological findings, but because of the nature of their data they are much more confident in stating that night terrors are precipitated by a lowering of psychological defense. They base their assumptions on the fact that in contrast to Broughton's finding of heightened cardiovascular and respiratory functioning, their subjects were recorded as having lower than usual functioning just prior to the onset of the attack. They interpret these findings as indicating a greater depth of sleep with a concomitant lowering of defenses or "ego regression." But even more important is the verbal content that they were able to record both during a night-terror episode and after awakening their subjects. By putting this material in the context of psychiatric interviews obtained prior to recorded night-terror episodes, they were able to evaluate the verbal content gathered during these stage 4 sleep episodes. They found that this material was indeed of such a conflictual nature as to easily trigger a full-scale panic or terror attack. Fischer et al. also noted that there was often a repetitive theme in a series of night terrors and even in anxiety dreams occurring in the same night. It is significant that when the night terror was compared to the REM anxiety dream, it was found that the dream demonstrated a greater capacity to modulate anxiety. This finding is consistent with the assumption that night terrors are the problem of the immature or the disordered mind.

In order to evaluate Broughton's views on the effect of environmental stimulation on the formation of night terrors, Fischer et al. added an experimental segment to their study. They sounded a buzzer while subjects were in stage 4 sleep and found that the buzzer did, at times, provoke a night-terror attack. Therefore they concluded that environmental as well as ongoing mental activity can serve as a source of night terror. Similarly, Rogozea and Florea-Ciocoiu (1983), in a study of 36 subjects who suffered from night terrors, found that these subjects showed a significantly more intense orienting reaction than did 72 control subjects. Conceivably this finding suggests that individuals who suffer from night terrors may, in general, be much more vulnerable to environmental intrusion and that they are more threatened by it.

In evaluating Fischer et al.'s results, it should be noted that all their subjects were adults, as opposed to Broughton's population of both adults and children. Roughly half of Fischer's subjects had suffered from night terrors starting when they were quite young. Keith (1975) notes that these subjects are comparable to Sperling's type 1 children. He points out that other subjects had developed night terrors after a specific traumatic event in adulthood (Sperling's type 2) and the content of the night terrors was in some way related to this trauma (Keith 1975:485) Possibly the differences in their physiological findings may in part have been due to the differences in their subject population. Moreover, the content gathered from Fisher et al.'s subjects is reflective of the extensive degree of psychopathology in this population. Therefore, it would seem that more data needs to be gathered from a more representative population.

Finally, Hartmann (1984:257), in referring to studies by researchers such as the Kales group, states that it is well established that during the period of withdrawal from such depressant medication as barbiturates, alcohol, and the benzodiazepine tranquilizers, many individuals suffer from nightmares, bizarre dreams, and intensely vivid dreams.

## Discussion

It would appear that the research findings regarding night terrors are at odds with psychoanalytically oriented, etiological theories of this disorder. It is possible, however, that the findings are not necessarily in conflict with classical Freudian theory. Freud always acknowledged that physical sensation can be a significant factor in dream formation. For example, he (Freud 1900) postulated three kinds of somatic sources of dreams: (1) objective sensory stimuli arising from external objects (Fisher et al.'s buzzer), (2) internal states of excitation of the sense organs having only a subjective basis (the pattern of light that is seen when the eyes are closed, ringing in the ears, etc.—W. Wundt, cited in Freud 1900:30), and (3) somatic stimuli derived from the interior of the body (respiratory distress or Broughton's predisposing physiological factors). Freud believed that any or all of these can play a part in the creation of a dream. He was, however, emphatic about his contention that the *overriding* reason for the formation of a dream was wish fulfillment.

> When external nervous stimuli and internal somatic stimuli are intense enough to force psychical attention to themselves, then—provided that their outcome *is* dreaming and waking up—they serve as a fixed point for the formation of a dream, a nucleus in its material; a wish-fulfillment is then looked for that shall correspond to this nucleus. . . . (Freud 1900:235)

Freud (1901) takes this issue up again in his essay on "The Psychopathology of Everyday Life." In this work Freud deals with the proposition that forgetting might lie in some functional problem of the brain (such as fatigue) versus his own psychological explanation of the role of the unconscious in determining our actions. He states (1901:21), "that would be to confuse the mechanism of a process, which is of the same kind in all cases, with the factors favouring the process, which are variable and not necessarily essential." To illustrate this point (ibid.) he proposes a hypothetical situation in which he goes into a deserted part of town where he is robbed. Freud then asks whether he should go to the police and say that "I was in such and such a street and there *loneliness* and *darkness* took away my watch and purse." Freud points out that to do so would be partially accurate but would also make him look crazy. The correct description of the situation would be "that *favoured* by the loneliness of the place and under the *shield* of darkness *unknown malefactors* robbed me of my valuables." In other words tiredness, circulatory disturbances, intoxication, etc. can all be factors which favor psychopathological forgetting. They do not explain why such forgetting also takes place under perfectly normal conditions. (Freud 1921:21–22).

Therefore Freud always recognized the role of factors other than conflictual material in symptom formation. But he adamantly asserts that these factors will be used in the service of the individual's own particular unconscious psychic predisposition. Taking into consideration Broughton's notion of the predisposing factor, it would seem quite likely that only the immature or disordered mind would allow conflictual material to emerge to such a degree that the sleeper would be catapulted out of sleep without really wakening, or to be much more likely to interpret urgent physiological data in terms of such dramatically conflictual material.

The data are, however, somewhat confusing (see Sperling's [1958] three types of night terrors). If all children go through intense conflict in response to "sucessive waves of spontaneous developmental processes" why don't all children suffer from night terrors, unless, indeed, some are predisposed to night terrors because of physiological immaturity? Yet the fact that so many of the children of Chowchilla suffered from night terrors definitely points to emergence of this disorder in response to psychic trauma. Does psychic trauma play the same role as physiological immaturity? Or perhaps, given enough stress, any child or adult (see dreams of traumatic war experiences) will experience night terrors which are perhaps a more primitive response to stress than the dream. Or perhaps predisposition and stress must come together to produce night terrors. Therefore, children and adults who are significantly predisposed to disordered arousal would invariably manifest night terrors in response to stress which would be handled through other channels by a less vulnerable individual. Even in normal individuals when there is significant trauma there will be a breakdown of defenses, and night terrors might emerge. On the other hand, physiologically vulnerable individuals might never suffer from night terrors. In other words night terrors may be a more primitive response which will emerge in those instances in which for psychological and/or physiological reasons anxiety cannot be contained in any other way.

## Treatment

Psychoanalysts have always felt that as young children progress through the psychosexual stages of development, they are subject to periodic episodes of intense symptom formation. Yet, if the child is reasonably healthy and if the environment is "good enough," these symptoms resolve themselves without outside intervention. Night-terror attacks can be particularly frightening for parents, but the child in most instances is relatively oblivious to their occurrence.

Therefore, if the attacks are confined to a brief period, approximately 3 to 4 months, child specialists such as Sperling (1958), Fraiberg (1950), Mack (1965), etc. suggest that other than reducing obvious sources of stress (i.e., sleeping in the parents' bedroom), no specific treatment is necessary. This approach would obviously be consistent with that of those writers who believe that night terrors represent a delay in maturation of the central nervous system. In other words, both groups for different reasons suggest that the child will outgrow the episodes. Keith (1975) suggests that more frequent episodes, i.e., at least 3 or 4 times a week for a period of months, indicate more serious pathology. Other evidence of anxiety or neurotic symptoms are also usually present. In these instances, Keith feels that the child and the parents should be evaluated and treated in order to prevent pathological character development.

When specific environmental trauma is the precipitant for night terrors, treatment may or may not be necessary to prevent subsequent pathological development. One of the most striking instances of traumatic night terrors was discussed by Terr (1979, 1981). In a study of the Chowchilla, California schoolbus highjacking, Terr states that 14 out of 23 parents reported that their children had begun suffering from night terrors immediately after the incident occurred. In most instances, these episodes subsided after several months without requiring psychological intervention. Some of these children, however, continued to have night-terror episodes until they received psychotherapy which dealt with the kidnapping. This finding and others suggest that when night terrors are clearly the result of a specific trauma, the child must be carefully observed to determine whether his or her resources are adequate to deal with the aftermath of the trauma. If not, psychological intervention may be required to allow for catharsis, resolution of conflict, and strengthening of the child's existing defenses.

Recently drug treatment of night terrors has become more and more popular. As early as 1971 Pesikoff and Davis reported successfully using the antidepressant drug imipramine in treating three children. Other drugs have since been tried with both children and adults. It is unclear, however, if the mixed degrees of success are due to the failure of the drugs or to the conditions for the study of these drugs, i.e., number of studies, subjects, dosages etc., were the problem. The use of drugs with adults is more prevalent in the literature. For example, Marshall (1975), Beitman and Carlin (1979), Burstein and Burstein (1983) report the successful use of imipramine with adults. Fischer et al. (1973a) and McLeod and Fischer (1978) report considerable success with diazepam. These researchers chose diazepam because J. Kales et al. (1970) had demonstrated that diazepam reduces stage 4 sleep. The Fischer group report fairly good results in 8 out of the 9 subjects studied. But neither Fischer et al. nor Glick et al. (1971), who used diazepam successfully with children, were able clearly to tie the success of this drug to the suppression of stage 4 sleep as opposed to "a larger, more comprehensive biochemical action on the brain, which independently suppressed the symptom and delta sleep" (Fischer et al. 1973a:258).

Reports of the use of psychotherapy in the treatment of adults suffering from night terrors are sparse. Perhaps most therapists see night terrors as just one of many symptoms of a larger core problem, and therefore, they would not discuss these episodes apart from a general discussion of the overall case. J. Kales et al. (1982) and Hartmann (1983) each report on successful psychotherapy with two adult patients. In both instances the patient started treatment wanting only to focus on the episodes, and treatment did not progress until they were able to move on to more general issues. Since the majority of writers agree that night terrors are always an indicator of moderate to severe pathology in adults, treatment is more important with adults than it would be with children. The choice of medication versus psychotherapy would most probably depend on the patient's willingness to engage in either or both. Interestingly enough, as with children, the impetus for seeking therapy usually comes from family members, who generally suffer more from the episodes than does the patient.

## Summary

Night terrors represent a dramatic but relatively infrequent clinical syndrome. It is for the most part a disorder of children, and many children outgrow it without requiring any treatment at all. When night terrors occur in adults, it is usually considered an indicator of serious pathology. Many of the adults reported to suffer from night terrors tended to have severe character disorders or were schizophrenic. Etiological theories can be divided as to whether psychodynamic or physiological factors are seen as the source of the episode. Psychoanalytic theory proposes that the episode is triggered by conflictual material which emerges owing to a lowering of defenses during sleep. The physiological manifestations of the episode represent the anxiety generated by this conflict. The alternative position has been offered by sleep researchers Gastaut and Broughton (1965) and Broughton (1968, 1970), who suggest that a physiological predisposition to a "disorder of arousal" results in the disturbing physiological sensations which the sleeper then interprets in terms of being choked, etc.

Conceivably, both physiological and psychodynamic factors are at work during an episode of night terrors. Night terrors may, indeed, be a primitive kind of response which will emerge in those instances in which, for psychological and/or physiological reasons, anxiety cannot be contained in any other way.

In situations in which treatment is deemed to be required, the literature seems to report equal success in using psychiatric medications such as diazepam or imipramine and in using analytic psychotherapy.

## References


Agrell, I., and A. Axelsson. 1972. The relationship between pavor nocturnus and adenoids. *Acta Paedopsychiatrica* 39:46–53.

Anthony, J. 1959. An experimental approach to the psychopathology of childhood: Sleep disturbances. *British Journal of Medical Psychology* 32:19-37.

Beitman, B. D. and A. S. Carlin. 1979. Night terrors treated with imipramine. *American Journal of Psychiatry* 136:1087–88.

Broughton, R. J. 1968. Sleep disorders: Disorders of arousal? *Science* 159:1070–78.

Broughton, R. J. 1970. The incubus attack. In E. Hartmann, ed., *Sleep and Dreaming,* pp. 188–92. Boston: Little, Brown.

Burstein, A. and A. Burstein. 1983. Treatment of night terrors with imipramine. *Journal of Clinical Psychiatry* 44(2):82.

Clardy, E. R. and B. C. Hill. 1949. Sleep disorders in institutionalized disturbed children and deliquent boys. *Nervous Child* 8:50–53.

Deutsch, H. 1951. *Psychoanalysis of Neurosis.* London: Hogarth Press (Original work published in 1930.)

Fisher, C., E. Kahn, A. Edwards, and D. Davis. 1973a. A psychophysiological study of nightmares and night terrors: The suppression of stage 4 night terrors with diazepam. *Archives of General Psychiatry* 28:252–59.

Fisher, C., E. Kahn, A. Edwards, and D. Davis. 1973b. A psychophysiological study of nightmares and night terrors. I. Physiological aspects of the stage 4 night terror. *Journal of Nervous and Mental Disease* 157(2):75–98.

Fisher, C., E. Kahn, A. Edwards, D. Davis, and J. Fine. 1974. A psychophsiological study of nightmares and night terrors. III. Mental content and recall of stage 4 night terrors. *Journal of Nervous and Mental Disease* 158(3):174–88.

Fraiberg, S. 1950. On sleep disturbances of early childhood. In R. Eissler et al., eds., *The Psychoanalytic Study of the Child* 5:285–309. New York: International Universities Press.

Freud, S. *Standard Edition of the Complete Psychological Works of Sigmund Freud.* James Strachey, ed. and tr. 24 vols. London: Hogarth Press, 1953–1974; New York: Macmillan.

1895. On the grounds for detaching a particular syndrome from neuresthenia under the description "anxiety neurosis." 3:87–117.

1900. *The Interpretation of Dreams.* Vols. 4 and 5.

1901. *The Psychopathology of Everyday Life.* Vol. 6.

Gardner, G. 1932. Night terrors and the mutilation threat. *Psychoanalytic Review* 19:182–99.

Gastaut, H. and R. Broughton. 1965. A clinical and polygraphic study of episodic phenomena during sleep. In J. Wortis, ed., *Recent Advances in Biological Psychiatry* 7:197–221. New York: Plenum Press.

Glick, B. S., D. Schulman, and S. Turecki. 1971. Diazepam (Valium) treatment in childhood sleep disorders. *Diseases of the Nervous System* 32:565–66.

Hallstrom, T. 1972. Night terrors in adults through three generations. *Acta Psychiatrica Scandinavica* 48:350–52

Hartmann, E. 1983. Two case reports: Night terrors with sleepwalking—A potentially lethal disorder. *Journal of Nervous and Mental Disease* 171(8):503–5.

Hartmann, E. 1984. *The Nightmare.* New York: Basic Books.

Jones, E. 1931. *On the Nightmare.* London: Hagarth Press. (Original work published in 1911.)

Kales, J., A. Jacobson, and A. Kales. 1968. Sleep disorders in children. In L. Abt and B. F. Riess, eds., *Progress in Clinical Psychology,* pp. 63–75. New York: Grune and Stratton.

Kales, J., R. L. Tan, T. A. Preston, and C. Allen. 1970. Stage 4 sleep: Studies of hypnotic, tranquilizing, and antidepressant drugs. *Psychophysiology* 7:342–43.

Kales, J., A. Kales, C. Soldatos, K. Chamberlin, and E. Martin. 1979. Sleepwalking and night terrors related to febrile illness. *American Journal of Psychiatry* 136(9):1214–15.

Kales, J., A. Kales, C. Soldatos, A. Caldwell, D. Charney, and E. Martin. 1980a. Night terrors: Clinical characteristics and personality patterns. *Archives of General Psychiatry* 37:1413–17.

Kales, J., C. Soldatos, E. Bixler, R. Ladda, G. Charney, G. Weber, and P. Schweitzer. 1980b. Hereditary factors in sleepwalking and night terrors. *British Journal of Psychiatry* 137:111:18.

Kales, J., R. Cadieux, C. Soldatos and A. Kales. 1982. Psychotherapy with night terrors patients. *American Journal of Psychotherapy* 36(3):399–407.

Keith, P. 1975. Night terrors: A review of the psychology, neurophysiology, and therapy. *Journal of the American Academy of Child Psychiatry* 14:477–89.

Klein, M. 1963. *The Psycho-Analysis of Children.* London: Hogarth Press. (Original work in published 1932.)

Mack, J. E. 1965. Nightmares, conflict, and ego development. *International Journal of Psycho-Analysis* 46:403–28.

McLeod, M. and P. Fisher. 1978. Pavor nocturnus in a schizophrenic patient: A review and case study. *American Journal of Psychiatry* 135(2):235–36.

Marshall, J. 1975. The treatment of night terrors associated with the posttramautic syndrome. *American Journal of Psychiatry* 132(3):293–95.

Pesikoff, R. B. and P. C. Davis. 1971. Treatment of pavor nocturnus and somnambulism in children. *American Journal of Psychiatry* 128:778–81.

Rogozea, R. and V. Florea-Ciocoiu. 1983. Responsiveness disturbances in patients with night terrors. *Revue Roumaine de Medecine Neurologie et Psychiatrie* 21(2):83–96.

Shackle, J. W. 1928. A note on night terrors. *Lancet* pp. 287–88.

Sperling, M. 1958. Pavor nocturnus. *Journal of the American Psychoanalytic Association* 6:79–94.

Stern, M. 1951. Pavor nocturnus. *International Journal of Psycho-Analysis* 32:302–9.

Still, G. F. 1900. Day-terrors (pavor diurnus) in children. *Lancet* p. 293.

Terr, L. C. 1979. Children of Chowchilla: A study of psychic trauma. In A. Solnit et al., eds., *The Psychoanalytic Study of the Child* 34:547–623. New Haven: Yale University Press.

Terr, L. C. 1981. Psychic trauma in children: Observations following the Chowchilla school bus kidnapping. *American Journal of Psychiatry* 138:14–19.

Waelder Hall, J. 1946. The analysis of a case of night terrors. In R. Eissler, et al., eds., *The Psychoanalytic Study of the Child* 2:189–227. New York: International Universities Press. (Original work published in 1935.)

# 11.

# The Nightmare and Child Development: Some Observations from a Psychoanalytic Perspective

AVA L. SIEGLER

## A Lack of Developmental Data

THE PECULIAR TERROR of the nightmare exerts an extraordinary claim on our imagination. Yet at certain points in childhood, nightmares are so frequent as to constitute an ordinary disruption of sleep.[1] Given the frequency with which they occur, and their episodic persistence throughout the course of life, it is striking that we have so few studies of this particular type of dream and no systematic devlopmental exploration of their structure and content. This seems particularly notable in light of the extensive scientific interest in sleep and dreaming since the classic REM studies of the 1950s (Aserinsky and Kleitman, Dement and Fisher)

1. In Germanic folklore, nightmares were attributed to an evil spirit that plagued the sleeper, sitting on his chest and attempting to suffocate him, a vivid metaphor for the sense of oppression and helplessness that the nightmare produces in us ("Mare" = Demon).

and the burgeoning of scientific interest in infancy and early childhood over the past decade.

A review of the available literature on children's dreams indicates a great deal of similarity among different studies of children living at different times and in different social and geographic settings (Ames 1964; Despert 1949; Nagera 1966; and Piaget 1950). All studies indicate the presence of specific developmental trends in dreaming, and some address the fact that the nightmare appears to represent one of the most common transient experiences of dream life, particularly at three distinct points in human development: (1) between 1½ and 2½ years (which appears to be the first reliable stage of onset); (2) at 4–6 years (which appears to be a stage of peak incidence for sleep disruption, and particularly for nightmares); (3) around 11–13 years (where, after a rather calm hiatus in sleep disturbances from 7–11, there is a resurgence of reported nightmares).

In an article on sleep behavior in preschool children Beltramini and Hertzig (1983) report their analysis of the data available on the 109 children who were subjects of the New York Longitudinal Study of Temperament (originally conducted by Chess and Thomas from 1956 to 1962). They report that 95 percent of these children (1–5 years old) were described by their parents as regularly crying or calling during the night as frequently as once a week, and 62 percent of the children were reported to have regularly experienced nightmares as often as once every two weeks at some point during the preschool period. All these bedtime and sleep behaviors peaked at 4–5 years.

Certain formidable obstacles have undoubtedly impeded efforts to elicit information about children's dreams in general, and children's nightmares in particular:

1. In the face of the child's night-time terror, the attentive parent responds by getting the child to forget the "bad" dream as rapidly as possible, and to resume sleep.

2. The limitations of the young child's cognitive development make it difficult for him/her to reliably identify and/or retrieve dreams. For example, it takes quite a long time for the child to become aware of the differences between dreaming and waking life. Even after this distinction has been made by the child,

he still may not absorb the fact that he, himself, creates his own dreams and invents his own terrors.

3. The child may experience some bewilderment about the fragile and confusing links in the dream's narrative, and therefore find the dream difficult to remember. (The child understands the dream as "nonsense" rather than as a "sensible" story.)

4. The experience of arousal in and of itself produces a cognitive discontinuity which the child must overcome. This altered state of consciousness—moving from a sleeping to a waking state of mind—may disrupt processes of recall.

5. It is much more difficult to subject children to REM studies with their accompanying electrode-monitoring, sleep-interrupting procedures.

6. It is possible that such experimental techniques actually discourage the production of nightmares. Fisher et al. (1970) make the point that in laboratory studies of REM dreaming, the dreams reported are usually mild to moderate in intensity, while Broughton (1968:757) observes:

> Quite probably the reduction in severity has to do with the fact that someone is present and in communication with the subject all night, thus reducing separation anxiety which plays an important role in nightmares. It is well known that mothers, in order to assuage the nightmares of their children, keep the lights on, the door open, or sit with the terrified child.

## Some Difficulties in Definition

In their study of the nightmare, Fisher et al. (1970:780) conclude that "Most frightening arousals subjectively experienced as nightmares are REM anxiety dreams of varying degrees of intensity." They remind us, however, that nightmares are reported as well in NREM stages of sleep, particularly stage 4 sleep, which is associated with the severe pavor nocturnus (night terror) of childhood.

In fact, if dreaming is defined as the mental activity of the REM periods, it appears that many of the more frightening experiences of children and adults do not take place during dreaming at all (sleepwalking, enuresis, sleep talking, pavor nocturnus).

Broughton (1968) has suggested that these types of sleep disorders are really "disorders of arousal," not of sleep, and suggest that there may be serious loss of reality testing and of the integrative functions of the ego at these points in the sleep cycle (produced by the experience of forced arousal from slow-wave sleep). Fisher et al. (1970:781) suggest that these so-called "nightmares" must be considered in a different category:

> It is best to consider that the Stage IV nightmare is not a dream at all in the ordinary sense, but a symptom, a pathological formation of NREM sleep brought about by a rift in the ego's capacity to control anxiety. . . . The REM anxiety dream, on the other hand, is a normal phenomenon present from infancy throughout life.

In the Beltramini and Hertzig (1983:156) study, pavor nocturnus was characterized as "episodes of intense crying accompanied by difficulty in arousal," and they were only reported by the parents of a total of 7 children (6 percent) during the preschool period. Other authors have noted the somatic manifestations which are present in these episodes of night terror (sweating, trembling, palpitations, etc.). They too observe that pavor nocturnus is a relatively rare occurrence in childhood, while nightmares, on the other hand, appear to be quite common. In "The Interpretation of Dreams," Freud (1900:95) describes pavor nocturnus as an attack of night terror that is accompanied by hallucinations. He felt that it exhibited "a form which belongs to anxiety neurosis." Certainly, the terrified child appears to have no recourse to the defensive functions of the ego, and remains overwhelmed by anxiety. This is probably not surprising, since stage 4 nightmares occur in the deepest phase of sleep, the point at which the ego functions of the child certainly would be the most regressed and unavailable. Fisher et al. (1970:776) state, "Rather than serving to master anxiety, these nightmares appear to represent a massive failure of the ego to control it, a failure that may be of lifelong duration." The appearance of the REM nightmare, however, seems to herald the child's newly formed capacity for signal anxiety. Parenthetically, it should also be noted that the dream structure binds anxiety in much the same way that defenses bind anxiety in the child's waking life. The distinction between the normal and the pathological, or the ordinary and the extraordinary, which has been established in relation to the nightmare versus pavor nocturnus, highlights certain structural and adaptive issues in child development which shall be addressed in the following sections.

## The First Appearance of the Nightmare: Developmental Considerations

On the basis of laboratory studies, we now know that even neonates display the discrete patterns of REMs associated with an EEG configuration that is characteristic of dreaming. What does this mean? Are neonates dreaming? Roffwarg, Dement, and Fisher (1964:68) observe:

> If by dreaming is meant the occurrence of hallucinatory visual imagery which is correlated with the specific spatial patterns of the REM's, as in adults, then the possibility of dreaming in the newborn infant must be negated [for] . . . it would be necessary to invoke some factor such as inherited racial memories in order to postulate that REM patterns represent hallucinated imagery in newborns. However, the presence of REM's in neonates is not entirely incongruous. They seem to be an attribute of a unique physiological sleep state which *later* becomes associated with patterned dreaming. . . . Infants spend a considerable amount of time in the physiological stage of sleep during which dreams are known to occur in adults.

For our purposes, the existence of such "dreams" is moot, since in preverbal stages of development we can have no access to these dreams, as there is no evocative mechanism capable of organizing and expressing them. Such a mechanism presupposes not only a capacity for conceptual intelligence, but also a capacity for mental imagery and spoken language. Piaget (1950:178), in his studies of children's dreams, takes the same position:

> It is very difficult to say at what point in the child's development dreams appear, since before the stage of language only behaviors can be analyzed. It is often assumed that all mammals dream, but a dog which growls in

its sleep is not necessarily evoking mental images, and its "dream" can be interpreted in terms of mere sensory-motor automatism. In the case of children, we have been unable to find evidence of authentic dreams before the appearance of language. . . . The first definite proof of dreams in the children we have observed came between the age of 1 year, 9 months, and two years, when the children talked in their sleep and gave an account of their dreams when they woke. . . .

It is in the early stage of dreaming that the nightmare makes its first appearance. Somewhere in the second year of life, the child's sleep begins to be interrupted. It is not surprising that the onset of the nightmare should come at this stage in development, when symbolization, memory, and speech become available to the child as means to structure and modulate anxiety.

In the course of ordinary development, both cognition and affectivity pass through phases which have been defined in the work of both Piaget and Freud. The nightmare has an important part to play in this developmental journey. Thus, the 2-year-old's nightmare that "a bear came to eat my fingers" signals the developmental attainment of object constancy, self and object representation, and castration anxiety. From an ego point of view the newly emerging self, now capable of conceptualizing a separate other, is also capable of fearing injury and attack. However, that imagined attack is no longer annihilative but rather a limited fear of injury to a part of the body. Anna Freud (1936) in her approach to the developmental lines of psychic growth, highlights the ego's expanding capacity to master anxiety, moving from the earliest fears of annihilation through the child's fear of the loss of the mother, to fear of the loss of the mother's love, and finally to the internalized accomplishment of conscience. The work of Margaret Mahler (1975) and her followers has focused our attention on the early structures of mental life in children under 3 years of age. The early aggressive conflicts, the sexual interest in the anatomical distinction between the sexes, early schematization of the outline of the body, and early representations of self and object all have important implications for our understanding of the occurrence of nightmares in children at around 1½–2½ years of age, an age in which a great many of these mental structures are first laid down. The growing complexity of the mental apparatus, the interpersonal entanglements of family relations, the newly acquired motor skills, the shifts in nap and sleep schedules, separation from the mother's orbit all contribute to the disruption of sleep behavior at this critical point in time, and invest this phase in development with multiple functions and multiple meanings.

## The Nightmare: Previous Views

### THE NIGHTMARE AS A DIAGNOSTIC INDICATOR

It is interesting to note that from the perspective of Freud's early view of dreams as the "guardian of sleep," nightmares represent dream failures: the child's sleep is violently interrupted, as the anxiety meant to be contained by the dream structure breaks through. According to Freud (1901), this type of flooding of the organism with excitation without adequate defenses provides the model for all later anxiety. Freud specified two types of dreams which he referred to as "typical anxiety dreams," (1901:395) where the manifest content was more or less constant. He cites these dreams as a consequence of certain developmental experiences which are characteristic of children who "suffer with anxiety." They are "dreams of falling," and "dreams of the nocturnal burglar . . . of being threatened with knives, daggers and lances" (Freud 1901:264, 372). Irving Harris (1951) has conducted studies of these two types of dreams which he calls the falling dream and the attacked dream. He locates the origins of these nightmares in certain specific crises in development. The former, referring back to preoedipal issues of separation anxiety (annihilative fears and fears of abandonment by the maternal object), the latter taking its reference point from later oedipal struggles (projected aggressive wishes and the emotional complexity of triadic object relations with their accompanying experiences of envy, jealousy, and guilt, etc.). He suggests that the occurrence of this type of nightmare can be used as a diagnostic indicator of individual pathology.

In a series of three papers published in 1948, Harris reports his investigation of 250 children at a Child Guidance Clinic in Illinois, ranging in age from 3 to 17, approximately 75 percent of them boys. Harris states that between 85 and 90 percent of the spontaneously reported "scariest" nightmares of the children could be classified in these two categories, with 23 percent of the children reporting the falling dream as "scariest" and 58 percent reporting the attacked dream. The remaining 19 percent of nightmares most concerned someone emotionally close to the dreamer, rather than the dreamer himself, who was in danger, hurt, dying, or dead. Harris goes on to link his findings with Freud's (1936) description of the psychic dangers which face the child in ongoing development. These dangers emerge in parent-child relations and are later incorporated and internalized by the child in the course of superego development: (1) loss of love or separation from the supporting object (separation anxiety); and (2) injury to or mutilation of the body or parts of the body (castration anxiety).

## THE NIGHTMARE AS AN EARLY WARNING SIGN

Sperling (1958), in her studies of sleep disturbances in young children, takes the point of view that nightmares are probably typical of certain stages of development, with their onset associated with the anal phase, and peak disturbance associated with the oedipal phase. She states that nightmares first manifest themselves at about the age of 1½–2 years and reminds us that from the ages of 2–5, even in the most favorable setting, every child "lives through a period of emotional frustration which leads to repression of sexual and aggressive impulses. . . . The oedipal phase is the classical period of sleep disturbance in children. During this age, from about three to five, almost every child experiences a transient period of disturbed sleep" (Sperling 1958:34). Her position on the first appearance and the peak appearance of nightmares is consistent with most of the authors who have explored this phenomenon from both a psychoanalytic and a psychophysiological perspective. However, persistent nightmares are seen by Sperling to be an early warning sign of serious pathology. She states (1958:360), "I wish to particularly emphasize that disturbances of sleep in children are the first reliable signs of emotional conflicts, and that this symptom precedes any other overt indications of them in the behavior of the child." In her view, any trauma experienced by the child is likely to be reexperienced in repetitive nightmares, and these nightmares indicate that the child is unable to master the trauma; "acute exacerbations leading to persistent sleeplessness are pathologic phenomena indicative of serious emotional disorder" (1958:359).

Sperling (1958) has described the type of nightmare that she associates with serious pathology in the child. She stresses its insidious onset in early childhood, its persistence, and its link to murderous impulses and primal scene experiences on the part of the child. She sees this type of nightmare as similar to a psychotic episode, but one which takes place only in the sleeping life of the child.

It is possible that the sleep disturbances that Sperling describes may, in fact, be stage 4 NREM "nightmares" (rather, night terrors—pavor nocturnus). There is no doubt that the child's sleep begins to be interrupted by both nightmares and night terrors somewhere in the second year of life. While we now have available to us a psychophysiological distinction between the two experiences which can be made in the laboratory (REM and NREM phenomena), in real life, or in clinical practice, this distinction can be difficult to make. An interesting clinical observation with respect to night terrors has been made by Brenner (1951), Esman (1962), and Schur (1966), who have all discussed cases where the night terrors initially experienced by their patients subsequently developed into acute visual hallucinations and psychotic states of mind.

## THE NIGHTMARE AS PHOBIC DEFENSE

Psychoanalytic developmental theory takes note of the links between the structure of a dream and the structures which underlie a phobia. Children are capable of forming phobic symptoms as soon as they are capable of dreams which involve dreamwork. The nightmare can be seen in this context, as a form of phobic transformation. The child's own sexual and aggressive impulses are externalized and perceived as fearful dangers.

Where Sperling (1949) emphasized dynamic considerations and pathological issues in regard to the nightmare, Mack (1965) and Herzog (1980) emphasize structural and adaptive considerations. The nightmare expresses the child's newly acquired representational and defensive skills. These skills are pressed into service to cope with the ordinary events of childhood: separations, accidents, illnesses, births, and deaths.

Many psychoanalytic observers have now placed the capacity to develop phobic symptoms earlier in the child's life than was previously believed. Several cases of children with highly developed phobias (where a sophisticated degree of symbolization disguises underlying drive-related conflicts) as early as 18 months have been reported in the literature (Renik et al. 1978). Mack (1965), in his paper on "Nightmares, Conflict, and Ego Development in Childhood," similarly assigns a symbolic and highly conflictive content to the child's nightmare in the first half of the second year (12–18 months). This places the use of structuralization and the presence of symbolic dreamwork six months earlier than other investigators have found. Herzog (1980:229), in his study of 18–28-month-old boys who had lost their fathers, reports that "Under the regressive and progressive sway of sleep a phobic transformation emerges in which the child's own aggressive impulses are seen as hostilely and mercilessly attacking the self in the guise of monsters, big birds, and so forth." The phobic content of the nightmare suggests to him that defensive structures are precipitated in these children under the special ego circumstances which emerge during sleep. These structures help them to deal with the traumatic loss of their fathers at this critical developmental juncture.

## Conclusion: The Nightmare, Developmental Organizer and Developmental Achievement

Clearly, the nightmare not only reflects conflict, anxiety, and the defensive struggles of the child; it also reflects the child's growing cognitive and affective capacities to organize and express these conflicts. This organization, then, stimulates further development.

If we recall that the first appearance of the nightmare coincided with the attainment of secondary-process thought, speech development, motor control, anal-phase development, the consolidation of narcissism, the beginnings of a clearly defined, anatomically distinct body image, object constancy, and self and object representations—we can observe that all these express massive achievements on the part of the ego. The onset of nightmares at this phase surely reflects the child's newfound ability to express dynamic, conflictive issues for the first time, in representational, structuralized terms (e.g., Anna, aged 2 years, 2 months: "I want to have breakfast, Mommy was not in her chair, and a big cat scratched me." Mathilda, aged 2 years, 4 months: "I had a bad dream . . . I was in the park. A big black witch took my Tiny Tears." Jeremy, aged 19 months: "Bad, bad snake go away . . . A snake bite my head off, bite my sweater.")

A review of both the psychophysiological and the psychoanalytic literature confirms that the peak incidence of the nightmare coincides with oedipal-phase development and the emergence of internalized superego processes, the consolidation of sexual identity, and the resolution of narcissistic and identificatory dilemmas, which are the outcome of this phase. The turbulence of powerful aggressive and rivalrous impulses, the fear of retaliation and retribution, and the loss of the dyadic, infantile relationship to the parents must all be renounced and resolved if the child is to move out into the world and away from the original incestuous ties to the family circle. It is not surprising that the child's sleeping life is as vulnerable as his waking life to these inevitable conflicts. By the age of 3, the narrative of the nightmare has become more complex, as cognitive and affective structures have become more mature. Freud's famous case of the Wolfman, for example, was named for the intricate and terrifying nightmare of wolves first dreamed by the suffering patient when he was 4 years old. Through an analysis of this dream, Freud lays bare the history and formation of the patient's symptoms. We can also see the relationship between the dream of wolves (the nightmare) and the fear of wolves (the wolf phobia). (This link also appears in the case of "Little Hans," with his fear of horses and his accompanying nightmares of biting animals.)

A 3½-year-old little girl (in treatment for panphobic behavior which greatly interfered with her functioning and required that she spend her time completely under the devoted care of her anxious mother) dreamed the following dream at the point in treatment where her rivalrous feelings toward her mother and her wish to be her father's "princess" and have his baby were beginning to surface in her play:

I had a scary dream last night, and I went into Mommy's bed. (Can you tell me about your dream?) I was a beautiful princess and I had a gold crown and I had glass shoes and I had a red pocketbook and I had a big, big, dress. You know, (gestures with her hands to indicate a dress that puffed out around her) ah . . . ummm . . . a fat dress. I was running and running and I fell down the stairs and my dress broke and a teeny-tiny kittie bit me.

In preadolescence there appears to be a resurgence in the incidence of nightmares, after a relatively calm pattern of dreaming throughout the years of latency:

There is a recurrence of nightmares which bother many children between the ages of 10 and 13 considerably more than at just-preceding and just-following ages . . . at least one-third of our subjects reported nightmares . . . such things as dragons, bad guys, animals, robbers, and being chased or killed. (Ames 1964:27)

Once again, recourse to a psychoanalytic understanding of the development of mind can be helpful in accounting for this resurgence. It is in preadolescent years that the child begins to experience what Blos has called the second separation-individuation, with its echoes of the 1½–2½-year-old's struggles, and its deep oedipal resonance. Now, with physical maturation preparing the child to take his/her place as a sexually active, competent adult, the old psychic conflicts over separation, autonomy, and identity take on new meaning. Nightmares reported at this age resemble adult dreams in their complex use of symbolization, condensation, and displacement.

In individuals, in the course of their development, certain stresses which are unique to their circumstances may, in fact, precipitate and consolidate new cognitive and affective attainments. Each child brings an idiosyncratic solution to the problems of his/her life. The dream life of the child also expresses what is unique and particular to that child. Despert (1949), in her classic study of children's dreams, made the observation that each child's dreams displayed highly characteristic themes, and that these themes tended to appear and reappear in the child's dreams throughout development with slight variation. Mack (1965) describes the nightmare as "part and parcel" of the child's ability to dream. Since all dreaming reflects the ups and downs of the mental life of the dreamer, both children and adults will have "good" and "bad" dreams, just as they have "good" and "bad" thoughts, and "good" and "bad" experiences.

If the nightmare is seen in the broad developmental context that we have been constructing, its presence need not be a primary indicator of psychic disequilibrium or emotional pathology, either in the internal or in the external world of the child. Rather, the appearance and reappearance of the nightmare may indicate the maturation and function of certain affective and cognitive processes which first appear at around 1½–2½ years, reach a peak during 3–6 years, and form a part of the profound contribution preoedipal and oedipal struggles make to ongoing human development.

In this manner, the nightmare also may be regarded as a "developmental organizer," similar in its appearance and function to other such organizers first noted by Rene Spitz in his classic observational studies of infants. Spitz (1965) maintained that the smiling response, stranger anxiety, and the verbalized "no" were points of consolidation and organization in development—each point signaling the attainment of cognitive and affective intrapsychic structures.

Ordinary processes of dreaming include the nightmare, which may be enlisted on behalf of development as the mind gains momentum. The consistent appearance of nightmares throughout the lifespan and their insistent claim upon the mental life at certain peak points in development indicate that they play a crucial role in the ontogeny of mind.

## Summary

The peculiar terror of the nightmare exerts an extraordinary claim on our imagination; yet no systematic developmental exploration of its meaning exists. There are difficulties in defining exactly what constitutes a nightmare during the course of childhood and distinguishing it (as a REM anxiety dream) from the NREM "pavor nocturnus" (night terrors) of childhood. An additional obstacle to a thoughtful exploration of children's nightmares is the fact that laboratory monitoring techniques may actually discourage the production of this type of dream: the dreamer is aware of the continued presence of another person throughout the night, and this may serve to soothe the very fears which stimulate the production of the nightmare.

Nevertheless, there appears to be rather widespread agreement that nightmares first occur at about 1½–2½ years, with peak incidence occurring during 4–6 years, and some resurgence during the preadolescent years (11–13). A psychoanalytic perspective on this phenomenon yields some interesting hypotheses about the nature and function of the nightmare. Previous psychoanalytic views have described the nightmare as a dream failure, an early warning sign of pathology, a diagnostic indicator, and a phobic symptom. Freud spoke of two types of "typical" nightmares which seem to reflect early developmental conflicts: dreams of falling, (preoedipal dyadic experiences of feared abandonment by the mother) and dreams of being attacked (which appear to reflect experiences of oedipal conflict and triadic object relations).

The frequency with which nightmares occur throughout the lifespan and their link to particular developmental phases indicate that they may play a major structural and adaptive role in human development. As such, they may be most fruitfully compared to other "developmental organizers" described by Spitz (the smiling response, stranger anxiety, and the appearance of the "no."). A. Freud, Spitz, Mahler, and other developmentally oriented psychoanalysts have emphasized the progressive differentiation and increasing capacities of the ego to articulate and master both endogenous and exogenous anxiety. The earliest structures of mental life leave the child vulnerable to the experience of anxiety without recourse to adequate defensive structures. The occurrence of the nightmare may signal the child's increasing cognitive and affective competence and could be considered a *developmental achievement.* Because the nightmare expresses developmental dynamic, structural, and adaptive processes, it gives us a unique opportunity to explore the ontogeny of mind.

## References

Ames, L. B. 1964. Sleep and dreams in childhood. In E. Harms, ed., *Problems of Sleep and Dream in Children,* pp. 6–29. New York: Macmillan.

Anders, T. F. and C. Guilleminault. 1976. The pathophysiology of sleep disorders in pediatrics. *Advances in Pediatrics* 22(1):137–49.

Aserinsky, E. and N. Kleitman. 1953. Regularly occurring periods of eye motility and concomitant phenomena during sleep. *Science* 118:273–74.

Beltramini, A. U. and M. Hertzig. 1983. Sleep and bedtime behavior in preschool-aged children. *Pediatrics* 71(2):153–58.

Bornstein, B. 1935. Phobia in a two-and-a-half-year-old girl. *Psychoanalytic Quarterly,* vol. 4.

Brenner, C. 1951. *A case of childhood hallucinosis.* In R. Eissler et al., ed., *Psychoanalytic Study of the Child,* vol. 6. New York: International Universities Press.

Broughton, R.J. 1968. Sleep disorders: Disorders of arousal? *Science* 159:1070–78.

Despert, J. L. 1949. Dreams in children of preschool age. In R. Eissler et al., eds., *Psychoanalytic Study of the Child,* 3-4:141–80. New York: International Universities Press.

Erickson, M. H. 1941. On the possible occurrence of a dream in an eight-month-old infant. *Psychoanalytic Quarterly,* vol. 10.

Esman, A. H. 1962. Visual hallucinoses in young children. In R. Eissler et al., eds., *Psychoanalytic Study of the Child,* vol. 17. New York: International Universities Press.

Fisher, C., J. Byrne, A. Edwards, and E. Kahn. 1970. A psychophysiological study of nightmares. *Journal of American Psychoanalytic Association* 18:747–82.

Fisher, C. and W. C. Dement. 1963. Studies of the psychopathology of sleep and dreams. *American Journal of Psychiatry,* vol. 119.

Foster, J. D. and J. E. Anderson. 1936. Unpleasant dreams in childhood. *Child Development,* vol. 7.

Foulkes, D. 1979. Children's dreams. In B. B. Wolman, ed., *Handbook of Dreams: Research, Theories, and Applications,* pp. 131–67. New York: Van Nostrand Reinhold.

Fraiberg, S. 1950. On the sleep disturbance of early childhood. In R. Eissler et al., eds., *Psychoanalytic Study of the Child,* 5:285–309. New York: International Universities Press.

Freud, A. 1936. *The Ego and the Mechanisms of Defence.* New York: International Universities Press.

Freud, S. *Standard Edition of the Complete Psychological Works of Sigmund Freud.* James Strachey, ed. and tr. 24 vols. London: Hogarth Press, 1953–1974; New York: Macmillan.

1900. *The Interpretation of Dreams.* Vols. 4 and 5.

1901. *On Dreams.* Vol. 5.

1905. *Three Essays on the Theory of Sexuality.* Vol. 7.
1918. *The History of an Infantile Neurosis.* Vol. 22.
1926. Inhibitions, symptoms, and anxiety. 20:75–172.
1933. *New Introductory Lectures on Psychoanalysis.* Vol. 22.

Friend, M. R. 1956. Report of panel: On sleep disturbances in children. *Journal of American Psychoanalytic Association* 4:514–25.

Furman, E. 1962. Some features of the dream function of a severely disturbed child. *Journal of American Psychoanalytic Association,* vol. 10.

Grotjahn, M. 1938. Dream observations in a two-year-four-months-old baby. *Psychoanalytic Quarterly,* vol. 7.

Guilleminault, C. and T. F. Anders. 1976. Sleep disorders in children. *Advances in Pediatrics* 22(2):151–75.

Harris, I. D. 1948. Observation concerning typical anxiety dreams. *Psychiatry* 11(3):301–9.

Harris, I. D. 1951. Characterological significance of typical anxiety dreams. *Psychiatry* 14(3):279–93.

Herzog, J. M. 1980. Sleep disturbance and father hunger in 18-to-28-month-old boys. In A. Solnit et al., eds., *Psychoanalytic Study of the Child,* 35:219–33. New Haven: Yale University Press.

Holt, R. R. 1967. The development of the primary process: A structural view. *Psychoanalytic Issues* 5(2–3):345–83.

Jones, E. 1931. *On the Nightmare.* London: Hogarth Press. (Original work published in 1911.)

Levy, D. 1945. Psychic trauma of operations in children. *American Journal of Disorders of Childhood,* vol. 59.

Lewin, B. 1952. Phobic symptoms and dream interpretation. *Psychoanalytic Quarterly,* vol. 21.

Mack, J. E. 1965. Nightmares, conflicts, and ego development in childhood. *International Journal of Psychoanalysis* 46(4):403–27.

Maenchen, A. 1942. On neurotic disturbances of sleep. *International Journal of Psychoanalysis,* vol. 23.

Mahler, M. S. 1975. *The Psychological Birth of the Human Infant.* New York: Basic Books.

Nagera, H. 1966. Sleep and its disturbances approached developmentally. In R. Eissler et al., eds., *Psychoanalytic Study of the Child,* 21:393–447. New York: International Universities Press.

Niederland, W. 1957. The earliest dreams of a young child. In R. Eissler et al., eds., *Psychoanalytic Study of the Child,* 12:190–208. New York: International Universities Press.

Piaget, J. 1950. *Play, Dreams, and Imitation.* New York: Norton.

Rangell, L. 1950. A treatment of nightmares in a seven-year-old boy. In R. Eissler et al., eds., *Psychoanalytic Study of the Child,* 5:358–90. New York: International Universities Press.

Renik, O., P. Spielman, and J. Afterman. 1978. Bamboo phobia in an eighteen-month-old boy. *Journal of the American Psychoanalytic Association* (Suppl.) 26:255–82.

Ritvo, S. 1974. Current status of the concept of the infantile neurosis. In R. Eissler et al., eds., *Psychoanalytic Study of the Child,* vol. 29. New Haven: Yale University press.

Roffwarg, H. P., W. C. Dement, and C. Fisher. 1964. Sleep-dream patterns in neonates, infants, children, and adults. In E. Harms, ed., *Problems of Sleep and Dream in Children,* pp. 60–71. New York: Macmillan.

Roiphe, H. and E. Galenson. 1973. Object loss and early sexual development. *Psychoanalytic Quarterly* 40(1):73–90.

Root, N. 1962. Some remarks on anxiety dreams in latency and adolescence. *Journal of American Psychoanalytic Association,* vol. 10.

Sarnoff, C. A. 1970. Symbols and symptoms: Phytophobia in a two-year-old girl. *Psychoanalytic Quarterly* 39:550–62.

Schur, M. 1966. *The Id and the Regulatory Principles of Mental Functioning.* New York: International Universities Press.

Sperling, M. 1949. Neurotic sleep disturbances in children. *Nervous Child* 8(1):28–46.

Sperling, M. 1952. Animal phobias in a two-year-old-child. In R. Eissler et al., eds., *Psychoanalytic Study of the Child,* vol. 7. New York: International Universities Press.

Sperling, M. 1955. Etiology and treatment of sleep disturbances in children. *Psychoanalytic Quarterly* 24:358–68.

Sperling, M. 1958. Pavor nocturnus. *Journal of the American Psychoanalytic Association,* vol. 6.

Spitz, R. 1965. *The First Year of Life: A Psychoanalytic Study of Normal and Deviant Development of Object Relations.* New York: International Universities Press.

Waelder, H. J. 1930. The analysis of a case of night terror. In R. Eissler et al., eds., *Psychoanalytic Study of the Child,* 2:189–227. New York: International Universities Press.

# PART FOUR: Studies of the Nightmare in the Psychology of Personality

# 12.

# Nightmares and Psychopathology

MICHAEL JOSEPH DAVIES

ALTHOUGH THE NIGHTMARE seems to be a universal human experience, it is still one of the least understood with respect to psychological phenomena. The lack of understanding about nightmares derives in part from the difficulty in making a direct study of psychic phenomena, and in part from a lack of consensus about the teleology and psychology of dreaming in general (Blum 1976). A further complication arises from the fact that few psychological studies have specified with much clarity the differences between nightmares and other kinds of dreams. Are nightmares qualitatively different from other dreams, for example? If so, in what respects do they differ? If not, how are we to explain their intensity and vividness as well as the unique appeal they have had on the imagination of people throughout history?

In the past, human mythology sought to attribute nightmares to demoniacal influence. As Friedmann (1980) has pointed out, the word "nightmare" comes from both the French "cauchemar" and the German "Nachtmahr"—"mahr" being a devil—and thus both the French word (a devil lying on top of one's chest) and the German word (a night devil) indicate that an evil spirit has interrupted the peace of sleep. Modern psychology, taking into account the findings of sleep research as well as dynamic psychiatry, does not credit demons with causing nightmares. However, there is still much confusion about what is "normal" and what is "pathological" about nightmares.

This chapter briefly reviews the recent psychological literature on nightmares. Then it discusses this literature in the light of the present author's own clinical data. The focus is on two questions. First, are nightmares "pathological" in and of themselves? That is, do they indicate the presence of psychopathology in the person who experiences them? Second, how do nightmares differ from other dreams in relation to psychopathology?

It is concluded that (1) nightmares are not in and of themselves psychopathological; (2) the anxiety which is a common characteristic of nightmares may often be caused by conflicts over aggression, either the impulse of aggression or the expression of that impulse in aggressive behavior; (3) nightmares are often caused by affects other than aggression; and (4) nightmares and other dreams have more similarities than differences.

Before discussing these issues, however, it is important to clarify some terminology.

## Terminology in the Study of Nightmares

The term "nightmare" has been used generically, and popularly, to refer to any kind of anxiety dream, and especially to an anxiety dream which disturbs sleep to the point that the person wakes up because of the dream's content. In the scientific literature the word "nightmare" is used more specifically to distinguish it from "night terror" (pavor nocturnus). In this sense a "nightmare" is considered by many authors (Broughton 1968; Friedmann 1980; Hartmann 1980; Kahn et al. 1978; Kales et al. 1974; Keith 1975) to refer to an anxiety dream occurring during rapid eye movement (REM) sleep, as opposed to night terrors which occur during non–rapid eye movement (NREM) sleep. In this sense nightmares are defined by Kales et al. (1981:439) as:

> nocturnal episodes of intense anxiety and fear associated with a vivid and emotionally charged dream experience. Nightmares are often accompanied by some vocalization and increased autonomic activity. They can be serious

cause of sleep disruption, since the events are most often followed by lengthy periods of arousal. Typically, the individual has detailed recall of the nightmare. The patient usually awakens easily, often spontaneously, from a nightmare, is lucid following arousal, and usually becomes quickly oriented to the environment, although it may take some time for him to separate nightmare dream content from reality.

Kales et al. (1974:407–9), drawing on the findings of Gastaut and Broughton (1964), distinguished the characteristics of nightmares and night terrors:

In the night terror, the child (or adult) suddenly, out of "deep" sleep, sits up with a piercing scream. Motor activity is intense with occasional sleepwalking, the child is confused and incoherent, and heart and respiratory rate are profoundly elevated. Subjectively there are feelings of intense anxiety and respiratory oppression, and a sensation of doom, while content recalled is usually limited to a single frightening image. In the REM nightmare, or frightening dream, autonomic changes, if present, are slight, the individual is more easily aroused and content recalled is more lengthy and developed.

Kahn et al. (1978:532) suggested that the "lesser intensity of the REM anxiety dream may be at least partially explained by the fact that during REM the physiological activation provides a buffer which prevents extreme terror."

Clarity in termination is difficult to achieve, however, because some authors (e.g., Broughton 1968) use the term "pavor nocturnus" when referring to children's night terrors and "nightmare" when referring to the NREM terror of adults. Other authors (e.g., Friedmann 1980) use the term "nightmare" to refer to all anxiety dreams generically, including night terrors. Friedmann reserves the term "REM nightmare" to distinguish nightmares from night terrors. A further complication comes from the occasional use of terms such as "incubus attack" (from the medieval notion of the male demon, *incubus,* thought to lie on women during sleep to have sexual intercourse with them) and "succubus attack" (the *succubus* lay under males in order to have sex with them) as synonyms for nightmare in the broadest sense.

In the present chapter the distinction between night terrors, occurring during NREM sleep, and nightmares, occurring during REM sleep, will be maintained.

## Are Nightmares Pathological?

From the literature the answer to this question appears to depend on the background of the respondent. Authors seem to take one or more of three positions. First there are the neurophysiological researchers who describe nightmares as sleep *disorders,* thereby implying some degree of neuropsychopathology. Evidence for such pathology may range from the simple assertion that nightmares involve involuntary arousal from sleep to the studies which have noted positive correlations between the administration of drugs such as reserpine, L-Dopa, or monoamine oxidase inhibitors and the presence of nightmares (Hartmann 1980).

A second group of authors have reported psychological characteristics of nightmare sufferers. Among these authors, Kales et al. (1980), along with their laboratory studies, reported findings of "relatively high levels of psychopathology" among subjects reporting nightmares as compared to a control group not reporting nightmares. The authors of this study described their nightmare sufferers in general as "distrustful, alienated, and emotionally estranged, and many showed a chronic schizoid pattern of adjustment" (1980:1197). Although not psychotic, these nightmare sufferers were described from MMPI data as having "considerable psychopathology" and "a common personality pattern for nightmare sufferers" (1980:1200).

Hartmann and Russ (1979) reported higher frequency of nightmares in people vulnerable to schizophrenia, for example relatives of schizophrenics, or in people themselves disposed to schizophrenia.

A third position has been taken by authors who are more clinically and less physiologically oriented. They have looked at the content of the nightmare as they would at the content of any other anxiety dream and have arrived at conclusions about the nightmare experiencer's psychological state. Dreistadt (1972:22) described a "new theory of nightmares" as follows:

> the sleeping person's censorship is sometimes powerless because he has already expressed and even partially fulfilled an angry hostile motivation *while awake.* The person is already starting to express an aggressive and hostile motivation while he is awake which he fears will lead him into

danger or disaster and so he cannot help turning the motivation against himself in his dreams, thereby turning his dreams into nightmares. The content of the nightmare itself consists of *consequences* that he fears will result from his hostile motivation and he depicts these terrible consequences *to warn and stop himself.* These consequences are directly expressed insofar as they are present dangers but are expressed in disguise if the consequence would involve the fulfillment of past repressed motivations. (italics in the original)

Harris (1951) described the "typical anxiety dream," without distinguishing nightmares from other anxiety dreams, as falling into two groups, "dreams of falling from heights" and "dreams of being attacked"—the former he associated with the psychic danger of loss of love or of separation of the loved one, and the latter with the danger of castration or somatic injury. Further, he listed characteristics of patients with falling dreams in terms of their object relationships. He concluded that the patients with falling dreams tended (1) to have problems in separating from the mother and in expressing aggression toward her; (2) to be more highly and naively "emotional" rather than rational in their overt behavior; (3) to be defensive about letting their conscious thoughts or feelings be known to others. In a later work Harris (1960:605) refined his views by speculating that "the falling dream reflects anxiety over loss of *a* love object, whereas the attack dream reflects anxiety over loss of *the* love object." In other words, the falling dream is seen as originating in conflicts derivative of a pre-object-constancy phase while attack dreams would originate in conflicts from an object-constancy phase. His conclusion is that neither kind of anxiety dream is of itself evidence of psychopathology:

Since both kinds of dream and their predominances are reported by persons in normal and abnormal samples, there is little evidence that the predominance of the dream type has much to do with whether the person is psychologically healthy or sick. The position which I believe it is safer to take is that the two groups represent two paths of a divergent characterological evolution, each with its particular strengths and limitations. (Harris 1960:610)

## The Distinction Between Nightmares and Psychopathology

Having sampled the pertinent literature, we can state some conclusions. First, *there is no clear, simple link between nightmares and psychopathology.* In other words, the experiencing of nightmares alone is not sufficient to warrant a psychopathological diagnosis. To those authors who point out that patients who present themselves as nightmare sufferers tend to show evidence of psychopathology, we can reply that, since mental health is not a discrete entity but is a descriptive term implying an appropriate level of intra- and interpersonal maturity, the same piece of behavior may be evidence of psychopathology in one case and not in another.

An analogy would be the experience of anxiety. For someone to be anxious is not evidence of psychopathology. In fact, in some instances the apparent lack of anxiety may be evidence of psychopathology. In general, however, we need to know the degree of anxiety and how it affects behavior before we can decide whether it is symptomatic of pathology.

Second, we can conclude that *the anxiety which is a common characteristic of nightmares may often be caused by conflicts over aggression, either the impulse of aggression or the expression of the impulse in aggressive behavior.*

Third, as a result of my own psychoanalytic work with patients, I would suggest that *nightmares are often caused by affects other than aggression.* Patients have reported that their sleep was disturbed by dreams which in their manifest content may have been, for example, overtly sexual and pleasurable. In some instances this happened when the dream content led them to reach orgasm, at which point their sleep was disturbed. On arousal, anxiety may or may not have been present along with the recollection of pleasurable sensations. Other qualities of nightmares listed earlier in this chapter may also have been present. When one recalls that REM sleep is also a time of sexual excitement, the presence of erotic affects in nightmares is not difficult to comprehend. This position—that nightmares are not only dreams of terror—is also proposed by Kellerman (this volume, chapters 15–18).

Even when the manifest content of the nightmare involves aggression, the latent content may imply other affects. For instance, a female patient began a psychoanalytic session by relating a dream she had had early that morning. She had woken up quite anxious. The dream involved her "murdering someone in a very bloody fashion or being murdered by someone." She described the dream as going on until "I woke up because it became more and more violent." Later in the session when she associated to the dream, she described herself as having to wake up "before something totally unacceptable happens." As the associations continued she was struck by her own phrase "totally unacceptable," this sounded to her like words her mother might have used rather than words she herself would use in everyday speech. What her mother had found "totally unacceptable" was the idea that her daughter in adolescence might become sexually active. For her mother sex was nothing more than a duty which a woman was obligated to perform passively and submissively in order to provide children for her husband. At this point in the session the patient had a strong emotional conviction that what had been so troubling about the dream was that she had really been dreaming about sexual relations with a man in which both she and he were very active aggressively and with much pleasure. What caused her anxiety in the dream was that her sexual behavior was strongly fused with aggressive elements and that such a fusion was immensely pleasurable. In psychoanalytic terminology, her superego, involving among other aspects the internalized prohibitions of her mother, found "totally unacceptable" the ideas that not only was sexual activity being enjoyed but that the patient was partaking with active lust. So intense was her aggressive enjoyment of sex that it appears that the sleep censor was alerted partially, that is, to the point that it could not allow the dream to continue, but because of the disguised nature of the dream content (aggressive masking the libidinal) not to the point that the dream's content had to be repressed.

## The Relation of Neurophysiological Research and Applied Clinical Work

Authors who are concerned with the neurophysiology of sleep are engaged in an important area of scientific discovery. Unfortunately, up to this point it has been difficult to apply their findings in a very relevant way to the field of dynamic, clinical psychology. The situation is analogous to research into schizophrenia. So much of the neurophysiology has shed light on the understanding and chemical alleviation of the symptom without shedding much light on the intrapsychic and interpersonal meaning of the problems whose presence is signaled by the symptoms. In this regard it is important to note that so far the important discovery of REM sleep by Aserinsky and Kleitman (1953) and the subsequent sleep research have not been translated into new or deeper understanding of the dynamic significance of dreams.

We can conclude then that the neuropsychological determination of nightmares as sleep *disorders* is not particularly helpful to us in our attempt to answer the question whether nightmares are pathological in a psychological sense.

A second group of authors apparently has tried to bridge the gap between neuropsychology and clinical psychology. They have done this principally by the addition of some psychological testing and interviewing of subjects who report experiencing nightmares. The consequent results have a number of shortcomings. At best they are tentative, and one must be warned against generalizing from scant data. Most of these studies generate correlations which do not of themselves prove causality. Further, a study which matches nightmare sufferers with a control group not reporting nightmares still has to avoid all the problems of sampling bias. Another criticism of such "controlled" studies is that it is easy to overgeneralize results obtained from psychological testing. There is also the danger of forgetting that psychological tests are useful only as adjuncts to the expertise of the clinician. In this respect findings of psychopathology in nightmare sufferers must be carefully evaluated, and further studies both new and replicative must be encouraged.

Also it is important to recall that psychopathology is not an entity that a subject "has" or "doesn't have" the way persons may "have" or "not have" a certain level of a drug in their bodies. Mental health refers primarily to a person's intrapersonal and interpersonal maturity (Grey and Davies 1981).

A third group of authors are more psychodynamically oriented. Harris (1951, 1960) explicitly and Dreistadt (1972) implicitly take the position that nightmares are not ipso facto evidence of psychopathology.

Dreistadt and Harris are further in agreement with each other on the important role which aggression plays in generating nightmares. For Dreistadt it is the aggression which has been partially expressed during waking hours, and thereby becomes anxiety-provoking because of anticipated "danger" or "disaster," that provokes the nightmare. Harris' "falling" and "attack" dreams both imply aggression. Harris concluded that the dreamer of the falling dream has conflicts (derived from an early, pre-object-constancy state of development) over the expression of aggression toward the mother. The "attack" dream implies the projection of the dreamer's own aggression onto others who are then portrayed as attacking him.

Harris and Dreistadt's emphasis on the role of aggression in the genesis of nightmares is of paramount importance. However, conflicts over aggression do not explain fully the occurrence of nightmares.

Dreistadt (1972:21), while criticizing Freud for failing to explain "why anxiety occurs *only* in *some* dreams when he theorizes that wishes and repressed wishes are fulfilled in *all* dreams" (italics in the original), offers data that lack clinical confirmation. Some of his conclusions seem naive. For example he "explains" the fact that some people wake up frightened from nightmares without remembering specific dream content by describing such anxiety dreams as "blind," that is, lacking "visual imagery." He then speculates "that this kind of nightmare may mean that the person is warning himself that he is walking too *blindly* into some situation that may be dangerous" (Dreistadt 1972:251; italics added).

Dreistadt appears to be further forcing his theory because of his neglect of the latent meaning of dream content. Although manifest dream content is a valid and reliable source of scientific data (Davies 1978), it cannot be studied as if there were no such thing as latent content. In fact, it is not clear that Dreistadt isn't in fact attempting to deny the unconscious meaning of dreams, which in itself would explain his opposition to Freud's views. It is also not clear what the danger or disaster is that people who have nightmares must fear when they begin to express their aggression during waking hours, as he hypothesizes results in the occurrence of the nightmare. Further, why must these people anticipate such danger and why do they wait until they have gone to sleep to react to it? Also his theory restricts the meaning of nightmares to recent experiences of aggression; otherwise, why would aggression felt in the past result in the subject's having to "warn and stop himself" in the present? To a clinician dynamically oriented, such exclusion of any meaning to dreams except in relation to the here and now is naive.

Harris, on the other hand, is aware of the importance both of the latent content of dreams and of their specific meaning. In the articles cited he is intentionally confining himself to the elucidation of two typical patterns of manifest dream content. The conclusions stated in this chapter are not necessarily in opposition to his theory. The present chapter simply attempts to take a larger, more encompassing view of nightmares and their origins.

## How Do Nightmares Differ from Other Dreams?

Our second question in this chapter asks how nightmares differ from other dreams in relation to psychopathology. The answer to this seems to be that nightmares and dreams have more in common than they have differing. All dreams, whether nightmares or not, in psychoanalytic terms are considered to be primary-process phenomena. Primary-process phenomena are not in themselves psychopathological. One of the main characteristics of primary process activity is that there is a high degree of cathectic mobility (Brenner 1973). This means that if one method of discharging drive energy is blocked, another means of discharge is easily found. In this sense nightmares occur when for some particular reason a person cannot discharge psychic energy without the interruption of sleep by the sleep censor. The sleep censor manages a partial blocking by preventing the continuation of the dream, but the ego manages to prevent further repression.

There is a need for additional research by clinicians on the reasons why in particular instances dreamers cannot discharge the psychic energy without the intervention of the sleep censor which interrupts the process. Is this curtailing of the dream by an interruption of sleep an attempt to continue a neurotic conflict or an attempt to resolve it? Are the reasons the same for different individuals or even for the same individual at different moments in life? Does the nightmare of a person in psychoanalysis who will work on analyzing it soon after in an analytic session have a different meaning in this sense from the nightmare of a person who is not at all introspective or interested in understanding dreams? Clearly the nightmare of a psychotic individual has different dynamic significance from the nightmare of the "healthy neurotic."

For the present author dreams and nightmares form a psychic continuum. Therefore, posing and attempting to answer such questions as the above are of more relevance than simply dismissing nightmares as "psychopathological."

## Summary

This chapter briefly reviewed the recent psychological literature on nightmares. It then discussed this literature in the light of the present author's own clinical data. The distinction between "nightmares" as anxiety dreams occurring during REM sleep and "night terrors" (pavor nocturnus) occurring during NREM sleep was described. In this chapter "nightmares" referred to the REM type of anxiety dream.

It was concluded that: (1) nightmares are not in and of themselves psychopathological; (2) the anxiety which is a common characteristic of nightmares may often be caused by conflicts over aggression, either the impulse of aggression or the expression of that impulse in aggressive behavior; (3) nightmares are often caused by affects other than aggression; and (4) nightmares and other dreams have more in common with each other than they have differences.

## References

Aserinsky, E. and N. Kleitman. 1953. Regularly occurring periods of eye motility, and concomitant phenomena during sleep. *Science* 118:273–74.

Blum, H. P. 1976. The changing use of dreams in psychoanalytic practice. *International Journal of Psychoanalysis,* 57:315–24.

Brenner, C. 1973. *An Elementary Textbook of Psychoanalysis.* New York: International Universities Press.

Broughton, R. J. 1968. Sleep disorders: Disorders of arousal? *Science* 159:1070–78.

Davies, M. J. 1978. The manifest content of initial dreams in psychotherapy: Their diagnostic and prognostic significance. Ph.D. dissertation, Fordham University.

Dreistadt, R. 1972. A unifying theory of dreams, a new theory of nightmares, and the relationship of nightmares to psychopathology, literature, and collective social panic behavior. *Psychology* 9(4):19–30.

Freidmann, C. T. H. 1980. Nightmares. In J. M. Natterson ed., *The Dream in Clinical Practice.* New York: Jason Aronson.

Gastaut, H. and R. Broughton. 1964. A clinical and polygraphic study of episodic phenomena during sleep. *Biological Psychiatry* 7:197–221.

Grey, A. and M. J. Davies. 1981. Mental health as level of interpersonal maturity. *Journal of the American Academy of Psychoanalysis* 9(4):601–14.

Harris, I. D. 1951. Characterological significance of the typical anxiety dreams. *Psychiatry* 14:279–94.

Harris, I. D. 1960. Typical anxiety dreams and object relations. *International Journal of Psychoanalysis* 41:604–11.

Hartmann, E. 1980. Sleep disorders. In H. I. Kaplan, A. M. Freedman, and B. Sadock, eds., *Comprehensive Textbook of Psychiatry III.* 3d ed. Baltimore: Williams and Wilkins.

Hartmann, E. and D. Russ. 1979. Frequent nightmares and the vulnerability to schizophrenia: The personality of the nightmare sufferer. *Psychopharmacological Bulletin* 15(1):10–12.

Kahn, E., C. Fisher, and A. Edwards. 1978. Night terrors and anxiety dreams. In A. M. Arkin, J. S. Antrobus, and S. J. Ellman, eds., *The Mind in Sleep: Psychology and Psychophysiology.* Hillsdale, N.J.: Lawrence Erlbaum Associates.

Kales, A., E. O. Bixler, and J. D. Kales. 1974. Role of the sleep research and treatment facility: Diagnosis, treatment, and education. In E. D. Weitzman, ed., *Advances in Sleep Research.* Vol. 1. Flushing, N.Y.: Spectrum.

Kales, A., C. R. Soldatos, A. B. Caldwell, D. S. Charney, J. D. Kales, D. Markel, and R. Cadieux. Nightmares: Clinical characteristics and personality patterns. *American Journal of Psychiatry* 1980. 137(10):1197-1201.

Kales, A., C. R. Soldatos, and J. D. Kales. 1981. Sleep disorders: Evaluation and management in the office setting. In S. Arieti, ed., *American Handbook of Psychiatry.* 2d ed. Vol. 7. New York: Basic Books.

Keith, P. R. 1975. Night terrors: A review of psychology, neurophysiology, and therapy. *Journal of the American Academy of Child Psychiatry* 14:477-89.

# 13.

# Nightmares, Hypnagogic Hallucinations, and Sleep Paralysis

Arthur A. Gray

THE EMPHASIS IN this chapter will be on the psychological significance and distinction of nightmares, hypnagogic hallucinations, and sleep paralysis. These sleep disturbances have long presented problems for psychological interpretation. Some authors have treated each sleep phenomenon separately, while others have discussed all of them together. From as early as the latter part of the nineteenth century to the present, these phenomena have been correlated with a wide variety of variables. For example, nightmares have been viewed as the result of lung disorder (Tissié, cited by Freud 1900) and were attributed to biophysical roots (Gruppé, cited by Freud 1900). Freud (1900, 1927), Jones (1949), and Schneck (1969) all understood nightmares, hypnagogic hallucinations, and sleep paralysis as anthropomorphic repressed impulses fighting for self-assertion in the psyche. Alexander (1909) in early studies supported the anthropomorphic approach by seeing in hypnagogic hallucinations the creative unconscious at work. More recently, Campbell (1981) related sleep paralysis to a neurological dysfunction of the reticular activation system, and Kellerman (1981) has emphasized that along with the familiar nightmare there has emerged in clinical practice the increased appearance of hypnagogic hallucinations, and sleep paralysis as part of the narcoleptic syndrome. Finally, Liddon (1967) indicated that while it is accurate to consider hypnagogic hallucinations and sleep paralysis as having a biological basis, it is more clinically productive to view these phenomena as features of the nightmare.

## Nightmares, Anxiety Dreams, and Night Terrors

Research (Fisher et al. 1970; Broughton 1968, 1970; Hartmann 1970) has identified different types of nightmares. While it is common for clinicians and lay people alike to identify REM anxiety dreams awakening the dreamer as being nightmares, the picture is more intricate. In addition to the REM anxiety dream/nightmare, Fisher et al. have added two other types of nightmares. First is the stage 4 arousal reaction nightmare and second is the stage 2 awakenings which are similar to stage 4 nightmares but are not as intense. These three forms of nightmares all have in common the presence of anxiety and the awakening of the person from sleep.

The authors here refer to the four stages of sleep in their formulations of the different types of nightmares. Stage 1 is REM sleep characterized by rapid eye movement and low-voltage random EEG patterns. Stages 2 to 4 are similar to each other, with 4 being considered the deepest level. These latter three stages are represented by an absence of REM and the presence of clearly delineated delta waves. Delta waves are "EEG activity with a frequency of less than 4 cycles per second" (Hartmann 1970). The deeper the sleep, the greater is the presence of delta waves in the EEG record.

Anxiety dreams take place in stage 1 sleep; that is, REM sleep. Imagery with anxiety themes is present. On the other hand, there is controversy as to whether or not stage 4 sleep contains any imagery. Broughton's (1970) research found no imagery present in stage 4 awakenings, while Fisher et al. did. Fisher et al.'s research revealed that in the stage 4 nightmare there is first a breakthrough of panic resulting in night terror, sleepwalking, or sleep talking with accompanying hallucinatory images. The hallucinatory images result from a state of psychological regression combining with early psychic trauma (Fisher et al. 1970). Broughton, on the other hand, found no imagery present during these stage 4 arousals, and he interpreted them as simply disturbances in the physiological arousal pattern.

Despite the controversy, it is established that in stage 4 nightmares, anxiety is first experienced somatically, leading to an awakened-like state in which associated imagery might emerge. On the other hand, in the REM or stage 1 nightmares, imagery emerges first. These images generate anxiety, ultimately leading to an awakening of the sleeper. Note that stage 2 and 3 nightmares are most easily thought of as less intense versions of stage 4 nightmares. It is probably simplest to distinguish only between stage 1 and stage 4 nightmares (Hartmann 1970); that is, REM and NREM nightmares. The REM sleep which defines the REM nightmare is also called D-sleep or paradoxical sleep. The NREM sleep which defines the NREM nightmares is often referred to as S-sleep (Hartmann 1970, 1984).

In summary, then, NREM nightmares are characterized by somatization of anxiety in the form of night terrors, sleepwalking, and sleep talking. These arousal states are possibly then accompanied by frightening imagery. On the other hand, in REM nightmares anxiety is experienced first through imagery. The sleeper somatically awakens to avoid or gain relief from the anxiety-laden imagery.

## Hypnagogic Hallucinations and Sleep Paralysis

Hypnagogic hallucinations and sleep paralysis have been described by Kellerman (1981) and others (Yoss and Daly 1957; Zarcone 1973) as part of the tetrad of symptoms diagnostic of narcolepsy. The other symptoms of the tetrad are narcolepsy proper and cataplexy. However, the hypnagogic hallucination and sleep paralysis also appear in nonnarcoleptics (Everett 1963; Kellerman

1981; Schneck 1969). Clearly, when these two symptoms—hypnagogic hallucinations and sleep paralysis—are detected, the presence of narcolepsy becomes a possibility.

The term "hypnagogic hallucination" was first formally coined by Maury in 1848. It is only over the past three decades that much interest in this phenomenon has developed. Hypnagogic images are hallucinations which occur in a period of drowsiness between wakefulness and sleep (Vihvelin 1948). They can also occur in the period of awakening from sleep. In this latter condition they are referred to as hypnopompic hallucinations. Whether before sleep onset or after sleep, the experience is one of seeing things that are not there (McKellar and Simpson 1954; Schacter 1976; Slight 1924; Vihvelin 1948). Hypnagogic hallucinations differ from nightmares in that there is a greater degree of waking consciousness present during the hallucination. The person experiencing the hypnagogic hallucination can still consciously look at the dreamlike imagery and is aware of this imagery, much as one by attending can be aware of one's waking fantasies. The imagery seems real and is observed in great detail. Because of the unusual combination of being conscious yet in a dreamlike state, people can often momentarily confuse the hypnagogic experience with reality. This temporary confusion with reality can easily take place since the hypnagogic experience can creep in so subtly. For example, while fatigued sitting at a desk studying for a long time, it is possible to close one's eyes for a moment's rest and fall into a hypnagogic state without noticing it. The difference between waking consciousness and sleep is blurred at this point. For most people, such hallucinations are not bizarre or terribly frightening.

There is, however, a special condition when the hypnagogic imagery can be frightening. This is when it occurs in the presence of sleep paralysis. During sleep paralysis the subject's mind is to some degree awake and therefore a sense of familiar waking consciousness exists. At the same time there is a dreaded sense of not being able to move physically—hence, the paralysis. During the sleep paralysis a person is completely immobile. This paralysis can last a few seconds or a few minutes. Surprisingly, although people with sleep paralysis report a profound paralysis during the attack, nevertheless this experience stands in stark contrast to the end of the attack. The end of the attack can be achieved by the mere physical touch of another person.

When sleep paralysis is combined with frightening, threatening hypnagogic hallucinations, a nightmare-like state can exist. Patients have reported this type of experience in which some important person seems to intrude into the room (Kellerman 1981; Vihvelin 1948). The intruder will rummage through the room and the person in bed is unable to respond physically. During the hallucination the imagined intruder can be experienced as within arm's reach of the dreamer. The dreamer can consciously think of reaching out to touch the intruder but is unable to move. In this conscious thought of reaching out, the wish to reality-test the hallucination is implied. But because of the paralysis, the attempt is futile. Moaning and some twisting or stirring motions are possible, but coordinated movement allowing the individual to confirm or deny the hallucinatory experience is not possible.

How does this differ from the nightmare? Kellerman (1981:54) suggests that in sleep paralysis accompanying the hypnagogic hallucination "the definition of REM sleep is not conventionally satisfied; a suppression of muscle activity occurs but the REM pattern and low voltage frequency in the EEG are atypical." During waking this phenomenon of the sleep paralysis emerges symptomatically as a cataleptic attack. There is a seizure-like loss of muscle control. In the process of waking from or going to sleep, the phenomenon occurs as the sleep paralysis. The hypnagogic hallucinations which accompany the sleep paralysis do not have the quality of sleepwalking, sleep talking, or night terrors, after which the persons in these states have no memory of them. It has been proposed that hypnagogic imagery is accessible to introspection (Slight 1924). These are images of something physical taking place that an outside observer can verify as clearly not there. Interestingly, Schacter (1976) found that people with the so-called less rigid authoritarian personality tended to experience the hypnagogic imagery as more dreamlike than real. This sort of finding suggests that the effect of such phenomena may be differentiated on the basis of various personality variables. Hartmann (1984:154–55) found that frequent nightmare sufferers showed elevated psychotic scales on the MMPI. He concluded that those who suffer from frequent nightmares had a strong tendency to be at least preschizophrenic. It could be valuable to continue this line of exploration with those who suffer frequent bouts of hypnogogic hallucinations in the frightening context of sleep paralysis. Whether sleep paralysis victims show similar or different personality characteristics from those who suffer frequently from nightmares is a relevant question.

## Sleep Disorders and Implications of Psychopathology

Taub (1978) clarified four major types of spontaneous awakenings from sleep. These are stage 4 night terrors, REM nightmares, stage 2 awakenings, and hypnagogic nightmares. All four have in common terror or intense anxiety. Most authors of studies on sleep disorders agree with this fourfold formulation. One question that now arises refers to the extent to which the presence of these sleep disorders signals severe pathology, or whether pathology in the psychological sense is applicable to all. Various studies have shown conflicting results. Hartmann (1970, 1984; Hartmann et al. 1981) found a greater frequency of nightmares in those who tended toward schizophrenic pathology than in those who did not. Kales et al. (1980) found in nightmare sufferers reports of much anxiety and tendencies toward schizoid personality organization but no significant tendencies to psychosis. The same conflicting results can be assumed for hypnagogic hallucination and sleep paralysis. Herson (1971) found nightmares to correlate highly with other forms of sleep disorders. Vihvelin (1948) would agree. However, Vihvelin would have added that the signal of pathology is when sleep disorders such as hypnagogic hallucinations take on highly anxious content.

Schacter (1976) takes issue with the tendency to view hypnagogic states in overly physiological terms or in anthropomorphic terms such as creativity or incestuous impulses. Leroy (1926) and Rapaport (1967a, 1967b) viewed the hypnagogic state as a unique synthesis of mental content. The approach of Leroy and Rapaport viewed the sleep disorders (hypnagogic hallucinations, sleep paralysis, and nightmares) as reflections of how a person experiences and organizes the content of mental life. Hartmann

(1984) has also elaborated on the organization of the mental life of those who suffered frequent nightmares; frequent nightmare sufferers revealed a greater degree of pathology than did less frequent nightmare sufferers. This approach—of seeing sleep disorders as a reflection of how one experiences and organizes the content of one's mental life—seems most fruitful in interpreting the sleep disorders discussed in this chapter, and could lead to a better understanding of the psychological implication of sleep-interruption phenomena. It seems that the presence of sleep disturbance is not automatically an indication of serious pathology.

## Structuralization

Is it possible to view the sleep disorders addressed here as containing information on the unconscious state in terms of the degree of organization of the self? As Freud (1900) stated, "The interpretation of dreams is like a window through which we can get a glimpse of the interior of . . . the mental apparatus." Kohut (1971) has further clarified that that glimpse is a look at the content of the mental apparatus; that is, how one experiences one's self. Pathology would be defined in terms of the greater or lesser degree of structuralization of the self experience (Kohut 1984). By "structuralization" is meant first the individual's ability to establish a whole, cohesive sense of self limited by the boundaries of one's skin. Second, this cohesive sense of self would remain fairly consistent over time and especially during periods of stress. Third, the structuralization would include the individual's ability to maintain predominantly positive, affective coloration of the self, also especially during stressful, anxiety-provoking experiences (Stolorow and Lachmann, 1980). Fourth, a resulting feature of structuralization of the self is one's ability to maintain clearly demarcated distinctions between self representations and object representations. Again, as in the first three features of the structure of the self (cohesion, continuity, self-esteem regulation), the important qualifier is that this feature of self-object distinction holds up under periods of stressful, anxiety-provoking experiences.

Since under untoward conditions nightmares, hypnagogic hallucinations, and sleep paralysis are perhaps ubiquitous, the important interpretation of these symptoms perhaps will exist within the nature of the imagery represented. The nature of the imagery would indicate the type of mental organization present. Serious pathology would be represented by the absence of structure (Kohut 1971, 1984; Stolorow and Lachmann 1980). Less serious pathology would be interpreted from imagery revealing more object-instinctual type of conflicts (Stolorow and Lachmann 1980), i.e., so-called neurotic disorders. Sleep-disorder imagery in people with structural deficits would reveal conflicts about the organization of the self. In the less pathological object-instinctual disorders, the imagery of the sleep disorders would reveal conflict between self and others.

But what of the condition, such as in night terrors, where there may be no imagery present? The prevailing understanding of night terrors seems to consider the absence of imagery during the episode to be expected. What could this absence of imagery imply about pathology? Two possible explanations are plausible. First, the lack of imagery could result from some disorder associated with brainstem physiology (Hartmann 1984). This could be drug-induced, such as is found in the chronic use of the antiparkinsonian drup levodopa (Sharf et al. 1978). Possibly, the disturbance in the brainstem physiology could also result from physical pathology in the brain system.

The second possible explanation for night terrors could be a psychological one. For defensive reasons one might need to deny severely disturbing object-instinctual conflicts. Such a person would have established a high degree of structure confronting him or her with threatening, highly conflicted issues between self and others. Unconsciously and defensively all attempts would be made to deny all imagery of the object-instinctual conflict. However, the anxiety associated with this conflict would break through in the form of image-free somatized awakenings. This psychological hypothesis could be assessed by comparing the dream and other sleep-disorder imagery of those suffering night terrors with those who suffer from sleep disorders in which imagery is present. The imagery of the night-terror sufferers should be more akin to that of sleep-disorder sufferers who reveal objective-instinctual (neurotic) conflicts as opposed to those suffering from structural deficits. Hartmann's (1984; 155) findings support this hypothesis.

It was stated earlier that while Hartmann (1970, 1981) found that frequent nightmare sufferers tended toward schizophrenic disorders, Kales et al. (1980) found otherwise. For Kales the tendency was toward schizoid personality organization. More recently Hartmann (1984) groups schizoid personality disorders with schizophrenic ones. The schizoid persons are simply more integrated but possessing a vulnerability to a schizophrenic condition. The theory of structural deficits versus object-instinctual conflict pathology neatly supports Hartmann's contentions of a range of pathology from schizophrenic to preschizophrenic in frequent nightmare sufferers. According to the theory here proposed of interpreting pathology according to degree of structuralization, the findings of Kales were among persons with a greater degree of structure than for those in Hartmann's earlier studies who showed a greater tendency to schizophrenia. Those people with greater degree of schizophrenic pathology could be hypothesized as having more structural deficits.

The remaining part of this chapter will consider the psychological interpretation of sleep disorders without reference to frequency of occurrence.

## Psychological Interpretation of Sleep Disorders

Where there is structuralization, anxiety becomes a signal of the presence of important conflict. This proposition raises the point that it is possible to view the presence of sleep disturbances as a barometer of intensely experienced anxiety. The sleep disorder then would indicate a state of stress. In this sense the imagery of the sleep disturbance—nightmare, anxiety dream, or hypnagogic hallucination—will signal the degree of pathological response to that stress. Where there is a higher level of personality organization (referred to here as structuralization), the stress is experienced less pathologically but more in terms of unresolved conflicted relationships between self representations and object representations (Stolorow and Lachmann 1980). The corollary would indicate that severe pathology is defined as the absence of structure. However, it is important to repeat that unconsciously it is possible for one to psychically defend against some object-instinctual conflict by attempting to deny one's clearly established structure. Three brief vignettes will be used to demonstrate the hypothesized psychological interpretation of sleep disorders. Restated briefly, the hypothesis suggests that: (1) where there are reported sleep disorders, there is a patient under a state of stressful anxiety; (2) if the patient lacks structure, the imagery in the sleep disorders will reveal a pathological effort to establish some boundaries of self during the stress; (3) a more mature personality organization (structuralization) would be revealed in sleep disorder imagery of unresolved object-instinctual conflict between already firmly established self and object (other) representations.

In his volume on sleep disorders Kellerman (1981) cites the clinical example of a 26-year-old, asocial man who sought treatment because of his inability to pursue his romantic interest toward a woman who, in turn, also found him attractive. This patient, Alvin, felt ill-prepared to cope with the experience of a mature relationship. Alvin's social context was essentially composed of living at home with his parents and five siblings. He was always indulged as a child and as an adult he was similarly catered to in every way. Because of his extreme dependency at home, he had not developed any real measure of a sense of autonomy. Rather, in the place of greater maturity there developed an equivalent experience of anxiety. He was singularly unable to be direct with anyone, and invariably he was left feeling frustrated and full of pent-up anger. The pressure and anxiety generated by the potential and impending relationship became expressed as a sleep paralysis experience—in his case, a hypnopompic hallucination; that is, a paralysis occurring during the stage of awakening from sleep rather than one that occurs while falling into sleep.

While awakening one morning, Alvin suddenly experienced a paralysis along with a hallucination in which he felt as if he was blowing up like a balloon, filling the entire room. Kellerman states, "His immediate problem was that his reservoir of anger was so great that it was literally *blowing him up* during the attack of sleep paralysis." His conflict reached intensely anxious proportions because he had almost decided to leave home, and the separation anxiety that resulted was too difficult for him to bear. Hence, he sought therapeutic intervention.

Alvin's sleep disorder points to the presence of poor structuralization in his personality. Being overly pampered and protected at home, he had little opportunity to experience himself as a whole and integrated person in a consistent fashion. Social interaction threatened his poorly established sense of self-esteem. While to the observer his hallucinating experience of "blowing up" was not real, this experience nevertheless was a real representation of his subjective experience of himself. Alvin was overwhelmed, and this was represented by the hypnagogic imagery of his being blown up out of proportion with the threat of exploding.

Mark is another case of hypnagogic hallucination with sleep paralysis presented by Kellerman (1981). Mark, in contrast to Alvin, indicated through his reported sleep disorder a tolerance for close contact with others. This implies a greater degree of structuralization. However, within the context of his more mature sense of himself, he experienced great conflict and was, in fact, narcoleptic.

While Alvin was exceedingly ambivalent regarding social contact, Mark tolerated it. However, social contact for Mark created severe conflicts resulting in "frequent fugue or automatic behavior states. He would continue to do whatever he was doing at any given time but would have total amnesia for the period of time in the fugue state" (Kellerman 1981:59). The degree of pathology sounds greater in Mark than in Alvin. However, looking at the reported hypnagogic hallucination accompanied by sleep paralysis, the imagery contained in the sleep disorder suggests otherwise. Mark's fugue state could be interpreted as an attempt to avoid the conflict by simply denying its existence.

Mark, during sleep paralysis, hallucinated the presence of an intruder in his room. The intruder was the superintendent of the building in which Mark lived. The intruder rummaged around and seemed as close as a few inches away. Mark, however, could not respond because of the experience of sleep paralysis. On awakening, it was difficult for him to believe that the intruder was not really present.

In Mark's hallucinations there are clearly distinct representations of self and objects. Both are intact. However, from a psychological point of view, the self, represented by Mark's lying paralyzed in bed, reveals Mark's sense of incapacity in coping with a dangerous intrusion on his self-experience. The intrusion did not threaten to destroy him. It simply and frighteningly made him aware that he was ill-equipped to handle it. He was not threatened by blowing up or any other fantasy of self-annihilation. Instead, he was faced with a task he was not equipped to manage.

When Mark was confronted in waking life with the subjective intrusion of being attracted to a coworker, he experienced a sense of nonexistence through a fugue or automatic behavior state. He had trouble experiencing his interaction with the woman in his office as manageable. As with the superintendent in his hypnagogic hallucination, subjectively this woman in his office rummaged around in his emotional life, but Mark had no sense of being able to manage the affective encounter he had established with her. Could Mark's automatic behavior response to his involvement with his coworker be a sign that Mark had indeed achieved a degree of structuralization in his past? As a hypothesis it may be speculated that Mark may have felt abandoned by important authority figures from his past who left him vulnerable to intense emotional experiences he wanted to encounter. These encounters presented him with object-instinctual conflicts he was not mature enough to handle on his own. The intact images in his hypnagogic hallucination and his willingness to encounter others, both in work and in romance, signal some degree of structuralization present for Mark. However, the actuality of following through on his involvements threatened the already established stability of his psychological maturity (structuralization). This conceptualization has its source in Kohut's (1971, 1977, 1984) notion of a self-object; that is, important objects (people) whose presence enables a psychological function within oneself until that self, unaided, is able to perform that function. A simple example of such a self-object function is the ability to soothe oneself when things go badly. For Mark there might have been a sudden loss of an important self-object when Mark was learning to handle his experiences autonomously. Yet it must be remembered that Mark had a full-blown narcoleptic syndrome, and this condition reveals some brain involvement (Kellerman 1981). The contribution here is to suggest that even in biological conditions important psychological variables can offer valuable information about the particular condition and personality problem.

From the two examples above it can be seen that both Alvin and Mark suffered intensely from their conflicted contact with others. But interpreting the content of the dream imagery along the lines of structure showed differences in the nature of the pathology. For Alvin, the conflict revealed more severe pathology resulting from structural deficits. For Mark, the conflict was pathological but not to the degree that it was for Alvin. For Mark, the problem was how to cope with the conflicted object-instinctual meanings presented by the event associated with strivings for independent self-assertion. Examinations of the vicissitudes of structuralization are further offered by Stolorow and Lachmann (1981), Lachmann and Beebe (1983), and Kohut (1984). These authors reveal that the understanding of structure here proposed has crucial implications for effective, curative, clinical psychotherapeutic interventions.

Just as it may be possible to use the imagery of sleep paralysis and hypnagogic hallucination as valuable tools that reveal degree of structuralization of personality, the same, perhaps, may be said for the nightmare. The example of a nightmare to follow reveals a patient who, possibly, fits the third part of the proposed hypothesis; that is, he possesses a mature personality organization revealed in the nightmare imagery of unresolved conflict between already firmly established self and object representations. While Mark, who suffered from narcolepsy, became fearful of being overwhelmed during his involvements with others, the following patient had firmly established a structuralized sense of himself during the course of treatment. However, there remained remnants of conflict around succeeding.

The following is a nightmare from a highly structuralized patient who it is proposed suffered from derivative castration anxiety problems.

Peter, a lawyer in his early 30s, grew up in a family in which his parents divorced soon after his birth. His mother, seeing herself as inept, physically withdrew. She absented herself from the home, leaving the patient to the care of a series of surrogate mothers. However, she maintained contact with the patient throughout his life. His father, a very successful man, would drift in and out of his life. He admired his father greatly at first but grew to hate him later, as his father always criticized the patient's school and play successes, characterizing them as being "short of the mark." When the patient succeeded, he was accused of cheating. When the patient failed, he was accused of being "lazy." Actually, this person is quite intelligent.

Faced with an assignment which would have ensured partnership in a major law firm, the patient had the following dream: he was driving south on the FDR Drive in New York City. He witnessed three accidents, each involving a woman being struck. None were dead. There was heavy traffic. Each time he drove by he reassured himself that the event was not too frightening, since others were assisting the injured woman. However, each time he passed he also attempted to look up the skirt of the woman lying there. In the second accident the woman's skirt was higher than the first, but he still could not see up her dress. Finally, in the third case he was able to see up the woman's dress and saw her vagina. At this point he felt truly panicked and attempted to leave the highway. The panic became so intense that he awakened from the dream.

Analysis of the dream revealed a correspondence between the Drive and his drive for success. It seemed that each accident was his frightened attempt to jump a new hurdle in his firm. Further analysis led to the hypothesis that the last accident referred to his present major assignment, leading him to think that he would have to leave the drive (perhaps a reference to abandoning his hopes for partnership). Continuing this line of analysis, his efforts to look up the dresses of women lying on the Drive could represent reassurance attempts, indicating that these dangers were happening to someone, definitely not him (they had vaginas). However, the women had other distinguishing features, reminding him of himself. Thus, whatever the extent of denial and projection, at the point of the awakening these defenses were not successful.

Clearly present were a sense of competence (driving the car), anxiety about the dangers of succeeding, recurring themes of castration anxiety reminiscent of his childhood—for example, his father's rejecting his successes as being the result of cheating instead of acknowledging them as a result of Peter's intelligence and resourcefulness. Also clearly present were self and object distinctions of being male rather than female. But there were attempts also to deny his anxiety, attributing them to women rather than to himself. These themes represented the patient's mature self-organization (structuraliztion) but with the presence of some conflicts around maintaining his positive self-esteem. He feared unconsciously that the partners in his firm would give him reason to doubt his sense of his own positive self worth, as his father had made him doubtful of this.

The mere presence of the nightmare did not suggest the presence or absence of pathology for Peter. Instead, the nature of the imagery in the nightmare confirmed his mature self-organization (structuralization). At the same time, the analysis of the content revealed an unconscious conflict around self-assertion in the work arena. The nightmare can reveal severe pathology or it can reveal disturbing conflict in a person with a mature personality organization.

These three vignettes demonstrate that the presence of nightmares, hypnagogic hallucinations, and sleep paralysis can be distinguished quite clearly and cannot be assumed to be universal harbingers of severe pathology in patients' reports. It is, of course, necessary to evaluate the nature of the imagery contained in these reports. Where dream-related imagery such as Alvin's shows little representations of objects and distorted representations of self, the structuralization is faulty at least around themes that generate anxiety. In the cases of Mark and Peter, the clear intact representations of self and others indicated a higher level of structuralization. The anxiety present in their sleep-related imagery illustrates to a lesser degree in Mark, and to a greater degree in Peter, a lively struggle, with significant conflict resulting from involvements with others. Maturity (structuralization), though, does not mean an absence of conflict. On the contrary, it can mean a willingness to confront conflict while being able to maintain a sense of oneself as cohesive, continuous in time, able to maintain reasonably positively affective self-esteem, and able to maintain clearly defined self and object representations.

## Summary

Three sleep disorders were discussed in this chapter: nightmares, hypnagogic hallucinations, and sleep paralysis. Nightmares are any anxiety dream which causes a person to wake up. These anxiety dreams included stage 4 awakenings, such as night terrors, which at the moment of occurrence do not contain imagery. Hypnagogic hallucinations are imagery occurring in the period of drowsiness between waking and sleeping. These hallucinations need not be frightening. However, when they are combined with sleep paralysis, they usually have a nightmarish quality. The sleep paralysis can also occur in the drowsy period between sleep and wakefulness. The experience in the paralysis is that of being paralyzed and is especially frightening when accompanied by a hypnagogic hallucination threatening to a person in this drowsy state. This chapter hypothesizes that these sleep disorders need not be automatically viewed as harbingers of severe pathology. Instead, these sleep disorders do reveal the presence of severe anxiety. The analysis of the content imagery in these unusual sleep states can reveal either pathological psychic organization or important conflict in an otherwise mature personality structure. Pathology is defined in terms of the degree of self-organization.

## References

Alexander, H. E. 1909. The subconscious in light of dream imagery. *Proceedings of the Society for Psychical Research* 8:623–34.

Broughton, R. J. 1968. Sleep disorders: Disorders of arousal? *Science* 159(819):1070–78.

Broughton, R. J. 1970. The incubus attack. In E. Hartmann, ed., *Sleep and Dreaming*. Boston: Little, Brown.

Campbell, R. J. 1981. *Psychiatric Dictionary*. New York: Oxford University Press.

Everett, H. C. 1963. Sleep paralysis in medical students. *Journal of Nervous and Mental Disease* 136:283–87.

Fisher, C., J. V. Byrne, A. Edwards, and E. Kahn. 1970. REM and NREM nightmares. In E. Hartmann, ed., *Sleep and Dreaming*. Boston: Little, Brown.

Freud, S. *Standard Edition of the Complete Psychological Works of Sigmund Freud.* James Strachey, ed. and tr. 24 vols. London: Hogarth Press, 1953–1974; New York: Macmillan.

1900. *The Interpretation of Dreams.* Vols. 4 and 5.

1927. *Dostoevsky and Parracide.* Vol. 19.

Hartmann, E., ed. 1970. *Sleep and Dreaming.* Boston: Little, Brown.

Hartmann, E. 1984. *The Nightmare.* New York: Basic Books.

Hartmann, E., D. Russ, B. van der Kolk, R. Falke, and M. Oldfield. 1981. A preliminary study of the personality of the nightmare sufferer: Relationship to schizophrenia and creativity? *American Journal of Psychiatry* 138(6):794–97.

Herson, M. 1971. Personality of nightmare sufferers. *Journal of Nervous and Mental disease* 153:27–31.

Jones, E. 1949. *On the Nightmare.* London: Hogarth Press. (Original work published in 1911.)

Kales, A., C. R. Soldatos, A. B. Caldwell, D. S. Charney, J. D. Kales, D. Markel and R. Cardieux. 1980. Nightmares: Clinical characteristics and personality patterns. *American Journal of Psychiatry* 137(10):1197–1201.

Kellerman, H. 1981. *Sleep Disorders: Insomnia and Narcolepsy.* New York: Brunner/Mazel.

Kohut, H. 1971. *The Analysis of the Self.* New York: International Universities Press.

Kohut, H. 1977. *The Restoration of the Self.* New York: International Universities Press.

Kohut, H. 1984. *How Does Analysis Cure?* A. Golberg and E. Stepansky, eds. Chicago: University of Chicago Press.

Lachmann, F. and B. Beebe. 1983. Consolidation of the self: A case study. *Dynamic Psychotherapy* 1(1):55–75.

Leroy, E.B. 1926. *Les Visions du demi-sommeil.* Paris: Librairie Felix Alcan.

Liddon, S. C. 1967. Sleep paralysis and hypnagogic hallucinations: Their relationship to the nightmare. *Archives of General Psychiatry* 17:88–96.

McKellar, P. and L. Simpson. 1954. Between wakefulness and sleep: Hypnagogic imagery. *British Journal of Psychology* 45:266–76.

Maury, A. 1848. Des Hallucinations hypnagogiques ou des erreurs des sens dans l'état intermédiare entre la veille et le sommeil. *Annales Médico-Psychologiques du Système Nerveux* 11:26–40.

Rapaport, D. 1967a. Cognitive structures. In M. M. Gill, ed., *The Collected Papers of David Rapaport.* New York: Basic Books.

Rapaport, D. 1967b. States of consciousness: A psychopathological and psychodynamic view. In M. M. Gill, ed., *The Collected Papers of David Rapaport.* New York: Basic Books.

Schacter, D. L. 1976. The hypnagogic state: A critical review of the literature. *Psychological Bulletin* 83:452–81.

Schneck, J. M. 1969. Personality components in patients with sleep paralysis. *Psychiatric Quarterly* 43:343–48.

Sharf, B., C. Moskovitz, M. Lupton, and H. Klawans. 1978. Dream phenomena induced by chronic levodopa therapy. *Journal of Neural Transmission* 43:143–51.

Slight, D. 1924. Hypnagogic phenomena. *Journal of Abnormal Psychology* 19:274–82.

Stolorow, R. D. and F. M. Lachmann. 1980. *Psychoanalysis of Developmental Arrests: Theory and Treatment.* New York: International Universities Press.

Taub, J. M., M. Kramer, D. Arand, and G. A. Jacobs. 1978. Nightmare dreams and nightmare confabulations. *Comprehensive Psychiatry* 19:285–91.

Vihvelin, H. 1948. On the differentiation of some typical forms of hypnagogic hallucinations. *Acta Psychiatrica et Neuroligica* 23:359–89.

Yoss, R. E. and D. D. Daly. 1957. Criteria for the diagnosis of the narcoleptic syndrome. *Proceedings of Staff Meetings, Mayo Clinic* 32:320–28.

Zarcone, V. 1973. Narcolepsy. *New England Journal of Medicine* 228:1156–66.

# 14.

# Personality Characteristics of Nightmare Sufferers and Some Speculations on the Meaning of the Nightmare

DANIEL P. JUDA

THIS CHAPTER (1) briefly reviews the small body of literature relating personality variables to recurrent nightmares and/or frequent nightmare sufferers; (2) summarizes self-psychology formulations regarding the function of the recurrent nightmare; and (3) suggests a possible differential diagnostic function that the nightmare might serve among psychopathic populations.

## A Brief Review of the Literature Relating Personality Characteristics to the Recurrent Nightmare and/or Frequent Nightmare Sufferer

### THE EARLY EMPIRICAL STUDIES

Herson (1971:27), in reviewing the literature on the personality characteristics of nightmare sufferers, wrote:

Although the reporting of nightmares frequently takes place in the clinical therapeutic situation, a perusal of the literature reveals very little of an empirical nature with respect to the characterological structure of the nightmare sufferers. Considerable theorizing about the etiology and course of the nightmare has appeared (Fenichel, 1945; Hadfield, 1954; Jones, 1949; Schneck, 1969; de Verteuil, 1962), objective physiological studies of the nightmare dream have been conducted (Broughton, 1968; Fisher, et al., 1968), the behavioral treatment of nightmare sufferers has been described (Geer and Silverman, 1967; Silverman and Geer, 1968), but with one exception (Feldman and Hersen, 1967) there are no studies known to this author relating personality variables to the frequency of occurrences of nightmares.

The Feldman and Hersen (1967) study, in which college students were examined, reported a significant positive relationship between scores on a ten-item Death Scale and the frequency of reported nightmares. The authors suggested that nightmare frequency in these subjects might be rooted in concrete (i.e., actual) experiences, since the more frequent nightmare sufferers had a history of greater numbers of deaths of relatives and close friends, particularly when they had experienced these deaths when they were under 10 years of age. Feldman and Herson (1967:425) summarize their findings as follows: "It is possible that frequent nightmare subjects can be characterized, more broadly, as anxious, fearful individuals, [and] therefore their heightened concern with death would be only a part of the general neurosis."

This, then, is one of the earliest empirically based findings regarding the personality of the nightmare sufferer; they seem to be "anxious," "neurotic," and "fearful" individuals.

Hersen's (1971) own study replicated this initial finding. Using inpatients in a large state hospital whose diagnoses included primarily psychotic disorders (but omitting subjects who were retardates, alcoholics, organics, and drug addicts), Herson found that frequent nightmare sufferers were characterized by high manifest anxiety when compared to their counterparts with less frequent or no nightmares. He also found an inverse relationship between nightmares and ego strength which, according to Barron's (1953) Ego Strength Scale definition, suggests that frequent nightmare sufferers are generally less physiologically stable, have poorer health, have a poorer sense of reality, have weaker feelings of adequacy and vitality, have a more restricted morality, display more prejudicial attitudes, are more emotionally restricted and stilted, and are less intelligent when compared with non-nightmare subjects. In short, frequent nightmare sufferers appear to exhibit greater pathology than their less frequent and non-nightmare comparison groups. (Hersen 1971:30)

These early controlled studies of nightmare sufferers confirmed reports from psychoanalysts that these psychological events were symptoms of pathological systems—were, in fact, disorders (of sleep). Later investigators confirmed and elaborated these early findings. Haynes and Mooney (1975) replicated Hersen's major finding and reported a significant correlation between nightmare frequency and MAS scores (i.e., Taylor's Manifest Anxiety Scale) in two separate experiments. Cellucci and Lawrence (1978) also replicated these findings and observed important individual differences among nightmare sufferers which suggested different treatment procedures (i.e., systematic desensitization for the serious anxiety sufferer versus alternative treatments such as stimulus or temporal control procedures when there is an absence of anxiety in individuals who nevertheless suffer from sleep problems). (See Knapp et al. 1976 for a review of behavioral approaches to insomnia, for example.)

## THE LATER EMPIRICAL REPORTS: HARTMANN'S STUDY OF NIGHTMARE SUFFERERS

In a study conducted in the Boston area, by placing ads in local newspapers Hartmann et al. (1981) found 38 subjects (27 male, 11 female) who had suffered from nightmares at least once a week for one year. The researchers carefully distinguished between night terrors (see Kales et al. 1980a) and nightmares and eliminated night-terror sufferers from their sample. Of the subjects, 35 had suffered nightmares since age 5 or earlier. The 3 others reported the onset of nightmares in later childhood or adolesence. The mean sample age was 23, with the ages ranging from 18 to 50 years. The mean number of nightmares in the sample was 3.8 nightmares per week. Interestingly, although 26 subjects had experienced one or more serious traumatic events (i.e., rape, incest, sudden death of a parent), these events invariably occurred long after the onset of the nightmares. Although the subjects reported that the frequency of nightmares increased during times of stress, they also claimed that their nightmares did not begin with identifiable traumatic events. (This is the only study in which subjects reported that they did not associate traumatic events with their nightmares.) The following characteristics of the group emerged:

(1) nearly all subjects had occupations or career plans relating to arts or crafts;

(2) 4 had been hospitalized (probably for schizophrenia);

(3) 29 had been or were in psychotherapy;

(4) many suffered from periods of derpression; 15 had seriously considered suicide; 7 had made suicide attempts;

(5) little overt psychosis was observed during the interviews;

(6) 4 met DSM-III criteria for schizophrenia; 9 for borderline personality; 6 schizotypal personality. The others were not "sick" (e.g., there were no typical neurotics, obsessives, or hysterics, no phobics or overtly anxious—they were all described as very openminded and nondefensive);

(7) almost all spoke of themselves as unusually sensitive since childhood, i.e., easily hurt, particularly sensitive to the feelings of others, and in some cases unusually sensitive to light and sound. Many said they were unhappy children, even in cases where there were no overt family problems;

(8) 22 subjects had a close relative who had been institutionalized for mental illness, or who had had a serious "nervous breakdown"; 8 had one or more relatives who had attempted or committed suicide; and,

(9) subjects did not describe patterns of loss or rejection by parents or siblings.

The content of the nightmares suffered in this sample most often involved being chased, being about to be hurt, or actually being hurt or wounded. Sometimes no specific person was chasing the dreamer. When a threatening figure appeared in recurrent nightmares, it was usually a large, unidentified man; in childhood nightmares the dreamer was usually chased by a large animal or monster. On the Cornell Index—a test measuring levels of anxiety and depression—the sample scored considerably higher than the population at large. The subscales that contributed the most to this deviant score were nervousness and anxiety and the startle reaction for female subjects; and depression for male subjects.

On the MMPI (Minnesota Multiphasic Personality Inventory)—a test designed to assess psychopathology—group means on the Schizophrenia and Psychopathic deviate scales for both men and women were about two standard deviations above normal. Men scored almost two standard deviations above normal on the Depression and Conversion Hysteria scales; women scored almost two standard deviations above normal on the Hypomanic scale.

On the Rotter Internal/External Locus of Control scale—a test of external or internal cue-based behavior—the mean for the entire sample indicated belief in external control of life (e.g., that situations are controlled by lucky chance, fate, or some all-powerful individual).

Nineteen subjects were given the Rorschach Ink Blots and all 19 showed problems in the areas of boundaries and penetration.

Hartmann et al. (1981:796) conclude:

> these Ss probably have a biological vulnerability to schizophrenia. However, most of them have not developed signs of chronic mental illness. Most have been able to pursue activities in areas involving art and creativity, perhaps making use of the sensitivity, openness, and vulnerability we have described. If our impressions are confirmed they could possibly have some importance in preventing mental illness. A large proportion of children aged 3–6 have nightmares, but frequent nightmares become increasingly rare in children over 6 years old. Therefore, children who continue to have frequent nightmares at the age of perhaps 10 or 12

could be considered a group at risk for the possible development of schizophrenia.

More recently Hartmann (1984:103–4) reports what seems to be almost a new personality disorder—different from schizophrenia, different from borderline, and different from neurosis—as predominating among nightmare sufferers:

The most striking finding is not the formal psychopathology of some, but rather the *openness* and *defenselessness* of almost all the nightmare sufferers. They have not developed the usual defenses and protections that most persons have. They are not armored; they are vulnerable in many respects. . . . Another term that comes to mind is *sensitive.* Nightmare sufferers appear to be unusually sensitive in a number of different meanings of the term. . . . Finally, the most accurate way I can sum up the characteristics of these persons is to say that they have *thin boundaries or permeable boundaries.* They do not keep things pigeonholed between rigid partitions; they 'let things through.'

Hartmann (1984:102) goes on to offer an interesting hypothesis about the relationship between these "vulnerable, open and sensitive persons with thin boundaries" and artistic and creative capabilities:

I also believe that the nightmare subjects we studied have definite artistic and creative tendencies and energies, although they may not necessarily have the specific talent required of a great artist. . . . I am suggesting that one important aspect of what makes a person an artist is having a psychological makeup of thin boundaries, which include the ability to experience and take in a great deal from inside and outside, to experience one's own inner life in a very direct fashion, and an ability (sometimes an unwanted ability) to experience the world more directly, more painfully than others. (1984:108)

This hypothesis, it must be remembered, does not arise from a study of the personality characteristics of a random sample of artists; therefore, it remains to be tested. It is also possible to hypothesize—on the basis of Hartmann's nightmare-suffering sample—either (1) that persons with thin boundaries try to "thicken" the boundaries by binding their energy and sublimating their "sensitivity" in artistic (e.g., concrete) forms; or (2) that some artists have this personality characteristic while others (perhaps most others) do not.

KALES'S CONTROLLED STUDY OF NIGHTMARE SUFFERERS

Kales et al. (1980b) studied 30 adult subjects between the ages of 39 and 77 (mean age 39.1; 27 females, 3 males) who suffered a minimum of 12 nightmares per year. The subjects, as in Hartmann et al.'s (1981) study, were solicited through media advertisements. Unlike Hartmann et al., however, Kales et al. developed a control group of 30 that was age- and sex-matched with no sleep-disorder history. The clinical data were as follows:

(1) 50 percent (i.e., 15) of the subjects had suffered from recurrent nightmares before age 10 (5 subjects between ages 11 and 20; 4 between ages 21 and 30; 3 between ages 31 and 40; 1 subject between ages 41 and 50; and 2 subjects between ages 51 and 60);
(2) the frequency of episodes was a mean of 2.5 nightmares per week;
(3) the mean duration of this sleep disorder was 21.6 years (range: 2–50 years);
(4) the occurrence of a major life event preceding the onset of the disorder was reported by 60 percent of the subjects;
(5) the content of the nightmares was associated with fear. Specific fears were reported by the following percentages: fear of attack, 73 percent; fear of falling, 73 percent; fear of death, 60 percent;
(6) 83 percent of the subjects reported experiencing recurring nightmares.

Kales et al. report the findings of their 1980 study as follows:

1. When compared with controls, the subjects (i.e., nightmare subjects versus the control subjects) had significantly higher mean values on all eight clinical MMPI scales. The three highest mean scores for nightmare sufferers were (highest to lowest) on the scales of Psychopathic Deviate, Schizophrenia, and Hysteria. The consistency of elevations on the Schizophrenia scale in the sample suggests, the authors state, long-term schizoidness and perhaps what Meehl (1973) termed "schizotypy." However, as in

Hartmann et al.'s (1981) study, there was no indication of any overt psychoticism.

2. Significantly more nightmare subjects than control subjects reported having had emotional problems and having considered committing suicide; they reported significantly more emotional problems in their families; and their family members had committed suicide significantly more than family members of control subjects.

3. Mental stress increased the frequency of nightmare episodes in 90 percent of the subjects. Kales et al. (1980b:1200) note: "Our findings in nightmare sufferers are similar to those of Cartwright (1979) in individuals with repetitive dreams, many of which were unpleasant. Specifically, she related repetitive dreams to periods of stress associated with strong affect during the day."

They conclude:

> The persistence of nightmares into adulthood in our Ss appeared to be correlated with the presence of serious psychopathology. . . . We consider morbid nightmares to be episodic releases of intense emotions in individuals with long-term schizoid adjustments and chronic difficulties in dealing with interpersonal resentments and fears of hostility from others. When the individual cannot adapt to the excessive fear and hostility resulting from conflictual and antagonistic object relations by sufficiently discharging them during the daytime, the fear and hostility may be expressed during sleep in the form of nightmares. (Kales et al. 1980b:1200)

And again a page later:

> Although monosymptomatic psychiatric conditions, such as chronic fears or phobias, may be responsible for nightmares, it is usually a more global psychological disturbance that causes nightmares in adulthood, as demonstrated in the present study. . . . Since the nightmare sufferer's emotional condition is often complicated rather than monosymptomatic, we would expect behavioral treatment (Geer and Silverman, 1967; Silverman and Geer, 1968; Cautela, 1968) to be effective only in selected cases but insight-oriented psychotherapies more likely to be effective in the vast majority of cases. (1980b:1201).

BIXLER'S STUDY OF NIGHTMARE-SUFFERING INSOMNIAC SUBJECTS

Bixler et al. (1977) contrasted 47 chronic insomniac patients with a past or current complaint of at least one nightmare per month and 82 chronic insomniac patients who claimed never to have had nightmares. Patients with a history of nightmares had a significantly greater number of emotional problems or "breakdowns," significantly more hospitalizations, and seriously considered suicide more frequently than the insomniac group with no nightmares. The nightmare group also viewed death more frequently in terms of endless sleep and escape than the non-nightmare group. Insomniac patients with a history of nightmares characterized their dreams as more frightening, intense, strange, and violent than the dreams of the non-nightmare insomniacs.

MMPI data were also contrasted. A number of scales in the nightmare group were found to be significantly elevated compared to the non-nightmare group. These included the following scales: L or Lie scale, Depression, Hypochondriasis, Psychopathic Deviate, Psychasthenia, and Schizophrenia. These data suggest, the authors conclude, that while insomniac patients in general have a significant degree of psychopathology, those with a history of current and past nighmares represent a more disturbed group of insomniacs.

The small set of empirically based data regarding the frequent and/or recurrent nightmare sufferer suggests that this individual represents a clinically distinguishable person who suffers from a significantly greater pathological personality structure when compared to the mentally ill, to other insomniacs (who claim to not suffer from nightmares) and college students, and to other "normal" persons (e.g., who claim to not suffer from nightmares). In particular, the nightmare sufferer shows greater levels of disturbance in many areas of personality, with especially strong "schizotypy" or "schizophrenic" vulnerabilities. However, these high levels of anxiety, "psychopathic" characteristics, and, in general, greater vulnerabilities to experience psychiatric difficulties, do not seem to result in producing individuals with overt psychotic behaviors in their waking state. This suggests the possibility that the nightmare in addition to contributing to disturbed sleep may perhaps also serve a therapeutic function.

## Self-Psychology Formulations Regarding the Function of the Recurrent Nightmare

### EARLY PSYCHOANALYTIC CONTRIBUTIONS: ELLA FREEMAN SHARPE AND THE DREAMING FUNCTION

The research on the personality characteristics of nightmare sufferers strongly suggests that these individuals are not contented, well-integrated, and psychologically sound; rather, they seem to be experiencing important to profound difficulties in their mental health spheres of functioning. The literature surveyed thus far, however, is not clear about what specific psychological difficulties these individuals are experiencing; nor does it suggest how the nightmare relates to specific psychological problems. All that has been established is that nightmare sufferers typically are "anxious," "neurotic," or more seriously disturbed when compared to non-nightmare-experiencing persons. Psychoanalysts, however, have utilized the case history method of investigation to develop more elaborate hypotheses regarding the personality characteristics of the nightmare sufferer, as well as the function of the nightmare itself.

Ella Freeman Sharpe (1937:197), for instance, believed that, "prolific dreaming indicates a great deal of unresolved internal conflict [and that] the dreams are attempts to deal with this. Conversely, the entire absence of dreams indicates some faulty working in the psychic apparatus" (the absence of dreams was not yet known to be physiologically impossible). Most interestingly, Sharpe sets forth the hypothesis (which cries out to be tested empirically) that the "analyzed" person

> will experience only rarely if at all 'anxiety' dreams. Nightmares seldom occur amongst analyzed persons, neither do dreams in which animals represent the animal nature of the dreamer. The 'analyzed' person will not experience the repetition dream nor will there occur long series of dreams representing parts of things as parts of bodies. The dreams tend on the whole to be much shorter than before analysis. . . . The main reason for this is the fact that analysis has made possible greater satisfaction in reality, as regards both direct instinct gratification and sublimation. Hence, a person whose achievements have been mainly in dreams and not executed in reality may well lose his pleasurable night dreams

but find his inhibitions in doing actual work in reality removed. (Sharpe 1937:197)

The "analyzed" person in this connection is defined as "one who has had analysis adequate enough to ensure not only ego-stability, that is the capacity to carry on an independent life effectively, but also one in which direct instinct gratification and sublimation is accompanied by zest and a feeling of well-being" (Sharpe 1937:192).

In other words, Sharpe believed that nightmares, especially recurrent and repetitive nightmares, both reflect destabilized or unstabilized egos and are "attempts to deal with this." Sharpe also believed that external trauma may also precipitate nightmares—even in "analyzed" individuals—under certain conditions. That is, the nightmare is a "natural" consequence of an ego under attack. She writes: "The most stabilized people when threatened by external disaster experience psychical stress which may manifest itself in disturbing dreams. Normal people who are not so psychically well-stabilized more often have nightmares or recurrent anxiety dreams" (Sharpe 1937:198).

For Sharpe, individual psychic stability results when we are experienced and prepared (by experience and working through) to "correlate external disturbing events with unconscious impulses, desires, phantasies and so to a great degree control and manage appropriately the associated affects" (1937:197). Unanalyzed people—or traumatized people—frequently encounter these ego-threatening unconscious phenomena in dreams and nightmares (since they tend to repress or try to avoid them in their waking state). It is only in those individuals who cannot "to a great degree control and manage appropriately the associated affects [to the trauma]"—those who wish only to repress, deny, or abandon the unexplored—whose egos cannot stabilize and therefore leave them vulnerable to experiencing these traumas again and again—that is, cause these individuals to fall prey to the repetitive or recurrent nightmare.

## SIGMUND FREUD AND THE NIGHTMARE AS A MANIFESTATION OF THE REPETITION COMPULSION

Freud also believed that anxiety dreams not only reflect trauma but provide the dreamer with repeated opportunities to control and manage the psychological fallout from trauma-experience as the nightmares tend to be repeated again and again (the repetition compulsion). "These dreams are endeavoring to master the stimulus retrospectively, by developing the anxiety whose omission was the cause of the traumatic neurosis" (Freud 1920:27). Freud, however, did not fully appreciate this function of the repetition compulsion as vitally adaptive; rather, he wrote of it as some sort of "daemonic" manifestation of the psychic apparatus and as a "wish" to return to an inorganic state (e.g., the death instinct). As I have written elsewhere (Juda 1983), it is more heuristic to construe the repetition compulsion—be it manifested in behavior, in obsessional thought, or in recurrent nightmares—as one manifestation of the organizing principle inherent in the physical and psychic nature of the central nervous system.

> It seems that when new information is admitted into our consciousness—be it externally, through unrepressible trauma, or internally, through unrepressible dreams, symptom formation, fantasies, thoughts, etc.—the human organism *cannot rest until this new data is assimilated and accommodated.* If our existing "laws," or schemata, by which we have understood our internal and external universes, are not capable of accounting for this new experience of our world, or if this new information is sufficiently radical that it places into question our most basic life assumptions, then we will remain profoundly unsettled until such time that a new accommodation, schema or principle is formulated. We must . . . repeat again and again our new experience until we have "mastered" it (e.g., reschematized our universe). This is the motive behind our repetition compulsions; failure to find new accommodations, as Horner (1979) describes, leads to severe mental dis-organization, dis-integration, and/or de-differentiation, with its parallel clinical manifestations. (Juda 1983:359–60)

The recurrent nightmare, in other words, is the psyche's means of maintaining threatening (to the ego or self) information about our universe (both our external and internal, i.e., unconscious, environments) in a vivid and emotionally meaningful state so that this vital information is available for us to learn about, to understand, and to master. In this manner we are able to *organize* our personal experience, and thus successfully adapt to our life's experience (see also Vaillant 1977). The nightmare not only reflects the state of our psychic affairs, but it is purposeful—it helps us to organize experiences that threaten to shatter our psychic well-being.

This is not an altogether new idea. Lerner (1967) has presented data to suggest that dreams, through their kinesthetic elements, function to strengthen the body image. Formulations of the problem-solving (Freud 1900), focal conflict-resolving (French and Fromm 1964), and trauma-integrating (de Monchaux 1978) functions of dreams may also be seen as special instances of "the role of dream symbolization in maintaining the organization of experience" (Atwood and Stolorow 1984:103).

## RECENT PSYCHOANALYTIC CONTRIBUTIONS: KOHUT'S "SELF-STATE DREAMS"

The so-called "self-state dreams" discussed by Kohut (1977:109) portray in their manifest imagery "the dreamer's dread vis-à-vis some uncontrollable tension-increase or his dread of the dissolution of the self." Kohut suggests that the very act of portraying these archaic self-states in the dream in a minimally disguised form "constitutes an attempt to deal with the psychological danger by covering frightening nameless processes with namable visual imagery" (ibid.); (thereby preserving this psychologically vital information in an emotionally and cognitively meaningful form so that it can be better understood and mastered). Socarides (1980), according to Atwood and Stolorow (1984:104), "has discovered a similar purpose fulfilled by dreams that directly depict perverse sexual enactments similar to those performed by the dreamer in his waking life. The hallucinatory visualization of the perversion during sleep, like the perverse enactment itself, shores up an imperiled sense of self and protects against the danger of its dissolution." I have also written (Juda 1986) of a recurrent, sexually perverse nightmare suffered by a homosexual pedophilic criminal following his imprisonment and have suggested that the function of his recurrent nightmare was to restore and maintain the intactness of this man's self and object representations and structuralizations, which were continuously threatened with dissolution—especially following his sudden removal from his self-object child-victims as a result of his imprisonment. In addition, the recurrent nightmare perhaps served to repeatedly, vividly, and meaningfully expose this troubled man to his fragile self and object structures—which helped to enlighten and convince him of his vulnerability and need for treatment.

## RECENT PSYCHOANALYTIC CONTRIBUTIONS: ATWOOD AND STOLOROW

Atwood and Stolorow (1984:103) have developed these ideas still further and set forth the hypothesis that dreams—in general—"are the *guardians of psychological structure,* and [that] they fulfill this vital purpose by means of concrete symbolizations." "As human subjectivity in purest culture, the dream constitutes a 'royal road' to the prereflective unconscious—to the organizing principles and dominant leitmotivs that unconsciously pattern and thematize a person's psychological life" (1984:98). And again: "We would expand the classical conception of the centrality of wish fulfillment in dreams into a more general and inclusive proposition that dreams always embody one or more of the dreamer's *personal purposes.* Such purposes include the fulfillment of wishes as discussed by Freud, but also a number of other important psychological purposes (self-guiding and self-punishing, adaptive, restitutive-reparative, defensive) as well" (1984:100).

They believe that the

> most distinctive and central feature of the dream experience [is] the use of concrete perceptual images endowed with hallucinatory vividness to symbolize abstract thoughts, feelings, and subjective states. . . . We are proposing that concrete symbolization in dreams and their resulting hallucinatory vividness serve a vital psychological purpose for the dreamer. . . . It is in the need to maintain the organization of experience, our supraordinate motivational principle, that we can discover the fundamental purpose of concrete symbolization in dreams. When configurations of experience of self and other find symbolization in concrete perceptual images and are thereby articulated with hallucinatory vividness, the dreamer's feeling of conviction about the validity and reality of these configurations receives a powerful reinforcement. Perceiving, after all, is believing. (Atwood and Stolorow (1984:102–3)

In other words, it is crucial to our adaptation to life that we "believe" the "validity" of the experience of our psychological selves—just as we believe in the validity of our physical selves and universe through the five senses—and that the dream provide this validity for us in a perceptual (e.g., hallucinatory) difficult-to-avoid-experiencing modality (e.g., the dream and nightmare). In this way, psychological processes (i.e., intangible forces such as self and object structuralizations and representations, unconscious wishes, motives, and fantasies, etc.) are made visual/perceptual and therefore all the more believable. In this manner, our psychological life is made "real," and thus organizable. That is, the more we recognize, experience, accept, and believe in the existence of our psychological selves, the more we can schematize life and organize our experience (i.e., assimilate and accommodate it).

Atwood and Stolorow also believe that there is a class of dreams different from those reported by them above which seem to be more in the category of anxiety dreams or nightmares—although these authors do not refer to them exclusively in those terms. They write:

> In another class of dreams, concrete symbols serve not so much to actualize particular configurations of experience, but rather to maintain psychological organization per se. Dreams of this second class occur most often in the context of developmental interferences and arrests, whereby structuralization of the subjective world has remained incomplete, precarious, and vulnerable to dissolution. . . . We have seen that for persons with severe deficits in psychological structure formation, concretization may serve a similar purpose in their waking lives as well, not only in the form of delusions and hallucinations, but also in the concrete behavioral enactments, often of a destructive or sexual nature, that are required to sustain the cohesion and continuity of a fragmenting sense of self or other. (Atwood and Stolorow 1984:104)

In the empirical findings reported in the first part of this chapter, the recurrent nightmare sufferer's personality was proposed to be deficient in the ego-functioning area, in its vulnerability to anxiety and "schizotypy"; perhaps these individuals are the same as those spoken of by Atwood and Stolorow as suffering from "severe deficits in psychological structure formation." If so, we may have discovered a theoretical orientation to account for the vulnerability of the nightmare sufferer to reexperiencing the sleep disorder again and again. Perhaps the nightmare sufferer is a member of Atwood and Stolorow's "second class" of individuals who need to dream nightmares—of a destructive and/or sexual nature—in order to "sustain the cohesion and continuity of a fragmenting sense of self or other."

Indeed, Atwood and Stolorow present a fascinating case of a female patient who, after unknowingly suffering from an undiagnosed brain tumor, felt her self falling apart. Finally, she was operated on and the tumor was removed. Her parents as well as the doctors were reportedly "highly insensitive." This she experienced as an overwhelming trauma and then suffered from a recurrent nightmare for years afterward. The authors report and discuss this dream as follows:

> In these dreams she stood alone in the small train station of her town as flames sprang up all around her. Soon the whole building was engulfed in fire. After the station had burned to the ground, two eyeballs lay quietly in the smoking ashes and then began to quiver and roll about, conversing with each other by means of movements and glances. . . . What psychological function can be ascribed to the patient's recurring dream of being burned down to isolated fragments? The repeated transformation of the experience of self-disintegration into an image of the physical incineration of her body enabled her to maintain the state of her self in focal awareness and encapsulated her effort to retain psychological integrity in the face of the threat of total self-dissolution. (Atwood and Stolorow 1984:106–7)

> . . . As she increasingly came to rely on the therapist as a selfobject for the maintenance of her psychological organization, the ritualized enactments [e.g., self-mutilations, etc. . . .] which she had formerly needed for this purpose, lessened and finally disappeared. The repeating nightmares of being burned to fragments came to an end simultaneously. (Ibid.:113–14)

## HYPOTHESES FROM THE SELF-PSYCHOLOGY FORMULATIONS

Although much further empirical research is needed to evaluate and corroborate the relationship between one's self and object structuralizations and the occurrence of nightmares, it is possible to hypothesize—on the basis of existing data and theory—that there is an inverse relationship here: the stronger the self and object structuralizations, the less likely the occurrence of nightmares; and, the weaker the self and object structuralizations, the more frequent (and the greater the need) for nightmares. Although traumatization in the external world may result in even "normal" persons dreaming nightmares, in cases of repetitive nightmares over long periods of time their duration may be due not to the severity of the trauma but to the severity of the psychological deficits existing prior to the trauma onset. These hypotheses must, however, be suggested as tentative and in need of additional support from both empirically controlled studies and psychoanalytic case material.

## Methodological Complications in Nightmare Research

Collecting data to validate or invalidate these hypotheses is a tricky and methodologically complicated task. Cartwright (1979) has warned that, for example, although many have proposed that the four or five dreams of the night represent a continuation of the cognitive processing of affective material made salient during the previous waking period (Freud 1900; French and Fromm 1964; Jones 1949), this proposition has proved difficult to test in any formal way. She writes:

> Which of all the emotional stimuli of the day are likely to carry over into the dreams, and how is one to recognize them if they do? The problem of establishing the validity of the idea that a dream element is the equivalent of a waking experience has been troublesome. Dream images are so unique that unless some repetitive elements or themes can be established to exist and to have the same meaning whenever they occur, obtaining agreement on what a dream represents will be hard to establish. (Cartwright 1979:131)

### CARTWRIGHT'S STUDY OF FEMALE NIGHTMARE SUFFERERS

Cartwright has utilized the survey method in an attempt to collect data about dreams. In her questionnaire, completed by 167 women ages 18–55 (71 undergraduates and 96 alumnae from the same university), Cartwright was able to collect interesting data regarding repetitive dreams. (She did not ask about repetitive nightmares per se, and it is not clear from her publication if her subjects were reporting nightmares, night terrors, or dreams.) She writes:

> These findings are only suggestive but appear to support the idea that recall of dreaming is related to the affect level being experienced during the prior waking period. Following stressful events and upset moods we are aware of dreaming more; when things are going well we are less aware of dreaming. Repetitive dreams seem to originate at different periods around points of stress. The earliest issues are: our physical safety, which is a paramount concern because we are small and unstable in a world of large immutable laws like that of gravity; and our social survival in interactions with important others who, we discover, are not always nurturing or benign. These experiences appear to be represented in repetitive dreams which are especially memorable. Later dreams of this kind mirror the succeeding developmental problems, such as maintaining self-esteem. . . . [Repetitive dreams] with the earliest age of onset most often involve threats to our physical existence or safety which we are ill prepared to handle when so young. In adolescence, dreams of competence as well as dreams of shame, failure, and incompetence increase. (Cartwright 1979:135–36)

It would be most helpful, in formulating a complete account of the personality characteristics of the nightmare sufferer, if research such as this not only clarified the nature of the repetitive dreams (e.g., nightmare versus night terror versus normal dream) but, in addition, evaluated the self and object structural stability of these individuals as well.

## The Nightmare and the Criminal

The dreams and nightmares of criminal offenders evidently have never been studied. A computer search of the literature failed to uncover a single publication in which dreams or nightmare experiences of criminals were investigated, and Charles Fisher (personal communication) has confirmed the absence of studies in this area. The lack of research is both surprising and unfortunate. It is surprising because the nightmare research strongly demonstrates—on the MMPI—that psychopathic characteristics correlate highly with nightmare sufferers. It is unfortunate because this population might be invaluable in providing data to support (or fail to support) the hypotheses set forth earlier in this chapter, and because invaluable differential diagnostic insight might be obtained regarding the criminal population through careful research into the relationship between their self-structuralizations, the frequency of their nightmares, and their recidivism rates.

An isolated and rare reference that discussed nightmares among criminals is found in W. H. Reid's (1978) book *The Psychopath: A Comprehensive Study of Antisocial Disorders and Behaviors,* in an article by J. E. Talley entitled: "A Jungian Viewpoint." In this fascinating and provocative chapter, Talley begins by reviewing Karpman's (1941) distinction between "true" psychopaths he called *anethopaths,* and all other psychopaths:

The psychopathic personality is amenable to psychotherapy, while the anethopath is not. Behaviorally, the two are on an antisocial continuum or spectrum ranging from minimal to profound. Yet behavior alone is not the differentiating factor. Besides their obvious value in the therapeutic situation, dreams can be helpful in diagnostically differentiating the patient with psychopathic characteristics from the true anethopath. Two dreams with similar imagery might serve as illustrations. The first is that of a young woman described by Kohut as having a narcissistic personality disturbance. (Many psychopathic personalities suffer from this problem). In the dream

"the patient is on a swing, swinging forward and backward, higher and higher . . . yet, there is never a serious danger of either the patient's flying off, or of the swing uncontrollably entering a full circle" (Kohut, 1971, pp. 4–5).

Kohut states that the person was amenable to psychoanalytic treatment. In contrast is the dream reported by von Franz (1974) of

"an international criminal who had already murdered 10 or 12 people, a kind of pathological creature who committed cold-blooded murder without the slightest reaction of conscience. . . . (he) killed an unknown, old man in the streets of Zurich, took his money, and got caught. Dr. Guggenbuhl-Craig had to give the court the psychiatric expert's opinion and ascertain whether or not the man was responsible for his deeds. . . . (Dr. Guggenbuhl) told us the man's dreams without telling us (anything of the dreamer). . . . The dream in question was very simple, It was one which was repeated frequently and in which the murderer went to an amusement park where there were big swings. He was on such a swing, swinging up and down, higher and higher, when suddenly the swing went too high and he fell into empty space. That was the end of the dream."

I thought "My God, swinging between opposites and taking it as a pleasure with no reaction towards it, taking it as fun!" And the lysis in the end sentence of the dream was "falling into empty space," without even the reaction of "I woke up with a cry." There was no emotional reaction. I could only say that this was a lost soul. . . . In the dream there is no attempt by nature (i.e., by the unconscious) to save the man by giving him a shock. . . . His unconscious tells him, just as cold-bloodedly as he murders, that he is lost! The first dream might be that of a non-anethopathic psychopath. The second, without question, is that of an anethopath. (Reid 1978:122)

It would be most interesting to follow up on this case history and discover if our most recalcitrant recidivist criminal offenders:

(1) experience nightmares;
(2) experience dreams;
(3) experience dreams which might ordinarily be experienced as nightmares by others, but are experienced by them as pleasurable; and
(4) suffer more (or less) than the nonrecidivist offenders from serious structural deficits.

Is it possible that anethopaths, through the acting out of their impulses and structural difficulties in waking life, somehow provide themselves with the necessary "positive" coloring of their self and object representations (albeit through heinous acts rather than through loving relationships), and thereby manage to develop stable structuralizations and avoid the need for nightmares to shore up their self-esteem? Do psychopathic criminals differ diagnostically (e.g., anethopaths versus psychopaths), and can this differentiation be made on the basis of the content of their nightmare dreams?

## Summary

A survey of the literature relating personality variables to the frequency of occurrences of nightmares suggests that frequent nightmare sufferers are more vulnerable to suffering from serious psychiatric disorders than individuals who rarely, if ever, report experiencing nightmares. Psychological test data reveal that nightmare sufferers tend to score significantly poorer on various scales: Death-Scale; Ego Strength Scale; Taylor's Manifest Anxiety Scale; DSM III criteria for schizophrenia, borderline personality, and schizotype personality; the Cornell Index (e.g., subscales of anxiety and nervousness, startle reaction, and depression—especially for men); MMPI (e.g., subscales of Schizophrenia, Psychopathy, Depression, Conversion Hysteria, Hypomania, Hypochondriasis, and Psychasthenia); and the Rotter Internal/External Locus of Control (indicating a strong external locus of control in this population).

In addition, nightmare sufferers were found to have had a significantly greater number of emotional problems or "breakdowns," had more hospitalizations, and had seriously considered suicide more frequently; they experienced their dreams as more frightening, more intense, strange, and violent.

With this empirical data as a basis for hypothesizing, psychoanalytic contributions to a more comprehensive theory of the personality characteristics of the nightmare sufferer were briefly explored—with particular emphasis on the formulations of self psychologists. It was suggested that the recurrent/repetitive nightmare was a manifestation of the repetition compulsion and, as such, served critical psychological functions for the dreamer: self-guiding, self-punishing, adaptive, defensive, and most significantly, restitutive-reparative.

Finally, it was proposed that the nightmare may be fruitfully investigated by observing its existence and nature (or lack of existence) among criminals. It was suggested that this population may be differentially diagnosed—by examining its dream/nightmare history—into two distinct subclasses: anethopaths (incurables) and psychopaths (curables). Further, it was suggested that the self psychologists' hypotheses regarding the inverse relationship between degree of psychic structuralization and frequency of nightmare experiences in individuals might be significantly elucidated by examining the criminal's nocturnal habits more carefully. Indeed, our theoretical propositions regarding psychopathy might need to be revised in basic ways if we discover that recidivist offenders are not a single class of individuals, but two (or more) classes—with regard to their self and object structuralizations, concomitant psychological vulnerabilities, and nightmare frequency.

## References


Atwood, G. E. and R. D. Stolorow. 1984. *Structures of Subjectivity: Explorations in Psychoanalytic Phenomenology.* Hillsdale, N.J.: Analytic Press.

Barron, F. 1953. An ego-strength scale which predicts response to psychotherapy. *Journal of Consulting Psychology* 17:327–33.

Bixler, E. O., C. R. Soldatos, D. S. Charney, D. J. Mitsky, and A. Kales. 1977. Nightmares as an index of psychopathology. *Sleep Research* vol. 140, no. 6.

Broughton, R. J. 1968. Sleep disorders: Disorders of arousal? *Science* 159:1070–78.

Cartwright, R. D. 1979. The nature and function of repetitive dreams: A survey and speculation. *Psychiatry* 42:131–37.

Cautela, J. R. 1968. Behavior therapy and the need for behavioral assessment. *Psychotherapy* 5:175–79.

Cellucci, A. J. and P. S. Lawrence. 1978. Individual differences in self-reported sleep variable correlations among nightmare sufferers. *Journal of Clinical Psychology* 34(3):721–25.

Feldman, M. J. and M. Hersen. 1967. Attitudes towards death in nightmare subjects. *Journal of Abnormal Psychology* 72:421–25.

Fenichel, O. 1945. *The Psychoanalytic Theory of Neurosis.* New York: Norton.

Fisher, C., J. Byrne, A. Edwards, and E. Kahn. 1968. NREM and REM nightmares. *Psychophysiology* 5:221–22.

French, T. and E. Fromm. 1964. *Dream Interpretation: A New Approach.* New York: Basic Books.

Freud, S. *Standard Edition of the Complete Psychological Works of Sigmund Freud.* James Strachey, ed. and tr. 24 vols. London: Hogarth Press, 1953–1974; New York: Macmillan.

1900. *The Interpretation of Dreams.* Vols. 4 and 5.

1920. *Beyond the Pleasure Principle.* Vol. 18.

Geer, J. H. and I. Silverman. 1967. Treatment of a recurrent nightmare by behavior-modification procedures: A case study. *Journal of Abnormal Psychology* 72:188–90.

Guggenbuhl-Craig, A. 1971. *Power in the Helping Professions.* New York: Spring.

Hadfield, J. A. 1954. *Dreams and Nightmares.* London: Penguin.

Hartmann, E. 1984. *The Nightmare: The Psychology and Biology of Terrifying Dreams.* New York: Basic Books.

Hartmann, E., D. Russ, B. Van der Kolk, R. Falke, and M. Oldfield. 1981. A preliminary study of the personality of the nightmare sufferer: Relationship to schizophrenia and creativity? *American Journal of Psychiatry* 138(6):794–97.

Haynes, S. and D. Mooney. 1975. Nightmares: Etiological, theoretical, and behavioral treatment considerations. *Psychological Record* 25:225–36.

Hersen, M. 1971. Personality characteristics of nightmare sufferers. *Journal of Nervous and Mental Disease* 153(1)27–31.

Horner, A. J. 1979. *Object Relations and the Developing Ego in Therapy.* New York: Jason Aronson.

Jones, E. 1949. *On the Nightmare.* London: Hogarth Press. (Original work published in 1911.)

Juda, D. P. 1983. Exorcising Freud's "Daemonic" compulsion to repeat: Repetition compulsion as part of the adaptational/maturational process. *Journal of the American Academy of Psychoanalysis* 11(3):353–75.

Juda, D. P. 1986. Comments on the usefulness of self psychology in understanding and treating a case of homosexual pedophilia. *Dynamic Psychotherapy.* Spring.

Kales, J. K., A. Kales, C. R. Soldatos, A. B. Caldwell, D. S. Charney, and E. D. Martin. 1980a. Night terrors: Clinical characteristics and personality patterns. *Achives of General Psychiatry* 37:1413–17.

Kales, A., C. R. Soldatos, A. B. Caldwell, D. S. Charney, J. D. Kales, D. Markel, and R. Cadieux. 1980b. Nightmares: Clinical characteristics and personality patterns. *American Journal of Psychiatry* 137(10):1197–1201.

Karpman, B. 1941. On the need of separating psychopathy into two distinct clinical types: The symptomatic and the idiopathic. *Journal of Criminal Psychopathology* 3:112.

Knapp, T. J., D. L. Downs, and J. R. Alperson. 1976. Behavior therapy for insomnia: A review. *Behavior Therapy* 7:614–25.

Kohut, H. 1971. *The Analysis of the Self.* New York: International Universities Press.

Kohut, H. 1977. *The Restoration of the Self.* New York: International Universities Press.

Lerner, B. 1967. Dream function reconsidered. *Journal of Abnormal Psychology* 72:85–100.

Meehl, P. E. 1973. *Psychodiagnosis: Selected Papers.* Minneapolis: University of Minnesota Press.

Monchaux, C. de 1978. Dreaming and the organizing function of the ego. *International Journal of Psycho-Analysis* 59:443–53.

Reid, W. H. 1978. *The Psychopath: A Comprehensive Study of Antisocial Disorders and Behaviors.* New York: Brunner/Mazel.

Schneck, J. M. 1969. Henri Fusell, nightmare, and sleep paralysis. *Journal of the American Medical Association* 207:725–26.

Sharpe, E. F. 1937. *Dream Analysis.* New York: Brunner/Mazel.

Silverman, I. and J. H. Geer. 1968. The elimination of a recurrent nightmare by desensitization of a related phobia. *Behavior Research Therapy* 6:109–11.

Socarides, C. 1980. Perverse symptoms and the manifest dream of perversion. In J. Natterson, ed., *The Dream in Clinical Practice,* pp. 237–56. New York: Jason Aronson.

Vaillant, G. E. 1977. *Adaptation to Life.* Boston: Little, Brown.

Verteuil, R. L. de. 1962. A psychiatric approach to the study of nightmare. *Canadian Psychiatric Association Journal* 7:151–58.

Von Franz, M. L. 1974. *Shadow and Evil in Fairy Tales.* New York: Spring.

# PART FIVE: The Nightmare and the Structure of Personality

# 15.

# Nightmares and the Structure of Personality

## I. Psychoanalytic Dream Theory and an Introduction to a Structural Theory of Nightmares

HENRY KELLERMAN

### Introduction to Psychoanalytic Dream Theory

IN HIS ENORMOUSLY influential book *The Interpretation of Dreams,* Sigmund Freud (1900) first proposed that the dream is the guardian of sleep. He postulated that the dream functioned to order all the amorphous bombardment of stimuli occurring internally during sleep so that potential interferences from such stimuli become relatively neutralized and harmless.

In his explanatory journey through the theory of dream construction and the appearance of nightmares, Freud utilized a staggering array of concepts to account for the phenomena he was studying. Among these concepts are dreamwork mechanisms, the latent versus the manifest dream, mental apparatus and mental censor, intrapsychic structure, primary-process thinking, wish fulfillment, the topographic system, unconscious impulses, cathected and decathected material, day's residue, motor versus sensory systems, therapeutic resistance, counterwish dreams, anxiety, and a number of collateral concepts. These are also reviewed and illustrated with examples by Altman (1969) and Nagera (1969).

Freud proposed that the transformation of potentially disturbing stimulation in the dream into some benign form was the function of the dreamwork—a process that utilizes a system of coping mechanisms. The purpose of these coping mechanisms is to disguise disturbing primary-process material. The ultimate transformation of this disturbing primary-process material—known as the latent content of a dream—distinguishes it from the manifest content, or the form to which the latent content is transformed. The dreamwork accomplishes its mission through use of coping mechanisms defined by Freud as the dreamwork mechanisms. They are: displacement, condensation, symbolism, and secondary elaboration.

## THE DREAMWORK MECHANISMS

*Displacement* is the mechanism in which surrogate subjects are chosen in order to deflect the dreamer's focus from the original subject of the latent dream. If these original subjects were perceived directly they would create distress for the dreamer. The mechanism of *condensation* operates to fuse or compress several meaningful and potentially disturbing latent-material events into another, single event—one that is not familiar or palpable. The mechanism of *symbolism* creates more neutral embodiments in a nonmaterial manner within the latent material. Finally, the mechanism of *secondary elaboration* uses the deflected subject matter of the displacement—the unitary compressed or condensed event, the intangible neutralized embodiment of symbols—and elaborates to connect it all by creating an intact, manifest, descriptive story—the dream. The result is a dream designed to produce something relatively innocuous for the dreamer, especially with respect to its underlying original and presumably threatening material.

According to Freud, when such coping mechanisms do not sufficiently disguise the latent dream, sleep will not be successfully guarded, the latent material will then emerge into consciousness, and the dreamer will awaken, having had a nightmare.

In addition to spelling out the principles of the dream-work mechanisms, Freud postulated that the mental apparatus contains a censor that helps to repress, disguise, and deflect all thoughts not permitted to emerge into consciousness. This censor is always vigilant with respect to the impulse product in the form of the primary-process dream. In the central core of this primary-process material, Freud postulated the existence of a wish.

## THE DREAM WISH FULFILLMENT

Freud was interested in constructing a consistent conception of the essence of the dream, and proposed the concept of wish fulfillment. The entire conception of dreaming revolved around this formulation of the wish-fulfillment nature of the dream.

In Freud's view in the course of evolution the dream developed with an essence. This central source of the dream relates to the process of fulfilling a wish. The wish is determined by and composed of impulse properties. Freud theorized that during sleep, the unconscious aspect of the mental apparatus provides the only available vehicle for the discharge of these impulses and the expression of the dream wish. Further, in order to preserve the condition of sleep, these impulses, which are indeed expressed, are also disguised. They then emerge in the manifest dream—the dream already transformed into a relatively innocuous story or a fragment of a story. When the transformation mechanisms of the dreamwork are not under stress and are not confronted with compelling material, a manifest dream is generated that is smooth, logical, and contains a complete story line. To the extent that the dreamwork mechanisms are under stress and the material confronting them is indeed compelling, to this extent does the manifest dream begin to break down and exhibit an absence of smoothness, a greater number of illogical events, and dream construction with an incomplete story line. This relative viability of the dream raises the possibility of primary process breaking into consciousness and threatening the sleep state. In a dream formed by a strong transformation and efficient working of the dream mechanisms, the dreamer is usually not threatened by the innocuous material of the manifest dream, and therefore the dreamer remains asleep. This entire process is conceptually treated by Freud as one that is possible because of the nature of the topography of the mental apparatus.

## THE TOPOGRAPHIC MODEL

Freud saw the topographic system of the mental apparatus—that is, conscious, preconscious, and unconscious—as the theoretical underpinning governing the mechanics of dream phenomena. Within this mental apparatus the unconscious remains active during sleep, while sleep holds its counterparts, the conscious and preconscious, in abeyance. Thus, because of the condition of sleep as applied to the systems conscious and preconscious, Freud considered that consciousness is almost entirely and effectively decathected. Only the active part of the apparatus—the unconscious—can threaten the sleep condition. Yet, there always exists a threat that emotionally charged material from consciousness can interfere with the dreamwork even though the systems conscious and preconscious are asleep and decathected. This is so because, according to Freud's conception of the latent dream, an association is created between unconscious impulses and experiences in thought and feeling of the actual day's events. Presumably, the original latent dream is formed through this association.

In Freud's view, the preconscious day's memory-residues are still somewhat cathected during sleep. Therefore, in association with unconscious impulses, some cathected material does indeed enter the unconscious. Because of the so-called contaminated unconscious, psychoanalytic practitioners are confident that the preconscious is always scanning the day's events in order to fix on any material that is congruent with unconscious wishes. It is a position that considers the dream to be always relevant in a person's psychological existence. The dream, then, in its importance as a historical recapitulation of past as well as recent events, reflects idiosyncratic conflict in an individual's life. In addition, this position—that some cathected material always enters the unconscious—enables the therapist to select dream elements for therapeutic work that resonate both with current residue material in the patient's life and with corresponding historical themes.

## THE DISTURBED DREAM

The dream finally exists as a sensory experience—that is, in a visual image or images. According to Freud, this occurs because during sleep the dreamer simply cannot express the wish of the dream in motor behavior. Rather, the wish is transported, as it were—from the unconscious to the sensory part of the mental apparatus.

Freud indicated that even in the nightmare—where motor behavior threatens to interrupt the dream and awaken the dreamer—the stressful dream can be a disguised wish fulfillment. In such cases the emotions of dread or fear would actually be transformed pleasure wishes. In addition, Freud identified some anxiety dreams as resistance dreams of patients in therapy who, because of their struggle with the therapist and resistance to the therapy, produce counterwish dreams. Another variation of this theme concerns the masochistic dream wish, which Freud viewed as a distorted pleasure dream attached to sexual strivings.

In a general Freudian sense then, disturbed dreams can occur when the wish of the dream confronts the preconscious with such force that the preconscious system is awakened. In anxiety dreams, it is presumably the sexual wishes that were repressed by the preconscious that become ultimately expressed as anxiety. During sleep, the preconscious repressive force is correspondingly inhibited, thereby releasing the anxiety. Finally, Freud saw the anxiety dream simply as an underdisguised wish-fulfillment dream where good and bad projections are embodied in different characters of the dream—no doubt a conceptual precursor to future split-object transferences of object relations thinking.

This, then, is the essence of Freud's position on dreams and nightmares. It is a beginning, an entrée into understanding of the nightmare within a psychoanalytic orientation, but fundamentally it is a theory of dreams. It does not constitute a bona fide theory of nightmares. Freud did not provide either a comprehensive or a more detailed view of the nightmare. He did not, for example, propose a system for understanding the implications of the variety of emotions that can cause a nightmare and the diagnostic meaning of such nightmares. Nor did he connect the appearance of the nightmare to a fuller understanding of the intrapsychic structure. He also did not offer any insight into the role that specific individual defenses play in the regulation of particular emotions as they precipitate the nightmare. Hartmann (1984) recognizes this absence of a comprehensive understanding of the nightmare; he notes that "Freud had surprisingly little to say about nightmares," basically relating in a general way traumatic nightmares to the repetition compulsion.

In this chapter a theory of nightmares will be presented that in part draws on a core of psychoanalytic conceptualizations regarding the understanding of nightmares. In this theory a host of personality variables can be organized around the structure of the nightmare. Questions to be answered include: how many kinds of nightmares are there—that is, are there a finite number? Do nightmares reveal intrapsychic etchings of the personality? How does a nightmare differ from an anxiety dream? In relation to nightmares, which defenses regulate which emotions? How do nightmares reveal diagnostic information? How is the nightmare embedded in the infrastructure of personality? Some of the propositions on the nightmare to be presented here have also been discussed elsewhere (Kellerman 1979, 1980).

## A CLARIFICATION OF THE CAUSE OF THE NIGHTMARE

It is proposed here (in contrast to Freud's position) that the kind of nightmare that awakens the dreamer is not determined solely by a breakdown of the dreamwork. Rather, when the dreamer's main defense system is not operating effectively, the dreamer will awaken with a nightmare in which emotion appears in its undefended and most intense form. The incapacity of defense means an incapacity of a given so-called ego-defense that manages or regulates a specific emotion. This incapacity of a specific defense releases a specific emotion that is then expressed at its highest intensity, and this is the only way in which the nightmare can occur. The nightmare is triggered *only* if a specific emotion-defense is impaired along with an impairment or some disorganization to dreamwork mechanisms so that these mechanisms are inoperative. In such a case the emotion is deregulated, while the primary-process material of the latent dream is similarly unregulated. Under such conditions, the highest intensity of the emotion is experienced, and the dreamer awakens. The important point to note here is the distinction made between defenses and dreamwork mechanisms. The dreamwork mechanisms regulate and manage the latent dream and its primary-process material, while defense mechanisms—those attributed to ego function in conventional psychoanalytic thinking—regulate the experience of particular emotions.

## Anxiety Dreams and Nightmares

This clarification of the cause of the nightmare allows the following formulation. Whenever the dreamwork mechanisms are impaired but ego defenses remain intact in their basic function as emotion coping devices, the dreamer will experience an anxiety dream—one in which the dreamer remains asleep; that is, latent material threatens consciousness, but the dreamer's emotion is controlled, and what the dreamer experiences is palpable anxiety. In contrast, in order for a nightmare to occur, the dreamwork mechanisms have to be impaired so that primary-process latent material can surface—but only along with an impairment of defense mechanisms and the consequent expression of emotion in its highest intensity. Under such conditions, the dream is now a full-fledged nightmare—one that awakens the dreamer—and not a typical anxiety dream where the dreamer remains sleeping, albeit uncomfortably.

In the definition of a nightmare, therefore, it is the emotion within the content of the dream that awakens the dreamer. This proposition considerably broadens the notion that nightmares are only dreams of terror (Kellerman 1979). It is obvious that individuals awaken because of a wide array of dream contents, not all of which are dreams of terror, panic, or fear. This point of view is quite different from that of Jones (1931), who focused mainly on terror nightmares as more or less comprising his universe of nightmares. Recent clinical understanding of the nightmare indicates that Jones's position at best barely touched the surface of a comprehensive understanding of the nightmare.

In this, and the following three chapters, it will be proposed that the system of nightmares reveals the intrapsychic designation of specific emotions that trigger the nightmare, and further reveals diagnostic information about the dreamer. In addition, it will be proposed that the nightmare reveals the intrapsychic function of each corresponding emotion-defense. When the nightmare occurs, the central underlying intrapsychic position of the dream is revealed. Furthermore, it is proposed that any nightmare that occurs reflects the dreamer's current diagnostic disposition. More specifically, it is probably the case that the nightmare is characterized by the basic emotion implied by any given diagnostic disposition, so that the expression of an intense emotion triggering a nightmare reveals diagnostic information. This also means that nightmares can be triggered by emotions of rage, grief, sexual feelings, mirth or laughter, surprise, etc.

In the following discussion an original conception of a system of nightmares will be presented—a theory proposing that there are only a few basic nightmare themes, although there may be an infinite number of dream contents. This system can reveal the specific underlying intrapsychic nature of each diagnostic state and the specific array of primary emotions that can cause nightmares. The system of nightmares and the resulting correlation with the entire personality organization of emotion, defense, diagnostic disposition, and intrapsychic forces suggest a series of postulates some of which are also elaborated in Kellerman (1979, 1980). These postulates will be presented in this and in the following three chapters. Next, a discussion will ensue that shows the several different kinds of nightmares that may occur and makes the point that nightmares can be caused by a number of emotions—not just the emotions of fear or terror.

## A Catalogue of Nightmare Themes

Although psychoanalytic as well as personality-theory literature on nightmares focuses mainly on nightmares of terror, nevertheless a perusal of the overall clinical literature on psychotherapy and psychoanalytic treatment, as well as a review of one's personal experience, reveals a much richer tapestry of emotions—not just terror—that correlate with the onset of nightmares. For example, therapists frequently describe treatment sessions in which patients report nightmares of grief. In such dreams, a loved one has usually died and the patient begins to sob until the grief becomes unbearable and awakens the dreamer. All illustration of this kind of grief nightmare occurred with a female patient who reported awakening while sobbing uncontrollably. This woman had always maintained an extremely warm relationship with her father and in fact admired him with the utmost consideration and respect. She reported that in her dream he died, and the emotion of grief simply gripped her and was overwhelming. She further reported that the scenario of his death in the dream was so real that it turned into a nightmare. When asked what exactly in the dream awakened her and when in the dream the awakening occurred, the patient responded, "When I realized he was dead and the sorrow overcame me, then the dream turned into a nightmare and I woke up."

From this example of a grief nightmare several phenomena about nightmares can be appreciated. First, nightmares can crystallize from dreams. Second, the basic definition or determining factor that distinguishes a nightmare from a dream centers on the point that in a dream the dreamer remains asleep, but in a nightmare the dreamer awakens from sleep because of the emotional content of the dream. Third, nightmares are not merely dreams of terror.

A second example of a nonterror nightmare concerns the dream in which the dreamer awakens because the subject of the dream revolves around the dreamer in the role of the aggressor. A male patient reported a dream in which he was physically struggling with someone who was threatening him. Usually a taciturn person who would avoid confrontation, in the dream the patient challenged his opponent, began feeling defiant and rageful, and then in a violent moment, killed his opponent. The patient awakened feeling quite surprised at his newfound courage and reported feeling refreshed. Here again, after close scrutiny it was determined that the triggering emotion in the dream that awakened this man was anger and not terror.

Regarding the other few emotions that can transform a dream into a nightmare, a survey of the literature, a compendium of nightmares reported clinically by patients, and a review of personal dream experiences suggest that the emotions that can cause nightmares include: terror, rage, sexuality, grief, surprise, laughter (or humor), revulsion, falling (or expectation), and feelings of paralysis. Examples of each of these emotion categories will be presented in the following sections. Dreams of sensory experiences such as flashing lights or tactile sensations that awaken a dreamer may be dream anomalies, non-REM night-terror products, or fragments of a dream that have been transformed into a nightmare but are instantly repressed (Kellerman 1981).

Consideration of the spectrum of emotions that can evoke nightmares creates the need for devising a parsimonious system that enables the range of nightmares to be understood, so that these basic nightmare themes can be correlated with their respective basic emotions as well as with the many other levels of personality description, such as defenses, diagnostic condition, and intrapsychic state.

## EMOTIONS, DEFENSES, AND NIGHTMARES

There are many researchers who have postulated systems of basic emotions (McDougall 1921; Scott 1958; Plutchik 1980). In fact, those researchers, clinicians, and philosophers who have been concerned with this domain of experience have uniformly concentrated on the issue of the number of basic emotions, as well as discussing a variety of other variables. In table 15.1, a sampling of the basic-emotion systems that have been proposed in the literature and throughout history is presented. This table shows that authors agree to 8 or 9 basic emotions or less, with most authors agreeing on 5 to 8 emotions.

In the earlier discussion eight distinct nightmare themes emerged as constituting the basic emotional range of all nightmares, and this proposal correlates best with the system of basic emotions formulated by Plutchik (1962, 1980). In this system Plutchik proposes the basic emotions of joy, sorrow, acceptance, disgust, expectation, surprise, anger, and fear. Essentially, the emotion of joy refers to pleasure responses including sexuality; the emotion of sorrow includes responses to loss and includes the response of grief; the emotion of acceptance is one in which there is a determined absence of criticality in the person, thereby permitting a naive and open condition of acceptance to exist (even, for example, as in the

TABLE 15.1. A Compendium of Basic Emotion Systems[a]

| *Chinese (during antiquity)* | *Descartes* | *Spinoza* | *Hobbes* | *McDougall* | *Bion's system for groups* | *Tomkins* | *Jorgensen* | *Plutchik* |
|---|---|---|---|---|---|---|---|---|
| Happiness | Joy | Joy | Joy | Elation | Sexuality | Joy | Happiness | Joy |
| Anger | Love | Desire | Love | Tender | Hope | Interest | Want | Acceptance |
| Sorrow | Admiration | Sorrow | Desire | Subjection | Depression | Surprise | Shyness | Surprise |
| Fear | Desire | | Hate | | | Rage | Anger | Expectation |
| | Hatred | | Grief | | | Disgust | Sorrow | Anger |
| | Sadness | | Aversion | | | Shame | Fear | Disgust |
| | | | | Disgust | Guilt | | | |
| | | | | | | Anguish | (Loathing)? | Sorrow |
| | | | | Fear | | | | |
| | | | | | | Fear | | Fear |

[a] In addition to those listed above, other systems include: Darwin's seven clusters of emotion; Cattell's ten factors of basic emotions; Murray's action tendencies; and, Scott's behavioral categories.

susceptibility in being surprised by the punchline of a joke); the emotion of disgust includes responses such as revulsion; the emotions of expectation and surprise include responses of falling and disorientation, respectively; the emotion of anger includes rage; and fear includes terror.

In Plutchik's conception of a basic-emotion system the eight basic emotions are conceived along an intensity dimension so that, for example, fear is the middle intensity level of its dimension while apprehension is a low-intensity and terror a high-intensity emotion on the same dimension. This is an important point in the discussion of emotions and nightmares because it is proposed here that all nightmares are caused by high-intensity emotion. In table 15.2 the basic emotion dimensions are presented with respect to their highest intensity levels along with indications of a sampling of the property of intensity of emotion within each dimension.

In a series of papers and books Kellerman (1977, 1979, 1980) has related these basic emotions to basic defenses. In Table 15.3 this correlation of emotion and defense is presented. The correlation is also an attempt to provide a similarity structure of defense mechanisms (which can be seen also in figure 15.1 below).

The idea that defense mechanisms are systematically linked with emotion has been alluded to in earlier studies by Brenner (1974, 1975) and Rado (1956). Yet, in all the studies on emotion, on defense, and on their linkage none have atempted to provide a way of understanding this linkage. In addition, only a few theorists and researchers have tried to determine the developmental levels of defenses. Although Freud (1926) took up the cause of outlining the defense system in his paper "Inhibitions, Symptoms, and Anxiety" he never provided a way to further link defenses to emotion or even to determine their inherent connection to psychosexual development. Lists of defenses and their vicissitudes are given by Coleman (1956), English and Finch (1964), Ewalt and Farnsworth (1963), Frazier (1975), Healy, Bronner, and Bowers (1930), Semrad (1967), and Vaillant (1976). Some of these authors consider hierarchical arrangements of defenses, and along with Blum (1953) and Fenichel (1945), provide the few theoretical studies in the psychoanalytic consideration of a systematic arrangement of defenses as correlated with other aspects of personality. Most of these

TABLE 15.2. The Basic Emotion Dimensions and the Property of Intensity of Emotion[a]

| *Intensity* | *Basic Emotion Dimensions* | | | | | | | |
|---|---|---|---|---|---|---|---|---|
| High | Voraciousness | Revulsion | Ecstasy | Grief | Vigilance | Amazement | Rage | Terror |
| Medium | Acceptance | Disgust | Joy | Sorrow | Expectation | Surprise | Anger | Fear |
| Low | Agreeableness | Dislike | Cheerful-ness | Gloom-iness | Set | Startle | Annoy-ance | Apprehen-sion |

[a] The intensity component of basic emotions displayed here is a formulation of Plutchik's (1980) psychoevolutionary theory of emotion.

TABLE 15.3. Basic Bipolar Emotion and Defense Dimensions

| *Emotion* | *Defense* |
|---|---|
| Acceptance | Denial |
| Disgust | Projection |
| Expectation | Intellectualization |
| Surprise | Regression |
| Fear | Repression |
| Anger | Displacement |
| Joy | Reaction formation |
| Sorrow | Compensation |

studies of the defense system are essentially influenced by Anna Freud's (1937) well-known work *The Ego and the Mechanisms of Defense,* in which a distinction is made between primitive and higher-order defenses, although no distinction is made between defenses used in character formation and those designed to manage transitory emotion. It should be noted that all these authors, starting with A. Freud, were also concerned with listing what they considered to be primary defenses. Most authors generated lists of defenses that overlapped, and the agreement between authors regarding the definition of these defenses was relatively high.

The method by which defenses are related to emotion in this chapter is given comprehensively elsewhere (Kellerman 1979, 1980). In these studies the emotions of displacement, repression, reaction formation, projection, undoing, isolation, intellectualization, sublimation, rationalization, denial, and compensation were designated as reflecting a defense system used in the personality to manage transitory emotion. The defenses of introjection, idealization, and identification were designated as reflecting a defensive level utilized in the service of trait formation or in the entrenchment of particular personality style. In figure 15.1, a similarity structure of the entire defense system is proposed. This structure shows the relation of one defense to another in terms of relative similarity and polarity of defenses as well as their relation to a circumplex similarity structure of the basic emotions.

A series of postulates can be formulated in order to contribute organizational power to the theoretical model that relates the domains of emotion, defense, and nightmares. Then, a discussion

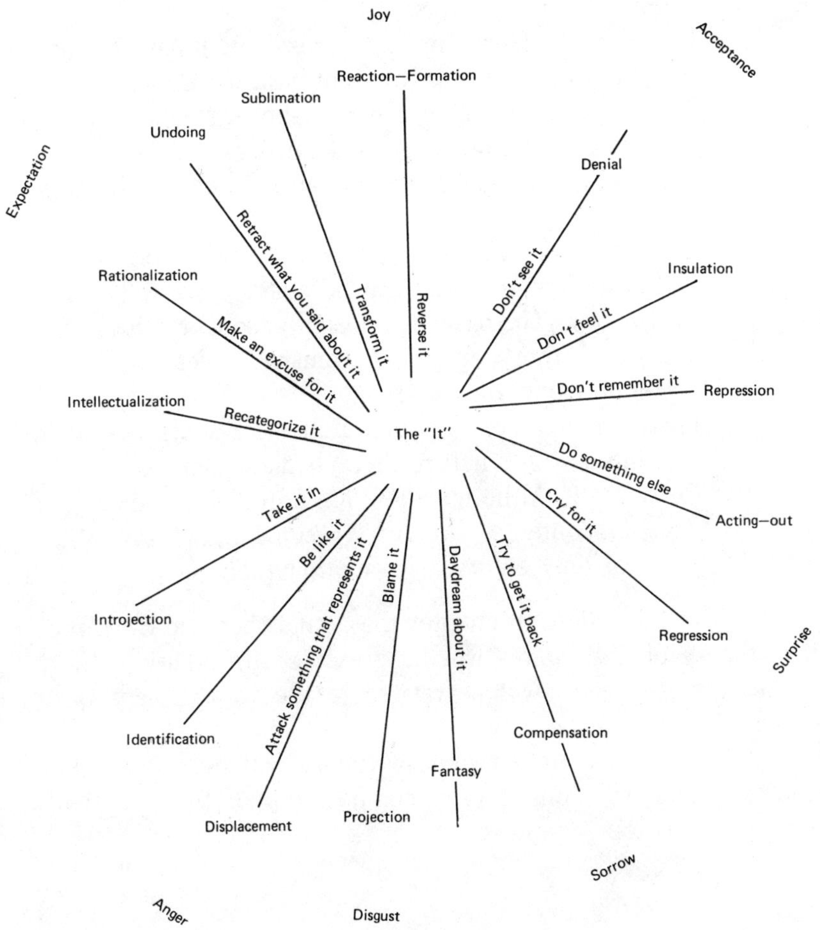


FIGURE 15.1: The "it"; a mnemonic device to create an image of each defense mechanism. A similarity structure of defenses is revealed by the continuous images around the circle. Corresponding emotions are indicated. *Source:* Kellerman (1979).

of the connections between these seemingly diverse domains will also be considered in the following three chapters.

Postulate 1. Defense mechanisms regulate emotions.

Postulate 2. Specific defenses are designed to manage specific emotions.

Postulate 3. There are eight basic defenses to manage eight basic emotions.

Postulate 4. There are eight basic nightmare themes- that correspond to the eight basic categories of the entire emotion-defense personality system.

Postulate 5. A nightmare is defined as a dream that, because of its emotional content, awakens the dreamer.

Postulate 6. Any basic nightmare is a reflection of the dreamer's current diagnostic state.

Postulate 7. The basic diagnostic personality types are derived from particular defensive styles and their emotion underpinnings.

Postulate 8. Each nightmare theme reveals the basic intrapsychic nature of each diagnostic state.

Postulate 9. Although there are an infinite number of dream contents, when they become nightmares they reveal only eight basic emotion themes.

In the following chapter the actual thematic categories of the theory of nightmares will be presented. In addition, these basic nightmare themes will be related to the various aspects of personality that have been outlined.

A summary of the entire theory will be offered after chapter 18 and will consist of a compendium of the postulates presented in all four chapters.

## Summary

In this chapter the study of the nightmare was introduced with a review of Sigmund Freud's formulations and discoveries relating to dreaming generally. In addition, a distinction between nightmares and anxiety dreams was presented and a new theory of basic nightmare themes was introduced. Finally, nightmares were related to a basic system of emotions and defenses.

## References


Altman, L. L. 1969. *The Dream in Psychoanalysis.* New York: International Universities Press.

Blum, G. S. 1953. *Psychoanalytic Theories of Personality.* New York: McGraw-Hill.

Brenner, C. 1974. On the nature and development of affects: A unified theory. *Psychoanalytic Quarterly* 43(4):532–56.

Brenner, C. 1975. Affects and psychic conflict. *Psychoanalytic Quarterly* 44(1):5–28.

Coleman, J. C. 1956. *Abnormal Psychology and Modern Life.* New York: Scott Foresman.

English, O. S. and S. M. Finch. 1964. *Introduction to Psychiatry.* New York: Norton.

Ewalt, J. R. and D. C. Farnsworth. 1963. *Textbook of Psychiatry.* New York: McGraw-Hill.

Fenichel, O. 1945. *The Psychoanalytic Theory of Neurosis.* New York: Norton.

Frazier, S. H. 1975. *A Psychiatric Glossary.* Washington, D.C.: American Psychiatric Association.

Freud, A. 1937. *The Ego and the Mechanisms of Defense.* London: Hogarth Press.

Freud, S. *Standard Edition of the Complete Psychological Works of Sigmund Freud.* James Strachey, ed. and tr. 24 vols. London: Hogarth Press, 1953–1974; New York: Macmillan.

1900. *The Interpretation of Dreams.* Vols. 4 and 5.

1926. Inhibitions, symptoms, and anxiety. 20:75–172.

Hartmann, E. 1984. *The Nightmare.* New York: Basic Books.

Healy, W., A. F. Bronner, and A. M. Bowers. 1930. *The Structure and Meaning of Psychoanalysis.* New York: Knopf.

Jones, E. 1931. *On the Nightmare.* London: Hogarth Press. (Original work published in 1911.)

Kellerman, H. 1977. Hate. In B. B. Wolman, ed., *International Encyclopedia of Neurology, Psychiatry, Psychoanalysis, and Psychology.* New York: Von Nostrand Reinhold.

Kellerman, H. 1979. *Group Psychotherapy and Personality: Intersecting Structures.* New York: Grune and Stratton.

Kellerman, H. 1980. A structural model of emotion and personality: Psychoanalytic and sociobiological implications. In R. Plutchik and H. Kellerman, eds., *Emotion: Theory, Research, and Experience.* Vol. 1. *Theories of Emotion.* New York: Academic Press.

Kellerman, H. 1981. *Sleep Disorders: Insomnia and Narcolepsy.* New York: Brunner/Mazel.

McDougall, W. 1921. *The Group Mind.* London: Cambridge University Press.

Nagera, H. 1969. *Basic Psychoanalytic Concepts on the Theory of Dreams.* New York: Basic Books.

Plutchik, R. 1962. *The Emotions: Facts, Theories, and a New Model.* New York: Random House.

Plutchik, R. 1980. *Emotion: A Psychoevolutionary Synthesis.* New York: Harper and Row.

Rado, S. 1956. *Psychoanalysis of Behavior.* New York: Grune and Stratton.

Scott, J. P. 1958. *Animal Behavior.* Chicago: University of Chicago Press.

Semrad, E. 1967. The organization of ego-defenses and object-loss. In D. M. Moriarity, ed., *The Loss of Loved Ones.* Springfield, Ill.: Charles C. Thomas.

Vaillant, G.E. 1976. Natural history of male psychological health. V. The relation of ego mechanisms of defense to adult adjustment. *Archives of General Psychiatry* 33:535–45.

# 16.

# Nightmares and the Structure of Personality

## II. The Basic Nightmare Themes and Their Relation to Personality

HENRY KELLERMAN

IN THE PRECEDING chapter, an introduction to the theory of nightmares was approached through an analysis of the psychoanalytic theory of dreams and by distinguishing dreams from nightmares. A series of questions and postulates was developed regarding the relationships among emotions, defenses, diagnostic dispositions, intrapsychic designations, and nightmares. In this and the following two chapters the assumptions and connections that underlie these postulates will be outlined. This discussion will draw upon theoretical and clinical material as presented by Kellerman (1979, 1980, 1983).

### Nightmares and Personality Structure

#### THE TERROR NIGHTMARE AND ITS EMOTION-PERSONALITY CORRELATES

In examining the terror nightmare and in the overall clinical understanding of this sort of nightmare it is generally accepted that the experience of the emotion of terror reflects a moment when the repressive defense is lifted. In other words, since repression is chiefly the defense mechanism regulating apprehension and fear, when this defense is incapacitated or actually lifted, a high-intensity fear—terror—emerges. Insofar as fear generates escape as well as withdrawal feelings, repression acts to eliminate threatening material from consciousness. Clinicians, in fact, often find that it is generally fearful patients who show the most intense repression.

Fear may concern unconscious feelings of anger, or it may be the desire to avoid painful memories. Further, although repression is the central quality that defines all defenses, it is most prominent in the management of the emotion of fear. In studies of hypnosis, for example, fears are frequently reported as becoming freed from their repressions. However, when repression is simply overcome by excessively threatening stimuli in the dream, the dreamer experiences a nightmare in which terror characterizes the dream content. Contents of such nightmares include running in terror from an attacker, being physically harmed, being unable to escape fast enough from an attacker, and variations on the terror theme.

In terms of diagnosis, the emotion of fear constitutes the underlying emotional state of the passive disposition, and repression is the specific defense designed to manage the fear and the passivity. The passive dispositional type is characterized by an inert, nonaction attitude. Whether the defensive posture of the passive dispositional type is to avoid anger or simply to defy the object through passivity, traits such as delay, procrastination, and general avoidance behavior chiefly characterize such a person. To maintain the passive stance, massive repression is brought to bear on day-to-day experiences, so that the repression constitutes the central defensive core of the passive personality. The repression then permits the main withdrawal and avoidance reactions to exist. The use of repression as the chief defensive function of the passive type implies the need for a tenth postulate to be added to the nine postulates on emotions, defenses, and nightmares that were presented in the previous chapter.

> Postulate 10. It is proposed that although all defenses contain a repressive element, repression was originally

developed to manage the emotion of fear, which is the chief underlying component of the passive dispositional diagnosis.

An example of a nightmare that was reported by a 42-year-old passive male patient is now presented. This nightmare seems to illustrate the connection between the terror nightmare, the defense of repression, and the passive diagnostic disposition. This man lived alone, never married, and never developed any significant enduring relationships, although he did have many acquaintances and friends. He was not withdrawn or particularly remote in the schizoid sense, but was a classic procrastinator and was basically inert and somewhat shy. He finally began a relationship with a woman that lasted for more than two years. In the therapy sessions he noticed that this was indeed his longest relationship, that friends were curious about any marriage plans, and that his woman friend had also suggested that they would probably marry. At this point he had the following dream:

I was sleeping in my bedroom and I heard someone break in the front door. I was terrified. I started saying "who is it?" but the terror was too much. I felt myself getting out of bed to run somewhere and I woke up mumbling to myself "who is it?" which in the dream was said very clearly, but when I heard myself as I woke up, it was just a mumble. I woke up half sitting in the bed. I was terrified.

The relationship this man was developing was apparently pushing back the barriers of repression. His terror reflected an intensely experienced fear about allowing someone in. This finding is consistent with the proposal that of the multitude of dream contents that may contain themes of threat, the specific nightmare itself, because of the impairment of the repressive defense, will always be characterized by the emotion of terror.

## THE RAGE NIGHTMARE AND ITS EMOTION-PERSONALITY CORRELATES

In examining the nightmare characterized by rage and in an analysis of the defensive mechanism designed chiefly to manage and regulate the anger emotion, there is a wide cross-disciplinary literature suggesting the intrinsic relationship between the emotion of anger and the defense of displacement. For example, in social psychological and psychoanalytic studies of scapegoating and hate, a generally accepted psychological principle concerns the proposition that when anger cannot be expressed directly it becomes indirectly expressed toward substitute target figures (Bychowski 1968; Kellerman 1977, 1980; Lasswell 1952). In ethological studies (Kaufman 1960; Kellerman et al. 1974; Lorenz 1966) it was shown that this phenomenon of indirect displaced attack even occurs in animals.

The typical diagnostic condition that includes anger as its central emotion and displacement as its chief defensive operation is the aggressive personality. In addition, typical behavior of the aggressive person reflects anger as the chief underlying emotion. Were it not for the operation of the mechanism of displacement, ongoing dissatisfactions in the personality would be continuously and directly expressed to on-target figures. Such behavior could cause untold upheavals, inappropriate reactions, and retaliations in many situations. Displacement permits the channeling of aggression toward substitute and safer figures and to those who may absorb the anger without its causing immediate repercussions.

The rage nightmare occurs when the mechanism of displacement is inadequate to block direct expression of anger or to create safe overflow channels for the expression of anger. The appearance of the rage or assertion nightmare means that the dreamer has produced a highly aggressive, confrontational or directly rageful dream in which the dreamer is the assertive figure. Of the many dreams in which the dreamer experiences rage directly, the nightmare is always a result of assertion or direct expression of the rage.

The same man whose terror nightmare was presented above, one year later at the age of 43 awakened with a nightmare that reflected a shift in his diagnosis from the passive dispositional state to the aggressive one. He was not yet married but was talking about it continually in sessions. He was no longer repressing as much as he had and was becoming more assertive. One month after reporting the following nightmare he was married.

I was sleeping in my bedroom and again I heard someone break into my house. I immediately remembered that I had dreamt this exact dream before and in a way I then knew it was a dream, but I still couldn't ignore what was happening. I was surprised. I was almost terrified again but I felt something get angry inside of me. The anger became high and strong and I felt my fear dip into the background. I never felt that before in my life. I felt strong and brave and even tough. I dreamed that I got out of bed and said, "Who is it? Come on in, I'm ready for you." I dreamed I was standing there with my fists clenched as though I was ready to fight. I woke up stirred up but I felt good.

Even though his assertiveness was becoming expressed through anger, nevertheless the displacement defense was ostensibly more restricted—that is, he didn't dilute his response by anchoring it to a less threatening figure—and this enabled him to become heroic in the dream.

Usual contents of such nightmares include harming another person, shooting or stabbing someone, and screaming at someone rather than playing the role of object of the confrontation. Thus, in persons of the aggressive dispositional type and in the absence of the displacement defense, all dream contents will develop into nightmares in which aggression and confrontation prevail.

When the terror and rage nightmares are compared, a correspondence appears that seems to show a polarity of emotion, defense, and diagnostic disposition. On the emotion level fear is opposite to anger. On the diagnostic level the passive and the aggressive dispositions are opposites. On the level of the nightmare, terror is opposite to rage, and on the level of defense, by inference based upon the respective functions of the two defenses, repression is proposed as the opposite of displacement, although the polarity is less apparent.

From this analysis of the terror and rage nightmares and their respective personality correlates, two further postulates can be proposed. An eleventh postulate to join the ten proposed earlier refers to the nature of the shift of diagnosis as a result of life experience. This shift is the result of the experience of relationships, as well as of therapy working through experience.

Postulate 11. Theoretically, any of the basic nightmare themes may be experienced. For example, a formerly passive person who, because of an alteration of defenses, is better able to be confrontational and as-

> sertive can experience nightmares of aggression. This shift of diagnostic expression is a reflection also of postulate 6—namely, any basic nightmare is a reflection of the dreamer's current diagnostic state.

In addition, in view of postulate 4 in which the parameters of the entire nightmare system are proposed—namely that there are eight basic nightmare themes that correspond to the eight basic categories of the entire emotion-personality system—the analysis of only two of these categories, the terror and rage nightmares, suggests that there may be an inherent organizational arrangement to the eight categories of the nightmare-personality system. Thus, a postulate accounting for the organizational powers of the system suggests itself. This postulate embodies the wide array of data from the diverse domains of emotion, defense, diagnostic disposition, and nightmares and interrelates these in a parsimonious manner.

> Postulate 12. The eight basic nightmare themes, emotions, defenses, and diagnostic dispositions, respectively, show the properties of both polarity and similarity.

(See Kellerman 1979, 1980 and Plutchik 1962, 1980 for a discussion of these properties.)

## THE PLEASURE NIGHTMARE AND ITS EMOTION-PERSONALITY CORRELATES

The sexual dream is one that can also develop into a nightmare when the dreamer is awakened by intense, undefended emotion. In the case of a sexual or pleasure dream that ultimately becomes a nightmare—that is, a dream that because of its content awakens the dreamer—the dreamer is stirred to wakening by sexual orgasm, near orgasm, or some erotic experience. Such a nightmare can only be possible when the defense of reaction formation, which acts to block an overflow of pleasurable-sexual impulses, becomes momentarily impaired, or for some other psychic reason becomes inadequate to its task. In the absence of reaction formation a person may be directing substantial energy toward sexual release.

It is proposed that the defense of reaction formation was originally designed to manage the joy-pleasure emotions. Correspondingly it has been proposed that the emotion of joy or feelings of pleasure constitute the underlying state of the manic disposition (Kellerman 1979, 1980). In any dreamer, especially in one with manic feelings, when the bombardment of erotic or pleasurable dream stimuli is too strong, and the defensive operation of reaction formation not sufficiently applied to manage such stimuli, then the dreamer will produce highly sexualized ecstatic dream content in which all prohibition dissipates. It is likely that a loss of control will result, and an orgastic or wet dream will awaken the dreamer. Such a nightmare thus is a result of the heightened sexuality that ordinarily would have been managed by some reasonable measure of reaction formation.

On the levels of emotion, diagnostic disposition, and defense, the manic type is an energized type who needs to be involved in multitudes of projects. Good feelings toward people and a gregarious and intense sociality characterize manic behavior. The manic type contains in its basic nature the potential for needing an overabundance of pleasurable stimuli. Therefore, the reaction formation has developed to manage undue amounts of pleasure-need in the personality. In psychoanalytic terms, the reaction formation results from superego prohibitions against the attraction to pleasurable stimuli—especially toward those objects that will become repressed on the basis of socialization requirements. One such example is the attraction to oedipal figures. These attractions contain sexual implications. The reaction formation acts to maintain a moderate degree of positive response to pleasurable perceptions by converting nonsocialized attractions of a sexual nature to opposite avoidance experiences and along with the defense of sublimation creates an abundance of work energy.

Contents of such nightmares include any playing out in the dream of sexual fantasies to a desired conclusion. This can include anything from the mere touching of various body parts to actual sexual intercourse, or may involve any other erotic gratification whatsoever.

A young man of 22 who was in psychoanalytic treatment and who was in the process of analyzing an oedipal conflict described a sexual obsession he had about a woman five years his senior whom he had known since adolescence. He had always been strongly attracted to her but believed she would never consider any relationship with him other than a casual one. This man was an active, productive, and exuberant person. After some time in therapy, he began to feel more mature and less inadequate. Apparently, his reaction-formation defense became less severe and he had the following dream after coincidentally meeting this woman at a party.

I was standing in a room near a couch. There were lots of people around. Denise walked by. She was wearing a tight black woolen sweater and she was big. I felt sexual toward her. The people were milling around but they gradually disappeared and we seemed to be alone. I had my hands out—like they were held out in front of me in a cupped fashion, palms away from me—like you'd help someone on with a coat. We seemed to be sitting on the couch now. She slowly turned toward me, and as she did, I didn't move my hands, so that they were slightly cupped and her breasts sort of fit—like a perfect fit. It reminds me of the docking maneuver of one space vehicle with another—a locking together—but it was gentle. I was feeling very excited, extremely excited. I instantly felt that she was firm, and as I got the feeling that she was firm, I had an orgasm and ejaculated in my sleep. The orgasm woke me up—rather the certainty that I was going to have the orgasm woke me up. I had the orgasm as I was waking up.

This dream-nightmare is one example of many possible eroticized dream contents, all of which will end in an erotic awakening presumably when the defense of reaction formation is impaired. The pleasure-joy nightmare and its theoretical analysis also suggest another postulate in establishing parameters of the nightmare. This new postulate reflects the fact that even when the dream is a pleasure dream, it can cause an awakening or a nightmare. Consideration of the question why this should be so reveals that all dreams that become nightmares contain a prohibitive component which is fundamentally breached. Thus, dream contents causing awakenings reflect wishes or needs that the dreamer finds, for whatever reason, to be unacceptable. The unacceptability of the dream content implies that the emotion of fear exists in every dream that turns into a nightmare—even dreams of pleasure. Thus, just as every defense mechanism contains the element repression, so too does every nightmare contain an element of the emotion of fear, in the sense of the fearfulness inherent in prohibitions that are breached. This idea is presented in the following new postulate,

> Postulate 13. Each nightmare contains a fear component. This postulate is also consistent with the observation that (a) each defense contains a repression component, and (b) repression is the defense designed chiefly to manage the emotion of fear.

## THE GRIEF NIGHTMARE AND ITS EMOTION-PERSONALITY CORRELATES

The nightmare of grief or crying is one that reflects intensely sorrowful feelings in the dreamer. It is proposed that the chief defense used to avoid feelings of depression or to manage potentially sorrowful feelings is that of compensation. This proposition is based on the fact that the compensatory defense is especially effective in helping to maintain higher self-esteem. It is also the defense mechanism through which restitutive processes are maintained; that is, in the period of reconstituting oneself from depressive or otherwise debilitating emotional states, it is the defense of compensation that is mainly used.

The depressed personality type primarily suffers from real or imagined object loss, from a loss of self-esteem, or from perceived low self-esteem. During object-loss experiences, identification with the object as an internalized symbol produces a sense that something inside was lost. This identity loss needs to be replaced, or in some way regained. The compensatory mechanism manages, through aggrandizing fantasy or expansive behavior, to accomplish this aim. It is an attempt to overcome the effects of a real or perceived loss. When the bombardment of loss stimuli in any dreamer overpowers the compensatory defense, the dreamer will experience a dream in which the dream content reflects grief. Even in nondepressed personalities what is seen in therapy is that when a significant conflict such as a dependency has been worked through, for example, a grief nightmare can occur. This grief nightmare simulates the depressive diagnostic condition because the giving up of a major defensive operation connected with dependency is experienced by the dreamer as a significant loss—

hence the grief or crying nightmare, usually taking the form of the death of a loved one.

Contents of such dreams frequently include this theme of death of a loved one or variations on it, and the dreamer often finds himself awakening and sobbing uncontrollably. In the dream, the dreamer experiences that something equivalent to a last chance has been forever and inexorably lost. Thus, in the absence of the compensation defense, the loss seems irretrievable. If sobbing or crying does not result from the nightmare, the loss experience will be reflected in a profound yearning or grieving. In the absence of compensatory mechanisms, nothing is left for the dreamer but weeping or admitting total helplessness. Such nightmares are so very vivid that even after awakening and realizing that the experience was only a dream, those who have had such nightmares report that the awful feelings of dread and grief seem to linger and to maintain their profound emotional impact—even superceding the conscious awareness that it was only a dream.

A 30-year-old man who was working through separation fears and who consistently defended against any expression of depressive feeling finally was able to admit to feelings of incapacity. He then could report that he was afraid to live alone and that he usually managed to divert his attention from his fears by engaging in compensatory behavior. Nevertheless, he was somewhat shy and relied heavily on his parents for emotional support. The day after he finally rented his own apartment he had the following dream.

I can't quite remember all the events. I know my father died. He was dead. It was too much for me to take. I loved him so much and now I would never see him again. I was crying. It seemed that grief was pouring all out of me. I felt miserable. I'd never experienced such misery. I woke up sobbing with tears streaming down my face. I forgot how I found it out, but someone told me he was dead. When I woke up and realized I'd had a nightmare I was relieved but still sobbing. It was the worst dream I have ever had.

In the discussion above on nightmares of terror and of rage, a postulate was proposed that suggested the existence of laws in the organization of personality structure. One such law concerned the appearance of a polarity with respect to nightmares and their emotion-personality correlates. Here too it is proposed that a polarity exists between the nightmares of pleasure-sexuality and those of grief. Further, on a diagnostic level, the manic state of the pleasure dimension seems opposite to the depressive disposition of the sorrow, dread, and grief dimension. In this sense, although there is not an apparent polarity, the systematic organization of personality domains points to a polarity between the defense of reaction formation of the pleasure dimension and the defense of compensation of the depressive dimension. In terms of descriptive content, orgastic or wet dreams are opposite to those of sobbing.

## THE REVULSION NIGHTMARE AND ITS EMOTION-PERSONALITY CORRELATES

In the revulsion nightmare, the dreamer awakens because of some drama that is so utterly revolting that the dreamer is virtually shaken out of the dream and awakens. This kind of nightmare is generally produced by the critical paranoid diagnostic type. The dreamer awakens feeling disgusted, revolted, and in addition, sometimes frightened and disoriented. Contents of such nightmares include watching while one's arm falls off, seeing one's penis split apart, and viewing other similar fragmentation of body parts. Such nightmares also generate nausea in the dreamer. These nightmares can be understood in terms of the overwhelming criticality of the paranoid dispositional type. Persons with the paranoid disposition generally utilize projection as their central defensive posture, and they constantly and critically aim at targets external to the self. Projection is a necessary defense in this diagnostic type because theoretically such persons experience a complete lack of inner solidity; that is, they really feel most critical towards the self, but such an attitude must be deflected and kept out of consciousness at all costs. Projection is the defense that enables such a person to be oblivious to ongoing feelings of inferiority by considering everyone else as inferior—hence the presence of a constant stream of criticism toward others. When the projection defense becomes incapacitated, the critical paranoid type who is always rejecting the ostensible imperfections of the world can no longer limit criticism to objects exclusively external to the self. In the absence of the projection defense, then, intense self-criticism occurs in the extreme form of lack of solidity or body fragmentation images. At such a point any dream produced by a person of this paranoid dispositional type or any person experiencing such critical feelings will likely be transformed into a nightmare because in the absence of the projection defense the person will experience a profound sense of personal imperfection.

This type of paranoid character defense as it is used in everyday life drives the person to experience a buyer's regret. This means that such a person finds it very difficult to accept or, so to speak, to buy anything without some qualifying intervention. The act of buying or affiliating would mean that something has been accepted. Should this acceptance occur, then the person is likely to generate a subsequent experience of regret. The regret is an attempt to reject the item or object that has been accepted. Of course, on the emotional level, feelings of distaste, dissatisfaction, and disgust are the central affects that constitute the rejection feelings of such a dispositional type, and the projection defense is designed to deliver the person from these dreadful feelings by attaching the feelings to others.

A 38-year-old man who consistently complained of somatic ailments reported the following dream that characterizes the confluence of a revulsion nightmare with the various personality properties being considered.

> I was walking along the street and a truck was backing into a driveway. I stopped and waited for the truck to clear the path along the sidewalk so that I could keep on walking. Suddenly, I looked down and noticed some of my clothes were gone. I don't know what happened but I saw my arm fall off. It was split down the middle. There was no blood. Then I looked down and my penis was lying on a table next to me on the sidewalk. It was detached from my body and it also seemed to be split down the middle. I could see the cross-section of tissue. I became horrified. I got nauseous and woke up with a feeling of great disgust.

This man was a severe paranoid character in that he was drawn to perceive the minutest imperfection in anything he decided to evaluate. His taste was finely tuned, and he was highly educated and cultured. All his energies and needs, rather than being directed into avenues of enjoyment and appreciation, were directed toward rejecting and disparaging attitudes as well as pervasive criticism. It was only after persistent therapeutic work with this theme of criticality that his symptomatically elevated blood pressure returned to normal, somatic complaints subsided, and his massive projective defensive operations abated. It was then that he could talk about his inferiority feelings. It was during this period of self-examination—when projection was less necessary, and a reduction of interpersonal anxiety was evident—that he experienced the body-fragmentation nightmare.

## THE LAUGHTER NIGHTMARE AND ITS EMOTION-PERSONALITY CORRELATES

As described above, the central traits most characteristic of the paranoid dispositional state are its criticality and implied mistrust. This means that such a person finds it almost impossible to accept anything, must reject everything through the use of qualifiers and criticism, and therefore is not at all suggestible. On the other hand, the hysterical dispositional type is highly suggestible and can be convinced of almost anything (and parenthetically is easily hypnotized). This can mean that such a person is generally highly trusting. The trusting quality of the hysteric does not necessarily reflect a mature attitude, because it is based upon the use of massive denial defenses. The hysteric type does not want to see any imperfections in the external world at all. Rather, this kind of person feels most comfortable accepting virtually everything. Because of this need to accept and not to be critical, such a person screens out negative feelings toward others. It may be proposed that in this sense the hysteric has an underdeveloped sense of even a normal critical attitude and frequently suffers from poor judgment. The use of denial ensures that what is perceived is only good; therefore the external object is accepted by the subject. The emotion of acceptance and the defense of denial are the structural components of hysterical functioning that permit this dispositional type to engage in the idealization of the perceived object; for example, hysterical types fall in love frequently. The idealization of the perceived object and the deflection or denial of any critical feelings toward the object are jointly the cause for what might be described as a repetitive swoon.

The kind of nightmare produced by this kind of person—that is, one who needs to screen out criticism—is characterized as a dream in which criticism toward the object breaks through and surprises the dreamer. This can take the form of sarcasm and wit, as in the punchline to a joke. Individuals from time to time report awakening from the dream because they found something to be funny and they began laughing. The laughing occurs because in the absence of the denial defense, critical feelings toward external figures are likely to emerge in the form of such sarcasm and wit. The dreamer awakens as a result of the ego-alien nature of the dream. When denial operations are incapacitated, the dreamer may experience a distinct boundary between those experiences that are internal and those that are external. Therefore, the possibility seems to be created that the external world is somehow different and may perhaps be criticized. The dreamer awakens laughing, but also feels perplexed. The laughter reveals tension in a hysterical fashion, and the laughing is a variant of hysterical laughter. The laughter usually reflects an acknowledgment of criticism toward others. When the denial operations were functioning adequately such criticism could not be expressed.

A 35-year-old man diagnosed as a hysteric personality usually experienced problems in his relationships with women. He was consistently unable to notice any negative qualities in women. He felt comfortable with men, yet depended on the women in his life for support, for evidence of self-importance, and for self-esteem. He was a happy-go-lucky type who was also socially immature. He was unemployed for a while and would not acknowledge the seriousness of his situation. After a therapy session in which he celebrated his one-year unemployment anniversary he reported the following dream.

I told someone a joke in the dream. I didn't know who it was, but the punchline was so funny that I broke up with laughter. It really was hysterically funny. It woke me up laughing. I can't remember what the joke was but it had to do with poking fun at someone.

In the systematic organization of nightmares and emotion-personality correlates, the revulsion nightmare in the form of body fragmentation—an expression of self-contempt or criticism toward the self—is the polar opposite of the laughing nightmare—

an apparent expression of the simple awareness of a critical attitude toward others. On the emotional level, disgust or rejection is opposite to the emotion of acceptance. And on the diagnostic level the paranoid and hysteric are polar dispositions especially with regard to their main characteristic features; that is, with respect to criticality in the paranoid, where nothing is ever accepted without qualification and almost everything is rejected, and with respect to the characteristic of suggestibility in the hysteric, where almost everything is accepted in an unqualified manner and almost nothing is ever rejected outright. On the defense level, although the polarity is not as descriptively apparent, the system reveals that projection is quite disparate and even opposite to denial.

## THE NIGHTMARE OF LOSS OF CONTROL AND ITS EMOTION-PERSONALITY CORRELATES

Loss-of-control dreams such as falling dreams or even bedwetting dreams are usually produced by overcontrolled individuals. When control defenses such as intellectualization, sublimation, undoing, and rationalization become impaired or otherwise minimized, then the nightmare of loss of control can occur. This defense cluster reflects the central dynamic operation of the obsessive dispositional type. The obsessive type is one who needs to control or map the environment. The emotions of expectation and anticipation are primary emotions that underlie the controlling attitude of this type. Vigilance, preparedness, and set or readiness are other intensities along this particular emotion dimension, and are other examples of the inherent control needs of the obsessive as revealed through corresponding emotions. Of the aggregate of defenses designed to manage this need for control, intellectualization is probably a good representative defense to reflect this entire defense cluster. On the emotional level, expectation is a middle-intensity emotion that can also represent the dimension. The entire defense syndrome acts to screen and sort all impulses in this obsessive type and therefore ensures a condition of secure controls. It is only when such control defenses are not exercised that nightmares of loss of control emerge. Typical contents of such nightmares include falling from a mountain precipice or from a high building. When reported by children, such dreams take the form of bedwetting dreams in which the child will describe a letting-go of control then followed by the bedwetting. In the bedwetting dream, rationalization is utilized to create a circumstance in which the child dreams of already being in the bathroom so that to urinate makes sense; that is, in the bathroom when one is about to urinate, permission to do so is assumed. However, the child then awakens in the process of urinating and, by default, in a wet bed. The child is always surprised when awakened by the bedwetting not to to be actually in a bathroom.

There is a common misconception regarding falling dreams in which it is believed that falling from a building or other high place and finally hitting the ground will actually prove fatal to the dreamer. This conception is theoretically and empirically entirely unfounded. Should the dreamer dream of hitting the ground but not awaken, then the dream cannot be considered a nightmare. Remaining asleep would imply that the controlling defenses are not impaired and that the phenomenon of falling in the dream has meaning other than loss of control.

A cogent dream that became a nightmare of falling was reported by a 36-year-old woman who was especially controlled and obsessional.

> I was high up on a cliff and I was dangerously close to the edge. Without realizing, I lost my footing, and I went over—falling, falling. I woke up.

This same woman reported that when she was a child she would frequently dream she was in the bathroom about to urinate. She would urinate only to awaken and realize that she had wet her bed. She was a bedwetter throughout her childhood, and each bedwetting incident always would be preceded by the rationale offered by the dream, thereby allowing her to urinate in bed.

## THE NIGHTMARE OF PARALYSIS OR OVERCONTROL AND ITS EMOTION-PERSONALITY CORRELATES

The nightmare of overcontrol usually occurs as the extreme of overcontrol, paralysis or some other form involving the inability to physically move. The dreamer awakens startled and deeply troubled by an excruciatingly experienced paralysis. This is the typical nightmare of the psychopathic dyscontrolled personality type. Contents of such nightmares include being buried alive, drowning, and being pursued by a dangerous and menacing figure. In each case the dreamer is unable to move. The psychopathic dispositional type on the contrary needs to feel especially free of physical restrictions. The main characterological requirement of such a condition in the psychopathic dispositional type is for the person to create endless external stimulations presumably in order to counteract a deadened internalized sense. In the absence of the main defense of regression used by this type is a feeling that external stimulation is absent, motor potential is inhibited, and consequently the feeling of paralysis seems to be all that remains. It is the deadened experience that is reflected in the condition of paralysis that emerges in the nightmare.

When the main defense of regression, designed to ensure a condition of movement and stimulation, functions well, the dreamer can have pleasant dreams. When this defense is impaired, however, then the dreamer will experience the paralysis nightmare. It is the defense of regression that is the central and pivotal defense of this type, because this defense, as it functions especially in children, ensures a condition of movement. This kind of person needs to maintain a control-free state amounting to an impulsive condition that permits the motoric expression of needs. The defense of regression enables the need for the constant expression of impulse to be satisfied, thereby also permitting a continual retreat to more immature patterns of behavior and gratification. It should be pointed out that the use of the term "psychopathic personality" refers to a personality dispositional style. It does not mean "sociopathic" as in delinquency. Rather, like the other personality dispositions listed, it contains solely psychological meaning involving a dyscontrol syndrome of motor behavior and regression. However, under extreme conditions it can become pathological in the same way that extreme conditions can cause deleterious effects in any dispositional type.

The emotion of surprise or the need for endless novelty characterizes the central emotional underpinning of the psychopathic dispositional type. Dreamers usually awaken from the paralysis nightmare in a panicked and startled state, and this startle reaction is simply another intensity level of the surprise emotion dimension.

A 25-year-old woman was referred to treatment because of a severe acting-out problem. She was usually in trouble with her family and friends and she relied heavily on drugs. She was always on the move and could never fully concentrate. She frequently would complain that things were boring—apparently an oblique reference to her need to be constantly confronted with stimulating events. She did not particularly like the idea that a therapy session was a standard and specified period of time. These observations of hers seemed to indicate that she was always worried about her position with respect to potential control by rules and regulations. During the second session she reported the following fragment of a nightmare.

> I was in a grave and I was being buried alive. I couldn't move. I was paralyzed. I tried to scream and woke up. I was amazed in the dream that I couldn't move, and the moment I felt that strong feeling of amazement that I couldn't move, I shook myself out of sleep.

In another dream she reported essentially the same nightmare theme except that the dream was one in which she was drowning and was unable to breathe. She again was strongly panicked and suddenly startled by this turn of events in the dream—that is, never expected to be in such a predicament—and again tried to scream and awakened. Thus, in the absence of the regression defense, which ensures an impulsive motor condition, the nightmare for this dispositional type consists of themes in which the dreamer is profoundly overcontrolled.

In terms of the internal consistency of this emerging theoretical model, on all levels of the personality system, a pattern of polarity and similarity is apparent. On the diagnostic level, the obsessive and psychopathic type are polar dispositional states. Emotionally, the obsessive pattern revolves around expectation while the psychopathic type reveals a central emotional position of surprise—startlement or amazement. Thus, the polar emotions of the obsessive and the psychopathic types are revealed to be expectation and surprise, respectively. On the defense level, the control defense of intellectualization seems to function for the obsessive in a manner similar to the way in which the defense of regression functions for the psychopathic type, and from the theoretical consistency of the system the defenses of intellectualization and regression are considered to be polar opposites. With respect to nightmares, then, the overcontrol or paralysis nightmare of the psychopath is opposite to the loss-of-control nightmare of the obsessive.

## The Internal Consistency of the Model

Figure 16.1 shows the internal consistency of the organization of basic nightmare themes, emotions, defenses, and diagnostic dispositions. In this figure, those states opposite to one another are considered most dissimilar, while neighboring states are most similar. For example, on the dream level of figure 16.1, a loss-of-control dream, a sexual dream, and a laughter dream represent a cluster on the circle that seem related one to the other and quite opposite to the cluster of paralysis dreams, crying dreams, and fragmentation dreams. On the diagnostic level, the dispositions of manic and hysteric are quite similar but also quite opposite to the dispositions of depressed and paranoid. This similarity structure also suggests that the personality system has not evolved in a random fashion. Rather, it may have developed to provide the best coping system for the individual. In this sense the proposition that aspects of personality are linked in a systematic fashion is perfectly reasonable. In the same sense, the nightmare becomes a rare window in which can be viewed the infra-formation of personality. This infra-formation of personality is composed at its core of the intrapsychic forces that constitute the texture and quality of each basic nightmare theme. Fundamentally, therefore, a new postulate regarding the nightmare and its intrapsychic nature can be proposed.

> Postulate 14. Intrapsychic forces are essences of basic emotions and become revealed in the nightmare when, in the absence of defense, these basic emotions are expressed at their highest intensities.

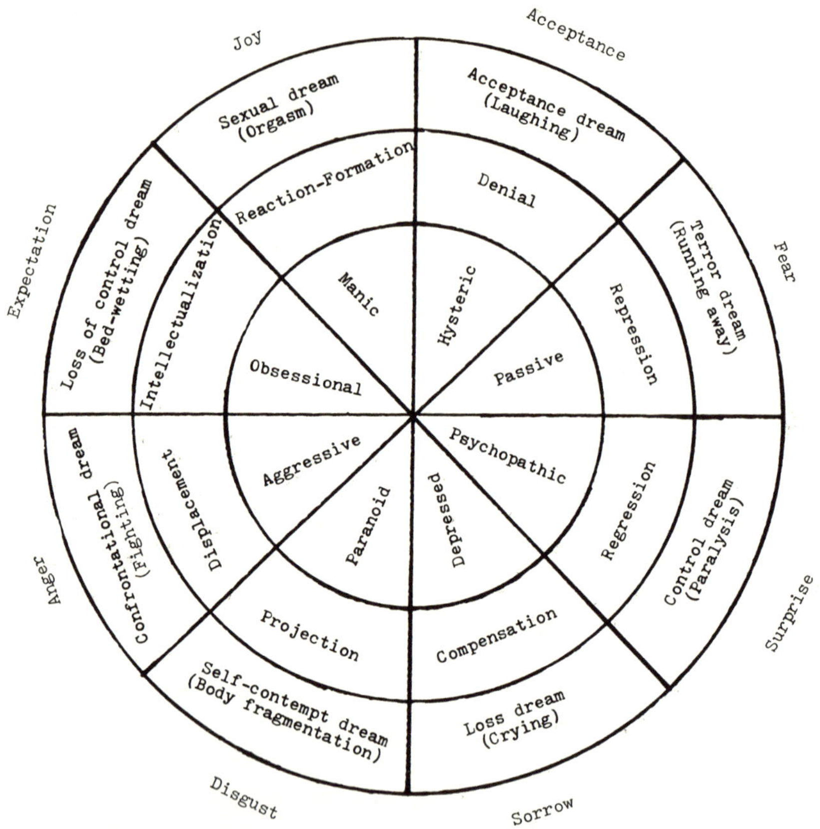


FIGURE 16.1 A similarity structure of diagnostic dispositions and nightmare themes. Intervening defenses are indicated. *Source:* Adapted from Kellerman (1979).

## Summary

In this chapter, the entire system of basic nightmare categories was made explicit and illustrated by vignettes of actual nightmares or fragments of nightmares. These vignettes illustrated the various connections of nightmares and corresponding personality variables. In the following chapter the basic nightmare themes will be analyzed with reference to their defense mechanisms and, in a deeper sense, the intrapsychic essence of each defense. The issue that will be addressed concerns the intrapsychic purpose of each basic defense and how this purpose relates to other personality variables and to the nightmare.

## References


Bychowski, G. 1968. *Evil in Man: The Anatomy of Hate and Violence.* New York: Grune and Stratton.

Kaufman, C. 1960. Some ethological studies of social relationships and conflict situations. *Journal of the American Psychoanalytic Association* 8(4):671–85.

Kellerman, H. 1977. Hate. In B. B. Wolman, ed., *International Encyclopedia of Neurology, Psychiatry, Psychoanalysis, and Psychology.* New York: Van Nostrand Reinhold.

Kellerman, H. 1979. *Group Psychotherapy and Personality: Intersecting Structures.* New York: Grune and Stratton.

Kellerman, H. 1980. A structural model of emotion and personality: Psychoanalytic and sociobiological implications. In R. Plutchik and H. Kellerman, eds., *Emotion: Theory, Research, and Experience* Vol. 1, *Theories of Emotion.* New York: Academic Press.

Kellerman, H. 1983. An epigenetic theory of emotions in early development. In R. Plutchik and H. Kellerman, eds., *Emotion: Theory, Research, and Experience.* Vol. 2, *Emotions in Early Development.* New York: Academic Press.

Kellerman, H., R. Buirski, and R. Plutchik. 1974. Group behavior in a baboon troop: Implications for human group process. In L. R. Wolberg and M. L. Aronson, eds., *Group Therapy 1974.* New York: Stratton Intercontinental Medical Book.

Lasswell, H. D. 1952. The psychology of Hitlerism as a response of the lower middle class to continuing insecurity. In G. Swanson, T. M. Newcomb, and E. L. Hartley, eds., *Readings in Social Psychology.* New York: Holt.

Lorenz, K. 1966. *On Aggression.* New York: Harcourt, Brace.

Plutchik, R. 1962. *The Emotions: Facts, Theories, and a New Model.* New York: Random House.

Plutchik, R. 1980. *Emotion: A Psychoevolutionary Synthesis.* New York: Harper and Row.

# 17.

# Nightmares and the Structure of Personality

## III. The Intrapsychic Function of Defense Mechanisms

HENRY KELLERMAN

IN THE PREVIOUS two chapters the various aspects of the personality structure were related to one another with respect to their structural correspondence, and the organization of nightmares revealed an infra-formation of the personality. In this chapter, the intrapsychic function of each defense mechanism will be outlined. It will be proposed that the intrapsychic management function of each defense operation permits a dynamic interplay of forces in the entire emotion-personality system. These dynamic relationships are revealed through the analysis of dreams and nightmares. The interplay of the intrapsychic forces of the personality will then be related to psychosexual developmental concepts.

### Nightmare Themes and the Intrapsychic Purpose of Corresponding Defense Mechanisms

When the nightmare occurs, the central underlying intrapsychic position of the dream is revealed; that is, under conditions where defense is not effectively regulating emotion, emotion will be expressed in its undefended and most intense form, and therefore the nature of the emotion can be readily inferred. Is the emotion an id emotion or a superego one, or is it a so-called ego emotion? This question implies that each basic nightmare also can be viewed as containing an intrapsychic nature. Is the nightmare reflecting id strivings or superego strivings?

In the following discussion the intrapsychic designation of each type of nightmare will be proposed. In addition, the defenses will be shown to play a pivotal role in the connection between emotions and their intrapsychic nature, as well as in dreams and the appearance of nightmares.

## NIGHTMARES OF TERROR AND THE INTRAPSYCHIC PURPOSE OF REPRESSION

The threatening terror dream of the passive dispositional type is quite inhibiting and punitive and reflects the superego nature of the emotion of fear. This sort of nightmare occurs when the repression defense is inadequate, so that the basic impulse of escape from threatening stimuli fails. The nightmare of terror in which fear, punishment, and the general feeling of dread prevail corresponds to a superego reference in which a sense that the dreamer is weak or bad exists. Since the dreamer is found in the role of the bad or unfortunate object, an implicit rationale exists for the presence of punishment themes. The emotion of fear is therefore presumed to contain superego elements and suggests a superego condition as the fundamental nature of the passive type. Terror nightmares therefore can be conceived as superego dreams. In addition, the defense of repression may now be understood as serving to regulate the superego impulses inherent in the emotion of fear.

In summary, it is proposed that the passive personality type, in which the basic emotion of fear is managed by the defense of repression, generates terror nightmares and is revealed to be a superego dispositional type; that is, a diagnostic type whose inherent superego nature is managed by the *impulse-releasing defense* of repression. Such a proposition also points out that superego aims can be achieved through the use of defenses that release impulse.

## NIGHTMARES OF RAGE AND THE INTRAPSYCHIC PURPOSE OF DISPLACEMENT

The nightmare of rage, in which there appears anger, execution of punishment, and a general feeling of permission to assault, is assumed to be based on an id formation in which there is a sense that the dreamer has been somehow vindicated. The nightmare occurs when the defense of displacement becomes inadequate in its task to block direct expression of anger or create safe overflow channels for the expression of this anger. Thus, in the absence of the blocking defense of displacement, anger is expressed in its fullest and most direct manner. The rage or assaultive nightmare reveals the id nature of the aggressive dispositional type. Instead of expecting punishment in the superego sense, as in the case of the passive type, this aggressive type becomes the attacker, is free of superego prohibitions, and because of the absence of the displacement defense is able to express anger in the form of rage, assault, or extreme assertion of an unbridled nature.

It is proposed, therefore, that the aggressive personality, whose basic emotion of anger is managed by the defense of displacement, produces a nightmare of rage or attack and is revealed to be an id dispositional type; that is, a diagnostic type whose inherent id nature is managed by the *impulse-blocking defense* of displacement.

Again, in terms of the intrinsic consistency of the model, as the passive is opposite to the aggressive type, fear opposite to anger, repression and displacement opposites in a functional sense, so too are superego and id proclivities opposite. Finally, the impulse-releasing defense of repression of the passive type is opposite to the impulse-blocking defense of displacement of the aggressive type.

In figure 17.1 is presented a circumplex organization of the intrapsychic relation to the entire personality system. The polarity of the passive versus the aggressive types across all aspects of personality may be seen in this figure. The continuing discussion of each of the basic nightmare categories and their respective intrapsychic nature also may be followed on this figure. These data and parts of the ensuing discussion are also found in Kellerman (1979, 1980, 1981, 1983).

## NIGHTMARES OF GRIEF AND THE INTRAPSYCHIC PURPOSE OF COMPENSATION

The nightmare of grief or crying, in which sorrow and general feelings of loss are experienced, corresponds to a superego formation in which there exists a sense that the dreamer has lost a last chance. In the absence of the compensatory defense, loss seems irrevocable. What this suggests is that in the personality of the depressive dispositional type there exist superego urges that

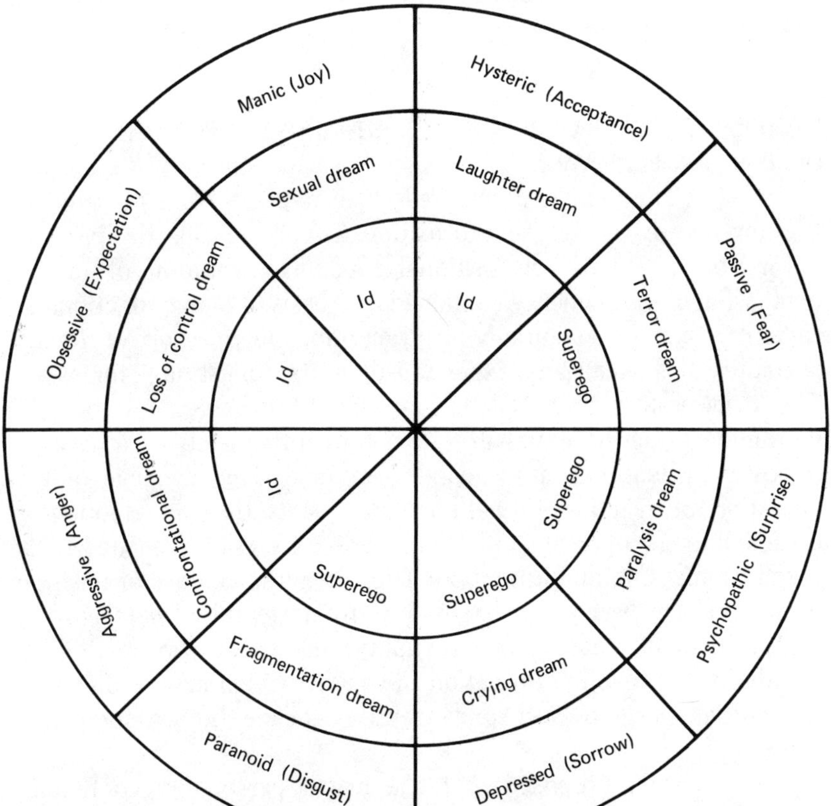


FIGURE 17.1 The intrapsychic structure of each of the eight basic emotion-personality categories. Typical nightmare themes are indicated. *Source:* Kellerman (1979).

generate feelings of inadequacy and a sense of extreme dependence on external figures for support and nurturance. The compensation defense is designed, therefore, as an impulse-releasing mechanism that increases self-esteem and manages feelings of loss by setting into motion a process of fantasies and behavior that are geared to regaining the lost object or reconstituting one's esteem level.

It is proposed that the depressed personality containing the primary emotion of sorrow and managed by the defense of compensation generates a nightmare of grief or crying and is revealed to be a superego dispositional type; that is, a diagnostic type whose inherent nature is managed by the *impulse-releasing defense* of compensation.

## NIGHTMARES OF PLEASURE AND THE INTRAPSYCHIC PURPOSE OF REACTION FORMATION

The sexual dream reflecting a great pleasure urge in the absence of the reaction-formation defense reveals the basic id nature of the manic dispositional type. The emotion of joy or expression of great energy contained as a basis of manic functioning, therefore, may be essentially an id emotion. In this sort of dream, sexuality or pleasure is experienced in its fullest id expression. The reaction-formation defense is used to manage and regulate inordinate pleasure-sexual urges by transforming such urges into opposite inclinations or avoidance reactions. This dynamic of the operation of reaction formation also reveals that an emotion is turned into its opposite only when the conversion was originally based on pleasure and attraction. Therefore, the defense of reaction formation may best be understood as fundamentally related to the management of pleasure and sexuality and the emotion of joy. In the absence of reaction formation the manic person may be directing substantial energy toward sexual release—hence the orgastic nightmare.

It is proposed that the manic personality containing the primary emotion of sorrow and managed by the defense of reaction formation generates a nightmare of sexuality, and is revealed to be an id dispositional type; that is, a diagnostic type whose inherent nature is managed by the *impulse-blocking defense* of reaction formation.

In terms of the internal consistency of the model, and as portrayed in figure 17.1, the depressed is opposite the manic disposition, sorrow is opposite joy, compensation and reaction formation serve opposite functional purposes, and so too is the superego nature inherent in the depressed type opposite to the id nature inherent in the manic type. Finally, the impulse-releasing defense of compensation of the depressed type is opposite to the impulse-blocking defense of reaction formation of the manic type.

## NIGHTMARES OF REVULSION AND THE INTRAPSYCHIC PURPOSE OF PROJECTION

The body-fragmentation or revulsion nightmare is associated with the critical paranoid diagnostic type. This sort of nightmare is based upon self-punitive feelings characteristic of persons who, to whatever extent, have lost the use of the projection defense which is designed to criticize the external world. This means that in the absence of the projective defense—a defense that releases impulse in order to serve critical ends—such persons are confronted with a profound sense of inferiority and strong critical feelings toward the self. Thus, it seems that in the basic nature of the paranoid dispositional type, a superego formation is indicated. This superego presence, in the absence of the projection defense, implies that the dreamer experiences a lack of solidity and unworthiness and feels subject to the punitive effect of a basic superego nature.

In summary, it is proposed that the paranoid personality, containing the central emotion of disgust or rejection and managed by the defense of projection, produces a nightmare of revulsion—usually in the form of body-fragmentation themes—and is revealed to be a superego dispositional type; that is, a diagnostic type whose inherent nature is managed by the *impulse-releasing defense* of projection.

## NIGHTMARES OF LAUGHTER AND THE INTRAPSYCHIC PURPOSE OF DENIAL

The laughter dream of the hysteric type is a yielding-to-impulse dream. The hysteric type is one who denies any critical feelings toward objects external to self. When the defense of denial is not properly functioning, impulse in the form of criticism toward the environment will be released. Thus, the use of denial is considered to be an impulse-blocking device preventing the hysteric type from seeing or expressing any negative feelings to external figures. In the absence of denial a release of impulse toward the environment reveals the id nature of the hysteric. When such denial mechanisms are incapacitated, the dreamer may then observe a distinct boundary between experiences that are internal and those that are external. The external world under such boundary conditions may indeed be criticized. When denial defenses operate smoothly, the absence of a critical attitude fuels and fortifies traits such as suggestibility and gullibility. The emotion of acceptance is then entirely reinforced and chiefly characterizes the emotional position of the hysteric. Thus, denial is the essential defense in all idealization, especially because the idealized object is accepted entirely and not only in part. Such types are surprised to experience any critical feelings at all. The laughter in the dream reflects this surprise, and the awakening moment, therefore, also reveals the ego-alien nature of the nightmare and paranthetically also seems to suggest that all nightmares represent ego-alien expressions of the personality.

It is proposed that the hysteric personality containing the primary emotion of acceptance and managed by the defense of denial generates a nightmare of laughter or other novel sensory experiences and is revealed to be an id dispositional type; that is, a diagnostic type whose inherent nature is managed by the *impulse-blocking defense* of denial.

Inspection of figure 17.1 shows the opposition of all levels of personality structure under consideration. On the diagnostic and emotional levels the criticality of the paranoid type is opposite the acceptance of the hysteric type. Projection and denial serve opposite purposes, and the superego nature of the paranoid type is opposite to the id nature of the hysteric. Finally, the impulse-releasing purpose of the projective defense of the paranoid is opposite to the impulse-blocking purpose of the denial defense of the hysteric.

## NIGHTMARES OF PARALYSIS AND THE INTRAPSYCHIC PURPOSE OF REGRESSION

The nightmare of overcontrol or paralysis becomes possible when the defense of regression is incapacitated. Instead of impulses being released, which is generally the case when regression is effectively working, impulses become blocked when regression is impaired. The dreamer, experiencing a sense that dire consequences exist, feels vulnerable. Instead of freedom of movement, which is usually necessary in persons of this type, in the absence of the regression defense, a deadened and dreaded immobility is experienced. It should be pointed out that the psychopathic type tries to create external stimulation in order to counteract a deadened internalized sense, and such attempts are generally made possible by the use of the regression defense. The immobile or stopped condition of paralysis generates a sense of vulnerability, implying the full punitive measure of the superego.

The nightmare of overcontrol is considered to be a reflection of the psychopathic diagnostic disposition and contains the emotion of surprise as the central wellspring of this entire personality syndrome. The emotion of surprise reflects an endless dyscontrolled condition and permits a continual reactivity to exist on the part of the subject. The regression aids in maintaining this motoric action orientation.

It is proposed that the psychopathic dyscontrolled personality, containing the central emotion of surprise and managed by the regression defense, produces a nightmare of panic-paralysis, and is revealed to be a superego dispositional type; that is, a diagnostic type whose inherent superego nature is managed by the impulse-releasing defense of regression.

## NIGHTMARES OF LOSS OF CONTROL AND THE INTRAPSYCHIC PURPOSE OF INTELLECTUALIZATION

The loss-of-control dreams of the obsessional type, in which falling or bedwetting are thematic examples, imply that the defense of intellectualization is designed to exert control over what appears to be emotion with an id nature. The entire obsessive defense syndrome is apparently designed to control impulses and to guard against loss of control. These are blocking defenses. This nightmare of loss of control suggests that inherent in the basic nature of the obsessive type is an id force. In the absence of controlling defenses, underlying id impulses become fully expressed. It even may be suggested that because id impulses inherent in the obsessive type are so intense, several symptoms become characteristic of this dispositional tendency. These include rituals, obsessions, compulsions, and ruminations. The control defenses of intellectualization, rationalization, undoing, and sublimation are used to manage any potential breakthrough of impulse. Intellectualization seems to best represent this aggregate of defenses. This is the control mechanism that permits all impulses to be screened and sorted. In order for the obsessive type to map and therefore attempt to control the environment, the central emotions of anticipation or expectation underlie all controlling attitudes. Expectation, mapping, controlling, and the use of intellectualization and the other obsessive defenses imply the need to maintain and ensure nonmotor transformation of impulses and thus to prevent motor or impulsive acting-out. In the nightmare, the loss of control—either falling or bedwetting or other similar contents—corresponds to an id reference in which, however momentary, an undefended motor sense of release takes place.

It is proposed, therefore, that the obsessive personality, expressing the central emotion of expectation and managed by the defense of intellectualization, produces a loss-of-control dream and is thereby revealed to be an id dispositional type; that is, to be a diagnostic type whose inherent id nature is managed by the *impulse-blocking defense* of intellectualization.

Of these basic dimensions of the personality—the psychopathic and obsessive—the system of polarity can again be seen with respect to all the aspects of personality that have been described. The motor needs of the psychopathic type are opposite to the control needs of the obsessive. On the emotion level, the orientation-mapping needs inherent in the emotions of anticipation and expectation of the obsessive are opposite to the disorientation-surprise need and emotion of the psychopathic type. The defense of regression serves the purpose of releasing impulse in the psychopathic dyscontrolled type while the defense of intellectualization serves the purpose of blocking impulse in the obsessive-controlled type. Finally, the obsessive is considered an id type and the psychopathic a superego type. Of course, on the level of nightmares, in the absence of necessary defense, the obsessive generates a dream of loss of control while the psychopathic type produces a nightmare of overcontrol. The entire similarity structure can be traced in figure 17.1, and the intrapsychic purpose of each basic defense as it relates to the entire personality system is presented in table 17.1. This table will show how defense mechanisms regulate the intrapsychic force of each diagnostic disposition. Also, in conjunction with figure 17.1, the theoretical structure shows the opposition of all levels of personality. This structure implies that the basic personality system is consistently paralleled by the id-superego opposition at all levels.

TABLE 17.1. The Intrapsychic Nature of Diagnostic States: The Relation of Defenses to Nightmares

| *Diagnostic disposition* | *Defense* | *Purpose of defense* | *Nightmare theme based upon impaired defense* | *Intrapsychic force revealed by nightmare* |
|---|---|---|---|---|
| Manic | Reaction-formation | To block impulse | Sexual-orgastic-pleasure | Id |
| Depressed | Compensation | To release impulse | Grief-sobbing | Superego |
| Obsessive | Intellectual-ization | To block impulse | Loss of control, falling-bedwetting | Id |
| Psycho-pathic | Regression | To release impulse | Paralysis, drowning, being buried alive | Superego |
| Aggressive | Displace-ment | To block impulse | Attack-stabbing-hitting | Id |
| Passive | Repression | To release impulse | Terror-running-escaping | Superego |
| Hysteric | Denial | To block impulse | Laughing–sarcastic wit | Id |
| Paranoid | Projection | To release impulse | Fragmentation–body parts falling off | Superego |

## The Intrapsychic System and the Ego

It now may be suggested that joy, acceptance, anger, and expectation are id emotions on the basis of their most intense expression in the absence of typical defenses. Similarly, sorrow, disgust, fear, and surprise may be superego emotions, since, in the absence of defense, their intense expression in nightmares reveals superego meaning. It also may be suggested on the same basis that manic, hysteric, aggressive, and obsessive diagnoses reflect id states, while depressed, paranoid, passive, and psychopathic diagnoses reflect superego states.

The system of personality presented here emerges as a parsimonious model especially from the point of view of understanding nightmares and how this understanding brings together in a coherent manner various and seemingly disparate domains of personality. The discovery that fundamental states reflect either an id or a superego nature also points to the possible formulation of a new and startling postulate regarding the relation of the defense system to the intrapsychic element of ego. In the conventional diagnostic and psychoanalytic sense, defenses are immutably derived from and associated with ego development. In the system presented here, this conventional psychoanalytic position regarding defenses and ego is unequivocally shifted. Rather, a new proposition holds that defenses are derived from emotion directly, and do not depend on ego development for their operation.

The analysis of defenses shows their intrapsychic regulating purpose and further reveals an intrinsic connection between emotion and defenses. Accordingly, as suggested elsewhere (Kellerman 1979), the ego forms as a function of development, and defenses simply may become more effective regulators of id and superego emotions as a result of this developmental experience. Yet, there may be justification for the theoretical position that shows a natural connection between ego and defenses. Defenses of the ego may be those that are utilized in the personality to maintain character formations and trait structure. These are ego-defenses of identification, introjection, internalization, and perhaps splitting and isolation.

In figure 17.1 it can be seen that the personality structure becomes an infra-formation composed of id versus superego. In this respect, defenses are viewed fundamentally as corresponding to emotions and not to ego. Even in infants and primates, and among other even less-developed species, in the absence of significant ego development, a wide range of emotions are expressed (Lorenz 1966; Scott 1958). The expression of emotion does not require the presence of ego, and the following postulates are based upon this finding.

Postulate 15. All basic defenses are emotion-defenses and not ego-defenses, and do not depend on ego development for their appearance.

Postulate 16. The purpose of defenses is to act as intrapsychic regulating devices—regulating id and superego strivings—designed either to block or to release impulse in the service of socialization aims.

Postulate 17. All nightmares represent emotional breakthroughs of the characterological defense structure and are therefore ego-alien expressions of the personality reflecting a moment of character reformation. As such, nightmares reveal the true undefended intrapsychic nature—either id or superego—of the personality.

The present theory proposes that the connections and links of the entire personality system are revealed through the nightmare. The nightmare is a phenomenon, therefore, that provides a powerful template which in a sense decodes the complex interconnections of personality. From this unraveling of the code of the infrastructural organization of personality the present theory views the entire personality system as existing in the substrate of emotion and the expression of this system as tied to object relations formation and to the vicissitudes of psychosexual development. The defense structure becomes salient during suitable developmental periods, and these periods also correspond to ego development. The differentiation process in the personality occurs through the resolution of conflict during these developing psychosexual stages. This differentiation process refers essentially to ego development.

However, it is proposed that id and superego predispositional forces are encoded within the basic-emotion structure.

In the following section, the connection of the personality system presented here and proposed to be etched within the emotion structure as an epigenetic phenomenon is discussed also with reference to the adaptational developmental process of the psychosexual stages.

## Personality and Psychosexual Stages

In the entire foregoing discussion, I have inexorably been led to the conclusion—by the strength of the theoretical data and by the power of the personality matrix with respect to its parsimony—that the etchings and dispositions within emotion are epigenetic phenomena. It is a system or program held in abeyance and awaiting its encounter with experience either to enhance the given program in bold relief or to alter the program. It seems that the program may be altered on the basis of a preponderance of one particular experience discrepant with the given program over another experience that might be in greater congruence with the system. In terms of intrapsychic formulations, a useful analogy would be: phylogeny is to id and superego as ontogeny is to ego. In this respect, psychosexual developmental periods are adaptational stages during which the internal conflict arena of id with superego intersects and influences the emerging ego. The operational process of this interaction of the epigenetic id-superego influence with that of ego adaptation continually requires the instrumentality of the defenses.

What has emerged from the findings discussed earlier on defense mechanisms is that they have two distinct functions: some have developed to permit impulse expression and some have developed to block it. This idea of defenses as either blocking or releasing mechanisms shows that defenses are performing an intrapsychic function relating to each basic diagnostic state; that is, defenses designed to block impulse are performing an id-management function while those designed to release impulse are performing a superego-management function. The superego is one that serves withholding, punitive, and controlling functions, while the id continually aims for release and expression. The job of the defenses, therefore, is to regulate these intrapsychic forces: to moderate both id and superego aims.

It should again be noted that these id and superego aims express the basic nature of the primary emotions and that therefore, with respect to psychosexual conflict, tasks of developmental stages become traversed or resolved on the basis of the extent to which the intrapsychic aims of each emotion are achieved; that is, whether the aims of id emotions and superego emotions are achieved. The ego emerges as one formed by the accumulation of both achieved and frustrated id-superego aims. This ego formation then, provides the bridge to the appearance of the identification mechanisms used in the development of personality-trait structure.

In the following section, the relationship of intrapsychic forces to psychosexual stages shall be proposed. Specifically, the question of intrapsychic aims during each psychosexual stage shall be hypothesized.

## Intrapsychic Aims of Psychosexual Stages

Conventional psychoanalytic thinking regards development of ego, id, and superego to be based upon object relations management within the confines of specific psychosexual stages. The theoretical construction proposed here suggests that object relations development within the context of psychosexual stages produces refinement of intrapsychic force but does not create intrapsychic force. Intrapsychic force in the form of id and superego formations is presumed to be present at birth. However, they become exercised and expressed, as it were, as a function of the working-through of object relations problems during salient psychosexual stages. This is what is meant by the refinement of intrapsychic forces as a function of development. Development of intrapsychic force as a function of the effects of psychosexual-stage conflicts and as an expression of diagnostic dispositional states is proposed in the following formulations.

## THE ORAL BIPOLAR DIAGNOSES: MANIC VERSUS DEPRESSED

Karl Abraham (1927) was among the early psychoanalytic pioneers to point out the relationship between the oral psychosexual stage and the manic-depressive diagnoses. The proposed intrapsychic aim of the manic type is to express id impulses inherent in underlying pleasure needs. The extent to which this aim becomes frustrated may determine how much superego becomes generated in the form of depressive, sorrowful feelings. The id aim, to express the basic nature of the manic type or to seek full gratification, cannot ever be fully met. Socialization demands make this id aim impossible to fulfill completely. The frustration of full gratification may create a condition in which superego elements emerge. Thus, the oral period may generate elements of id and superego on the basis of socializing demands. The relation of id and superego to diagnostic states was discussed on the intrapsychic analysis of nightmares and in the previous chapter.

## THE ANAL BIPOLAR DIAGNOSES: OBSESSIVE VERSUS PSYCHOPATHIC

It is proposed here that the intrapsychic aim of the obsessive dispositional type is to express underlying id impulse. The extent to which this aim becomes frustrated may determine how much superego emerges in the form of impulses that are withheld. When the control features of the obsessional type frustrate underlying urges for impulses to be expressed, what remains are stopping experiences or superego feelings of paralysis previously discussed on the intrapsychic nature of the nightmares of the psychopathic type. In a sense, the particular intrapsychic frustrations of the anal period generate obsessive-psychopathic conflict in the form of an id-superego compromise formation. These quantities of expression of id and superego are also based upon socializing demands.

## THE PHALLIC BIPOLAR DIAGNOSES: PASSIVE VERSUS AGGRESSIVE

The aim of the aggressive dispositional type is to express id impulse and release anger directly. This aim cannot be fulfilled because of socialization demands and, in psychoanalytic terms, because of castration fears. When id aims are frustrated during this phallic psychosexual period, it is proposed that superego force in the form of passive, fearful feelings will emerge. The relation of superego force to the passive diagnosis was also discussed previously on the intrapsychic analysis of nightmares.

## THE OEDIPAL BIPOLAR DIAGNOSES: HYSTERIC VERSUS PARANOID

The aim of the hysteric type is to express id impulses. Incorporation needs may even include the taking in of noxious stimuli. The extent to which such needs are blocked determines how much superego force inherent in opposite and rejecting paranoid features will substitute. This seems to indicate that if acceptance or incorporation fails to occur fully, what is left is superego force in the form of rejection inherent in the paranoid disposition.

Table 17.2 shows the relation between psychosexual conflict stages, diagnoses, and intrapsychic forces. In this table it may be seen that in any polar pair the two diagnostic types correspond to a single psychosexual stage but contain separate id or superego forces.

TABLE 17.2. Relation Between Psychosexual Stage, Diagnostic State, and Intrapsychic Force

| *Psychosexual Stage* | *Diagnosis* | *Intrapsychic Force* |
|---|---|---|
| Oral | Manic<br>Depressed | Id<br>Superego |
| Anal | Obsessive<br>Psychopathic | Id<br>Superego |
| Phallic | Aggressive<br>Passive | Id<br>Superego |
| Oedipal | Hysteric<br>Paranoid | Id<br>Superego |

In summary, it may be proposed that personality-trait structure and the refinement of ego/id and superego structure are based upon biological as well as developmental factors. Vicissitudes of psychosexual developmental experiences become superimposed on existing basic personality structure, in part, lending meaning to the psychosexual developmental experience. For example, it may be expected that id or superego emotions help make logical those events that evoke them during salient developmental periods. This process further contributes to the refinement of id and superego intrapsychic formation. In a sense, early and ongoing parental identifications and introjections, the basic nature of object relations, generate more differentiated elements of an existing program.

The present way of viewing the intrapsychic apparatus allows for the belief that infants experience the full basic-emotion system even with only minimal ego development, and, in addition, express a refinement of this system as a function of ego development. When the adaptational experience of each psychosexual period does indeed reinforce and enhance the given epigenetic emotion program, then the individual's motivational or cognitive style would emerge in sharper focus. In addition, this emotion program then also supplies the component emotions ultimately frozen into position as character traits. These traits are derived from the emotion program but are largely placed into position by object experiences during psychosexual developmental periods. The aims of id and superego emerge with respect to object experiences and then the intrapsychic expressions and object experiences reciprocally influence each other. In this sense, whatever precognitive qualities may be contained within the deep structure of basic emotions also become represented during id-superego expressions of psychosexual experiences. In terms of the epigenetic program presented here, it is proposed that cognitive qualities—or uncrystallized thought in the form of mood or intuition—are also infused in the structure of basic emotions.

In the discussion of the relation of intrapsychic aims and psychosexual development, and as an introduction to the presentation of the relation of cognitive styles to the epigenetic emotion program, two further postulates can be formulated.

Postulate 18. Id and superego are epigenetic encodings of emotion. In contrast, ego is adaptational. The ego develops out of the interaction of the epigenetic emotion program as it is affected by the compromise of intrapsychic id-superego aims during psychosexual periods.

Postulate 19. Cognitive styles correspond to the basic-emotion system, indicating that emotion is the wellspring of cognition.

In the following chapter the relation of emotion and personality to basic cognitive categories will be proposed. In addition, the nightmare will be defined as a state of the personality in which previously bound anxiety is unbound, further implying that some psychophysiological symptom has been altered. In order to better understand the alteration of psychosomatic or psychophysiological symptoms, the psychosomatic connection to the entire emotion-personality system also will be proposed.

## Summary

In this chapter the intrapsychic function of each defense mechanism was described, and the particular organization of dreams and nightmares revealed that the operation of such forces regulated the interaction of the entire emotion-personality system. These intrapsychic forces were then related to psychosexual development.

## References

Abraham, K. 1927. Psychoanalytical studies on character formation. In K. Abraham, *Selected Papers on Psychoanalysis.* London: Hogarth Press.

Kellerman, H. 1979. *Group Psychotherapy and Personality: Intersecting Structures.* New York: Grune and Stratton.

Kellerman, H. 1980. A structural model of emotion and personality: Psychoanalytic and sociobiological implications. In R. Plutchik and H. Kellerman, eds., *Emotion: Theory, Research, and Experience.* Vol. 1, *Theories of Emotion.* New York: Academic Press.

Kellerman, H. 1981. *Sleep Disorders: Insomnia and Narcolepsy.* New York: Brunner/Mazel.

Kellerman, H. 1983. An epigenetic theory of emotions in early development. In R. Plutchik and H. Kellerman, eds., *Emotion: Theory, Research, and Experience.* Vol. 2, *Emotions in Early Development.* New York: Academic Press.

Lorenz, K. 1966. *On Aggression.* New York: Harcourt, Brace.

Scott, J. P. 1958. *Animal Behavior.* Chicago: University of Chicago Press.

# 18.

# Nightmares and the Structure of Personality
## IV. Cognitive and Psychosomatic Structures

HENRY KELLERMAN

IN THIS FINAL of four chapters on the nightmare and personality structure the cognitive dispositional style associated with the emotion program is proposed. In addition, an analysis of the nature of anxiety, character-trait formation, and psychosomatic symptomatology as these phenomena relate to the nightmare will conclude the analysis of the levels and aspects of personality as they form a coherent system. These theoretical connections are also discussed by Kellerman (1979, 1980, 1983) in a series of publications that set forth various aspects of the personality system.

### The Relation of Emotion and Cognitive Dimensions: An Epigenetic Structure

Basic cognitive categories are proposed that are derived from the epigenetic emotion program. These categories have been formulated with respect to how each cognitive concept relates to corresponding basic-emotion dimensions (including defenses and diagnostic dispositions). In the following listing of cognitive elements, these connections will be further suggested. In addition, in table 18.1 the entire proposed emotion substrate of the epigenetic program is portrayed with respect to the connection between basic emotions and traits, diagnostic dispositions, regulatory emotion-defenses, intrapsychic elements, and cognitive dimensions of each of these basic emotions along with a listing of each proposed psychosomatic organ system to be more explicitly described in the last section of this chapter.

## ACCEPTANCE: ATTENTION-DISTRACTION

The cognitive dimension representing the emotion of acceptance and reflecting the diagnostic as well as defensive elements associated with this emotion is proposed as an *attention-distraction* dimension. Together, the emotion of acceptance and the cognitive element of attention reflect interest and positive focus on the object.

On the cognitive level, attention or positive focus on the object is a derivative form in a sequence of events that lead to acceptance or absorption of the object. This kind of focus on the object can also be characterized in cognitive terms as assimilating certain positive information about the object and in interpersonal terms as loving the object. The defense used in the service of loving the object is denial. In the hysteric, denial is invoked to prevent or minimize any critical view of the object. In a corollary sense the extent or success of the operation of this defense may be understood in terms of the extent of the subject's *distractibility.* That is, denial acts to distract the subject from expressing a critical view. Correspondingly, the focus on the object—or *attention* on the object—in this context essentially means acceptance of the object. In the use of denial, then, only positive acceptance experiences occur, and potentially negative rejecting responses are avoided.

Hence, it is proposed that the cognitive dimension here labeled *attention-distraction* corresponds to the diagnostic disposition of hysteric and defense of denial, and each of these are derivative aspects of the basic emotion of acceptance. The relation between the emotion of acceptance and the cognitive dimension of attention-distraction generally concerns the issue between subject and object of *taking-in.*

## DISGUST: CERTAINTY-UNCERTAINTY

It is further proposed that the cognitive dimension representing the emotion of disgust and reflecting the diagnostic as well as defensive elements of this emotion be designated as a *certainty-uncertainty* dimension. The cognitive quest for certainty is here defined as a need to reinforce distinctions between self and object. Together, the emotion of disgust and cognitive element of certainty reflect a negative focus on the object. The chief characteristic used to distinguish self from object is the critical stance toward the object that achieves the certainty that self and object are indeed different.

On the cognitive level, achieving certainty in the distinction between self and object (largely through the critical attitude toward the object) is a derivative aspect of a sequence of events that leads to rejection of the object. This kind of focus on the object can also be characterized in cognitive terms as identifying certain negative information about the object, and in interpersonal terms as being suspicious of the object, feeling guarded toward the object, or even hating the object. The defense used in hating the object is projection. In the paranoid, projection operates in terms of ascertaining the subject's degree of certainty or uncertainty with respect to the self-object difference. Thus, the projective defense that reinforces a critical stance toward the object acts to generate certainty in the subject of the distinction between self and object and correspondingly minimizes whatever uncertainty may exist. In projection, then, only negative experiences occur, and potentially positive accepting responses are limited within this paranoid sequence.

Hence, it is proposed that the cognitive dimension here labeled *certainty-uncertainty* corresponds to the diagnostic disposition of paranoid and defense of projection, and each of these are derivative aspects of the basic emotion of disgust. The relation between the emotion of disgust and the cognitive dimension of certainty-uncertainty generally concerns the issue between subject and object of *maintaining separation.*

TABLE 18.1. A Proposed System of the Epigenetic Structure of the Substrate of Emotion: Its Relation to the Nightmare and Psychosexual Stages

| *Nightmare* | *Emotion* | *Intrapsychic component* | *Emotion defense* | *Defense function* | *Diagnostic disposition* | *Trait element* | *Cognitive orientation* | *Cognitive theme* | *Psychosomatic organ systems* | *Adaptive correlate of epigenetic system: Psychosexual stages* |
|---|---|---|---|---|---|---|---|---|---|---|
| Orgastic-sexual | Joy | Id | Reaction-Formation | To block impulse | Manic | Gregarious | Purposiveness-aimlessness | Loss | Respiratory | Oral |
| Crying-grief | Sorrow | Superego | Compensation | To release impulse | Depressed | Depressed | Rumination-relinquish-ment | Loss | Reproductive | Oral |
| Loss of control | Expectation | Id | Intellectual-ization | To block impulse | Obsessive | Control | Analysis-Scatteredness | Control | Skeleto-muscular | Anal |
| Paralysis | Surprise | Superego | Regression | To release impulse | Psychopathic | Dyscontrol | Impatience-paralysis | Control | Dermatolog-ical | Anal |
| Attack | Anger | Id | Displacement | To block impulse | Aggressive | Aggressive | Condensing-reconstituting | Focus (remembering) | Circulatory | Phallic |
| Terror-flight | Fear | Superego | Repression | To release impulse | Passive | Timid | Recalling-forgetting | Focus (remembering) | Nervous | Phallic |
| Laughing | Acceptance | Id | Denial | To block impulse | Hysteric | Trustful | Attention-distraction | Autonomy | Sensory | Oedipal |
| Body part fragmentation | Disgust | Superego | Projection | To release impulse | Paranoid | Distrustful | Certainty-uncertainty | Autonomy | Digestive | Oedipal |

SOURCE: H. Kellerman, "An epigenetic theory of emotions in early development," in R. Plutchik and H. Kellerman, eds., *Emotions in Early Development*, vol. 2, *Emotions: Theory, Research, and Experience*. © 1983 by Academic Press Inc., New York. Reprinted by permission of the publisher.

Inspection of table 18.1 again reveals the polarity within the system of basic states. On a cognitive level, the attention-distraction element within the acceptance dimension is practically observed in the intuitive approach of the hysteric personality—one in which the object does not attend to details. Rather, the subject becomes concerned primarily with reinforcing positive feelings within an interpersonal context. Conversely, on a cognitive level, the certainty-uncertainty element of the disgust dimension is observed in the paranoid character with regard to this person's great attention to detail as a way of exercising critical judgment. Whereas the hysteric is highly suggestible and noncritical, the paranoid is highly critical and resists suggestion. The emotion-cognition theme of taking-in the object or separating from the object concerns the overall issue of *autonomy.*

## JOY: PURPOSIVENESS-AIMLESSNESS

The cognitive dimension representing the emotion of joy and reflecting the diagnostic and defensive elements of this emotion is here labeled *purposiveness-aimlessness* (or *randomness*). The correspondence between the emotion of joy and the cognitive quality of purposiveness is suggested by the theoretical framework which identifies the diagnostic state reflecting the emotion of joy as the manic state. The manic state becomes a bridge for understanding the relationship between the emotion of joy and cognitive quality of purposiveness because of the typical energized industriousness as well as apparent gregariousness of the manic person. Of course, as a clinical problem, mania is more than simply an example of industriousness in a person. In the manic state, industriousness and gregariousness are translated into the need to be involved in multitudes of projects, each ostensibly aiming toward a goal or containing a *purpose.* In this sense, the emotion of joy is proposed here to be related cognitively to the quality of purposiveness—a goal-oriented attitude. This purposiveness is one that seeks to accomplish enormous work aims. Although joy is a representative pleasure emotion that has its roots in sexuality, it is further proposed that through the reaction-formation defense and compensatory mechanisms, sexual energy is transformed into work energy. Inherent in the purposive cognitive orientation, therefore, is the drive involved in motivation and search for work.

Together, the emotion of joy, the defense of reaction formation, and the cognitive element of purposiveness reflect a nonsexual focus on the object. Through goal-oriented aims, the object is possessed in a work frenzy: a symbolic expression of the accomplishment of its aim. Therefore, the cognitive element of purposiveness as a derivative form of the emotion of joy also represents one aspect of a behavioral sequence that results in the possessing of the object in the form of accomplishment. The relationship between the emotion of joy and the cognitive dimension of purposiveness-aimlessness generally concerns the issue between subject and object of *fusion with, or possession of, the object.*

### SORROW: RUMINATION-RELINQUISHMENT

It is proposed that the cognitive dimension representing the emotion of sorrow and reflecting the diagnostic as well as defensive elements of this emotion be designated as a *rumination-relinquishment* dimension. Together, the emotion of sorrow and cognitive element of rumination reflect a continuous focus on the lost object. The cognitive element of rumination as a derivative form of sorrow represents one aspect of a behavioral sequence resulting in a repetitive attempt to reintegrate the lost object.

On the cognitive level, rumination or the attempt by the subject to retain the object is actually an attempt not to acknowledge loss of the object; rather, attempts at reintegration of the object occur through rumination in memory and fantasy. Therefore, rumination represents a continuous compensatory focus ostensibly on the presence—or on the image—of the object. In the absence of the compensatory mechanism, a *relinquishment* of the object is experienced by the subject, along with the appearance of the emotion of sorrow. The state of depression becomes a diagnostic expression for this entire syndrome.

In terms of this syndromal formulation, it is proposed that the cognitive dimension here labeled *rumination-relinquishment* corresponds to the diagnostic disposition of depression and defense of compensation, and each of these are derivative aspects of the basic emotion of sorrow. The relation between the emotion of sorrow and the cognitive dimension of rumination-relinquishment generally concerns the issue between subject and object of *reintegration.* The emotion-cognition theme of possessing the object and regaining the object concerns the overall issue of *loss.* The relationship between loss and reintegration is elaborated by Plutchik (1980).

In table 17.1 and in figure 16.1, the polarity of all levels of the personality are seen. To this now may be added that on a cognitive level, the purposiveness-aimlessness element within the joy dimension, reflecting a possession of the object, is opposite to the rumination-relinquishment element of the sorrow dimension that reflects a loss of the object and an attempt at repossession.

## EXPECTATION: ANALYSIS-SCATTEREDNESS

The cognitive dimension representing the emotion of expectation and reflecting the diagnostic as well as defense elements of this emotion is proposed here as an *analysis-scatteredness* dimension. Together, the emotion of expectation and the cognitive element of analysis reflect a process of scanning and control of the object in order to understand how subject and object can be related.

In interpersonal terms, *analysis* of the object can be considered control of the object. In the obsessive, intellectualization is used to examine, categorize, discover, or control the object. Intellectualization helps the subject maintain ties with the object rather than reinforce a scatteredness and dissolution of ties. The tie with the object, however, is characterized by the subject's need to control. Hence, it is proposed that the cognitive dimension here labeled *analysis-scatteredness* corresponds to the diagnostic disposition of obsessive and defense of intellectualization, and each of these are derivative aspects of the basic emotion of expectation. The relation between the emotion of expectation and the cognitive dimension of analysis-scatteredness generally concerns the issue between subject and object of *control.*

## SURPRISE: IMPATIENCE-PARALYSIS

It is proposed that the cognitive dimension representing the emotion of surprise and reflecting the diagnostic as well as defensive elements of this emotion be designated an *impatience-paralysis* dimension. As expectation is related to analysis and control of the object, surprise is related to a dyscontrol element, impulsivity, or impatience toward the object; that is, a state of dyscontrol in the subject prevents the object from controlling the subject.

On a cognitive level, the disorientation or dyscontrol is expressed as impatience (or short attention span). The relation between the emotion of surprise and the cognitive dimension of impatience-paralysis generally concerns the issue between subject and object of *the subject remaining uncontrolled.*

On all levels of the personality system within any basic polar pair the phenomenon of opposites is evident and is also proposed here with respect to cognitive dispositions. Correspondingly, on the cognitive level, the analysis-scatteredness element within the expectation dimension is used by the subject to control the object whereas the impatience-paralysis element within the surprise dimension is used by its subject to neutralize any control of subject by the object. The emotion-cognition theme of controlling the object or undermining control by the object concerns the overall issue of *control.*

## ANGER: CONDENSING-RECONSTITUTING

It is proposed that the cognitive dimension representing the emotion of anger and reflecting the diagnostic as well as defensive elements associated with this emotion be designated a *condensing-reconstituting* dimension. Together, the emotion of anger and the cognitive element of condensing reflect displaced negative expression toward the object. In this sense, on a cognitive level, such displacement is transposed as a condensing or coding capacity.

This kind of focus on the object dilutes negative feelings, thereby minimizing a direct expostulation or reconstitution of anger toward the object. In interpersonal terms, the displacement of anger permits the relationship between subject and object to remain relatively undisturbed. Hence, it is proposed that the cognitive dimension here labeled *condensing-reconstituting* corresponds to the diagnostic disposition of aggressive and defense of displacement, and that each of these are derivative aspects of the basic emotion of anger. The relation between the emotion of anger and the cognitive dimension of condensing-reconstituting generally concerns the issue between subject and object of *attenuating the expression of dissatisfaction.*

## FEAR: RECALLING-FORGETTING

It is proposed that the cognitive dimension representing the emotion of fear and reflecting the diagnostic and defensive elements associated with this emotion be designated a *recalling-forgetting* dimension. Generally, the relation between fear and recall concerns the idea of remembering a threatening event. In the passive syndrome, repression as a major defensive orientation facilitates forgetting of the event. On a cognitive level, recalling is a response by the subject to the ever-present conflict of suppression of memory through repressive defense versus the possibility of remembering the event; that is, the operation of repression creates a conflict between hiding or losing the memory and the tendency toward retaining or finding the memory. The relation between the emotion of fear and the cognitive dimension of recalling-forgetting generally concerns the issue between subject and object of *remembering or focusing.*

The entire personality cross-section of the anger-fear polarity is also revealed here in terms of respective cognitive dispositions. The condensing-reconstituting element within the anger dimension is considered opposite to the recalling-forgetting element within the fear dimension. The emotion-cognition theme of alternating and recalling dissatisfaction concerns the overall issue of asserting consciousness or *remembering, or focusing.*

These basic emotions, defenses, and diagnostic dispositions are related in a number of publications that spell out in considerable detail the various connections of the epigenetic emotion program; from specific emotion-diagnostic connections to corresponding defense and trait elements of each emotion (Kellerman 1976, 1977, 1979, 1980, 1981; Kellerman and Burry 1981; Kellerman and Plutchik 1968, 1977, 1978; Plutchik and Kellerman

1974; Plutchik, Kellerman, and Conte 1979). The analysis of the emotion system itself within a psychoevolutionary context is thoroughly explicated by Plutchik also in a number of publications (1955, 1958, 1960, 1962, 1980a, 1980b). The personality system and its internal theoretical correlations are similarly spelled out in greater detail by Kellerman (1979, 1980). Therefore, although the presentation of the relations of basic emotions with corresponding cognitive orientations has been considered in this section as a tentative organization of ideas and concepts, nevertheless this presentation is guided in its formulations by a larger theoretical matrix containing a measure of construct validity derived from theoretical as well as empirical studies.

## Structure and Dynamics of the System: An Introduction

The explication of this theoretical model is made with the system in place as a hypothetical pure entity. Each level of the personality is frozen into position so that the structure can be easily seen and understood. In this sense the model is mostly a structural one with the exceptions of the introduction of correlations to psychosexual stages and in the implied intrapsychic function of defense mechanisms revealing a dynamic interplay of forces in the actual functioning of the system. Further publications of this model will attempt to expand the analysis of the dynamics of the system.

There is another point in the system where ingredients of personality are unfrozen and where it is suggested that the individual is indeed in a transition period—able to reform and reshape aspects of personality. This point of remolding is indicated by the appearance of the nightmare. The nightmare is different from normal dreaming and is presumed to reflect characterological changes in the dreamer that are not reflected by normal, undisturbed night dreams.

Kadis et al. (1968) indicate that the dream will reveal information on diagnosis and defenses, and Foulkes and Anthony (1965) indicate that symptoms need to be defined by the therapist so that patients can see both sides to the conflict—the need to hide something, a character formation, and the need to have something understood, a potential character reformation, and the need to have something understood, a potential character reformation. The nightmare signals a moment of character reformation. This is so because the experience of a nightmare means that anxiety that was formerly bound as a symptom has now been freed. In this sense, a nightmare signals the dissolution of a fixed-character formation. This position is consistent with that expressed by Jones (1931) and Mack (1970). Because one's defenses are no longer serving to reinforce a particular character pattern, the appearance of a nightmare means that something has become ego-alien (Altman 1969). The likelihood is that the ego-alien element is reflected by the dissolution of a physical symptom and the consequent freeing of anxiety. This can likely mean that the nightmare signals a change in or the extinction of some psychosomatic symptom. Tension has become physically unbound. It may not remain unbound, but could develop into another symptom indicating a tension rebinding. It is proposed, therefore, that the occurrence of a nightmare represents a dissolution of a psychosomatic symptom, the beginning phase of a new one, or both, and that this period of fluidity and characterological uncertainty reflects a point in the structural explication of the theory where dynamics of the personality and its operation can be seen and understood with greater clarity.

In the following section, the relation of psychophysiological organ systems to the entire emotion-personality model will be proposed. The discussion will accept the assumption that anxiety becomes bound in symptoms and becomes unbound as signaled by the nightmare. This discussion is taken from Kellerman (1979) and elaborated here.

## Psychosomatic Symptomatology and Nightmares

Foulkes and Anthony (1965) indicate that the understanding of symptoms and the repressed unconscious is akin to the deciphering of a code. Kanzer (1959) also indicates that the basic symbolic communications are those of somatic conditions and dreams. Greenleaf (1973) adds that dreams have the same structure as symptoms. To this is now added the proposition by Alexander (1950:68) that "Every emotional state has its own physiological syndrome." Alexander further suggests that certain personality types are predisposed to certain diseases and that "physiological responses to emotional stimuli vary according to the nature of the precipitating emotional state." This is a theory of psychosomatic disorders proposing that specific disorders relate to specific emotions. It is a proposition of the specificity of the psychosomatic process also considered by Kubie (1953).

In more contemporary research on psychophysiological manifestations, the link between emotion-personality clusters and psychosomatic symptomatology is usually a multidimensional correlation. However, the Alexandrian proposition linking specific emotions with specific organ-symptom patterns is supported from a structural point of view by the present theory. This Alexandrian correlation between emotion and symptom also seems to provide a better first approximation that permits the entire psychosomatic organ system to become structurally integrated in the emotion-personality theory proposed here and revealed through the understanding of the organization of nightmares.

In this section a system of psychosomatic structure will be proposed. This system, as it functions in an individual personality, will be related to the overall structure of emotion, defense, and diagnostic disposition described above. This discussion will attempt to use the concepts relating dreams and the appearance of nightmares to anxiety, the acting-out of anxiety, and the binding of anxiety into character engravings of the personality of which psychophysiological or psychosomatic symptomatology is a part.

It is an accepted psychological principle that the appearance of symptoms is the result of anxiety that has been converted and expressed in body language, When individuals are anxious, but also unable either to examine or to manage their tension, then it may be likely for such persons to experience physical symptoms that in some way are tension equivalents. Spotnitz (1973) says that psychosomatic symptoms may be understood to be acting-out equivalents; that is, whenever basic anxieties cannot be managed they may tend to become expressed in action rather than for tension to continue. Anxiety then may become expressed as a rudimentary or prepsychosomatic condition. When one is conscious of intrapsychic conflict, acting-out probability decreases and the appearance of psychosomatic symptomatology also subsides.

The pioneers in the research on psychosomatic symptomatology were concerned with defining and determining how many basic psychophysiological systems actually comprised one whole basic system, and what basic emotions best reflected a correspondence with each organ system. The work by Alexander (1950) is a good example of this sort of approach in the understanding and organizing of the entire system of psychophysiological effects in the personality. Although the correlational approach has since been expanded and revealed to reflect a more complex interaction of systems in the personality, nevertheless, a compendium of the lists of basic organ systems developed by researchers will usually include the respiratory, reproductive, sensory, digestive, skeletomuscular, dermatological, nervous and cardiovascular systems. Some authors include the hemic, lymphatic, and endocrine systems, but these correlate to emotionality in only a general way. It is proposed here that a correlation can be determined connecting each of the eight organ systems with one of the eight basic emotions, and defense mechanisms, to reveal an underlying psychosomatic system inherent also in diagnostic composition.

## Personality Types and Corresponding Psychosomatic Organ Systems

It is proposed that eight basic psychosomatic types exist to which all psychosomatic symptomatology relates. Some systematic relationships between diagnostic type and psychosomatic symptomatology are offered by Alexander (1950), Gruenberg et al. (1968) and Weiss and English (1957), among many other sources. The entire literature on psychosomatics is highly theoretical. Generally, it lacks a systematic formulation based upon some unifying underlying structural organization. One possible unifying system will be offered in the following section. It should be noted that many of the symptoms listed in the following section and attributed to psychosomatic origins may also develop from physical causes. Each psychosomatic organ system contains a cluster of symptoms, so that while symptoms may overlap from one psychosomatic system to another, it is the entire cluster or syndrome that identifies any particular psychosomatic system. The relation of personality types with psychosomatic symptomatology suggests a new postulate.

> Postulate 20. Psychosomatic organ-system dispositions correspond to the basic-emotion system.

In the description of eight basic psychosomatic types presented here, each will be related to emotion, defense, diagnostic disposition, and psychosexual level of development. On the basis of the discussion of intrapsychic representation in the previous chapter each psychosomatic type also will be intrapsychically designated in terms of its basic nature. These relationships may be examined in table 18.1 and figure 18.1

## Gregarious versus Depressed

### GREGARIOUS: THE RESPIRATORY SYSTEM

The gregarious type expreses high energy in all social behavior. Joy or pleasure represents the emotion of this category. Defensively, reaction formation governs the basic sexual orientation of this type. On a clinical level, the manic disposition expresses the diagnosis of the gregarious type. On an empirical level, clinicians working with tubercular patients and patients with other respiratory problems frequently notice that manic or highly energized paranoid types are unduly represented in this symptom category. The point is that high-energy types seem to develop all kinds of respiratory disorders. Weiss and English (1957) also report the appearance of pulmonary tuberculosis in high-energy types. They as well as Wittkower (1949) indicate that such patients are fatigued and undernourished. Other respiratory disorders associated with high-energy personalities include hyperventilation, colds, allergy, sinu-

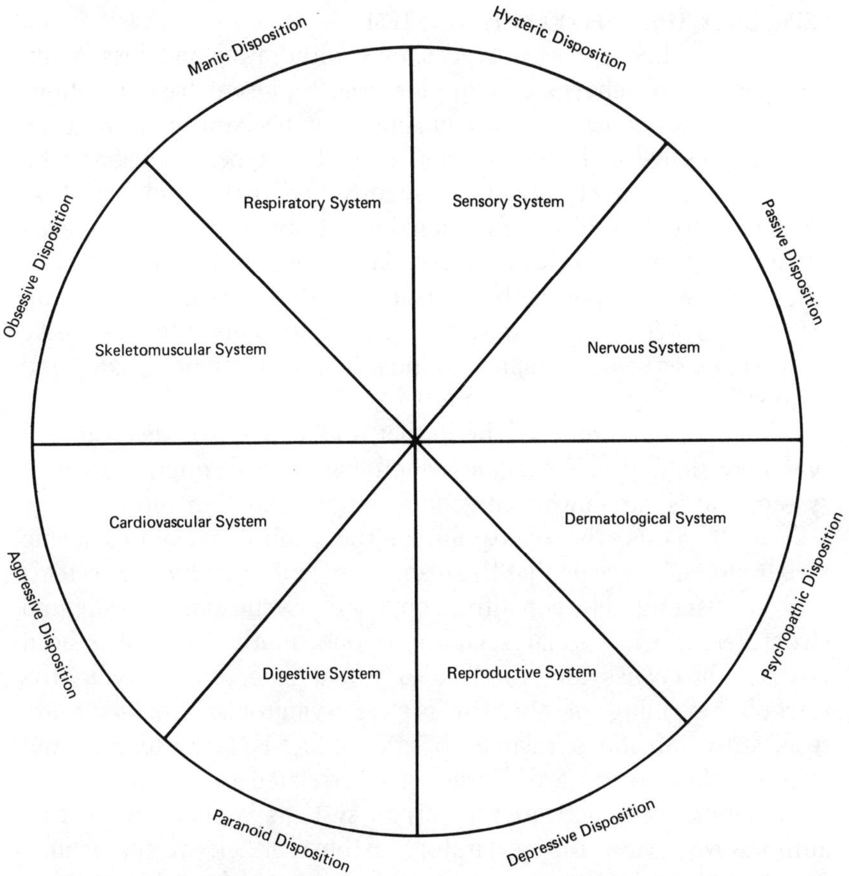


FIGURE 18.1 The relationship of psychosomatic organ systems to basic diagnostic types. *Source:* Kellerman (1979).

sitis, vasomotor rhinitis, asthma, sighing, coughing, and throat clearing. These correlations have been reported by Halliday as early as 1937. The high-energy or manic quality associated with respiratory disorders has also been related to aggression, ambition, argumentativeness, hysteria, repressed sexual tension, and underachievement.

It is proposed therefore, that the gregarious-manic type is dispositionally predisposed toward expressing psychosomatic symptomatology through respiratory disorders.

DEPRESSED: THE REPRODUCTIVE SYSTEM

The depressed type shows withdrawal and loss of interest in social behavior. Sorrow or grief represent basic emotions of this category. Defensively, compensatory mechanisms govern the basic depressive and loss experiences of this type. Clinicians who work with depressed patients frequently find that impotency, frigidity, menstrual problems, functional infertility, and premature ejaculation are the initial physical complaints offered by such patients. These are also reported by Alexander (1950), Gruenberg et al. (1968) and Weiss and English (1957). Causes of the depressive quality are offered as repressed hostility, fear, shame, hate, and disgust.

It is proposed here that the depressive dispositional type may show psychosomatic symptomatology through the organ system that is variably called genitourinary, sexual, or reproductive.

Thus, the opposition of the clinical categories manic and drepressive reveals that the respiratory and reproductive systems may correspondingly constitute opposite psychosomatic symptom structures. Their special relation to one another has also been reported by Weiss and English to reveal some similarity in the symbolic meaning of their respective symptoms. Not only are respiratory infections related to intense needs for attention and affection, but so too are depressions correlated to common colds. This simultaneous activation of organ systems is also proposed by authors who view the respiratory asthma attack of the manic-energized type to be the suppressed cry of the depressive type.

Finally, a possible relationship between psychosomatic organ-system expression and psychosexual development is offered in an early classic study by Saul (1939) who indicated that dermal and respiratory mechanisms are related to oral ones and imply a dynamic involving the mother figure. These mechanisms are influenced by psychological functioning. Saul further suggests that psychosexual mechanisms affect skin and respiratory allergies in a way that is similar to the role of oral mechanisms in the gastrointestinal disorders.

It is proposed here that the gregarious-manic and deprived-depressive dispositions express their respective opposite psychosomatic conditions of respiratory and reproductive disorders, and that these psychosomatic conditions perhaps may be better understood as those reflecting psychosexual problems of an oral nature. Problems of depression are also understood by psychoanalysts to reflect derivative oral problems.

## Controlled versus Dyscontrolled

### CONTROLLED: THE SKELETOMUSCULAR SYSTEM

The controlled type expresses feelings of expectation and anticipation as basic emotions. Defensively, intellectualization and other obsessional mechanisms operate to meet one's needs for control. On a clinical diagnostic level, obsessive highly controlled types seem to develop skeletomuscular disorders. Disorders of arthritis, rheumatism, aches in muscles and joints, lower back pain, muscle cramps, and generalized tension headaches are some examples. The prevailing psychodynamic interpretation of such psychosomatic expressions revolves around needs for control. For example, persons who develop these disorders are considered to be demanding and exacting. They experience great hostility and strong needs to manipulate and sometimes develop compelling feelings to serve others or to act deferentially. Such behavior reflects an attempt to keep hostility repressed. Weiss and English (1957) indicate that such persons alleviate guilt by serving others. Male patients show chronic inhibited but rebellious hostility—a reaction against dependent feminine trends that are unconscious. These types overcompensate with aggressiveness. There is some evidence that they are accident prone and behave in ways designed to relieve guilt. The authors further attribute the appearance of skeletomuscular disorders to persons who are uncommunicative. They are unable to fight directly. Therefore, they must control their environment completely or "seethe or boil within."

### DYSCONTROLLED: THE DERMATOLOGICAL SYSTEM

Weiss and English also propose that opposite to the controlled type is an impulsive one who tends to act out conflicts. The dyscontrolled type is an impulsive type. The emotion of surprise, defined as a behavioral disorientation, is the basic emotion of this category. The defense of regression permits the dyscontrolled type to persistently express impulse. On a clinical level a psychopathic disposition expresses the diagnosis of the dyscontrolled type. The impulsivity and acting-out characteristic of this type reflects an eruption of sorts through boundaries. Boundary violations are expressed physically in disorders of the skin. Dermatological conditions such as psoriasis are conditions that acting-out patients report. Conditions such as blushing, itching, edema, dermatitis, pruritus, alopecia areata (loss of hair), eczema, excessive sweating of hands and feet, acne, urticaria, nail biting, and eczema of ear, scalp, and nape of neck are some examples of dermatological disorders in acting-out personalities.

Psychodynamically, itching and scratching may be understood to be a symbol sequence of impatience and impulsivity. In an early study, Klander (1935) indicates that masochistic tendencies have a close affinity to the skin in the sensation of pain. Scratching constitutes an expression of the hostile impulse. In pruritus ani and vulvae, itching may reflect an inhibited sexual excitement. Scratching then becomes a source of conscious erotic pleasure and a masturbatory equivalent. It also has been correlated to regression (Gillespie 1938; Stokes 1932). In some respects impulsive types are also exhibitionistic. Weiss and English (1957) observe that the skin is the border between the inner and outer life and that scratching is related to aggression.

It is proposed here that the controlled-obsessional type and the opposite dyscontrolled-psychopathic type express their psychosomatic disorders through the skeletomuscular and dermatological systems respectively. In a structural sense, then, the skeletomuscular system is opposite to the dermatological system. Furthermore, the basic control and dyscontrol properties of these respective types may be regarded in psychosexual terms as anal-derivative elements. Macalpine (1953) and Weiss and English refer to anal-derivative dynamics for dermatological conditions. Macalpine (1953:507) states that the "origin can be traced to a reactivation in adult life of infantile fantasies about procreation centering around the anal function which preceded genital interest and the knowledge of sex." In addition, most clinicians generally understand the issue of obsessional-control and psychopathic-dyscontrol to be one that reflects anal-derivative problems.

## Timid Versus Aggressive

### TIMID: THE NERVOUS SYSTEM

The timid type expresses apprehension and fear as basic emotions. Defensively, a general repression mechanism enables a person of this type to inhibit both feeling and action. On a clinical level, a passive disposition reflects the diagnosis of the timid type. The defense of repression is used to maintain this timid style. A wide variety of nervous-system disorders are associated with this type. These include insomnia, fainting, weakness, vertigo, numbness, tingling of extremities, ringing in ears, ocular and visual phenomena, epilepsy syndrome, and migraines. Correlated behavior can include trepidation and lethargy. The level of introspection in such a person in exceedingly low, and interpersonal confrontations are scrupulously avoided.

It is proposed that the timid-passive type may show psychosomatic symptomatology through the organ system referred to as the nervous system.

### AGGRESSIVE: THE CARDIOVASCULAR SYSTEM

The aggressive dispositional type expresses or experiences anger and rage as basic emotions. Defensively, displacement mechanisms are designed to manage anger. On a clinical level, this disposition is expressed through direct aggressive behavior or through displaced aggression. Clinicians probably would agree that the aggressive type, whether outwardly angry or inwardly smouldering, is prone to cardiovascular disorders.

The essential psychodynamic of the correlation between the aggressive type albeit a smouldering passive-aggressive one and the appearance of cardiovascular problems is proposed by Alexander (1950:150):

> The individual who has become excessively inhibited under the influence of his early experiences will find it much more difficult to handle his

> aggressive impulses efficiently in adult life. He will tend to repress all his self-assertive tendencies and be unable to find some legitimate outlet for the expression of these tendencies. The damming up of his hostile impulses will continue and will consequently increase in intensity. This will induce the development of stronger defensive measures in order to keep the pent up aggressions in check. The over-complaint, over-polite, submissive attitudes found in patients with hypertension are precisely such defenses, but they do not prevent the accumulation of tension. Consequently, feelings of inferiority develop which, in turn, stimulate aggressive impulses; and the vicious circle is perpetuated. Because of the marked degree of their inhibitions, these patients are less effective in their occupational activities and for that reason tend to fail in competition with others, so that envy is stimulated and their hostile feelings toward more successful, less inhibited competitors is further intensified.

Saul (1939) proposes the same aggression-cardiovascular correlation, offering a similar illustrative case.

Other psychosomatic symptoms of the cardiovascular system may include fainting, palpitation, grinding of teeth, arrhythmia, migraine, high blood pressure, dizziness, and insomnia. Again, Weiss and English attribute these symptoms to an inability to express aggression directly, but within the context of an underlying consistent feeling of resentment and anger. Hamilton (1955) also states that tensions will become expressed through the circulatory system because of chronically displaced rage. This aggressive type has been reported to be overly concerned with social status, prestige, and material success (Dunbar 1943).

It is proposed that the timid-passive type and the opposite aggressive type express their respective psychosomatic disorders through the nervous and cardiovascular systems. Furthermore, it seems evident, as Alexander (1950) points out, that focal themes of the passive and aggressive types relate to issues of assertiveness. In psychosexual terms, this constitutes a phallic-level derivative theme.

## Trustful Versus Distrustful

### TRUSTFUL: THE SENSORY SYSTEM

The trustful type expresses agreeableness and positive attitudes. There is a distinct absence of criticality in such a person.

Acceptance is the basic emotion of this category. Defensively, denial mechanisms govern the basic suggestibility of this type. On a clinical level, a hysterical disposition expresses the diagnosis of the trustful type. Clinicians working with hysterical patients frequently find that these patients are sensory types and that they actually report many unusual sensory experiences. Some sensory symptoms include vertigo, dizziness, ringing in ears, taste distortion, hysterical deafness, hearing and visual problems including hallucinatory experiences, tunnel vision, blurriness, auras, and hysterical blindness. Generally, therefore, it seems that the sensory system reflects hysterical diagnostic dynamics.

## DISTRUSTFUL: THE DIGESTIVE SYSTEM

The distrustful type expresses suspicion and criticality. Disgust and rejection constitute the basic emotions of this category. Defensively, the projection mechanism is designed to keep the external world imperfect so that a personal sense of imperfection remains out of awareness. On a clinical level, the distrust is reflected as a paranoid dispositional style.

There has been much controversy in the literature regarding the basic psychodynamics of paranoid character and associated psychosomatic symptomatology. The paranoid as a projector and as one who expresses disgust as a basic emotion is presumably also making some digestive or gastrointestinal statement. This connection is also made by Alexander and Menninger (1936) in an early paper relating persecutory delusions to the digestive system. Persecutory delusions and melancholia were observed in constipated patients who were typically expressing distrust and rejection. The implicit self-instruction of the paranoid type is "I must hold on to what I have." Another self-instruction indicates that this person must not take in any foreign substance. Paranoid distrustful types also show a whole set of swallowing problems.

Symptoms of digestive disorders include chronic diarrhea, constipation, spastic colitis, ulcerative colitis, irritable colon, indigestion, peptic ulcers, belching, vomiting, biliary tract problems, and a wide variety of intake swallowing problems starting with exaggerated appetite and progressing to vomiting, nervous vomiting, esophageal neurosis or choking on food, cardiospasm, reporting metalic tastes, and anorexia nervosa. The proposed psychodynamics of digestive-tract disturbances have ranged from definitions of dependency reactions to underachievement, frustration, depression, anxiety, the appearance of "feminine" traits in males, and finally reactions of disgust generated by separation problems. Other emotions cited by Alexander relating to gastrointestinal disorders and constituting a paranoid emotion cluster include intense rage, greed, jealousy, and envy. Still other paranoid-obsessive features to this psychosomatic system can include stubbornness, overambitiousness, and overconscientiousness. When the paranoid type becomes exceedingly critical, according to Weiss (1944), this individual will behave as if existing conditions cannot be swallowed or tolerated. Some paranoid psychosomatic symptoms, such as swallowing problems, at times also appear to be hysteric.

It is proposed here that the trustful-hysterical type and the opposite distrustful-paranoid type express their respective psychosomatic disorders through the sensory and digestive systems. Furthermore, as a connection to psychosexual level of development, the hysterical-sensory and paranoid-digestive types seem to express oedipal conflict; that is, the hysteric-sensory type is forever loyal, and this loyalty is supported in its motive by the high suggestibility and posture of total acceptance of the hysteric. In contrast, the paranoid-digestive type is loyal to no one, and this lack of loyalty is supported in its motive by the need to criticize. It is this loyalty-disloyalty issue that theoretically ties the hysteric and paranoid types on the psychosexual level. The clear opposition of suggestibility and criticality also shows the polar connection between these types in terms of their respective underlying personality inclinations. The relationship of psychosomatic organ systems to basic diagnostic types is shown in table 18.1.

To summarize, it is proposed here that the appearance of a nightmare in an individual signals the modification or transformation of some psychosomatic physical symptom. The nature of the physical symptom is determined by the set of existing defenses and the basic dispositional tendency of the dreamer. These psychosomatic symptoms and the relation of nightmares to dispositional types were explored earlier. Now it is possible to relate dispositional types, defenses, nightmares, and psychosomatic symptoms.

Impairment of manic and depressed defenses will produce nightmares reflecting modification in respiratory and reproductive symptoms, respectively. Impairment of obsessional and psychopathic defenses will produce nightmares reflecting changes in skeletomuscular and dermatological symptoms, respectively. Impairment of passive and aggressive defenses will produce nightmares reflecting changes in nervous and circulatory or cardiovascular symptoms, respectively. Impairment in hysteric and paranoid defenses will produce nightmares that reflect modifications in sensory and digestive symptoms, respectively.

In the foregoing, an attempt was made to outline some basis for understanding the appearance of psychosomatic symptomatology as it is derived from a basic epigenetic emotion-personality system which is essentially entirely uncovered through the analysis of nightmares. Understanding the organization of nightmares, then, permits a rare view into the infrastructure of personality. Stekel (1943) indicated that the dream is a phantasmagorical phenomenon in which the present is forgotten, the past is reexperienced, and the future foretold. The present is unformed and unhistorical. The aim and direction to the unbinding of anxiety enables, so to speak, a foretelling of the future, a projected time of new character patterns—a glimpse of which may be gotten in the work on dreams and nightmares. Yet, although a final postulate will stress the genetic underpinning of personality predisposition, nevertheless, as I have stated elsewhere (Kellerman 1979:300), "the biological predispositional personality program may be an opaque and faintly inked one onto which cultural experiences—those adaptational influences—impress themselves only to then reveal the impressed parts of the program. Impressions made upon the biological-genetic program may be transformed by these cultural forces, and other impressions then may be made." One such cultural impression is the therapy experience, in which working-through becomes in the awake state what the nightmare is to the dream—that is, a resolution and recasting of rigidified perspectives, acting-out, and general self-defeating behavior. The transformation and new impression making of the program also constitute a raising of consciousness and enhancement of ego. This flexibility of the program attests to its evolutionary viability.

Several new postulates may now be proposed that are based upon the above discussion.

Postulate 21. Although the emotion-personality program is an epigenetic one, adaptational influences can have a profound effect on one's nature.

Postulate 22. Precursor personality dispositions are encoded in emotion. This finding reveals a genetic imperative in which the emotion-personality system is proposed to exist in virtual state within the genetic code etched in the emotion structure.

Postulate 23. The nightmare provides the rarest of opportunities to see the entire engraved emotion infrastructure in its basic decoded form.

The following chapter is a summary and conclusion of the four chapters on the nightmare and the structure of personality, forming a compilation of all postulates that were proposed throughout.

## Summary

In this chapter cognitive dispositions were related to the emotion-personality system. An analysis of anxiety, character trait formation, and psychosomatic symptomatology, as these phenomena are related to the nightmare, was also developed.

## References

Alexander, F. 1950. *Psychosomatic Medicine.* New York: Norton.

Alexander, F. and W. C. Menninger. 1936. Relation of persecutory delusions to the functioning of the gastro-intestinal tract. *Journal of Nervous and Mental Disease* 84:541.

Altman, L. L. 1969. *The Dream in Psychoanalysis.* New York: International Universities Press.

Dunbar, F. 1943. *Psychosomatic Diagnosis.* New York: Hoeber.

Foulkes, S. H. and E. J. Anthony. 1965. *Group Psychotherapy: The Psychoanalytic Approach.* Baltimore: Penguin.

Gillespie, R. D. 1938. Psychological aspects of skin disease. *British Journal of Dermatology* 50(1):1–16.

Greenleaf, E. 1973. Senoi dream groups. *Psychotherapy: Theory, Research, and Practice* 10(3):218–22.

Gruenberg, E. M. ed. *Diagnostic and Statistical Manual of Mental Disorders.* 2d ed. Washington, D.C.: American Psychiatric Association.

Halliday, J. L. 1937. Approach to asthma. *British Journal of Medical Psychology* 17:1.

Hamilton, M. 1955. *Psychosomatics.* New York: John Wiley and Sons.

Jones, E. 1931. *On the Nightmare.* London: Hogarth Press. (Original work published in 1911.)

Kadis, A., J. D. Krasner, C. Winick, and S. H. Foulkes. 1968. *A Practicum of Group Psychotherapy.* New York: Hoeber Medical Division, Harper and Row.

Kanzer, M. 1959. The recollection of the forgotten dream. *Journal of the Hillside Hospital* 8:74–85.

Kellerman, H. 1976. The sociobiology of group psychotherapy and the physics of group boundary structure. Paper delivered at the Association of Science, Psychotherapy, and Ethics, New York. November.

Kellerman, H. 1977. Hate. In B. B. Wolman, ed., *International Encyclopedia of Neurology, Psychiatry, Psychoanalysis, and Psychology.* New York: Von Nostrand Reinhold.

Kellerman, H. 1979. *Group Psychotherapy and Personality: Intersecting Structures.* New York: Grune and Stratton.

Kellerman, H. 1980. A structural model of emotion and personality: Psychoanalytic and sociobiological implications. In R. Plutchik and H. Kellerman, eds., *Emotion: Theory, Research, and Experience.* Vol. 1, *Theories of Emotion.* New York: Academic Press.

Kellerman, H. 1981. *Sleep Disorders: Insomnia and Narcolepsy.* New York: Brunner/Mazel.

Kellerman, H. 1983. An epigenetic theory of emotions in early development. In R. Plutchik and H. Kellerman, eds., *Emotion: Theory, Research, and Experience.* Vol. 2, *Emotions in Early Development.* New York: Academic Press.

Kellerman, H. and A. Burry. 1981. *A Handbook of Psychodiagnostic Testing: Personality Analysis and Report Writing.* New York: Grune and Stratton.

Kellerman, H. and R. Plutchik. 1968. Emotion-trait interrelations and the measurement of personality. *Psychological Reports* 23:1107–14.

Kellerman, H. and R. Plutchik. 1977. The meaning of tension in group therapy. In L. R. Wolberg, M. L. Aronson, and A. R. Wolberg, eds., *Group Therapy 1977—An Overview.* New York: Stratton Intercontinental Medical Book.

Kellerman, H. and R. Plutchik. 1978. Personality patterns of drug addicts in a therapy group: A similarity structure analysis. *Group* 2(1):14–21.

Klander, J. V. 1935. Psychogenic aspects of diseases of the skin. *Archives of Neurology and Psychiatry* 33:221.

Kubie, L. S. 1953. The problem of specificity in the psychosomatic process. In F. Deutsch, ed., *The Psychosomatic Concept in Psychoanalysis.* New York: International Universities Press.

Macalpine, I. 1953. Pruritis ani: A psychiatric study. *Psychosomatic Medicine* 15:499–519.

Mack, J. E. 1970. *Nightmares and Human Conflict.* Boston: Little, Brown.

Plutchik, R. 1955. Some problems for a theory of emotion. *Psychosomatic Medicine* 17:306–10.

Plutchik, R. 1958. Outlines of a new theory of emotion. *Transactions of the New York Academy of Science* 20:394–403.

Plutchik R. 1960. The multifactor analytic theory of emotion. *Journal of Psychology* 50:153–71.

Plutchik, R. 1962. *The Emotions: Theories, Facts, and a New Model.* New York: Random House.

Plutchik, R. 1980a. *Emotion: A Psychoevolutionary Synthesis.* New York: Harper and Row.

Plutchik, R. 1980b. A general psychoevolutionary theory of emotion. In R. Plutchik and H. Kellerman, eds., *Emotion: Theory, Research, and Experience.* Vol. 1, *Theories of Emotion.* New York: Academic Press.

Plutchik, R., and H. Kellerman. 1974. *The Emotions Profile Index: Test and Manual.* San Francisco: Western Psychological Services.

Plutchik, R., H. Kellerman, and H. Conte. 1979. A structural theory of ego defenses. In C. E. Izard, ed., *Emotions, Personality, and Psychopathology.* New York: Plenum Press.

Saul, L. J. 1939. Hostility in cases of essential hypertension. *Psychosomatic Medicine* 1:153.

Spotnitz, H. 1973. Acting-out in group psychotherapy. In L. R. Wolberg and E. K. Schwartz, eds., *Group Therapy 1973—An Overview.* New York: Stratton Intercontinental Medical Book.

Stekel, W. 1943. *The Interpretation of Dreams.* Vol. 1. New York: Liveright.

Stokes, J. H. 1932. The nervous and mental component in cutaneous disease. *Pennsylvania Medical Journal* 35:229.

Weiss, E. 1944. Cardiospasm: A psychosomatic disorder. *Psychosomatic Medicine* 6:58.

Weiss, E., and O. S. English. 1957. *Psychosomatic Medicine.* Philadelphia: Saunders.

Wittkower, E. 1949. *A Psychiatrist Looks at Tuberculosis.* London: The National Association for the Prevention of Tuberculosis.

# 19.

# Nightmares and the Structure of Personality

## Conclusion and Compilation of Postulates

HENRY KELLERMAN

THESE FOUR CHAPTERS have underscored the point that the personality of the individual contains a deep structure rooted in an emotion matrix. A series of hypotheses and postulates has been advanced to indicate that these emotions are marked with important dispositional information concerning aspects of personality, such as defenses, as well as cognitive, diagnostic, and psychosomatic elements. This epigenetic program expresses its imperatives in the person so that the program is influenced by and also influences external experience. Accordingly, the nature of emotions in development suggests a highly complex epigenetic program, the elements of which have been subject to theoretical exposition in these chapters.

The following twenty-three postulates essentially recapitulate the thematic strands that tie together the variety of elements of the system, including: nightmares, emotions, traits, defenses, defense functions, diagnostic dispositions, intrapsychic formulations, psychosexual stages, cognitive orientations, anxiety, ego, characterology, psychophysiological or psychosomatic organ systems, and the overall similarity structure of the personality.

Postulate 1. Defense mechanisms regulate emotions.

Postulate 2. Specific defenses are designed to manage specific emotions.

Postulate 3. There are eight basic defenses to manage eight basic emotions.

Postulate 4. There are eight basic nightmare themes that correspond to the eight basic categories of the entire emotion-defense personality system.

Postulate 5. A nightmare is defined as a dream that, because of its emotional content, awakens the dreamer.

Postulate 6. Any basic nightmare is a reflection of the dreamer's current diagnostic state.

Postulate 7. The basic diagnostic personality types are derived from particular defensive styles and their emotion underpinnings.

Postulate 8. Each nightmare theme reveals the basic intrapsychic nature of each diagnostic state.

Postulate 9. Although there are an infinite number of dream contents, when they become nightmares they reveal only eight basic emotion themes.

Postulate 10. Although all defenses contain a repressive element, repression was originally developed to manage the emotion of fear, which is the chief underlying component of the passive dispositional diagnosis.

Postulate 11. Theoretically, any of the basic nightmare themes may be experienced. For example, a formerly passive person who, because of an alteration of defenses, is better able to be confrontational and assertive can experience nightmares of aggression that are characteristic of that person's feelings at the time of the dream. This shift of diagnostic expression is a reflection also of Postulate 6—namely, any basic nightmare is a reflection of the dreamer's current diagnostic state.

Postulate 12. The eight basic nightmare themes, emotions, defenses, and diagnostic dispositions, respectively, show the properties of both polarity and similarity.

Postulate 13. Each nightmare contains a fear component. This postulate is also consistent with the observation that (a) each defense contains a repression component, and (b) repression is the defense designed chiefly to manage the emotion of fear.

Postulate 14. Intrapsychic forces are essences of basic emotions and become revealed in the nightmare when, in the absence of defense, these basic emotions are expressed at their highest intensities.

Postulate 15. All basic defenses are emotion-defenses and not ego-defenses, and do not depend on ego development for their appearance.

Postulate 16. The purpose of defenses is to act as intrapsychic regulating devices—regulating id and superego strivings—designed either to block or to release impulse in the service of socialization aims.

Postulate 17. All nightmares represent emotional breakthroughs of the characterological defense structure and are therefore ego-alien expressions of the personality reflecting a moment of character reformation. As such, nightmares reveal the true undefended intrapsychic nature—either id or superego—of the personality.

Postulate 18. Id and superego are epigenetic encodings of emotion. In contrast, ego is adaptational. The ego develops out of the interaction of the epigenetic emotion program as it is affected by the compromise of intrapsychic id-superego aims during psychosexual periods.

Postulate 19. Cognitive styles correspond to the basic-emotion system, indicating that emotion is the wellspring of cognition.

Postulate 20. Psychosomatic organ-system dispositions correspond to the basic-emotion system.

Postulate 21. Although the emotion-personality program is an epigenetic one, adaptational influences can have a profound effect on one's nature.

Postulate 22. Precursor personality dispositions are encoded in emotion. This finding reveals a genetic imperative in which the emotion-personality system is proposed to exist in virtual state within the genetic code etched in the emotion structure.

Postulate 23. The nightmare provides the rarest of opportunities to see the entire engraved emotion infrastructure in its basic decoded form.

# Epilogue

HENRY KELLERMAN

THE DEPTH OF chapters and the breadth of sections of this volume create an opportunity for the reader to assess the range of the field of nightmare study specifically and dreams and sleep generally. After reading these contributions individually, and understanding the work as a compendium in all its aspects, one can no longer think of the nightmare in a perfunctory manner. Further, one can certainly no longer simplistically identify nightmares merely as dreams of terror.

This volume distinguishes among disturbed dream phenomena and indicates that these phenomena are not subsumed only under the general rubric of nightmare. The analyses made throughout this volume demonstrate that a host of disturbed dream states exists. In addition to the nightmare, these states include, at the least, anxiety dreams, hypnagogic hallucinations, and night terrors. The literature is clear that so-called nightmares may emerge from several different stages of sleep and that these can actually be differentiated. For example, nightmares can be distinguished from stage 4 night terrors, REM anxiety dreams, stage 2 awakenings, and hypnagogic nightmares.

In a sense, in sampling the field of inquiry in the nightmare, this book has shown the range of theory that applies to this area of research; from the thinking of Francis Crick, who sees the dream generally as an attempt to remove certain undesirable modes of interaction in networks of cells in the cerebral cortex, to the deterministic id theory of Sigmund Freud, who attributes specific dynamic and structural motives to the nightmare. In addition, there are the physiologists, pharmacologists, neurologists, and laboratory sleep researchers engaged in a mapping of the nightmare from a nonpsychodynamic tradition as well as those psychoanalysts who understand the nightmare as containing psychodynamic interpersonal messages and as reflecting personality and diagnostic information. Clinicians who would minimize the use of the nightmare as a mode for furthering the treatment process on the basis that the state of the nightmare is an incompleted dream must now—because of the clinical chapters in this volume—appreciate the point that the nightmare is actually a ready-made technology affording an opportunity to enter the personality in order to examine emotions, characterological organization, defenses, diagnostic disposition, the psychic structure, and most other aspects of personality.

From the psychoanalytic and psychodynamic tradition, Freud started out in 1900 with the formulation of wish fulfillment as the energy fueling the dream. This tradition has gradually led to the examination of nightmares as correlated with the repetition compulsion, aggression, defenses, and ego-functions. In eighty years, Freud's understanding of the nightmare as a phenomenon influenced by the id has evolved to a point where the nightmare can be considered from several theoretical vantage points: from conflict psychology or ego psychology, from object relations psychology with a focus on the ego, from the perspective of separation anxiety or that of conflict resolution. Further, in connection with current understanding of the nightmare, studies in this volume that have explored the nightmare with respect to psychopathology dispel the popular notion that nightmares reflect illness or exist in simple positive correlation with disturbed personality functioning. They may simply be reflections of characterological structure at a given time. This observation regarding the lack of association between the nightmare and a particular pathology applies to children as well as adults. The basic nightmare themes, then, are reflections of ongoing adaptational events. They are not necessarily psychopathological. In fact, as applied to children, the studies have pointed out that the experience of nightmares reveals normative data according to developmental considerations. A context is developed in this volume that serves the purpose of clarifying that the nightmare—especially in children—exists in a specific social-familial environmental framework and that personality factors, family relationships, and the psychology of bedtime behavior are integral to the understanding of nightmares. It is even proposed that from a developmental point of view the experience of the nightmare can signal vital developmental achievement.

An important implication of this volume is that the nightmare has emerged as a legitimate field of study containing biological, chemical, neurological, and physiological underpinnings along with psychological imperatives. In addition, it is made clear that an individual's nightmare and nightmare-equivalent states need to be understood in the contexts of the psychophysiology of sleep, emotional-psychological variables, and the social-relational fabric of that individual's life. The study of the nightmare as such is located within the broader arenas of the study of sleep, sleep-disruption phenomena, and the relation of the sleep context to one's psychosocial existence. This realization that the nightmare must be understood in a particular, larger context—one that consolidates intrapersonal with interpersonal data—also reveals that this larger context is actually a distinct field of concentration that includes sleep, sleep-related problems, sleep-disruption phenomena, disturbed dreams, and nightmares. In this spirit, the present volume may encourage clinicians and researchers to join forces in cross-disciplinary research in order to finally elaborate the entire morphology of the nightmare—including its physiological basis, its psychological infrastructure, and its social implications.

The overriding theme emerging from this volume, therefore, concerns the need to strengthen interest in the study of the nightmare and its contextual spheres as a major field of concentration. In addition, this volume can contribute some assurance that this field of concentration and its physiological, psychological, and social contexts among theoreticians, researchers, and clinicians will be sustained and treated as a matter of primary importance.

# AUTHOR INDEX

# SUBJECT INDEX